Applied Data Science in FinTech

This textbook offers a comprehensive introduction to data science and financial technology, with a focus on advanced tools, data modeling, and their applications in FinTech. Adopting an inquiry-based approach, it integrates detailed case studies, clear definitions of financial terms, and practical examples to guide readers through core concepts and methods.

Step-by-step illustrations demonstrate how programs are developed, making the material accessible for students. Dedicated chapters explore cutting-edge applications such as AdviceTech, AgTech, PropTech, chatbots, and sentiment analytics. To support hands-on learning, the book also provides sample code and data sets, enabling readers to experiment, practice, and ultimately design their own programs.

Designed for those with a basic foundation in programming, this book is an ideal companion for applying data science techniques to financial and technological contexts. It is particularly valuable for postgraduate and advanced students in FinTech, Business Analytics, and Data Science programs.

Juraj Hric is Co-Founder and Chief Executive Officer at Zyanza Technologies. He is a course convenor for banking, finance and financial technology modules at the University of New South Wales, Australia.

Yiping Lin is Co-Founder of Alt Data Tech, a leading provider of alternative data. He is also the director of undergraduate and postgraduate FinTech programs at the University of New South Wales, Australia.

Applied Data Science in FinTech

Models, Tools, and Case Studies

Juraj Hric and Yiping Lin

Routledge
Taylor & Francis Group
LONDON AND NEW YORK

Designed cover image: Getty Images via derrrek

First published 2026
by Routledge
4 Park Square, Milton Park, Abingdon, Oxon OX14 4RN

and by Routledge
605 Third Avenue, New York, NY 10158

Routledge is an imprint of the Taylor & Francis Group, an informa business

British Library Cataloguing-in-Publication Data
A catalogue record for this book is available from the British Library

ISBN: 978-1-032-76258-6 (hbk)
ISBN: 978-1-032-76257-9 (pbk)
ISBN: 978-1-003-47774-7 (ebk)

DOI: 10.4324/9781003477747

Typeset in Goudy
by Apex CoVantage, LLC

Access the Support Material: www.routledge.com/9781032762579

Contents

About the Authors

Juraj Hric is Co-Founder and Chief Executive Officer at Zyanza Technologies, AI PaaS and DaaS platform, on a mission to cross the divide between applied AI, data science and finance and to help asset allocators to embrace the new digital paradigm. Juraj has over two decades of proven practical experience in global markets building and utilizing trading and risk platforms with deep understanding of multi-asset management, quant strategies, trading, hedging and structuring and is a strong proponent of digital technology driven solutions in this space.

Aside, Juraj is an adjunct lecturer and course convenor teaching in the areas of banking, finance and financial technology with research interests in applied artificial intelligence, financial mathematics, portfolio management, asset pricing, tokenization, quant trading and investing and behavioral finance. He is passionate about teaching and developing the next generation of future leaders across the industry. He is an AI advocate and speaker in FinTech, venture capital, innovation and strategy.

Dr Yiping Lin is the Co-Founder of Alt Data Tech, a leading provider of alternative data. He is a senior lecturer in data science and financial technology and currently directs both undergraduate and postgraduate FinTech programs at the University of New South Wales. Previously, he designed and taught flagship data science courses at the Chinese University of Hong Kong, Shenzhen.

Passionate about bridging academia and industry, Yiping's research on market microstructure and FinTech has been showcased at top international conferences. He also brings hands-on experience from Nasdaq, the Singapore Exchange, and the Capital Markets Cooperative Research Center. With this unique blend of academic expertise and industry know-how, Yiping offers powerful insights into the future of data science and the fast-changing FinTech landscape.

Glossary of Key Terms

Recurrent neural networks (RNNs) Artificial neural networks whose connections between neurons include loops, well suited for processing sequences of inputs, which makes them highly effective in a wide range of applications, from handwriting, to texts, to speech recognition.

Convolutional neural networks (CNNs) Artificial neural networks in which the connections between neural layers are inspired by the organization of the animal visual cortex, the portion of the brain that processes images, well suited for visual perception tasks.

Generative adversarial networks (GANs) These usually use two neural networks contesting each other in a zero-sum game framework (thus "adversarial"). GANs can learn to mimic various distributions of data (for example text, speech, and images) and are therefore valuable in generating test data sets when these are not readily available.

Supervised learning Given a set of inputs/independent variables/predictors $\mathbf{x}$ and outputs/dependent variables/targets $\mathbf{y}$, the goal is to learn a function $f(\mathbf{x})$ that approximates $\mathbf{y}$. This is accomplished by supervising $f(\mathbf{x})$, that is, providing it with examples $(\mathbf{x}1, \mathbf{y}1) \ldots (\mathbf{x}n, \mathbf{y}n)$ and feedback whenever it makes mistakes or accurate predictions.

Unsupervised learning Given several objects/samples/transactions $\mathbf{x}1 \ldots \mathbf{x}n$, the goal is to learn a hidden map $h(\mathbf{x})$ that can uncover a hidden structure in the data. This hidden map can be used to "compress" $\mathbf{x}$ (aka dimensionality reduction) or to assign to every $\mathbf{x}i$ a group ck (a.k.a. clustering or topic modelling).

Reinforcement learning Given an environment formed by several states $\boldsymbol{s}1, \boldsymbol{s}2 \ldots \boldsymbol{sn}$, an agent, and a reward function, the goal is to learn a policy π that will guide an agent actions $\boldsymbol{a}1, \boldsymbol{a}2 \ldots \boldsymbol{ak}$ through the state space so as to maximize occasional rewards.

Deep learning Deep learning algorithms attempt to model high-level abstractions in data by using multiple processing layers, with complex structures or otherwise, composed of multiple nonlinear transformations. Hence, the mapping function we are attempting to learn can be broken down into several compositional operations $f(\mathbf{x})=f1\circ f2\circ f3\circ \ldots \circ fn(\mathbf{x})$.

Adversarial learning Adversarial machine learning is a technique employed in the field of machine learning which attempts to "fool" models through malicious input. More formally, assume a given input $\mathbf{x}$ associated with a label $\mathbf{c}$ and a machine learning model f such that $f(\mathbf{x})=\mathbf{c}$, that is, f can perfectly classify $\mathbf{x}$. We consider $\mathbf{x}*$ an adversarial example if $\mathbf{x}*$ is indistinguishable from $\mathbf{x}$ and $f(\mathbf{x})\neq\mathbf{c}$.

Transfer/Meta-Learning These two learning paradigms are tightly connected, as their main goal is to encapsulate knowledge learned across many tasks and transfer it to new, unseen ones.

"Big" data Extremely large data sets analyzed computationally to reveal patterns, trends and associations, especially relating to human behavior and interactions.

Financial, economic and social media sources A computer program "scrapes" data from online sources or extracts data from human-readable output coming from another program. Company filings, Federal Reserve Bank of St. Louis, Twitter, and Instagram are example sources.

Alternative data sources Data gathered from outside of traditional financial and economic sources. Alternative data finance refers typically to data used to obtain insight into the investment process.

Multiple data sources Data integration involving combining data coming from multiple disparate information sources and repositories to providing users with a unified view of these data.

Natural Language Processing (NLP) The application of computational techniques to the analysis and synthesis of language and speech.

Sentiment analysis The process of computationally identifying and categorizing opinions expressed in a piece of text, especially in order to determine whether the writer's attitude towards a particular topic, product, etc., is positive, negative, or neutral.

Behavioral analytics An area of data analytics that focuses on providing insight into the actions of people, usually regarding online purchasing, interaction or social behavior.

Predictive analytics The practice of extracting information from existing data sets in order to determine patterns and predict future outcomes and trends; an example being the prediction of crime.

ABI Application Binary Interface for a smart contract is a standardized way to interact with its functions and data, essentially acting as a bridge between the human-readable code (like Solidity) and the machine-executable bytecode on the Ethereum Virtual Machine (EVM).

Ethereum Ethereum is a decentralized blockchain platform that enables developers to build and deploy smart contracts and decentralized applications (dApps).

Bitcoin Bitcoin is a decentralized digital currency that operates without a central authority like a government or bank.

LSTM Long-Short Term Memory is a type of recurrent neural network (RNN) aimed at mitigating the vanishing gradient problem commonly encountered by traditional RNNs.

Modern portfolio theory Developed by Nobel Laureate Harry Markowitz in the 1950s, it is a framework for constructing optimal investment portfolios.

Quantum computing This is a novel type of computation that leverages the principles of quantum mechanics to solve complex problems that are intractable for classical computers.

AI Agent A software program that acts on behalf of a user or another system to perform tasks, utilizing AI to make decisions, plan actions, and adapt to its environment.

GenAI Uses sophisticated algorithms to organize large, complex data sets into meaningful clusters of information to create new content, including text, images and audio, in response to a query or prompt.

Algorithm A process or set of rules to be followed in calculations or other problem-solving operations, especially by a computer.

Forward propagation Input data is fed through a neural network, in a forward direction, to generate an output. The data is accepted by hidden layers and processed, as per the activation function, and moves to the successive layer.

Backward propagation Process that works by calculating the error between the network's predicted output and the actual output, then propagating this error backward through the network to adjust the weights in a way that minimizes the overall error.

VADER Valence Aware Dictionary for sEntiment Reasoning. A pre-built sentiment analysis model for social media text, product reviews and other short text passages.

Preface

FinTech is all about dealing with different types of data across the financial services industry. It is essential to learn about the various types of data structures, modeling frameworks and available toolboxes, as well as about their pros and cons. There is no one-size-fits-all solution when it comes to dealing with predictive analytics and data in the age of generative artificial intelligence. This book will help readers to understand which data structures, predictive models and databases to use given the characteristics of the data, which can be either quantitative or qualitative, structured or unstructured. After completing this book, readers are expected to develop data management skills and be able to deal with many different data issues that can emerge in real-world circumstances.

This is a practical and hands-on book. Readers undertake an individual data-driven projects. The projects require all stages and steps to be fully contemplated, from idea generation to implementation. The book will draw on concepts, problems and practical implications from textbooks, academic papers, financial press articles as well as relevant financial regulators and government agencies. The aims of this book are as follows:

- Develop skills in data handling in the context of banking and finance
- Gain introductory exposure to state-of-the-art data modeling and analytics
- Get familiar with **genAI techniques and tools**
- Get familiar with **FinTech product design in FIGMA studio**
- Get familiar with **FinTech data design utilizing Python libraries**

This book is thus designed and developed for readers aiming to understand the connections between banking, finance, and technology. In this book we expose various data handling, analytics and computational methodologies in applied form as part of assisting you with a build-up of your practical FinTech techniques and skills. To develop skills in data handling in the context of banking and finance, we introduce various data handling methods. To gain an introductory exposure to state-of-the-art data modeling and analytics, we introduce various methods in applied format:

- Time Series Analytics
- Clustering
- Modern Portfolio Theory
- Predictive Analytics
    - Autoregressive Integrated Moving Average (ARIMA)
    - Recurrent Neural Networks (RNN)

- Long-Short Term Memory Recurrent Neural Networks (LSTM RNN)
- Natural Language Processing Basics (NLP)
- Large Language Models Basics (LLM)

Who Should Read This Book

You should find this book relevant if you are an analyst, data scientist or business graduate with an understanding of financial and capital markets and have a keen interest to explore applied AI and data science techniques used in finance and banking sector. You should also find this book informative if you are an investment professional looking to stay ahead in your field and to breach the gap between finance concepts and theories and practical applications and advances in AI techniques. By integrating scientific concepts with practical applications, the book provides valuable insights that can transform your understanding and approach to finance.

On the other hand, if your background is in computer science, software engineering or machine learning (ML) and artificial intelligence (AI), you may be able to skip some of the introductory material in this area. Last section of the book, *Section 3: FinTech Applications* covers applied techniques in finance and banking broken down into specific applied use cases. The book assumes that you want to proceed to learn about this rather dynamic area, that is the connection between finance and technology. For this purpose, we include numerous academic references and additional resources linked in the GitHub repository.

One of the key concepts explored is the **digital data factory (DDF)**, a new approach that leverages digital data to enhance financial analysis and decision-making processes. This book provides a comprehensive introduction to how ML and AI techniques can add value to the design and execution of FinTech solutions. It is structured into three sections that cover different aspects of data management, visualization and modeling moving into the technical exploration of recent AI techniques and concluding with a number of conceptual examples in finance and banking arena.

Section 1: Data Science for FinTech

The first section covers data fundamentals and core aspects of digital data factory concepts. This is a base, a stepping stone exposing the readers to the world of data literacy. It focuses on the data and data handling processes that drive the ML and AI algorithms and strategies discussed throughout this book.

Chapter 1, Data Science for FinTech. This chapter starts with the introduction to data literacy. We expose the reader to this skill as it applies to finance and banking profession. Then, we proceed and discuss algorithms and why we consider algorithms to be at the core of any FinTech solution. At this stage, we introduce the reader to a new programmatic concept, *pseudocoding*. Across the rest of the book we utilize pseudocoding sequences to talk to *AI copilots* and other chatbots. Lastly, we dive deeper into data governance covering important concepts such as data AI ethics, data integrity and data security.

Chapter 2, Data Management for FinTech. In this chapter, we look into the intricacies of data management from the perspective of **digital data factory (DDF)** concept. Data management from a digital data factory concept perspective involves the creation of a data lake, prompt and feature engineering, model design, and implementation stages or stations as we define these terms. These processes are essential in helping businesses to optimize their operations, improve the customer experience, and drive growth.

Chapter 3, Data Visualization. Firstly, we introduce schematic approach to data structures and data process flowcharts. Then we expose the visualization of structured and unstructured data structures utilizing state-of-the-art programmatic libraries. We conduct this exposition using cryptocurrencies and relevant textual data flows, such as cryptocurrency related news. Lastly, we dive deeper into **Streamlit** and **Figma** to expose these tools available to FinTech professionals to enhance and build highly dynamic and engaging visually driven FinTech products.

Chapter 4, Data Modeling in FinTech. In this chapter we connect data modeling and cutting-edge AI technologies implementing **digital data factory (DDF)**. Given the inherent complex nature of FinTech applications and services, AI tools such as chatbot and Co-Pilot and AI Agent are not in position to deliver on the entire FinTech solution or the entire product yet. Hence, the notion of introducing a logical sequence of steps, "stations," we break down the data modeling and application development process into these "pockets of similar tasks" and narrow down the purpose to use AI Agents. As a result, we introduce the reader to new cutting-edge techniques to use AI tools in this context, following the notion of DDF data flows.

Section 2: Advanced Tools for Finance and FinTech

The second section introduces fundamental supervised and unsupervised learning algorithms that can add value in finance and banking applications. In the context of the DDF concept, this section focuses on *DDF Model Selection* phase. This section introduces state-of-the-art tokenization approach and then various unsupervised learning techniques to extract high-quality signals and information from key source of alternative data, limited to text data format throughout this book.

Chapter 5, Bitcoin and Tokenization. This chapter starts with the introduction to cryptocurrencies, namely **bitcoin**. Then, we proceed and discuss the notion of tokenization within the **decentralized finance (DeFi)** framework. At this point, we introduce **blockchain** as a technology with a potential utility across finance and banking use cases. Finally, we expose the reader to practical examples of utilizing smart contracts from programmatic perspective. We use **Ethereum** and **Solana** platforms to build a smart contract application using Python scripting sequences. The focus of this chapter is on the process of asset tokenization.

Chapter 6, Machine Learning Tools for Finance and FinTech. In this chapter, we place the reader squarely into the *DDF Model selection* section and expose recent developments in ML and AI techniques as applied to finance and banking arena. We start with a simple **ordinary least square (OLS)** model and proceed to exposing **recurrent neural network (RNN)** architecture from mathematical and programmatic standpoints. Next we dive deeper into the intricacies of **long-short term memory recurrent neural network (LSTM RNN)** to provide the reader with core mathematical and conceptual formulations necessary for sentiment analytics and **large language model (LLM)** expositions in Chapter 7 and Chapter 8.

Chapter 7, Language Analytics for Finance and FinTech. This chapter starts defining and exposing unstructured data in a textual format. In this book, we use text format only to expose the readers to ML and AI techniques. Then, we dive deeper into the ways we use these techniques to extract information, or sentiments, from text and how these techniques can be used within finance and banking space. We showcase the use of various models, such as **VADER** in this context. Lastly, we use *machine poetry* to illustrate the limitations these techniques are prone to when used in heavily regulated space, such as finance and banking applications used within the industry. We conclude the chapter by highlighting the benefits however showcasing the potential limitations in these AI techniques.

Chapter 8, Chatbot for Sentiment Analytics. This chapter integrates the previous two chapters and illustrates how to build an **AI Agent**, a dedicated chatbot tool to analyze sentiment from various data sets as applied in finance and banking. We focus on official company filings and other fundamental data sets for exposition. We conclude the chapter with a practical use case from crypto markets building news sentiment index connecting the quantitative, prices, data streams with qualitative, textual, data streams in the process. All of this is in the context of *DDF Model Selection* phase.

Section 3: FinTech Applications

The third section illustrates practical and hand-on use cases from finance and banking industry. It focuses on DDF exposition and approach in a practical setting.

Chapter 9, FinTech Application: AdviceTech. In this chapter we connect the content from previous Section I and Section II covered in this book. The chapter starts with an outline of a use case from AdviceTech. We introduce the reader to the problems faced by practitioners in this area and provide potential solution by implementing step-by-step use case within the confines of DDF concept delivering a core outline of a FinTech solution utilizing **Modern Portfolio Theory** approach. In this simulation, the reader assumes a position of finance practitioner within roboAdvisory provider and is tasked to solve a predefined problem and to deliver a technology-driven solution.

Chapter 10, FinTech Application: AgTech. This chapter starts with an outline of a use case from agTech. We introduce the reader to the problems faced by practitioners in this area and provide potential solution by implementing step-by-step use case within the confines of DDF concept delivering a core outline of a FinTech solution utilizing **Predictive Analytics** approach. In this simulation, the reader assumes a position of finance practitioner within a banking institution and is tasked to solve a predefined problem and to deliver technology-driven solution.

Chapter 11, FinTech Application: PropTech. This chapter starts with an outline of a use case from propTech. We introduce the reader to the problems faced by practitioners in this area and provide potential solution by implementing step-by-step use case within the confines of DDF concept delivering a core outline of a FinTech solution utilizing **Asset Tokenization** approach. In this simulation, the reader assumes a position of finance practitioner within propTech provider and is tasked to solve a predefined problem and to deliver technology-driven solution.

Chapter 12, Data Frontiers in FinTech. Understanding current state of ML and AI techniques and tools, in this chapter, we look further into the frontiers of possibilities in FinTech. On the intersection of finance, banking and technology we introduce the reader to a number of topics related to other data formats, such as video and sound, then the topics related to **quantum computing** and potential advances in this space and lastly to the use of advanced LLMs and **cryptosecurity** approaches as related to finance and banking.

Toolbox

The book assumes limited programming background using Python 3+ and scientific computing libraries such as NumPy, pandas, SciPy, PyTorch or Tensorflow. Some experience with ML and AI tools would be helpful; however we do cover the basics starting with introducing the readers to the use of application programming interface (APIs) and basic ML and AI workflows and reference numerous resources in this area.

The GitHub Repository

The practical and hands-on nature of the exposition of the book's material is hosted on GitHub in a form of code repositories organized so that each chapter has its own self-contained directory. We have included relevant references and specific resources.

Data Sources

We use publicly available data sets from financial and capital markets, government agencies, fundamental, alternative and crypto markets and data providers. Each chapter is self-contained and includes detailed exposition to data handling and API calls whenever required with companion Python coding snippets. We refrain from using data web scrapping methods as we believe the appropriate approach to data extract and data handling is via official API channels offered by any given data provider.

Conventions

There are a number of text, mathematical and programmatic conventions used throughout this book.

A block of code, code snippet, is set as an example here:

```
import numpy as np
dt = np.dtype([('Name', 'S10'), ('Age', 'i4'),
               ('Height', 'f'), ('Children/Pets', 'i4', 2)])
s = np.array([('Smith', 45, 1.83, (0, 1)),
              ('Jones', 53, 1.72, (2, 2))], dtype=dt)
print(s)
print(s['Name'])
print(s['Height'].mean())
print(s[1]['Age'])
```

Words, statements or declarations of importance or a new term are denominated in **bold font**. Code formulas or functions or variables within a text narrative are shown as *code in text*.

SECTION 1

Data Science for FinTech

Chapter 1

Data Science for FinTech

1.1 Introduction

Data science has been rapidly gaining popularity in the banking and finance industry due to its ability to provide insights and analytics that help finance and banking professionals make better decisions. The emergence of FinTech has further increased the demand for data scientists and business analysts who can leverage technology and data to improve financial services. Data science is essentially the process of extracting insights and knowledge from data, using various statistical and computational techniques.

In the context of FinTech, data science is used to analyze vast amounts of transactional data and identify patterns that can help businesses optimize their operations and provide personalized services to customers. It allows FinTech companies to understand customer behavior, predict market trends and improve risk management. With the help of data science, FinTech companies can offer innovative and customized services that traditional banks may not be able to provide. The future of the banking and finance industry is heavily reliant on data science. As more and more financial transactions move online, the amount of data being

DOI: 10.4324/9781003477747-2

generated is increasing exponentially. This data can be leveraged to improve customer experience, reduce operational costs, and mitigate risk. With the help of data science, FinTech companies can create a more efficient and secure financial ecosystem.

In short, the introduction of Data Science in FinTech has revolutionized the way banking and finance companies operate. It has enabled the finance operators to leverage data to provide better services to customers, reduce costs, and improve risk management. The future of the industry is heavily reliant on Data Science, and it is essential for businesses to invest in these technologies to stay competitive. As the demand for skilled Data Scientists continues to grow, it is a promising field for those looking to enter the world of FinTech.

This chapter starts with the introduction to data literacy. We expose the reader to this skill as it applies to finance and banking profession. Then, we proceed and discuss algorithms and why we consider algorithms to be at the core of any FinTech solution. At this stage, we introduce the reader to a new programmatic concept, *pseudocoding*. Across the rest of the book we utilize pseudocoding sequences to talk to *AI copilots* and other chatbots. Lastly, we dive deeper into data governance covering important concepts such as data AI ethics, data integrity and data security.

Learning Outcomes

At the end of this chapter the reader will be able to do the following:

- Discuss importance of data science in banking and finance
- Define data literacy and data skills competencies
- Explain what algorithms represent and cover
- Introduce the notion of pseudocoding and applied Python coding
- Introduce data governance and AI ethics

1.2 Data Literacy

What Is Data Literacy?

Much like "regular" literacy, data literacy commonly refers to an individual's ability to read, understand, create and derive meaningful information from data, and also encompasses aspects of data quality, data governance, open data and big data. As with any form of literacy, the aim is to comprehend the intricacies and complexities involved in any given topic. In this case, the topic is financial data streams. Anything that relates to understanding as to the source, authenticity, generation capabilities, storage and processing, handling and securing and ultimately analyzing, visualizing and utilizing in decision-making processes.

Data literacy is the ability to understand, evaluate and apply data effectively in various settings. It involves a combination of skills, knowledge and attitudes that enable individuals to comprehend and use data to make informed decisions. Data literacy is becoming increasingly important in today's world, where data is abundant and ubiquitous.

Data comprehension is an essential component of data literacy. It involves the ability to read, analyze and interpret data accurately. Individuals with strong data comprehension skills can identify patterns, draw conclusions, and make predictions based on data. They can also evaluate the reliability and validity of data sources and assess the quality of the data. Data management is another critical aspect of data literacy. It involves the ability to organize, store and retrieve data efficiently. It also includes understanding the different types of data and how to manage them effectively. Individuals with strong data management skills can create and maintain databases, use data visualization tools, and ensure data security and privacy. Also it is the ability to use data to solve real-world problems. It involves applying data comprehension and management skills to make informed decisions and take appropriate actions. Individuals with strong data application skills can use data to identify trends, optimize processes, and improve outcomes. They can also communicate data insights effectively to different audiences.

To develop data literacy, individuals need a framework that provides a structured approach to learning. A framework can include various components, such as learning objectives, assessment methods and learning resources. It can also include a curriculum that covers different aspects of data literacy, such as data comprehension, management and application.

Data literacy plays a pivotal role in the intersection of data science and financial technology, empowering professionals to navigate the complex landscape of modern finance. At its core, data literacy in FinTech involves the ability to **read, interpret, and communicate data effectively**, enabling informed decision-making in an increasingly data-driven industry. For finance professionals and business executives, this skill is crucial for extracting meaningful insights from vast data sets, identifying market trends and assessing risk. Data scientists leverage their advanced literacy to develop sophisticated algorithms and models that drive innovation in areas such as predictive analytics and automated trading. Meanwhile, students aspiring to enter the FinTech field must cultivate strong data interpretation skills to prepare for the challenges of this dynamic sector. As financial services continue to evolve with technology, data literacy and the way how to utilize recent technological advancements in this

Figure 1.1 Data Literacy Skills and Competencies

field, via copilots, has become an *indispensable competency* for anyone looking to thrive in the world of FinTech.

As per the following, data management falls under the "Data Literacy Skills and Competencies" form and cannot be looked at in isolation. In this book, we combine data management under the umbrella of data literacy and integrate our discussions with respect to data applications, data collection and data evaluation.

In the first section of the book, we focus on practical aspects of data collection, data evaluation, data modeling and data application using pseudocoding and Python programming language.

1.3 Algorithms

What Is an Algorithm?

> **A set of mathematical instructions that must be followed in a fixed order, and that, especially if given to a computer, will help to calculate an answer to a mathematical problem.**

Algorithms are the backbone of modern computing, shaping the way we interact with technology in our daily lives. From the simplest calculator to the most complex artificial intelligence systems, algorithms play a crucial role in problem-solving and decision-making processes. Their impact extends far beyond computer science, influencing fields such as machine learning, data analysis and even social media recommendations.

Next is an enhanced definition of algorithms as applied in capital markets.

- Computational statistics
  - Basic pricing and valuation algorithms with closed mathematical solutions
- AI algorithms
  - Knowledge or rule-based systems
  - Machine learning (ML)
  - Deep learning (DL)
  - Large language models (LLM)
- Complex systems
  - Quantum-driven AI algorithms

In the field of computational statistics, algorithms are an essential component for the development of various models and tools used in pricing, valuations, and finance. From a mathematical perspective, an algorithm is a step-by-step procedure or set of rules used to solve a problem or perform a specific task. These rules are based on mathematical concepts, such as arithmetic, algebra, and calculus and are designed to efficiently process large amounts of data.

In essence, an algorithm is a recipe that outlines the necessary actions to achieve a desired outcome. Just as a recipe produces consistent results, algorithms ensure reliable and replicable outcomes for a wide range of tasks in the digital realm. They can be expressed in various forms, such as natural language, pseudocode, flowcharts, or programming languages.

Key Characteristics of Algorithms

Algorithms possess several essential characteristics that define their effectiveness and usability:

- Well-defined steps: An algorithm consists of clear and unambiguous instructions that can be followed precisely.

- Input and output: Algorithms take input data, process it, and produce at least one output.
- Finiteness: Every algorithm must terminate after a finite number of steps, ensuring it doesn't run indefinitely.
- Definiteness: Each instruction in an algorithm should be precise and easy to interpret, leaving no room for ambiguity.
- Effectiveness: Algorithms should be designed using basic, simple, and feasible operations that can be traced using just paper and pencil.
- Efficiency: Algorithms aim to solve problems in a timely manner, optimizing the use of computational resources.

Algorithms consist of several key components that work together to solve problems efficiently. These components form the foundation of algorithmic design and implementation. The *input component* of an algorithm represents the data or information that needs to be processed. It serves as the starting point for the algorithm's operation. Inputs can come from various sources, such as user input through a keyboard or mouse, sensor data, Internet of Things (IoT) or preexisting data sets. For example, in a sorting algorithm, the input would be an unsorted list of numbers or letters or any combination. **The quality and accuracy of the input directly impact the algorithm's performance and the validity of its output.**

The *process component* encompasses the core operations and steps that the algorithm performs on the input data to achieve the desired result. It involves a series of well-defined instructions that transform the input into the output. These instructions can include mathematical calculations, comparisons, logical operations, and data manipulations. The process component is where the algorithm's logic and problem-solving approach are implemented. In most of the FinTech project, this is the component that usually defines the business intellectual property, own algorithm. For instance, in a generic non-patented binary search algorithm, the process involves repeatedly dividing the search space in half until the target element is found or determined to be absent.

The *output component* represents the final result or solution produced by the algorithm after processing the input data. It is the information or action that the algorithm generates to address the problem it was designed to solve. Outputs can take various forms, such as numerical results, text, images, or even actions triggered by the algorithm. In a machine learning algorithm, the output might be a prediction or classification based on the input data. Lastly, the termination condition is a crucial component that determines when the algorithm should stop executing. It ensures that the algorithm does not run indefinitely and provides a clear endpoint for the computation. Termination conditions can be based on various factors, such as reaching a specific number of iterations, achieving a desired level of accuracy, or exhausting all possible solutions. For example, in a genetic algorithm, the termination condition might be set to stop after a predetermined number of generations or when there has been no improvement in the population for a certain number of iterations.

Pseudocode

In this book we use pseudocoding as one of the main tools to deliver potential solutions to complex problems in finance and banking based use cases. Pseudocode is a powerful tool in the world of programming and algorithm design. It serves as a bridge between human thought processes and computer code, allowing developers to outline their ideas in a structured yet flexible manner. This informal language combines natural language with programming constructs, making it easier to plan and communicate complex algorithms before diving into actual coding.

Pseudocode is an informal way of describing a program's flow without adhering to strict programming language syntax or underlying technology considerations. It summarizes a program's structure while excluding underlying details. Essentially, it's a detailed yet readable description of what a computer program or algorithm should do, written in a formal yet accessible style that uses natural syntax and formatting.

One of the key characteristics of pseudocode is that it cannot be compiled into an executable program. Instead, it uses short terms or simple English language syntaxes to write code for programs before it's converted into a specific programming language. This approach helps identify top-level flow errors and understand the programming data flows that the final program will use, ultimately saving time during actual programming as conceptual errors have been addressed early on. In our case, we use pseudocoding to express our algorithms and solutions and once we establish appropriate level of delivery, we use these pseudocode sequences in copilots to produce Python programming script for further processing and review. The notion of using pseudocode is to establish controlled syntax when "talking" to AI machines (algorithms) via copilot platforms.

Pseudocode plays a vital role in the software development process for several reasons:

- Efficient Planning: It serves as an efficient key principle of an algorithm, allowing programmers to sketch out the structure of the program before actual coding takes place.
- Collaboration Tool: When incorporated into the development process, designers, lead programmers, and other key players can use pseudocode to design, collaborate on, and evaluate the logic behind the program or algorithm.
- Error Detection: Catching errors during the pseudocode stage is less costly than identifying them later in the development process. This early error detection can significantly streamline the coding phase.
- Readability: Pseudocode improves the readability of any approach. While code is generally not very readable, pseudocode is in plain English, allowing readers to understand it quickly even without reading the entire line.
- Documentation: It works as a rough documentation, making it easier for other developers to understand the program. In the era of open source, many industries deem it necessary or essential to employ the approach of documentation, and that's where pseudocode proves vital.

Pseudocode serves as a bridge between human thought processes and computer code, allowing FinTech developers to outline their ideas in a structured yet flexible manner. To effectively use pseudocode and proceed further in our quest, it's essential to understand its core components, which include variables and data types, control structures, and input/output operations.

Variables are fundamental elements in pseudocode that store values and data of different types. They allow programmers to reference and manipulate data throughout their algorithms. In pseudocode, variables can store five different types of data: Boolean, Integer, Character, String, and Float/Decimal/Real.

To declare variables in pseudocode, developers simply mention the variable name and assign a value to it. For example:

```
name ← "John" age ← 25
```

Constants, on the other hand, are variables whose values never change during program runtime. To distinguish constants from regular variables, their names are typically written in capital letters. Control structures, on the other hand, are essential components of pseudocode that represent the logic and flow of control in an algorithm. There are six specific structured programming constructs commonly used in pseudocode, namely:

- SEQUENCE: Actions are performed in the order they are written, from top to bottom.
- IF-THEN-ELSE: Used for binary choices based on a Boolean condition.

```
IF age > 17
    THEN     Display "You can vote."
    ELSE     Display "You can't vote."
ENDIF
```

- WHILE: Specifies a loop with a test at the top.

```
count ← 0 WHILE count < 5
    Display "I love computers!"
    Increment count
ENDWHILE
```

- REPEAT-UNTIL: Similar to WHILE, but the test is performed at the bottom of the loop.

```
count ← 5 REPEAT
    Display "Blast off is soon!"
    Decrement count
UNTIL count < 1
```

- FOR: A specialized construct for iterating a specific number of times.

```
FOR x ← 0 TO 4
    Display "Are we having fun?"
END FOR
```

- CASE: Indicates a multiway branch based on mutually exclusive conditions.

```
CASE OF age
    0 TO 17: Display "You can't vote."
    18 TO 64: Display "You're in your working years."
    65+: Display "You should be retired."
ENDCASE
```

These constructs can be embedded within each other, and proper indentation is used to make the structure clear.

Pricing European Call Option Example

In this example we apply simple pseudocode and Python implementation to a simple financial algorithm. We use Black-Scholes-Merton (BSM) pricing methodology to showcase the use of data and algorithms in banking and finance. Specifically, a **call option** is a financial contract that gives the buyer the **right**, but not the obligation, to purchase a specific quantity of an underlying asset (such as a stock) at a predetermined price (known as the **strike price**) within a certain period of time. The buyer pays a premium for this right. If the market price of the asset rises above the strike price before the expiration date, the buyer can exercise the option and buy the asset at the lower strike price, potentially making a profit. If the market price does not exceed the strike price, the buyer may choose not to exercise the option, losing only the premium paid [1.1].

Step 1: Design Financial Product and Algorithmic Solution

For valuation purposes we define these valuation parameters relevant to an asset:

- Initial asset price $S_0 = 100$.
- Strike price of European Call $K = 105$
- Time to maturity $T = 1$ year
- Flat riskless rate $r = -1\%$ (yes, this is negative 1%)
- Flat volatility $\sigma = 38\%$
- Normal standard distribution z

Then, to value a European call option using the BSM algorithm, we can write pseudocode and the Python code based on the following algorithm definition:

$$C = S_0 * N(d_1) - K * e^{(-rT)} * N(d_2)$$

$$d_1 = \left(ln\left(\frac{S_0}{K}\right) + \left(r + \sigma^2 / 2\right)T \right) / \left(\sigma * \sqrt{T}\right)$$

$$d_2 = d_1 - \sigma * \sqrt{T}$$

The data here comprises of asset parameters such as historical price observations, interest rates and time to maturity. We rely on the authenticity and accuracy of the observed data to provide accurate results as derived by utilizing BSM formula.

Step 2: Design Pseudocode Interpretation

Next is a pseudocode interpretation for valuing a European Call option using the Black-Scholes formula with the given parameters:

```
// Function to calculate the cumulative standard normal distribution (N(x))
function N(x):
    return standard_normal_CDF(x)

// Function to calculate the value of a European call option
function BlackScholesCall(S, K, T, r, σ):
    // Calculate d1 and d2
    d1 = (ln(S / K) + (r + (σ^2) / 2) * T) / (σ * sqrt(T))
    d2 = d1 - σ * sqrt(T)

    // Calculate the call option value
    call_price = S * N(d1) - K * exp(-r * T) * N(d2)

    return call_price

// Example parameters from the user
S = 100          // Initial price
K = 105          // Strike price
T = 1            // Time to maturity in years
```

```
r = -0.01        // Negative risk-free interest rate (-1%)
σ = 0.38         // Volatility (38%)

// Calculate the call option price
call_value = BlackScholesCall(S, K, T, r, σ)
print("The value of the call option is: ", call_value)
```

In the previous pseudocode we first define relevant support function to calculate standard normal distribution, then proceed in writing BSM call option function as per previous BSM algorithm.

Step 3: Generate Python Code Implementing Defined Algorithm and Pseudocode

Next is the Python code interpretation to calculate the value of European call option as indicated previously:

```
import numpy as np
from scipy.stats import norm
# Parameters
S = 100   # Initial asset price
K = 105   # Strike price
T = 1     # Time to maturity (1 year)
r = 0.03 # Risk-free rate (3%)
sigma = 0.38 # Volatility (38%)

# Black-Scholes formula components
d1 = (np.log(S / K) + (r + (sigma ** 2) / 2) * T) / (sigma * np.sqrt(T))
d2 = d1 - sigma * np.sqrt(T)

# Calculate the call option price
call_price = S * norm.cdf(d1) - K * np.exp(-r * T) * norm.cdf(d2)

# Display the result
call_price
```

An alternative approach is to utilize Monte Carlo simulation methodology and based on the BSM model the asset index level at maturity S_T is defined as.

With **pricing algorithm** defined as follows:

1. Draw I random numbers from $z(i)$ from standard normal distribution
2. Calculate all resulting index levels at maturity S_T for given $z(i)$
3. Calculate all inner values of the option at maturity $h_0 = max(S_T - K, 0)$
4. Estimate the option present value via the Monte Carlo estimator

The simulated asset index level at maturity T is defined as follows:

$$S_T = S_0 * exp^{\left(\left(r - \frac{1}{2}\sigma^2\right)T + \sigma * \sqrt{T} * z\right)}$$

whereby the price of the call option is defined as discounted average payoff value, $max(S_T - K, 0)$, from maturity T to today:

$$C_0 = exp^{-rT} * \frac{1}{I} * \sum h_T(i)$$

We convert previous pricing algorithm to the world of Python.

```
'''
Comments: Show how to apply Monte Carlo algorithm
'''
from numpy import *

# Parameters
I = 1000000
S0 = 100  # Initial asset price
K = 105  # Strike price
T = 1    # Time to maturity (1 year)
r = 0.03 # Risk-free rate (3%)
sigma = 0.38 # Volatility (38%)

#Comment:
#Step1
z=random.standard_normal(I)
#Step2
ST=S0*exp((r-0.5*sigma**2)*T+sigma*sqrt(T)*z)
#Step3
hT=maximum(ST-K,0)
#Step4
C0=exp(-r*T)*sum(hT)/I
#print result
print("Value of European Call is %5.3f" %C0)
```

In this book we follow similar steps by defining algorithmic solution, creating pseudocode interpretation following up with Python code sequence and finally applying this solution to a practical use case in FinTech. This previous pricing algorithm returns a theoretical price of a derivative contract, in this case Call Option over a hypothetical asset. We have implicitly made numerous assumptions such as the price of the asset follows normal distribution and the data we have used in our calculation is unbiased, clean and without any errors.

Algorithms are used in a wide range of financial applications, including risk management, portfolio optimization and asset pricing. For example, in the field of valuations, algorithms are used to calculate the fair value of financial assets, such as stocks and bonds or relevant derivative instruments. These algorithms take into account various factors, such as market trends, historical data and economic indicators, to provide accurate valuations.

In finance, algorithms are used to automate various processes, such as trading and investment management. These algorithms are designed to analyze market data and make investment decisions based on predefined criteria. For example, a trading algorithm may be designed to buy or sell a stock based on specific market conditions, such as price movements or volume changes. The use of algorithms in finance has been the subject of much debate, with some arguing that their widespread use has led to increased market volatility and the creation of systemic risks. Nevertheless, the benefits of using algorithms in finance cannot be ignored. They are essential tools for financial institutions to manage risk, make investment decisions, and ensure effective pricing and valuations.

Overall, algorithms are a crucial component of the mathematical foundation underlying computational statistics. They are used extensively in finance to automate various processes and provide accurate pricing and valuations. While their use has been criticized, their benefits cannot be ignored, and they will continue to play a critical role in the financial industry in the years to come.

Algorithms and Data Design

Why are algorithms and data design in finance and banking driving data management requirements?

In today's digital age, the use of algorithms and data design has become increasingly important in the finance and banking industry. The rise of FinTech has created a need for financial institutions to stay competitive by using these tools to improve their trading capabilities, risk management and customer experience. As a result, data management has become a critical requirement for these institutions.

The use of algorithms and data design in finance and banking has revolutionized the way that financial institutions operate. These tools have made it easier to analyze large amounts of data quickly and accurately, making it possible to make better-informed decisions. Algorithms are used to analyze market trends, identify potential risks, and optimize trading strategies. Data design is used to create intuitive dashboards and interfaces that enable traders and analysts to access and analyze data in real time. However, the increased use of algorithms and data design has also led to an increase in data management requirements. Financial institutions must now manage vast amounts of data, and it is critical that they can do so efficiently and effectively. Data management involves collecting, storing, processing and analyzing data. Financial institutions must have robust data management systems in place that can handle the large volumes of data generated by these tools.

In addition to the technical aspects of data management, financial institutions must also consider the legal and regulatory requirements related to data privacy and security. They must ensure that they are collecting and storing data in compliance with local and international regulations. Failure to do so can result in significant legal and financial consequences.

The use of algorithms and data design in finance and banking has driven the need for robust data management systems. Financial institutions must invest in these systems to stay competitive and comply with legal and regulatory requirements. The benefits of using these tools, such as improved trading capabilities and better risk management, make the investment worthwhile. FinTech data management forms an integral part of the "new" algorithmic approach to providing business solutions.

Lastly, within our **digital data factory (DDF)** perspective, more on this in Chapter 2, there is a vast scope of opportunity for FinTech enterprises to step in and provide valuable solutions. Generally, banks and other financial institutions are still exploring projects at scale in the areas where running FinTech solutions can be deployed at scale and speed, for instance, Know Your Client (KYC) and Anti-Money Laundering (AML) or Cash Management or product design or fee leakage reduction activities, as we explore in further chapters. In this book we elevate data above algorithmic solutions.

Let us start by looking at various business problems. In the next graphic, a problem type defined, say, by "anomaly detection" is designed to use vector machines, k-nearest neighbors or neural networks as core AI models. In a FinTech context, anomaly detection techniques are best used in anti-money laundering (AML) solutions. Here the model is looking for any deviation from averages or predefined norms.

As per the previous diagram in Figure 1.2, various business "problem" types are using different algorithmic techniques. Another example is personalized recommendations, likely using collaborative filtering or ranking techniques to depict the most optimal recommendations as results as can be seen in Figure 1.3.

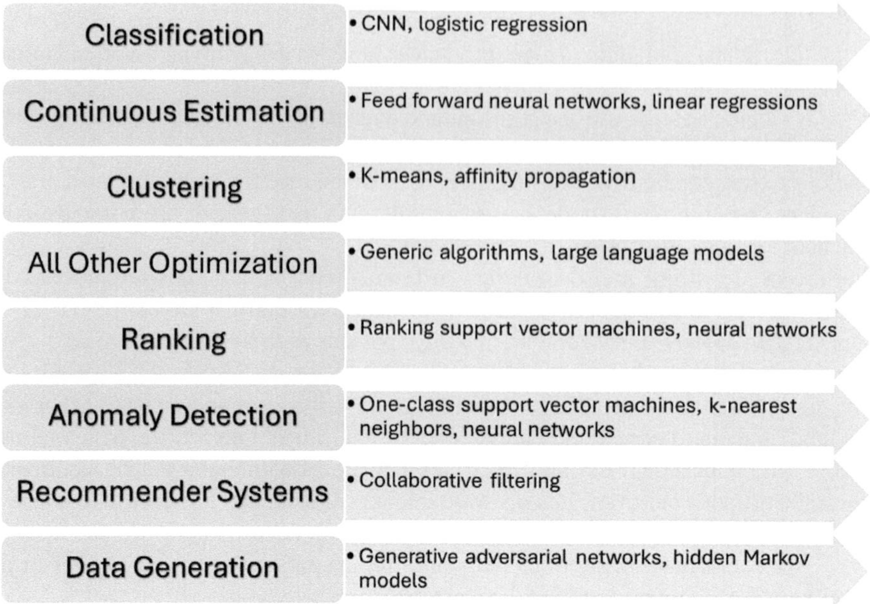

Figure 1.2 Problem Types and Sample Techniques

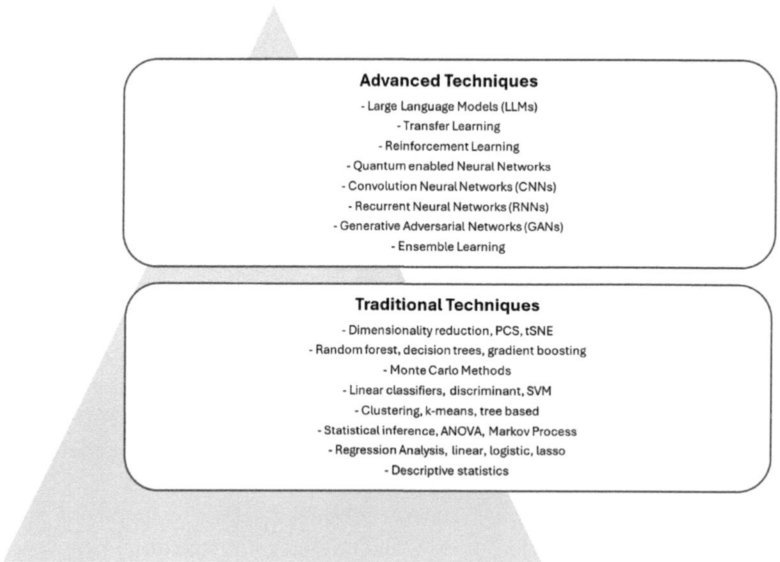

Figure 1.3 Traditional and Advanced Techniques

Specifically, in this book we study and apply the following techniques in detail:

- Descriptive statistics
- Regression analysis
- Autoregressive Moving Average (ARIMA)

- Recurrent Neural Networks (RNN)
- Large Language Models (LLM)

Large language models (LLMs) LLMs are advanced machine learning models that are designed to understand, generate, and manipulate natural language text. These models are built using neural networks, particularly deep learning architectures like transformers, which allow them to process large amounts of data and capture complex relationships in language. They are "large" because they contain millions or even billions of parameters (adjustable elements that the model learns from data). The more parameters a model has, the more sophisticated it becomes at understanding and generating human-like text. LLMs are typically trained on extensive corpora of text, including books, websites, articles, code and more. This allows them to capture a wide range of linguistic patterns, facts and structures. Most LLMs use transformer architecture, a type of deep learning model that relies on mechanisms like attention to process and relate different parts of input text efficiently. This enables the model to handle long sentences and context across large documents.

LLMs can perform a variety of natural language processing (NLP) tasks, such as:

- Text generation (writing coherent text or completing sentences)
- Text classification (e.g., sentiment analysis)
- Question answering
- Machine translation
- Summarization
- Code generation (for certain models trained on programming data)

LLMs are typically trained in a self-supervised manner, meaning they learn by predicting missing parts of text in a sentence or document without needing explicit human annotations.

Validation and Backtesting

In the rapidly evolving landscape of FinTech, the significance of rigorous model validation cannot be overstated. Backtesting and validating model algorithmic solutions have become paramount, especially when leveraging cutting-edge AI copilots to enhance decision-making processes and operational efficiency during service or product development stages. There are two angles to incorporating AI tools within FinTech solutions. One angle is to use already available or in-house created AI tools to assist with search, coding or ideation steps. The other angle is to build own AI driven solutions using in-house created and utilized modeling frameworks. Both approaches require validation and backtesting to be ingrained in the final FinTech based service or a product.

Backtesting in FinTech: This crucial practice involves applying a trading strategy or predictive model to historical data to verify its validity. By simulating past market conditions, financial institutions can do the following:

- Assess the potential performance of their algorithms
- Identify weaknesses or biases in their models
- Refine strategies before real-world implementation

For instance, a hedge fund developing a new algorithmic trading strategy would backtest it against years of market data to evaluate its effectiveness across various economic cycles.

However, trading strategy is never developed by using backtesting. Trading strategies must be based on a theory, either mispricing based or other economic driven derivations, and not purely on backtested historical simulations. This is a critical point: validation and backtesting are techniques used to back up a predefined trading strategy based on a solid theory, not vis-à-vis. In the financial services industry, the performance of predictive models used in trading strategies is crucial for making informed decisions and mitigating risks. Key metrics such as root square error (RSME), coefficient of determination (R^2), and precision-recall are essential for evaluating these models. RSME provides a measure of the average magnitude of errors in predictions, helping to identify models that offer higher accuracy. The coefficient of determination (R^2) indicates how well the model explains the variability of the response data, thus ensuring the robustness of predictions. Precision-recall metrics, on the other hand, are vital for assessing the trade-off between the true positive rate and the precision of the predictions, particularly in scenarios where the cost of false positives is high. By leveraging these metrics, data scientists and machine learning engineers can enhance trading strategies, leading to more reliable and profitable outcomes. Ultimately, the application of these performance metrics in trading strategies empowers financial institutions to navigate market complexities with greater confidence and precision.

Model Validation: Beyond backtesting, comprehensive model validation ensures that algorithmic solutions perform as intended and remain robust under diverse scenarios. This process typically includes:

1. **Stress testing**: Evaluating model performance under extreme market conditions
2. **Sensitivity analysis**: Assessing how changes in input parameters affect outputs
3. **Out-of-sample testing**: Verifying model accuracy on data not used in its development

A prime example is credit scoring models used by banks. Rigorous validation ensures these models accurately assess credit risk across different customer segments and economic conditions.

State-of-the-Art AI Copilots and AI Agents: The integration of advanced AI technologies has revolutionized FinTech operations. These AI copilots:

- Enhance decision-making processes by analyzing vast amounts of data in real-time
- Improve risk management through predictive analytics
- Automate complex tasks, allowing human experts to focus on high-level strategy

For example, robo-advisors utilize AI copilots to provide personalized investment advice, continuously learning from market trends and individual client behaviors. The synergy between robust model validation and AI copilots is evident in fraud detection systems. Banks employ machine learning algorithms to identify suspicious transactions, but these models require constant validation and refinement to adapt to evolving fraud tactics. When deploying AI-driven financial models, particularly in trading strategies, it is crucial to consider overfitting, model generalization, and hyperparameter tuning. Overfitting occurs when a model is too closely tailored to the training data, leading to poor performance on new, unseen data. This can result in significant financial losses if the model's predictions do not generalize well to real-world scenarios. To combat this, model generalization ensures that the model performs well on various data sets, enhancing its robustness and reliability. Hyperparameter tuning further refines the model by optimizing the parameters that govern its learning process, striking a balance between bias and variance. For data scientists, business analysts, machine learning engineers, and fraud detection specialists in the financial services industry, mastering these aspects is essential to developing effective, reliable, and profitable trading strategies or apply AI methodology successfully. By focusing on these considerations, we can drive business transformation and achieve transparent outcomes, ultimately empowering the financial services sector. In this book, we structure our solutions with an inbuild integration defaulting to backtesting and model validation methodologies.

1.4 Data Governance

Data governance is the critical link between algorithms as described previously and data being utilized across businesses. Data governance is a crucial aspect of data management that ensures data quality, integrity and security. It involves the development and implementation of policies, procedures and standards to manage data effectively. Data governance helps to enhance the effectiveness of data management practices, and it is especially important in industries such as FinTech where data is a critical factor for success.

Data governance involves several key components, including data design, metadata management, data quality management and data security. Data design involves the creation of data models and schemas that define the structure and relationships between data elements. Metadata management involves the management of information about data, such as data definitions, data lineage, and data ownership. Data quality management includes the development of processes to ensure that data is accurate, complete and consistent. Data security involves the protection of data from unauthorized access, alteration, or destruction.

In the context of FinTech, financial institutions deal with sensitive financial data, and any errors or breaches could have significant consequences. Data governance helps to mitigate these risks by ensuring that data is managed in a controlled and secure manner. Effective data governance requires a collaborative effort between various stakeholders, including business leaders, technology professionals, data analysts and data stewards. These stakeholders work together to develop and implement data governance policies and procedures that align with business goals and objectives. Additionally, data governance requires ongoing monitoring and evaluation to ensure that data management practices remain effective and up-to-date. Across the book we apply best practice in data governance on model design and algorithmic levels.

AI and Data Ethics

In addition to data governance, model and data ethics forms a critical component of any FinTech organization's data management strategy. Algorithms are a key component of data governance and ethics. They are used to analyze data and make predictions, but they can also perpetuate biases and discrimination if not properly managed. It is essential to ensure that algorithms are designed and implemented with a focus on fairness, transparency, and accountability. Additionally, data must be used in a responsible and ethical manner, with a focus on protecting the privacy and rights of individuals.

Ethical behavior is a critical component of data governance. It requires organizations to establish a code of conduct that guides employees' actions and decision-making processes. This includes implementing training programs to ensure that employees understand the importance of ethical behavior and the potential consequences of unethical actions. In this course, we elevate ethical constraints in all data management stages as outlined in the following chapters.

AI ethics in finance refers to the principles and guidelines that govern the responsible development and use of artificial intelligence in banking and financial services. As AI becomes increasingly prevalent in the industry, it is crucial to establish ethical frameworks to ensure fairness, transparency and accountability in AI-driven decision-making processes.

AI ethics in finance encompasses a set of moral principles and values that guide the implementation of AI technologies in banking and financial services. These ethical considerations are essential to maintain public trust, protect customer interests, and mitigate potential risks associated with AI adoption. The importance of AI ethics in finance cannot be overstated, as it helps to ensure that AI systems are designed and deployed in a manner that aligns with societal values and regulatory requirements.

The ethical use of AI in banking and finance is crucial for several reasons. Firstly, it helps to prevent bias and discrimination in financial decision-making processes, such as credit scoring and loan approvals. Secondly, it promotes transparency and explainability in AI-driven decisions, allowing customers and regulators to understand how these decisions are made. Lastly, it safeguards customer data privacy and security, which is paramount in the financial industry.

Integrity

Data integrity is a crucial aspect of any organization that deals with data, especially in the FinTech industry. It refers to the accuracy, consistency, and reliability of data over its entire life cycle, from creation to deletion. In simple terms, data integrity ensures that the data is accurate and trustworthy and that it has not been tampered with or corrupted in any way.

The process of maintaining data integrity involves implementing high standards of ethical behavior and using algorithms that are designed to identify and prevent data errors and inconsistencies. It requires a deep understanding of the data, its sources, and all the related processes that govern its use. It also involves regular monitoring and auditing of the data to ensure that it remains accurate and consistent. In the FinTech industry, data integrity is of utmost importance because it deals with sensitive financial information. Any data breach or error in the data can have severe consequences for both the customers and the business. Therefore, FinTech companies must adhere to strict data integrity policies and implement advanced security measures to protect their data from unauthorized access.

One of the key aspects of data integrity is maintaining a clear and accurate record of all data transactions. This includes logging all changes made to the data, who made those changes, and when they were made. This helps to maintain accountability and transparency in the data management process and ensures that any errors or inconsistencies can be traced back to their source, the source of truth.

In this book, data integrity is considered to be a critical aspect of any organization that deals with data, particularly in the FinTech sector. It requires high standards of ethical behavior, advanced algorithms, and regular monitoring and auditing to ensure that the data remains accurate and consistent. By implementing strict data integrity policies, businesses can protect their customers' sensitive information and maintain their trust in the organization.

Security

Data security is yet another critical aspect of any business operation, especially in the modern era where data breaches and cyberattacks are becoming increasingly common. In essence, data security refers to the measures put in place to protect sensitive information from unauthorized access or disclosure. This includes personal data, financial information and other sensitive data that could be used for fraudulent purposes. As a business in the FinTech domain, you are the custodian of your customer's data.

One of the key components of data security is the use of algorithms to encrypt and decrypt data. Encryption is the process of converting plain text into a code that can only be deciphered with a specific key or password. This prevents unauthorized access to sensitive information, thereby mitigating the risk of fraud. In addition, data security also involves the use of firewalls, antivirus software, and other tools to prevent malicious attacks on digital systems. To maintain high standards of data security, FinTech businesses must adopt ethical behavior when handling sensitive data. This includes ensuring that employees are trained on data protection best practices, implementing strict access controls, and regularly monitoring and auditing digital systems for vulnerabilities. Furthermore, businesses must also adhere to regulatory requirements such as GDPR to ensure that data is processed and stored in accordance with the highest quality standards.

In the FinTech industry, data security is of utmost importance given the sensitive nature of financial information. With the increasing adoption of digital banking and payment solutions, FinTech companies must ensure that their systems are secure and that customer data is protected at all times. This involves implementing robust security protocols, conducting regular security audits and ensuring that all third-party vendors adhere to the same high standards of data security. As a business in the FinTech domain, you are the custodian of your customer's data.

In this book, data governance is a critical aspect of data management that is essential for ensuring data quality, integrity and security. It is especially important in industries such as FinTech where data is a critical factor for success. Data is considered as the new gold, and algorithms are the engines that drive the digital world. Algorithms are complex mathematical models that help in analyzing vast amounts of data to derive insights and make predictions. However, for algorithms to be effective, they need to be fed with high-quality data that is accurate, reliable and consistent. This is where data governance comes into the picture. Data governance is the process of managing the availability, usability, integrity and security of the data used by an organization.

Data governance is the critical link between algorithms and data. The quality of the data used to train the algorithms determines the accuracy and effectiveness of the algorithms. If the data is inaccurate, inconsistent or incomplete, the algorithms will not be able to provide reliable insights or make accurate predictions. Data governance ensures that the data used by the algorithms is of high quality and meets the standards set by the organization.

1.5 Summary

This chapter outlines the significance of **Data Science for FinTech**, emphasizing its transformative impact on the financial sector. We explain the role of data science in improving decision-making in finance, especially through the rise of FinTech. This chapter also covers **data literacy**, essential skill for interpreting financial data streams and enabling informed decision-making, which has become increasingly critical in a data-driven industry. Also discussing the role of **algorithms**, their characteristics, pseudocode, and application of Python scripting in providing financial solutions. Finally, we emphasize the importance of **data governance**, addressing concerns about AI ethics, data integrity, and security, which are paramount in handling sensitive financial data.

Data science has been rapidly gaining popularity in the banking and finance industry. With the rise of FinTech, there is a greater need for financial institutions to adopt data-driven approaches to stay ahead of the competition. Data science has the potential to transform the way that banks and other financial institutions operate, from improving risk management to enhancing customer experience. The future of banking and finance lies in the frontiers of data science, where advanced analytics and machine learning can help financial institutions make better decisions. Data science can help banks identify new opportunities to increase profitability, while also reducing operational costs. By analyzing customer data, for example, banks can gain insights into customer behavior and preferences, which can inform product development and marketing strategies. However, as with any new technology, there are concerns around ethics and integrity. The use of data in banking must be done responsibly and with transparency, ensuring that customer privacy is protected. Financial institutions must also ensure that their algorithms are not biased or discriminatory in any way. In conclusion, data science has the potential to revolutionize the banking and finance industry, providing new insights and efficiencies that were previously impossible. However, it is important that financial institutions approach new technologies with caution, ensuring that ethical and integrity concerns are addressed. By doing so, FinTech operators as well as banks or other financial institutions can gain a competitive advantage and provide better services and products to their customers.

1.6 Concept Questions and Answers

Q1: What is data literacy and why is it crucial in the financial services industry?

A1: Data literacy is the ability to read, understand, work with and communicate data effectively. It's about understanding the source of data, its quality and how it can be used to solve problems and make informed decisions. In the world of finance, data is constantly generated through transactions, customer interactions, market movements and more. Being data literate means finance professionals can do the following:

- Extract meaningful insights from complex data sets: Identify trends, assess risks and make better-informed decisions.
- Develop data-driven strategies: Optimize investments, improve customer experiences and create innovative financial products.
- Communicate data effectively: Share findings with stakeholders, explain complex concepts and build trust through transparency.

Q2: What are algorithms and how are they used in FinTech?

A2: Algorithms are sets of well-defined instructions that solve problems or perform specific tasks. They are the building blocks of computer programs and are crucial for automating processes and analyzing data. Here's how algorithms impact FinTech:

- Algorithmic Trading: Automatically execute trades based on pre-set rules and market conditions, enabling faster and more efficient trading.
- Risk Management: Analyze large data sets to identify and assess potential financial risks, leading to more informed risk mitigation strategies.
- Personalized Financial Services: Offer tailored recommendations and services based on individual customer data and financial goals.

- Fraud Detection: Identify unusual patterns in transactions to detect and prevent fraudulent activities.

Q3: What is pseudocode and how does it help in developing FinTech solutions?

A3: Pseudocode is a simplified way of describing a program's logic without using the strict syntax of a specific programming language. It's like a blueprint for your code, written in a way that is easy for humans to understand. Benefits of pseudocode:

- Enhanced Planning: It helps developers plan the structure and logic of their programs before writing actual code, reducing errors and rework.
- Improved Collaboration: Makes it easier for teams to communicate and discuss ideas, as it's more accessible than complex code.
- Error Detection: Helps identify logic errors early in the development process, leading to more robust and efficient solutions.

Q4: What is data governance and why is it essential for financial institutions?

A4: Data governance is the overall management of the availability, usability, integrity, and security of data within an organization. It involves establishing policies, procedures, and responsibilities to ensure that data is managed effectively and ethically. Importance in finance:

- Regulatory Compliance: Meeting stringent regulatory requirements for data privacy, security and reporting.
- Risk Management: Minimizing risks associated with inaccurate data, data breaches and data misuse.
- Data Quality: Ensuring data accuracy, consistency and reliability for effective decision-making and business operations.
- Trust and Reputation: Building and maintaining trust with customers and stakeholders by demonstrating responsible data management.

Q5: How AI Ethics play a role in financial services?

A5: Ethical considerations in AI for finance:

- Bias and Fairness: Ensuring AI models do not perpetuate existing biases, leading to discriminatory outcomes in lending, credit scoring or other financial decisions.
- Transparency and Explainability: Making AI-driven decisions understandable and interpretable to customers and regulators.
- Data Privacy and Security: Protecting customer data from unauthorized access and misuse, especially in the context of increasingly sophisticated AI systems.
- Accountability: Establishing clear lines of responsibility for AI-driven decisions and their potential consequences. Key principles:
- Fairness: AI systems should treat individuals fairly and avoid creating or reinforcing biases.
- Transparency: The decision-making process of AI systems should be understandable and explainable.
- Accountability: There should be clear mechanisms for holding individuals and organizations accountable for AI-driven decisions.
- Privacy: Customer data should be protected and used responsibly, in line with privacy regulations.

1.7 Exercises

Exercise 1.1

E1: Replicate call option valuation steps from the previous text:

i) design the financial product, call option and define the pricing algorithm,
ii) define the solution using pseudocode and
iii) write Python code all with previously predefined input parameters, however use this to price a put option and then utilize combination to show the viability of put-call parity. Interpret actual numerical results. Use AI Copilot and check and review all AI outputs. Discuss your results.

1.8 Further Reading

- Cormen, T. H., Leiserson, C. E., Rivest, R. L., & Stein, C. (2022). Introduction to Algorithms, 4th Ed, Massachusetts Institute of Technology.
- Dickerson, A., & Hric, J. (2024). FINS5545 Financial Market Data Literacy Course Notes, UNSW Business School.
- Hull, J. C. (2005). Options, Futures and Other Derivatives, Prentice Hall.
- Kleppmann, M. (2017). Designing Data-Intensive Applications, O'Reilly.
- Lopez de Prado, M. (2020). Machine Learning for Asset Managers, Cambridge University Press.

1.9 Reference

[1.1] Black, F., & Scholes, M. (1973). The pricing of options and corporate liabilities. Journal of Political Economy, 81(3), 637–654.

Chapter 2

Data Management for FinTech

2.1 Introduction

In the world of FinTech, data is an essential component that fuels the industry's growth and innovation. Data management is the process of collecting, processing, storing, analyzing and visualizing data to ensure that it is accessible, accurate, reliable, and secure. It involves the systematic and organized handling of data throughout its life cycle, from data generation to data disposal.

Data generation is the first step in data management, where data is created through various sources such as transactions, customer interactions, social media, and other digital channels. Data collection is the process of gathering this data through various means, including automated systems, surveys and manual inputs. Data processing is the next step, where the

DOI: 10.4324/9781003477747-3

collected data is cleaned, transformed and standardized to make it suitable for analysis. Data storage is critical in data management, where the data is stored in various formats such as databases, data warehouses and data lakes. Data management ensures that the data is secure and accessible to authorized personnel. Data analysis is the process of extracting insights from the data using statistical and analytical tools to identify patterns, trends and relationships. Data visualization is the final step in data management, where the analyzed data is transformed into visual representations such as charts, graphs and dashboards. This helps stakeholders to understand the data and make informed decisions based on the insights gained.

Data management is crucial in FinTech as it enables financial institutions to leverage data to develop innovative products and services, enhance customer experiences and improve operational efficiency. With the increasing volume, velocity and variety of data, FinTech companies need robust data management strategies to ensure that the data is accurate, reliable and secure. Overall, data management is a critical component of the FinTech industry, where data is the lifeblood of innovation and growth. By effectively managing data through its life cycle, FinTech companies can unlock the full potential of data and create value for their stakeholders.

In this chapter, we look into the intricacies of data management from the perspective of **digital data factory (DDF)** concepts. Data management from a digital data factory concept perspective involves the creation of a data lake, prompt and feature engineering, model design and implementation stages or stations as we define these terms. These processes are essential in helping businesses to optimize their operations, improve the customer experience and drive growth. By leveraging these processes, businesses can gain valuable insights into their operations and make data-driven decisions that can lead to long-term success. Finally, we link hereabove data management concepts to basic data architecture designs and conclude the chapter with sample of data structure formats as implemented using an industry case study.

Learning Outcomes

- Introduce digital data factory (DDF) concept
- Outline data management life cycle
- Explain essential attributes of data infrastructure
- Understand how cloud capabilities are used in FinTech
- Overview data structures and data types
- Explore relevant real-life case studies

2.2 Digital Data Factory (DDF)

The process of data management begins with the creation of a data lake, which is a centralized repository that allows businesses to store and analyze large amounts of structured and unstructured data. A data lake is an important aspect of data management as it enables businesses to store, manage and process vast quantities of data in real time.

Prompt and feature engineering are also essential when it comes to data management. Prompt engineering involves the creation of a prompt system that prompts users to take specific actions based on their behavior. Feature engineering, on the other hand, is the process of transforming raw data into features that can be used by machine learning algorithms. The process of prompt and feature engineering is crucial in data management as it enables businesses to identify patterns and trends that can be used to optimize their operations.

Model design is another critical aspect of data management as it involves the creation of predictive models that can be used to forecast future trends and behaviors. This involves the use of machine learning algorithms, which are designed to analyze large sets of data and identify patterns that can be used to make predictions. Model design is a crucial aspect of data management as it enables businesses to make data-driven decisions that can improve their operations and drive growth.

Implementation is the final stage of data management in the context of this book, and it involves the deployment of models and strategies that have been designed to optimize business operations. This involves the use of data analytics tools, which allow businesses to monitor and analyze their data in real time. The process of implementation is critical as it enables businesses to leverage their data assets to enhance the customer experience and improve overall business performance.

From a practical standpoint in this book, we look at data management from the perspective of digital data factory floor. Going forward, we use the notion of the digital factory floor with workstations as our guiding principles in solving complex FinTech/data management tasks. In short, instead of producing "physical widgets" we are producing a digital FinTech product or a service.

In generic terms, we define our data factory floor comprising of four distinct stations. This is a fully secured environment, as we know FinTech operates in a heavily regulated environment. Hence, digital cryptographic security is an absolute prerequisite while dealing with issues relevant to data management. This digital data factory can be deployed on your private servers or cloud environments such as AWS, Azure, Google.

Digital data factory (DDF) floor concept shown next:

As per Figure 2.1, inside the secured walls of the data factory floor we operate four distinct workstations:

- Station #1: Data Lake ETL (Extract, Transform, Load)
- Station #2: Prompt and Feature Engineering
- Station #3: Model Design
- Station #4: Implementation

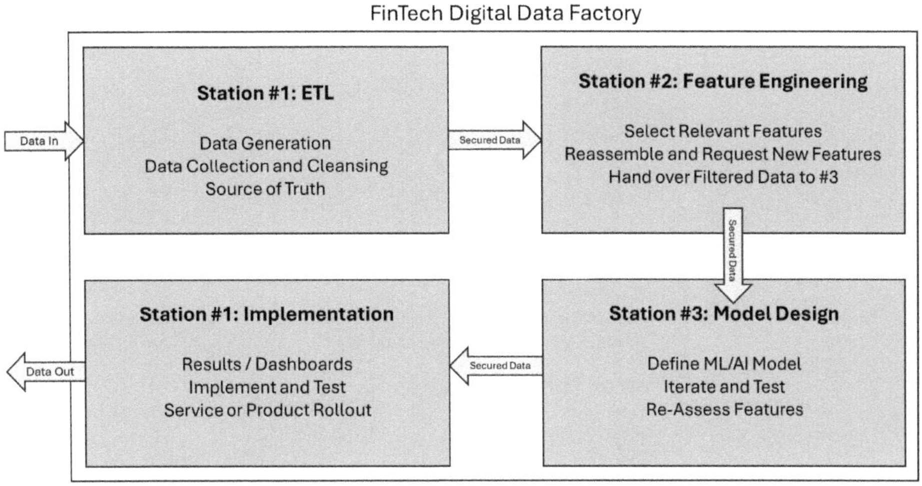

Figure 2.1 Data Factory Concept

These stations are all interconnected with the arrows depicting application programming interfaces (API) ensuring seamless internal communication across these conceptual data workstations.

- **Station #1: ETL (Extract, Transform, Load)**
  - Generation
  - Collection
- **Station #2: Feature Engineering**
  - Prompting
  - Processing
- **Station #3: Model Design**
  - Modeling
  - Analysis
- **Station #4: Implementation**
  - Visualization
  - Interpretation

As per Figure 2.2, in the context of data life cycle, information life span of the data is determined by its relevance to the business, and data that is no longer useful is archived. The data life cycle involves generation, collection, prompting, processing, modeling, analysis, visualization and the eventual end of information life span. Each stage is essential in ensuring that businesses leverage their data to gain insights and make informed decisions. Effective data management is critical in optimizing the value of data and driving business growth. In this book, we look at data management from the perspective of a simulated digital data factory floor. We proceed by introducing the four workstations.

Station 1: Data Lake

Data management is an integral part of any organization's day-to-day operations. In the extract, transform and load stage of the data management process, data is extracted from various sources and transformed into a format that can be easily understood by the system. This stage is crucial

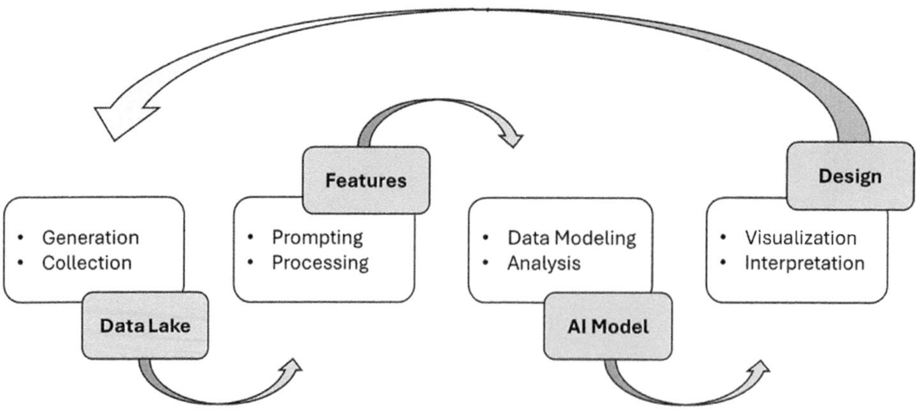

Figure 2.2 Data Factory Concept Data Life Cycle

because the data that is passed on to the next stage, that is, prompt and feature engineering, needs to be authentic and clear. This is a critical first station, and you are responsible for data clarity and authenticity. You guarantee the data source of truth. You are the gatekeepers.

The data lake stage is where the data is stored in its raw form. It is a centralized repository where data from various sources is collected and stored. The data lake is an essential component of the data management process because it provides a single source of truth for all the data that is used in the organization. This means that all the data that is stored in the data lake is authentic, and there is no ambiguity about its accuracy. We must guarantee the data's authenticity by ensuring that it is sourced from reliable sources and has not been tampered with in any way. We must also ensure that the data is clear and easily understandable by removing any ambiguity or redundancy. As gatekeepers, we must guarantee the data's authenticity and clarity to ensure that the data that is passed on to the next stage is tailored to the specific needs of the organization.

Task

Your task is to collate, collect, search and find and amass all relevant data streams – this could be structured as well as unstructured data formats. **Authenticity of the data is critical** in this stage. Secondly, your task is to ascertain and cleanse all received and onboarded data streams and store and secure access to all relevant points. Moreover, this workstation is responsible for daily data maintenance and workflow. Lastly, load and store is an integral part of workstation one tasks.

Techniques and Skills

Given the clarity of the task in Station #1, next are the required steps and techniques. In this book we cover the following data handling techniques:

- Data input/output
- Data preservation
- Data curation and conversion
- Data manipulation
- API access

Ensuring compliance with GDPR and PSD2 is paramount for managing financial data securely and effectively. The General Data Protection Regulation (GDPR) [2.1] mandates stringent data protection measures, requiring financial institutions to safeguard personal data and uphold individuals' privacy rights. Meanwhile, the Payment Services Directive 2 (PSD2) [2.2] aims to enhance payment services across the EU by promoting innovation and competition while ensuring secure transactions. Adhering to these regulations not only protects sensitive financial information from breaches and misuse but also fosters trust among clients and partners. For data scientists, business analysts, and machine learning engineers, understanding and implementing GDPR and PSD2 compliance is crucial in developing robust, secure and innovative financial solutions that meet regulatory standards and drive industry transformation. It is at this gatekeeper phase, Station 1: Data Lake, FinTech business is in a position to implement these regulatory measures to safeguard the entire solution.

All of the aforementioned is covered in practical pseudocode and Python-driven exercises to build up your skills from simple to more advanced data handling techniques. The skills needed in this station are predominantly technical and operational in nature, and you are not required to know the business landscape.

Station 2: Prompt and Feature Engineering

Prompt and feature engineering workstation is responsible for the selection of the most appropriate features to be passed on to the next Station #3 Model Design. Data features are relevant data points or streams, relevant in terms of the business problem at hand. In short, you are responsible for correct and optimal use of the vast data points collected in Station #1.

A prompt is a message or question that is presented to a user in order to elicit a response or action. In the context of a chatbot, a prompt could be a request for information, a suggestion, or a call to action. The purpose of a prompt is to guide the user towards a desired outcome or goal. User here can be an AI algorithm or a team of technologists. In order to create effective prompts, it is important to have a thorough understanding of the user's needs and preferences. This requires a deep understanding of the user's behavior patterns, preferences and expectations.

Feature engineering is the process of selecting and extracting the most relevant features from a data set in order to optimize the performance of a machine learning model. The goal of feature engineering is to create a model that is accurate, efficient and effective at predicting model behavior. The data that is passed on to workstation #3 for model design must be carefully selected and prepared in order to ensure that it is both relevant and useful. Data utility refers to the extent to which data can be effectively used to achieve a desired outcome. In the context of a chatbot, data utility might refer to the ability of the data to accurately predict model behavior, or to provide insights into model preferences and needs. In order to maximize data utility, it is important to have a deep understanding of the business knowledge and context in which the AI tool or a team of technologist will be used. This requires a broad understanding of the industry, customer needs and competitive landscape. Prompt and feature engineering is important stage in the data management process.

Task

Your task is to consume and fully utilize provided data streams from Station #1 and provide well-defined filtered data features for further processing in Station #3. **Utility of the data is critical** in this stage. Understanding of the data and the business requirements is an integral part of this task.

Techniques and Skills

In this station we expose you to the following skills and techniques:

- Data analytics
- Graphical data visualization
- Data manipulation
- Prompt engineering

In the realm of financial decision-making, the integration of AI has brought remarkable advancements, yet it has also spotlighted critical issues of bias and fairness. AI systems, if not carefully designed and monitored, can inadvertently perpetuate existing biases, leading to unfair outcomes in credit scoring, loan approvals, and fraud detection. For instance, historical data reflecting societal inequalities can skew AI algorithms, disproportionately affecting marginalized groups. FinTech operators, data scientists, business analysts, and machine learning engineers, must prioritize developing fair and unbiased models via prompt engineering. Ensuring fairness in AI-driven financial services is not just a technical challenge but a moral imperative to foster trust and transparency in the industry.

All of the aforementioned is covered in practical pseudocode and Python-driven exercises to build up your skills from simple to more advanced data handling techniques. The skills needed in this station are predominantly analytical in nature, and you need to understand the business landscape and contemplate potential biases across your solutions.

Station 3: Model Design

Model design workstation is responsible for analytics and model design. Authenticity and utilization given the collection of available data as combined with the business problem at hand forms the core brains of this station. Your job here is to consume Station #2 prompts and features and build a sustainable modelling framework to deliver business-critical and actionable results. Your results are being passed on the last Station #4 for final implementation.

A model design workstation is an important component utilizing the field of predictive analytics. It is responsible for creating models that can accurately forecast future outcomes. The success of these models is resulting in the clarity and parsimony of the results. A clear and concise model design can help businesses make informed decisions and stay ahead of the competition. The model design workstation utilizes advanced techniques such as neural networks and chatbots to create models that are both efficient and effective. A neural network is a machine learning technique that has been gaining popularity in recent years. It is a system of interconnected nodes that are designed to function like neurons in the human brain. This technology is capable of analyzing large amounts of data and identifying patterns that can be used to make predictions. The model design workstation uses neural networks to create models that can accurately forecast future outcomes.

Chatbots are another technology that is utilized in the model design workstation. These are computer programs that simulate human conversation. They are designed to interact with customers and provide them with information and assistance. Chatbots are particularly useful in the field of predictive analytics as they can gather data from customers and use it to create more accurate models.

Forecasting is a key component of predictive analytics. It involves analyzing historical data and using it to predict future outcomes. The model design workstation uses advanced algorithms to analyze data and create models that can accurately forecast future trends. This technology is particularly useful in industries such as finance, where accurate forecasting can help businesses make informed decisions and stay ahead of the competition.

Task

Your task at this stage is in converting, modeling and analyzing pre-processed and cleansed data streams into actionable business decisions. **Clarity and parsimony of the resulting data is critical** in this stage. You are delivering the state-of-the-art modelling results for your business and often ask, "So what?!"

Techniques and Skills

In this station we expose you to the following skills and techniques only, from the vast array of possible models:

- Regression
- Portfolio optimization
- ARIMA forecasting
- Recurrent neural network
- Large language models

It is at this stage, model evaluation plays a critical role. How accurate is the model prediction? How relevant are the results? What is out of sample model performance? Addressing these questions is of utmost importance. As an example, designing fraud detection model and evaluating the performance of predictive models for fraud detection is crucial to ensure accuracy and reliability. Techniques such as root mean square error (RMSE), precision-recall and AUC-ROC curves play pivotal roles in assessing model performance. RMSE provides a measure of the model's prediction errors, while precision-recall metrics help in understanding the trade-off between the model's ability to identify fraudulent transactions and its tendency to produce false positives. The AUC-ROC curve further aids in evaluating the model's overall ability to discriminate between fraudulent and non-fraudulent cases. Additionally, implementing cross-validation techniques is essential to prevent overfitting, ensuring that the model generalizes well to unseen data. By leveraging these evaluation methods, data scientists and machine learning engineers can enhance the robustness and effectiveness of fraud detection models, ultimately safeguarding financial institutions against fraudulent activities.

All of the aforementioned is covered in practical pseudocode and Python-driven exercises to build up your skills from simple to more advanced data handling techniques. The skills needed in this station are predominantly mathematical and analytical in nature, and you need to understand the business landscape and be able to simplify complex frameworks for further presentations.

Station 4: Product Implementation

The product implementation stage is the final step in the FinTech data management process and an essential component of the customer journey. This is the stage where your product is exposed to the final consumer in a production environment. It is at this stage that you consume results from Station #3 and package and sell the results in the form of a product or a service. In addition, you are responsible for providing all stakeholder feedback to Station #3.

At this stage, the product or service created by an organization is delivered to the customers or clients. It is a critical stage as it determines the success of the entire business. The product implementation stage involves a detailed and systematic approach to ensure that the final product meets the customer's expectations.

The first step in product implementation is to ensure that the product is of high quality and matches the look and feel that the customers expect. The final product should be visually appealing, easy to use, and intuitive, ensuring that customers have a positive experience. This step requires close collaboration between the development team and the designers to ensure that the product is aesthetically pleasing and easy to use.

The next step in product implementation is to ensure that the product is optimized for data monetization. This step involves ensuring that the product is designed to capture data effectively, allowing the organization to extract insights that can be used to generate revenue. The product should be designed to capture data at every stage of the customer journey, allowing the organization to gain a complete understanding of customer behavior.

Finally, the product implementation stage involves testing and validation to ensure that the product meets the desired outcomes. The testing process involves performing various tests to ensure that the product functions as intended and is free of any defects. The validation process involves ensuring that the product meets the customer's expectations and addresses their pain points. This stage requires close collaboration between the development team, designers and other stakeholders to ensure that the final product is a success.

Task

Your task is to interpret your business requirements and interpret and connect your business data results and create saleable, competitive and concise product or service delivery. **Added value of your data solution is critical** in this stage. You are delivering the final product to your clients and stakeholders abiding by and responding to strict regulatory and business requirements.

Techniques and Skills

In this last station, we expose you to the following skills and techniques:

- Data visualization
- Data interpretation
- Data reporting and presentation
- Ethical consideration

As an example, implementing automated credit scoring models, while innovative, raise significant ethical concerns that must be addressed to ensure fair and equitable financial services. One of the primary issues is **bias**; these models can inadvertently perpetuate existing inequalities if they rely on biased historical data. For instance, certain demographic groups may be unfairly disadvantaged due to systemic biases embedded in the data used to train these models. **Transparency** is another critical concern. The opaque nature of many machine learning algorithms makes it difficult for individuals to understand how their credit scores are determined, leading to a lack of trust and accountability. Furthermore, there is the issue of **accountability**. When decisions are made by automated systems, it becomes challenging to hold any entity responsible for errors or unfair outcomes. Addressing these ethical concerns is crucial for building trust and ensuring that automated credit scoring models serve all individuals fairly and justly.

All of the aforementioned is covered in practical pseudocode and Python-driven exercises to build up your skills from simple to more advanced data handling techniques. The skills needed in this station are predominantly technical and business-focused.

2.3 Essential Data Architecture

Based on our hypothetical digital data factory setup, we explore some core design attributes and address following questions: How would you set up your FinTech enterprise? How can you ensure compliance and data governance and data protection? What is the essential data architecture of your digital data factory floor?

Platform Attributes

We outline a core list of attributes needed to be in place for a platform or as defined by our digital data factory floor attributes of our FinTech architecture:

- Platform agnostic
- Light, flexible and agile
- API secured
- On-demand pricing, storage and computational power enabled
- Scalable
- Crypto secured
- Quantum computing adaptable
- Hybrid cloud, analytics engines, blockchain and R&D-enabled

There are several essential data architecture components that are crucial in building FinTech software applications that are platform agnostic, light, flexible, agile, on-demand, secured, scalable and API enabled.

One of the most important data architecture components is platform agnosticism. This means that the software application should be able to run on any platform without any issues. It allows for greater flexibility and adaptability, as it enables the application to work seamlessly with different systems and technologies. Another critical component is the application's lightness and flexibility, which ensure that it can handle large volumes of data and transactions without slowing down or crashing.

Agility is also a crucial component of data architecture, as it enables the application to respond quickly to changes in the market or user needs. This means that the application should be able to adapt to new technologies, regulations and customer preferences quickly. On-demand access to data is also essential in FinTech software applications, as it allows users to access and analyze data in real-time. This enables them to make informed decisions about financial transactions and investments, for example.

Security is another critical data architecture component in FinTech software applications. It ensures that sensitive financial data is protected from cyber threats and unauthorized access. Scalability is also vital, as it enables the application to handle growing volumes of data and transactions without any issues or downtime. Finally, API enablement is crucial in FinTech software applications, as it allows for seamless integration with other systems and technologies.

These components and features ensure that the application can effectively manage financial data and transactions while providing users with seamless access to data and analysis. As such, they are critical in building FinTech software applications that can meet the needs of customers in a rapidly evolving digital landscape. Within this framework and again from a conceptual standpoint, let us draw a basic data architecture next.

As per Figure 2.3, the backbone of the data architecture is based on "Data Lake," as seen in the previous section. This is the space allocated to host your databases, storage accounts, data cleansing tools and internal API gateways. Data inputs into this data lake consist of data streams, one being live data (such as Twitter or chat conversations); the other consists of data enrichments (such as weather observations or supply chain statistics). Data outputs

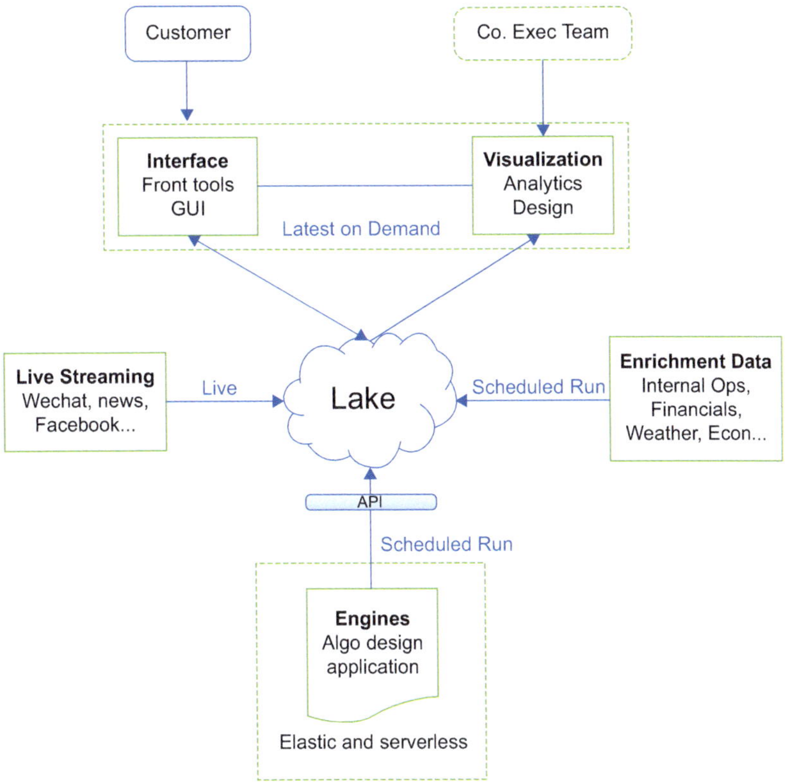

Figure 2.3 Data Factory Flow Concept

from this data lake consists of internal data streams delivered to your ultimate data consumers and main stakeholders. Station #1 ETL and Station #2 Feature Engineering teams operate in this environment.

Station #3 Model Design team operates within the "Engines" space. This is allocated to host your computing capabilities and internal API gateways. This is the area where models are being developed and released. Lastly, Station #4 Implementation team operates in the "Interface/Visualisation" space above. This is the space allocated to provide interaction between the business and technology platform. Your stakeholders have a tangible view of your FinTech product or service offering.

Figure 2.4 depicts essential data architecture concept in a form of features or components. This view links your external customer journey to your internal data journey.

2.4 Cloud Computing Application in Finance

The world of FinTech has been revolutionized by the emergence of cloud computing applications. Cloud infrastructure has enabled FinTech companies to leverage the benefits of agility, scalability and cost-effectiveness. It has also enabled faster software implementation, allowing companies to quickly adapt to changing market trends and customer preferences.

One of the major concerns for FinTech companies is data security, and cloud computing has been a game-changer in this regard. Cloud providers invest heavily in security measures,

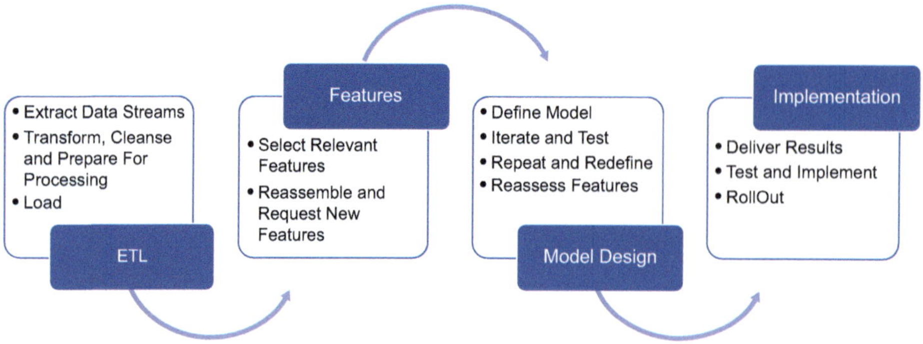

Figure 2.4 Essential Data Architecture Concept

such as encryption, access controls and monitoring, to ensure the protection of sensitive customer data. This has given FinTech companies the confidence to store and process data in the cloud, freeing them from the burden of maintaining their own infrastructure and security protocols. However, with the increasing use of cloud computing in FinTech, there has also been a greater focus on regulation. Regulators are becoming more stringent in their requirements for ensuring data privacy and security. FinTech companies need to ensure that their cloud providers comply with these regulations and standards and have appropriate measures in place to monitor and control data access.

Another advantage of cloud computing application in FinTech is the ability to collaborate and share data across multiple platforms. This has allowed for greater integration between financial institutions and technology companies, leading to the development of innovative financial products and services. The future of FinTech is inextricably linked to the cloud, and potential hybrid cloud solutions and companies that embrace this technology will be well-positioned to succeed in the years ahead.

Microsoft Azure Infrastructure

From a practical standpoint, we mirror the previous data architecture onto Microsoft (MS) Azure Cloud environment.

Figure 2.5 interposes our conceptual data architecture onto one of the cloud providers, MS Azure platform. In order to implement our data architecture, several MS Azure tools are selected (to name a few):

- Azure Data Lake
- Azure Factories and Storage Accounts
- API Gateways
- Azure ML Studios
- Power App
- Power BI
- Azure Web Services

To expand our understanding of the intricacies of "current" data architecture we explore a more advanced example from MS Azure, specifically focusing on Azure Kubernetes Service (AKS) as per Figure 2.6. To build, deliver and scale containerized apps faster, MS Azure

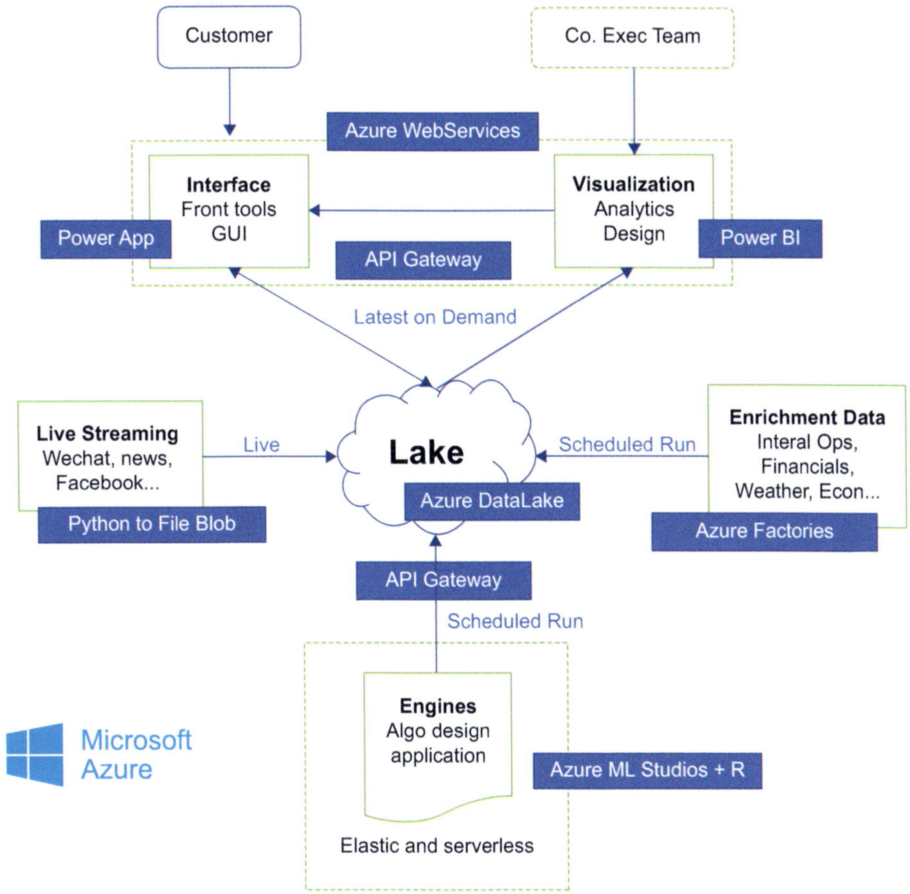

Figure 2.5 MS Azure Cloud Environment

offers open-source Kubernetes tools for deploying and managing those containers at scale – microservices style.

Exercise

No. 1 Read the AKS reference to get familiar with current state-of-the-art data architecture delivery platforms [2.3]. No. 2 Read (Optional) ML Architecture article and compare this AI/ML approach to current “standard” architecture designs [2.4].

Note, a similar exercise can be conducted by looking at other cloud providers. In this book, we refrain from using any particular cloud provider as we focus our attention on data management components within the four walls of our digital data factory. We stay on the lower layers of the data architecture focused on programming implementations and enhancing our data management skillsets by handling various data components and programmatically dealing with FinTech like business challenges. On that note, we move to the next sample for demonstration purposes.

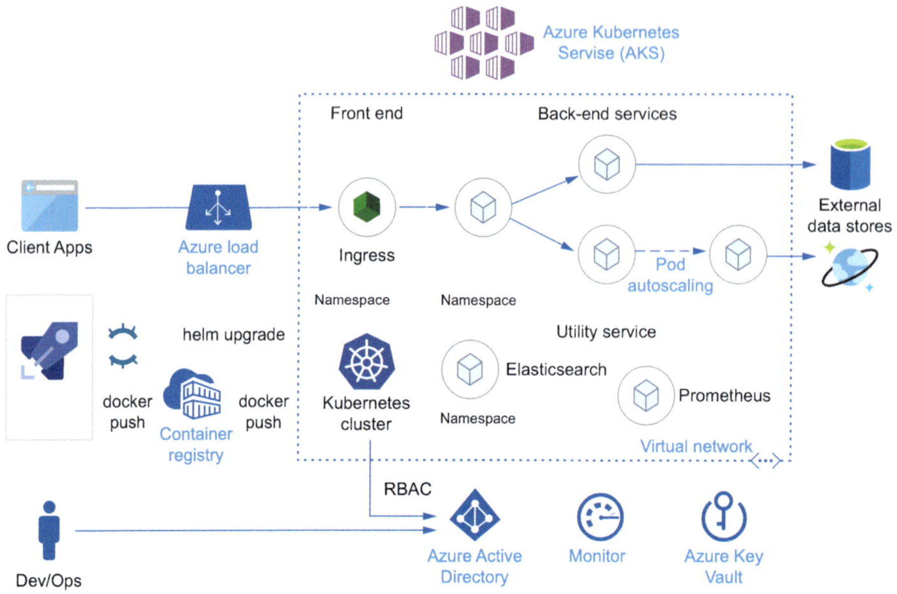

Figure 2.6 MS Azure Kubernetes Service Example

Amazon AWS Infrastructure

Amazon Web Services (AWS) is a leading cloud platform that offers a wide range of capabilities to support infrastructure and digital transformation. The platform is designed to provide a flexible, scalable and cost-effective solution for hosting applications, managing data, and running infrastructure. One of the key advantages of AWS is that it provides a cloud-based infrastructure that enables businesses to easily scale their operations up or down as needed. This means that businesses can quickly respond to changes in demand, without having to invest in expensive hardware or software.

AWS also offers a range of data services, including AWS Data Factory, which enables businesses to integrate, transform, and process structured and unstructured data from various sources. This helps businesses to better understand their customers, optimize their operations and make data-driven decisions. With AWS Data Factory concept, businesses can easily create data pipelines that move and transform data between different systems and applications.

Figure 2.7 interposes our conceptual data architecture onto one of the cloud providers, MS Azure platform. In order to implement our data architecture, several MS Azure tools are selected (to name a few):

- AWS S2
- AWS Factories and Storage Accounts
- API Gateways
- AWS Lamdba
- AWS Route 53 WebServices

Similar to MS Azure, AWS provides a flexible and cost-effective solution that can help businesses to achieve their goals. With its cloud-based infrastructure, data services and security

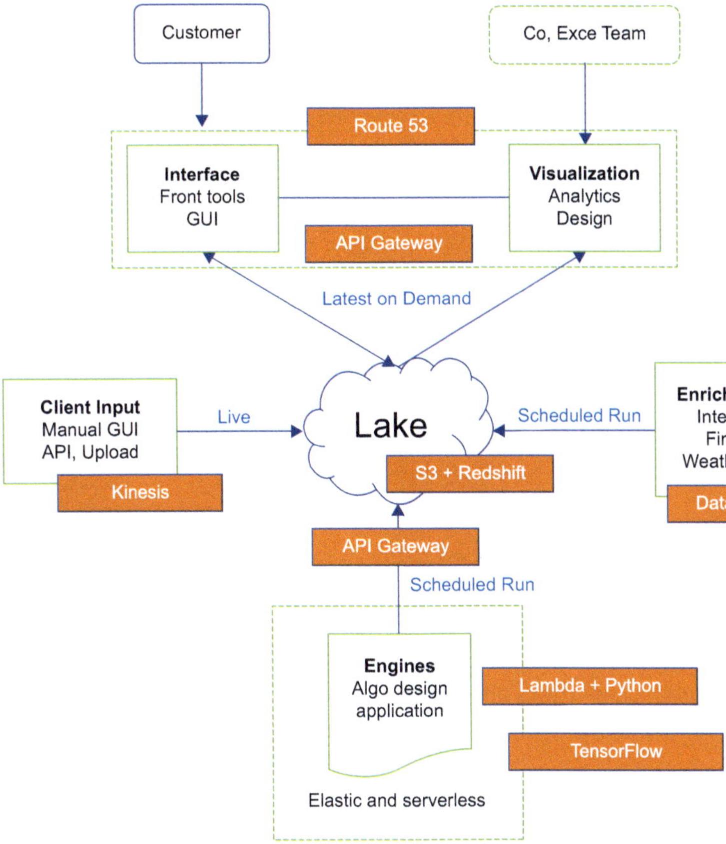

Figure 2.7 AWS Cloud Environment

features, AWS is a powerful platform that can help businesses to succeed in today's fast-paced and ever-changing business environment.

2.5 Essential Data Structures

The world of data is constantly evolving, and with it, the need for efficient data structures that can handle the vast amounts of information generated every day. Data can be broadly classified into two categories – structured and unstructured data. Structured data refers to information that is organized and follows a specific format, making it easy to store and access. On the other hand, unstructured data refers to complex information that does not follow a specific format, making it difficult to store and access.

Structured data represents only about 20% of the total data generated, while the remaining 80% is unstructured data. Structured data is typically stored in a database and organized using a predefined schema that outlines the data's structure and relationships. This makes it easy to store, access, and retrieve information quickly and efficiently. Structured data is commonly used in applications such as customer relationship management (CRM), enterprise resource planning (ERP) and financial systems.

Unstructured data, on the other hand, is more complex and challenging to store and access. This type of data includes things like social media posts, images, videos and audio files. Unstructured data does not follow a specific format, and the relationships between the data elements are often unclear. As a result, storing and accessing unstructured data require more sophisticated storage and access mechanisms. Unstructured data is commonly used in applications such as content management systems, social media analytics and data mining.

When it comes to storage, structured data is typically stored in a relational database, while unstructured data is often stored in a NoSQL database or object storage service. Structured data can be easily queried and indexed, making it simple to retrieve specific pieces of information quickly. Unstructured data, on the other hand, requires more complex search algorithms and indexing mechanisms to access specific pieces of data. With the growing amount of data generated every day, it is essential to have a clear understanding of these data structures to effectively manage and analyze data.

In Figure 2.8, we look at the variations in data structures [2.5].

Based on the previous statements, the astonishingly obvious observation, as per Gartner, is that

> **around 20% of enterprise data is in structured format whereas around 80% of enterprise data is in unstructured formats.**

Interestingly, and generally speaking, our data literacy at school and university levels have been focused on building skills and proficiencies inclusive of statistical and econometrics methodologies in those 20% structured data formats predominantly.

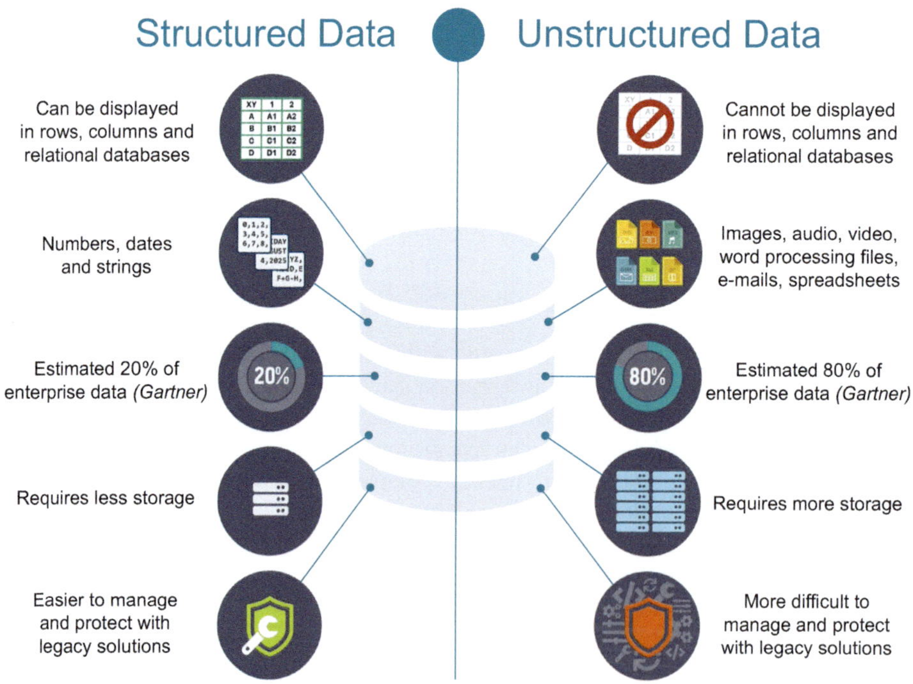

Figure 2.8 Structured vs Unstructured Data

In this book, we expose you to both **structured data** (easy to derive and store and follow in simple data format structures such as rows/columns/tables) as well as **unstructured data** (easy to derive not easy to store or follow with complex data format structures such as text, json, strings, voice, video). Moreover, let us assume we, as a team, are stationed on a **virtual digital factory floor** – data factory floor, to be more exact, comprising of four distinct sections.

Data Business Types

Digital data factory is a powerful tool for businesses to enhance their understanding of essential business data types. It provides a centralized platform for storing and analyzing a variety of data, including fundamental data, market data, generated data and alternative data. Fundamental data refers to financial and economic data that is fundamental to a company's operations, such as revenue, earnings, and cash flow. Market data includes data on stock prices, trading volumes and market trends. Generated data is data that is generated by business operations, such as website traffic, customer behavior and sales data. Alternative data refers to nontraditional data sources, such as social media sentiment and satellite imagery.

Digital data factory enables businesses to combine and analyze these different types of data, allowing them to gain deeper insights into their operations and make more informed business decisions. For example, by combining market data with generated data, businesses can gain a better understanding of consumer behavior and market trends, allowing them to adjust their marketing strategies accordingly. Furthermore, digital data factory allows businesses to easily visualize and analyze their data through interactive dashboards and reports. This not only enhances their understanding of the data but also provides a more efficient way to communicate insights to stakeholders.

Across all workstations of our digital data factory we enhance our understanding of essential data components:

- Data business types
- Data structures
- Data schema

In this section, we introduce a broad spectrum of business data types. All the following data types are provided in structured as well unstructured formats. This is from the perspective of data generators.

Fundamental Data

- Governments
  - Basic macro and microeconomic indicators
  - Government fiscal policies
  - Taxation
  - Regulatory policies
- Companies:
  - Company, sector and industry-level data
  - Annual reports
  - Regulatory filings
  - General market news

Market Data

- Governments:
  - Central bank monetary policies
  - Interest rates
  - Financial news
  - Announcements
  - FX
- Exchanges:
  - Stock prices, volumes, liquidity
  - Commodity prices, volumes, liquidity
  - Capital markets data streams

Generated Data

- Analysts forecasts and reports
- Sell-side and buy-side reports
- Financial institution reviews, reports and analyses
- AI Machine-generated news
- AI Machine-generated reports and analytics

Alternative Data

- Web-based information delivered by scraping
- Weather patterns
- Supply chain traffic
- You: your data footprint
  - Social media profiles
  - Web browsing
  - Personal banking
  - Spending patterns
  - GPS Location

With the ability to combine and analyze fundamental data, market data, generated data and alternative data, businesses can stay ahead of the competition and make data-driven decisions that drive growth and success.

Data Structures

In the previous section, we looked at data types and whoever is the generator of these data streams. Now, we dive deeper into the technical aspects of data capture in terms of data structures. Further discussion using Python is provided in the following lesson on dataframes.

Data structures are an essential component of any programming language. They provide a way to organize and store data in a way that can be easily accessed and manipulated. In the context of structured and unstructured formats, data structures serve as the backbone for both basic and advanced data storage and retrieval.

One of the most basic data structures is the list. A list is a collection of items that are ordered and can be accessed by their index. Lists are commonly used for storing data in a linear format, such as a list of names or numbers. Another common data structure is the dictionary. A dictionary is a collection of key-value pairs that can be accessed by their key. Dictionaries are commonly used for storing data in a nonlinear format, such as a list of attributes for a particular item. When it comes to structured formats, two of the most common file types are CSV and JSON. CSV stands for comma separated values and is a file format that stores data in a tabular format, with each row representing a record and each column representing a field. JSON, on the other hand, is a lightweight data interchange format that is used to store and exchange data between different systems. JSON data is stored in key-value pairs and can represent complex data structures.

Unstructured formats, such as video, voice, and pictures, require more complex data structures for storage and retrieval. These formats require specialized data structures that can handle large amounts of data, such as binary trees or hash tables. Input/output (I/O) operations are also critical for managing these types of data structures, as they allow for efficient reading and writing of data. Whether working with CSV or JSON files, or dealing with more complex data formats like video and voice, data structures are the foundation for effective data management.

Basic Data Structures

As per detail exposition provided in ***Toolkit for FinTech***, basic data structures or formats in this context are heavily used across FinTech businesses with some core formats as shown here:

- Numbers
- Lists
- Strings
- Tuples
- Dictionaries
- Arrays
- Matrices
- Pictures
- Videos
- Voice recordings

Advanced Data Structures

Input I/O Output Operations

Generally speaking, most data in the context of banking and finance is stored on hard disk drives (HDDs) or solid-state disks (SDDs) or form of hybrids, be it in local server farms or cloud-based solution providers such as Amazon AWS, Microsoft Azure or Google Cloud. There is an intricate process of moving data between your hard drive or storage locations into your internal random access memory (RAM) that is light and fast and internalized in your desktop or laptops. I/O operations are therefore very important when dealing with a vast amount of data and trying to utilize the full capacity of your computing capabilities (CPU) or (GPU) levels.

Frankly, big data is just a term used to capture attention, most of the real-world analytics operations in banking and finance process ~100GB of input/output at one go. This is good news for Python and current inbuild I/O tools that we cover here (as opposed to Hadoop/MapReduce, Mongo DB like solutions). Python contains solid in-build functions to serialize and store any objects on disk and to read it back into RAM, utilizing SQL style of handling. This form is perfect for structured data as we understand it in this course.

I/O with Pandas

Here we get exposed to more advanced techniques as used currently on the street, looking at important formats of data variations:

- CVS (comma-separated value)
- SQL (structured query language)
- XLS/XLSX (Microsoft Excel)
- JSON (JavaScript Object Notation)
- HTML (HyperText Markup Language)

Basic I/O

Python can operate with SQL as well as non-SQL-based databases with ease. A good example of an inbuild package is SQLite3. It is shown in practice here:

```
import sqlite3

class MySum:
    def __init__(self):
        self.count = 0

    def step(self, value):
        self.count += value

    def finalize(self):
        return self.count

con = sqlite3.connect(":memory:")
con.create_aggregate("mysum", 1, MySum)
cur = con.cursor()
cur.execute("create table test(i)")
cur.execute("insert into test(i) values (1)")
cur.execute("insert into test(i) values (2)")
cur.execute("select mysum(i) from test")
print(cur.fetchone()[0])
```

The previous example shows how easy it is to generate and create SQL tables directly in-memory on RAM as opposed to a physical disk location. Here we created a simple table with two rows and one column (i) then asked SQL language-wise to return the sum of the values inserted into those fields.

Now, let us look at a more practical example of data generation and data storage in memory replicating simple structure: date, value1, value2. You can think about this to be equivalent to a stock price observation on a given date with close price and close volume:

```
import sqlite3
import numpy as np
import datetime as dt
```

```
con = sqlite3.connect(":memory:")
cur = con.cursor()
cur.execute("create table tester (dates, mark, volume)")

# Generate random numbers in a matrix 10 rows by 2 columns rounded to 2
decimals
data = np.random.standard_normal((10,2)).round(2)

for row in data:
    # This is the qmark style:
    cur.execute("insert into tester values (?, ?, ?)", (dt.datetime.now(), row[0],
row[1]))

# And this is the named style:
cur.execute("select * from tester")

print(cur.fetchmany(10))
```

In these examples, we are using in-memory SQL tables and processing (we look at these processes using Python IDE on your machines). Figure 2.9 depicts in memory SQLite database setup.

From SQL to Array and Plot

To solidify these ideas let's look at another example:

```
import sqlite3
import numpy as np
import datetime as dt
import matplotlib.pyplot as plt

con = sqlite3.connect(":memory:")
cur = con.cursor()
cur.execute("create table tester (value1, value2)")

# Generate random numbers in a matrix 100 rows by 2 columns rounded to 2
decimals
data = 10*np.random.standard_normal((100,2)).round(2)

for row in data:
    # This is the qmark style:
    cur.execute("insert into tester values (?, ?)", (row[0], row[1]))
```

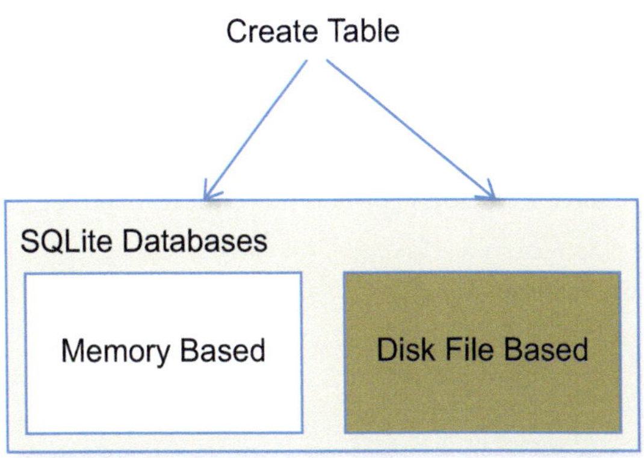

Figure 2.9 In Memory vs On Disk Operations

```
# And this is the named style:
res = np.array(cur.execute("select * from tester").fetchall())
print(res[:,0])

plt.plot(res[:,0],res[:,1],'ro')
plt.savefig('plot.png')
```

In the previous example, we generate random numbers into two columns and SQL table, then we extract all these data points and combine the results into "res" variable, and lastly, we link the results into a plot function to show on the screen.

From SQL to Pandas

There is a more appropriate way to deal with a larger amount of data loading into pandas DataFrames. For now, we run similar data generation into an in-memory table and then we extract it all into pandas DataFrames. The point being, if you are able to load static data points into memory, your data handling is going to be much faster than when using hard disk storage or I/O internet traffic to move large data chunks around.

```
import pandas.io.sql as pds
import sqlite3
import numpy as np
import matplotlib.pyplot as plt

con = sqlite3.connect(":memory:")
cur = con.cursor()
cur.execute("create table tester (value1, value2)")

# Generate random numbers in a matrix 100 rows by 2 columns rounded to 2
decimals
data = 100+10*np.random.standard_normal((100,2)).round(2)

for row in data:
    # This is the qmark style:
    cur.execute("insert into tester values (?, ?)", (row[0], row[1]))

df = pds.read_sql("select * from tester", con)
print(df.head())

plt.plot(df.value1,df.value2,'ro')
plt.savefig('plot.png')
```

From Pandas to JSON

The last example we look into is a very important data format, JSON. This format is used across banking and finance for being light and powerful in handling and representation as shown here:

```
import pandas.io.sql as pds
import sqlite3
import numpy as np
import json

con = sqlite3.connect(":memory:")
cur = con.cursor()
cur.execute("create table tester (name, value1)")
```

```
# Generate random numbers in a matrix 10 rows by 2 columns rounded to 2
decimals
data = 100+10*np.random.standard_normal((10,2)).round(2)

for row in data:
    # This is the qmark style:
    cur.execute("insert into tester values (?, ?)", ('stock1', row[1]))

df = pds.read_sql("select * from tester", con)
print(df.head())

df_JSON_format = df.to_json()
print(df_JSON_format)
```

Data Schema

The database schema is a core component of any database management system (DBMS). It is the structure of a database that provides a formal description of the data stored within it. The schema defines the types of data that can be stored, the relationships between them, and the rules for accessing and manipulating the data. One of the key benefits of a well-designed database schema is that it allows for efficient data retrieval and processing. By structuring the data in a logical and organized manner, the DBMS can quickly locate and retrieve the data needed to perform queries and other operations.

In recent years, there has been a growing trend towards using structured data formats such as FIBO (Financial Industry Business Ontology) to describe database schemas. FIBO is a standardized ontology that provides a common language for describing financial concepts and relationships. By utilizing a standardized format like FIBO, businesses can ensure that their database schemas are consistent and compatible with other systems. However, not all data is structured in a way that can be easily described using a formal schema. There is also a growing amount of unstructured data being generated by businesses and other organizations. This can include things like social media posts, emails, and other types of content that don't fit neatly into predefined categories. To address this challenge, many organizations are turning to data factories and other tools that can help them extract meaning from unstructured data. These tools use advanced algorithms and machine learning techniques to identify patterns and relationships within the data, allowing businesses to gain valuable insights and make more informed decisions.

Figure 2.10 shows the connection between data structures and possible database solutions. On one side, structured data format, SQL databases would be the solution. Most of the recent FinTech solutions operate in semi-structured and structured space, for instance, utilizing MongoDB as the core database solution.

While structured data formats like FIBO are becoming increasingly popular, there is also a growing need to process unstructured data. By leveraging data factories and other advanced tools, businesses can gain valuable insights from this unstructured data to drive better decision-making.

Let us enter the more "techy" topic of data schema before we venture any further and conclude with a comprehensive example. You, as a user of a credit card, would likely see something like this depicted in Figure 2.11:

A FinTech specialist would view the previous image from the lens of JSON format like the following one, as shown in Figure 2.12.

What does it mean?

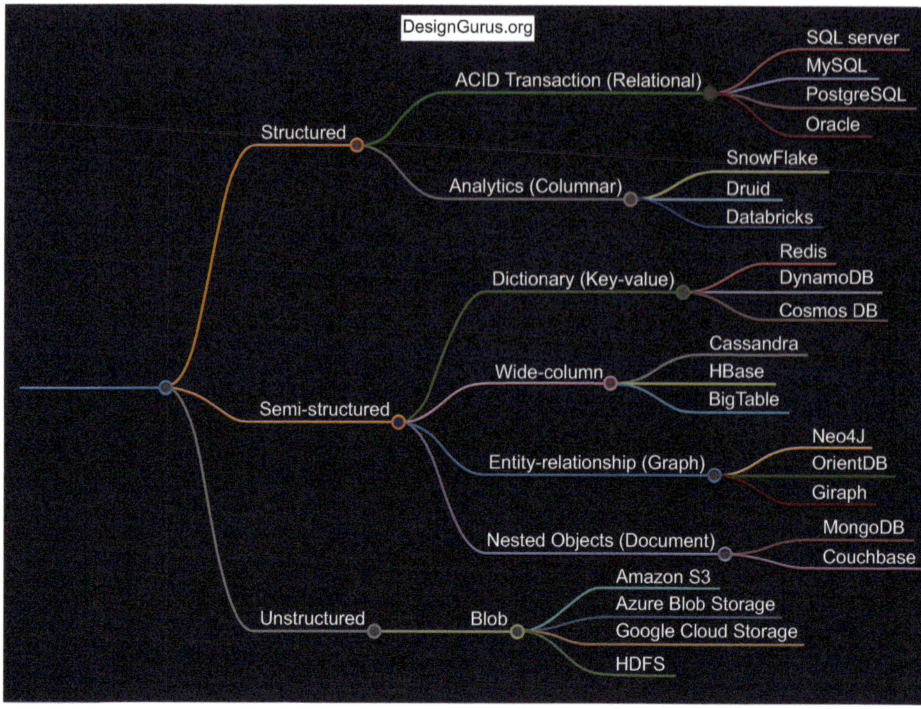

Figure 2.10 Data vs Database
(source: designgurus.org)

Figure 2.11 Credit Card

It shows a connection between your product – VISA CARD in physical external world – and your internal data platform. The previous schema depicts JSON format view of Financial Industry Business Ontology (FIBO) credit card specification [2.6].

As per FIBO, data structures and schemas are designed to streamline the exchange of financial data across the financial systems. Here we extend our VISA example and look at a financial product: investment or deposit: deposit account.

JSON-LD

```
<script type="application/ld+json">
{
 "@context": "http://schema.org",
 "@type": "CreditCard",
 "name": "Wells Fargo Secured Visa® Credit Card",
 "requiredCollateral": "Requires a minimum $300 security deposit.",
 "amount": {
   "@type": "MonetaryAmount",
   "minValue": "300",
   "maxValue": "10000",
   "currency": "USD"
 },
 "offers": {
   "@type": "Offer",
   "offeredBy": {
    "@type": "BankOrCreditUnion",
    "name":"Wells Fargo"
   },
   "priceSpecification": {
    "@type": "UnitPriceSpecification",
    "price": "25",
    "priceCurrency": "USD",
    "referenceQuantity": {
     "@type": "QuantitativeValue",
     "value": "1",
     "unitCode": "ANN"
    }
   }
 },
 "annualPercentageRate": "18.99",
 "feesAndCommissionsSpecification": "https://www.wellsfargo.com/credit-cards/secured/terms/"
}
</script>
```

Figure 2.12 Credit Card JSON Format

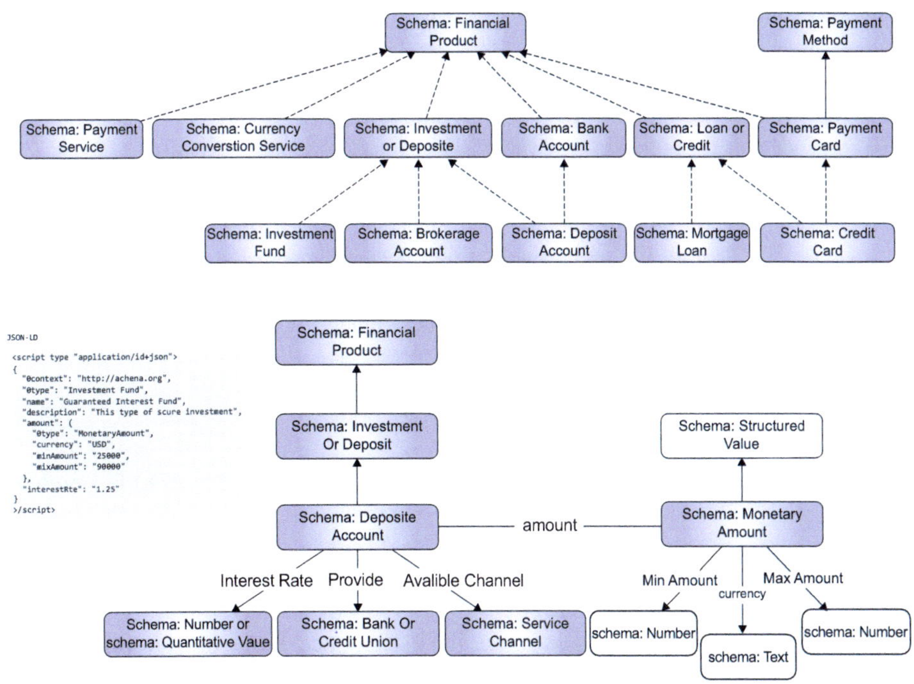

Figure 2.13 FIBO Schema Deposit Account (i and ii)

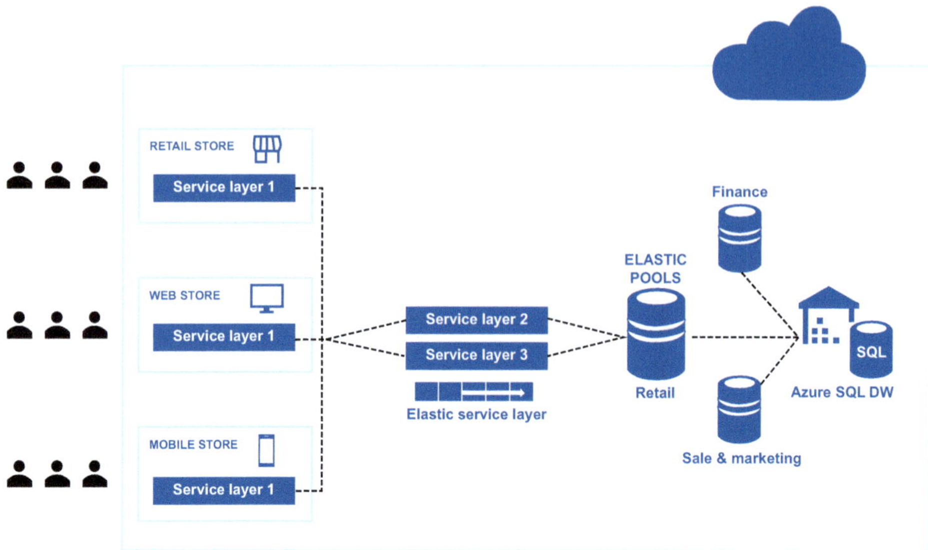

Figure 2.14 MS Azure Big Data and Analytics

Conceptually, to describe the deposit account we are looking to collect several informational components, namely (i) interest rate, (ii) provider, (iii) channels and (iv) amount, (v) currency. As per the previous schema shown in Figure 2.13, these informational components encapsulate the notion of a deposit account. Furthermore, having collected these details it is now possible to calculate and derive further data points, such as actual cash amount equivalent to interest rate accrued on the deposit account. Having this data schema available allows for clearer data handling and manipulations. Hence, it is critical to accommodate data schema across all data stations in our data factory floor.

To conclude this chapter, we bring the previous topics together in the next exercise.

Exercise

Read the article and get familiar with current state-of-the-art data architecture delivery platforms as depicted by Azure "Big Data and Advanced Analytics" example, specifically focusing on the use of SQL (structured query language) data schema and formats [2.7]. Figure 2.14 provides a guide to the exercise.

2.6 Summary

Data management function is a crucial aspect of any organization that deals with data-driven decision-making. This chapter covers various components, including data collection, data storage, data processing, data analysis and data usage. The data lake is a popular data storage mechanism that allows organizations to store vast amounts of data in its raw form. The data lake provides an efficient and cost-effective way of storing data, which can be used for various purposes such as analysis, machine learning, and data science. Prompt and feature engineering stage is a crucial step in the data management processes that involve identifying and extracting relevant features from the raw data. The prompt is a set of instructions that guide the data processing, while feature engineering involves the process of selecting and transforming the relevant features into a format and content that can be easily used for analysis. These steps are critical in ensuring that the data is accurate and relevant, which, in turn, leads to better decision-making. Model design is another essential step in the data management process that involves creating a model that can be used to predict future outcomes based on past data or effectively describe and summarize past events. The model design is important in ensuring that the data is used effectively to make informed decisions. Implementation is the final step in the data management process that involves the deployment of the model into the organization's system. Implementation ensures that the model is used effectively to make data-driven decisions that lead to better business outcomes.

The data life cycle is an encapsulating aspect of the data management process that describes the stages that data goes through from creation to disposal. The data life cycle includes data creation, data storage, data processing, data analysis, and data disposal. Understanding the data life cycle is essential in ensuring that the data is used effectively and efficiently, and that it is disposed of properly when it is no longer needed.

In this chapter, we have also, conceptually, connected generic data infrastructure with data structures simulated across our concept of digital data factory. In addition, we have looked at a number of practical use cases.

As we conclude this chapter, it is clear that a strong data infrastructure is crucial for any digital data factory based software application. In order to effectively simulate and manipulate data structures, it is important to have a solid foundation of data types and structures to work with. By connecting these two elements, we can create a seamless system that allows for efficient data processing and analysis. Data types play a critical role in defining the characteristics and properties of digital data. From integers to strings, each data type has a distinct set of rules that dictate how it can be used and manipulated. Understanding the intricacies of data types is essential for ensuring accurate data processing and analysis. It is important to note that data types are not limited to simple values like numbers and text. Complex data types, such as arrays and objects, are also used in modern digital data factories to represent more intricate data structures.

Data structures are the building blocks of digital data factories. They provide a means of organizing and storing data in a meaningful and efficient way. By defining data structures, we can ensure that data is stored and processed in a consistent and logical manner. By understanding data types and structures, we can create a powerful system that is capable of handling vast amounts of data. This system allows us to effectively analyze and draw insights from digital data, making it an invaluable tool for businesses and organizations of all sizes.

2.7 Concept Questions and Answers

Q1: What is a digital fata factory (DDF) and how does it relate to data management in FinTech?

A1: A digital data factory (DDF) is a conceptual framework for managing data in the FinTech industry. It simulates a factory floor with four distinct workstations: data lake, prompt and feature engineering, model design and implementation. Each station plays a crucial role in the data life cycle, from collecting raw data to delivering a final product or service. This approach ensures that data is managed efficiently, securely and in compliance with regulations.

Q2: What is the role of a Data Lake in the DDF?

A2: The Data Lake (Station 1) acts as the central repository for all data, both structured and unstructured. Its primary function is to ensure data authenticity and clarity. The team at this station acts as "gate keepers," guaranteeing a single source of truth by collecting, cleansing and storing data securely while maintaining daily data workflows.

Q3: How does prompt and feature engineering contribute to the DDF process?

A3: Prompt and feature engineering (Station 2) focuses on refining the vast data collected in the data lake. It involves understanding the business problem and selecting the most relevant data features for further processing. Prompt engineering guides users or AI algorithms towards specific actions, while feature engineering transforms raw data into usable features for machine learning models. This station ensures the utility of data for analysis and model building.

Q4: What happens at the model design stage of the DDF?

A4: Model design (Station 3) leverages the refined data features to create predictive models that address specific business needs. This station uses advanced techniques like neural networks, chatbots and forecasting algorithms to generate actionable insights. The goal is to build a sustainable modeling framework that delivers clear, concise and impactful results for the business.

Q5: How does product implementation conclude the DDF process?

A5: Product implementation (Station 4) transforms the results from the model design stage into a tangible product or service. This station packages the insights, ensuring they are marketable, competitive, and meet regulatory requirements. It also provides feedback to the model design team for continuous improvement. The focus here is on delivering value to clients and stakeholders through a well-defined product.

Q6: What are the essential attributes of a robust data architecture for a FinTech DDF?

A6: A robust data architecture for a FinTech DDF needs to be platform-agnostic, light, flexible, agile, API secured, scalable, crypto secured, and adaptable to emerging technologies like quantum computing. It should also enable on-demand pricing for storage and computational power. Cloud environments like AWS and Azure are often used to implement these attributes effectively.

Q7: What are the key data structure formats used in FinTech data management?

A7: FinTech utilizes both basic and advanced data structures. Basic structures include numbers, lists, strings, tuples, dictionaries, arrays, matrices, pictures, videos and voice recordings. Advanced structures involve input/output (I/O) operations, enabling efficient data transfer between storage and RAM. Popular formats include CSV, SQL, XLS/XLSX, JSON and HTML.

Q8: What is the importance of data schema in FinTech and how is it connected to data structures?

A8: Data schema defines the structure and relationships within a database, ensuring consistency and compatibility across systems. Structured data formats like FIBO (Financial Industry Business Ontology) offer a standardized language for describing financial concepts. This structured approach, alongside tools for handling unstructured data like social media posts, allows for a comprehensive and efficient data management system in FinTech. Data schema essentially acts as a blueprint that guides the organization and interpretation of various data structures, ensuring meaning and coherence within the DDF.

2.8 Further Reading

- Dickerson, A., & Hric, J. (2024). FINS5545 Financial Market Data Literacy Course Notes, UNSW Business School.
- Gamma, E., Helm, R., Johnson, R., & Vlissides, J. (1995). Design Patterns, Addison Wesley.
- Kleppmann, M. (2017). Designing Data-Intensive Applications, O'Reilly.

2.9 References

[2.1] General Data Protection Regulation (GDPR): https://gdpr-info.eu/
[2.2] Payment Services Directive 2 (PSD): https://www.ecb.europa.eu/press/intro/mip-online/2018/html/1803_revisedpsd.en.html
[2.3] Azure Kubernetes Services (AKS): https://azure.microsoft.com/en-au/resources/cloud-computing-dictionary/what-is-kubernetes/#overview
[2.4] Databaseline. (2020). A Tour of End-to-End Machine Learning Platforms: https://databaseline.tech/a-tour-of-end-to-end-ml-platforms/
[2.5] Lawtomated. (2019, April 7). Lawtomated. Retrieved from Structured vs Unstructured Data: https://lawtomated.com/structured-data-vs-unstructured-data-what-are-they-and-why-care/
[2.6] Financial Industry Business Ontology (FIBO). Retrieved from Schema.org: https://schema.org/docs/financial.html
[2.7] Microsoft Azure. Retrieved from Azure: https://azure-scenarios-experience.azurewebsites.net/big-data.html

Chapter 3

Data Visualization

DOI: 10.4324/9781003477747-4

3.1 Introduction

The purpose of this chapter is to extend and enrich our previous coverage on data structures, algorithms and the digital data factory (DDF) concept and to move into data visualization space. In the fast-paced world of banking and finance, **data visualization** has emerged as a powerful tool, transforming raw numbers into actionable insights. This innovative technique allows financial institutions to **paint a vivid picture** of complex data sets, making them easily digestible for both experts and novices alike. From tracking market trends to analyzing customer behavior, data visualization breathes life into financial information, enabling professionals to spot patterns and anomalies at a glance. For banking executives or FinTech professionals, it offers a **bird's-eye view** of organizational performance, while data analysts can dive deep into granular details with interactive charts and graphs. Even the general public benefits, as user-friendly visualizations demystify personal finance, empowering individuals to make informed decisions about their money. In an industry where time is literally money, data visualization is reshaping how we understand and interact with financial data.

Data visualization has become a **game-changer**, at the heart of this revolution lies the ability to harness both **structured** and **unstructured data**. Structured data, neatly organized in traditional databases, provides the backbone for financial reporting. However, it's the unstructured data – from social media sentiment to news articles – that adds depth to financial analysis, offering a **360-degree view** of market trends, for instance, exposed via sophisticated and dynamic dashboards. However, dashboards are just the tip of the iceberg. **Visual products** in finance have evolved to include sophisticated heat maps, network diagrams and even augmented reality displays. These tools do not just present data; these tools are designed to tell stories, making complex financial concepts accessible to stakeholders across the board. The impact of these visual tools on decision-making cannot be overstated. The tools are built to shorten reaction times to market changes, improve risk assessment and democratize financial insights.

Firstly, we introduce schematic approach to data structures and data process flowcharts. Then we expose the visualization of structured and unstructured data structures utilizing state-of-the-art programmatic libraries. We conduct this exposition using cryptocurrencies and relevant textual data flows, such as cryptocurrency related news. Lastly, we dive deeper into Streamlit and Figma to expose these tools available to FinTech professionals to enhance and build highly dynamic and engaging visually driven products. We conclude with industry case study. This chapter builds on Chapter 1 and Chapter 2 by introducing the reader to critical data techniques and tools related to the digital data factory (DDF) implementation phase.

Learning Outcomes

At the end of this chapter the reader will be able to do the following:

- Understand the importance of data visualization in banking and finance
- Get familiar with Python visual libraries
- Introduce additional packages for data visualization
- Introduce visualization tools, Streamlit and Figma
- Analyse FinTech case study: Simply Wall St

3.2 Data Processing Flow

Data processing flows and flowcharts are essential visual tools that illustrate the step-by-step progression of data through various operations within a system. These diagrams use standardized symbols to represent different processes, decisions and data flows, providing a clear road map for how information is collected, transformed and utilized. By depicting the logical sequence of data handling, flowcharts enable analysts and stakeholders to identify bottlenecks, optimize workflows and ensure data integrity throughout the processing life cycle. From input and storage to manipulation and output, each stage is meticulously mapped out, offering a comprehensive overview of the entire data journey. Understanding these flowcharts is crucial for effective data management, as they serve as a foundation for system design, troubleshooting and continuous improvement in data-driven organizations. In this, and the following two sections, for illustrative purposes, we use CryptoCompare data source to illuminate data processing and visualization capabilities [3.1].

Data Flows

Suppose we build our hypothetical FinTech application to show various analytical insights and potential trading strategies covering all currently available and traded digital assets, globally. To start with a use case, we need to extract data from a reliable data source, in our case CryptoCompare. Creating a data flowchart for extracting Bitcoin (BTC) vs. USD prices from the CryptoCompare API involves outlining the logical steps of the process. Next is a textual description of the flowchart:

1. Start
    - Begin the process.
2. Input Parameters
    - Define inputs:
    - API Key (if required)
    - Cryptocurrency (e.g., BTC)
    - Fiat Currency (e.g., USD)
    - Base URL for CryptoCompare API.
3. Prepare API Call
    - Construct the URL with query parameters:
    - Example: https://min-api.cryptocompare.com/data/price?fsym=BTC&tsyms=USD
4. Send HTTP Request
    - Use an HTTP client (e.g., Python's requests library) to send a GET request to the constructed URL.
5. Receive API Response
    - Get the JSON response containing the BTC to USD price.
6. Check for Errors
    - Validate response status:
    - If successful (200 OK), proceed to parse data.
    - If error, log the issue and retry or terminate.
7. Parse JSON Data
    - Extract the BTC price in USD from the response object.
8. Store or Display Data

- Store the extracted data in a database, file or variable.
- Optionally, display the data in the UI or console.

9. End
   - Complete the process.

Given the previous logical and sequential steps we generate data flowchart as depicted in Figure 3.1.

Figure 3.1 visualizes a simple data request and relevant data flow to trigger an application programming interface (API) call (Steps 4. and Step 5. as per previous description) from our

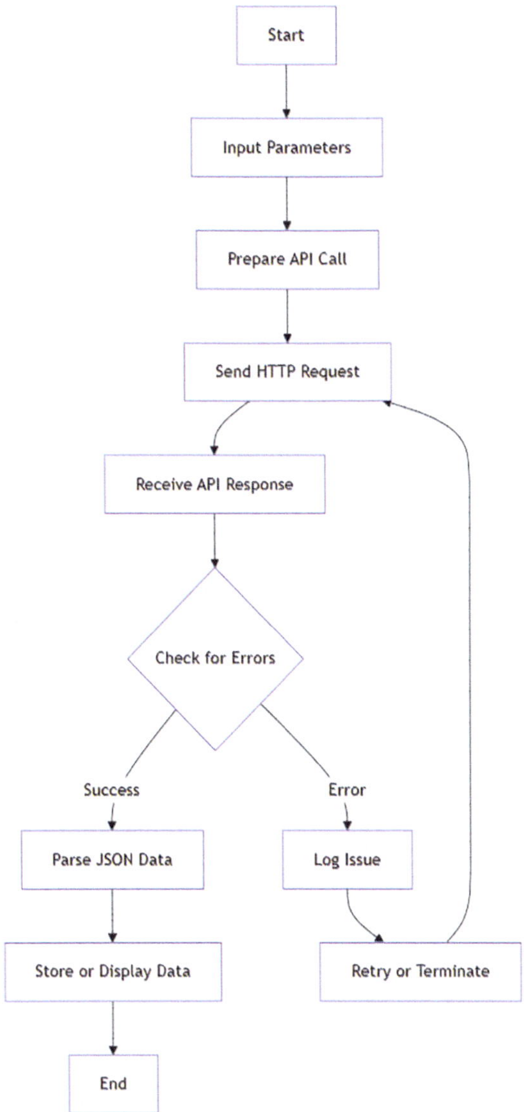

Figure 3.1 Data Flowchart to Extract BTC/USD Exchange Rate

FinTech application to CryptoCompare server and data store application to retrieve Bitcoin vs USD market rates back into our FinTech environment. The diagram is a neat visual interpretation of the logical and sequential step we take on this journey. Please note the graphical depiction of the steps using various "shapes"; each shape represents a predefined function or an activity. The diamond shape represents a decision point where the request is checked for validity, for example. At this point, let us step into the world of APIs as we extensively use APIs across this book in various activities.

Data Streams

An application programming interface (API) serves as a crucial bridge in the digital world, enabling different software applications to communicate and share data seamlessly. At its core, an API is a set of protocols, routines and tools that define how software components should interact. Think of it as a waiter in a restaurant taking requests from the customer (one application) to the kitchen (another application) and delivering the results back. APIs power many everyday experiences we often take for granted. For instance, when you use a weather app on your smartphone, it's likely retrieving data from a weather service's API. For developers, APIs offer a way to leverage existing services and data, significantly speeding up the development process. Businesses benefit from APIs by easily integrating third-party services, enhancing their offerings without building everything from scratch. In today's interconnected digital ecosystem, APIs have become indispensable, driving innovation and efficiency across industries.

In general, APIs are a set of rules and definitions that enable the integration of different systems, services and applications. This is done internally, within your own platform whereby your design and platform solution use APIs channels and connections to communicate within your environment. In our context, internally within your own digital factory space. Externally, APIs form channels to an external world as depicted in Figure 3.2.

APIs work through a series of requests and responses. A client, your FinTech application, makes a request to the APIs service, usually authorized. The APIs process the request and returns a response in a form of JSON or XML data formats, utilizing HTTP methods commonly used such as GET, POST, PUT or DELETE. The request can include parameters and headers to specify the query, in addition to required authorizations. The API responds with the requested data, which you can process further within your own FinTech environment.

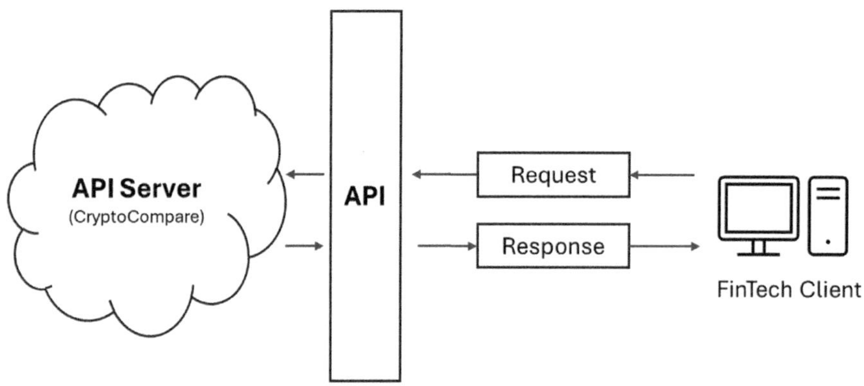

Figure 3.2 API Example

Python has libraries like *requests* and *http.client* to interact with APIs. Basic steps to query APIs:

1. Import relevant libraries into your Python environment
2. Define API endpoint and necessary parameters
3. Send request and capture the response
4. Process the response data

Figure 3.3 visualizes generic steps being conducted within an API call. Client, our FinTech platform, sends "GET" request to extract predefined data streams from the API service. If the

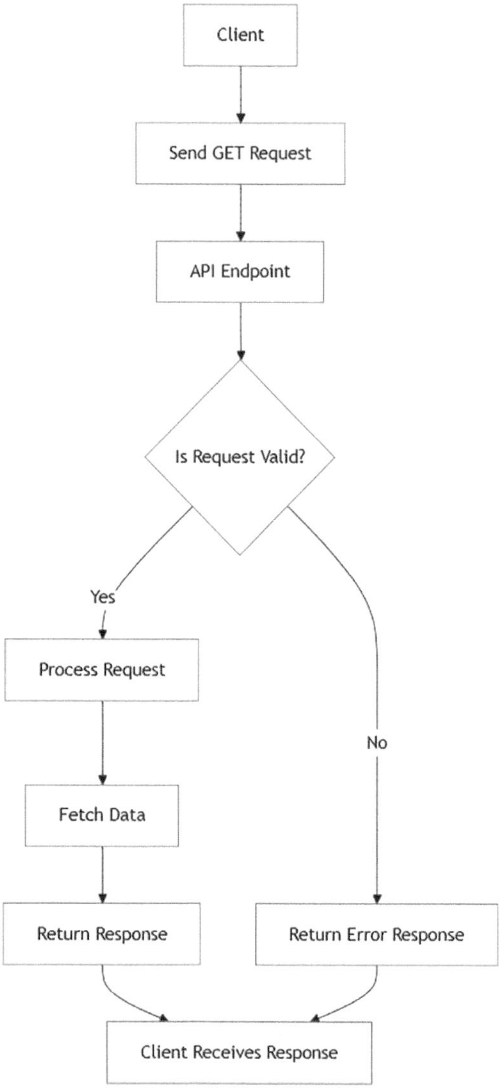

Figure 3.3 Generic API Get Flowchart

request is valid and authenticated, the API processes the request by providing data streams from the storage, in addition to sending a response message code "200". Our FinTech platform receives a package in the form of a JSON file [3.2].

In our use case, Crypto Compare is CCData's market-leading API that provides institutional-grade digital asset data stream across global exchanges. We focus on asset data, such as latest digital asset prices, as well as alternative data streams, such as historical and real-time news and sentiment data. Utilizing GET API endpoint: *https://min-api.cryptocompare.com/data/price?fsym=BTC&tsyms=USD,JPY,EUR* with pre-specified and required input parameters *fsym* and *tsyms* we get the current price of any cryptocurrency in any other currency [3.3].

The results are delivered in a light data format, usually utilizing JSON text delivery as an example in a standard key:value pair data structure. Here we have a price of "BTC," "USD" and "EUR" in terms of Ethereum "ETH":


```
{
  "BTC": 0.03792,
  "USD": 3629,
  "EUR": 3455.7
}
```


Next we derive a JSON file with latest news from Crypto Compare API GET call *https://min-api.cryptocompare.com/data/v2/news/?lang=EN* delivering JSON objects packaged into a structure. For the purposes of our exposition related to alternative data streams we focus on "body," "url" and "tags" among other sections.


```
 1: Object
id: "37653792"
guid: "https://ambcrypto.com/?p=452217"
published_on: 1734224415
imageurl: "https://images.cryptocompare.com/news/default/ambcrypto.png"
title: "ALGO still down 88% from ATH DESPITE recent 480% hike - What next?"
url: "https://ambcrypto.com/algo-still-down-88-from-ath-despite-recent-480-hike-
what-next/"
body: "ALGO's Open Interest has been slowly trending lower, as has the spot
CVD."
tags: "Altcoin|Analysis|HideCryptopanic|News|News 1|No Homepage|Social|Trading
View|ambcrypto"
lang: "EN"
upvotes: "0"
downvotes: "0"
categories: "ALGO|ALTCOIN|MARKET"
source_info: Object
name: "AMB Crypto"
img: "https://images.cryptocompare.com/news/default/ambcrypto.png"
lang: "EN"
source: "ambcrypto"
```


Pseudocode

Given we gained understanding of a simple "GET" API call via visualization of the data flows, as it relates to our CryptoCompare use case, we can start to build a programmatic solution to automate these data flows and steps necessary for our final FinTech product implementation.

Next is a simple pseudocode sequence outlining previous steps we took while dissecting API call. Pseudocode, as mentioned in Chapter 1, forms an integral part of any successful FinTech solution. **Pseudocode**, a powerful tool in the scientific and programming realms, serves as a bridge between human thought and machine logic. This informal, high-level description of an algorithm or program logic uses a mixture of natural language and simplified programming constructs. Unlike actual code, pseudocode isn't meant to be executed by a computer; instead, it *acts as a blueprint* for developers and scientists to outline their ideas before diving into the intricacies of a specific programming language. By allowing creators to focus on the problem-solving aspect without getting bogged down in syntax details, pseudocode facilitates clearer thinking and more efficient program design. Imagine it as a **universal language of logic**, enabling collaboration across different scientific disciplines and programming backgrounds. In essence, pseudocode embodies the scientific method's planning phase, providing a structured yet flexible way to approach complex problems and pave the way for innovative solutions in various fields of study.

As indicated in the next section, we step through logical sequence to extract Bitcoin data using CryptoCompare API service (Step 4). In this step, we express the need to proceed if we receive correct status from the API call via response equal to "200" (positive response). Then, we indicate the need to parse the received package, data flow, and place the results into a database (if any) or proceed and display the results.

```
BEGIN

    // Step 1: Input Parameters
    API_KEY ← "your_api_key_here"    // Optional, if CryptoCompare requires an
API key
    BASE_URL ← "https://min-api.cryptocompare.com/data/price"
    CRYPTO_SYMBOL ← "BTC"
    FIAT_SYMBOL ← "USD"

    // Step 2: Prepare API Call
    API_URL ← BASE_URL + "?fsym=" + CRYPTO_SYMBOL + "&tsyms=" + FIAT_SYMBOL
    IF API_KEY is required THEN
        API_URL ← API_URL + "&api_key=" + API_KEY
    END IF

    // Step 3: Send HTTP Request
    RESPONSE ← Send GET Request to API_URL

    // Step 4: Receive API Response
    IF RESPONSE.status_code = 200 THEN
        // Step 5: Parse JSON Data
        JSON_DATA ← Parse RESPONSE.body as JSON
        BTC_PRICE ← JSON_DATA[FIAT_SYMBOL]

        // Step 6: Store or Display Data
        PRINT "Bitcoin price in USD: " + BTC_PRICE
        STORE BTC_PRICE in database or file
    ELSE
        // Handle Errors
        PRINT "Error: Unable to fetch data. Status Code: " +
RESPONSE.status_code
        PRINT "Response Message: " + RESPONSE.body
    END IF
END*
```

Python

It is at this point, post visual evaluation of relevant data flows and pseudocode preparation, that we are in a position to encode a solution, using Python. Python, a **versatile and powerful programming language**, has revolutionized scientific computing and data analysis. Born from a desire for simplicity and readability, Python has become the *go-to tool* for researchers and scientists across disciplines. Its elegant syntax and vast ecosystem of in-build or externally integrated libraries, such as NumPy and SciPy, empower users to tackle complex problems with ease. Imagine a quantitative analysts or traders, racing against time to model global digital asset prices and valuation trends. With Python's data visualization capabilities, as we cover in the following sections, they can transform intricate data sets into compelling visual narratives, making their findings accessible to their stakeholders. This seamless blend of computational power and user-friendliness has catapulted Python to the forefront of scientific innovation and this is one of the reasons we use Python across the book.

In the next section, the Python code snippet shows an enclosed function, *fetch_btc_price()*, delivering JSON data format from CryptoCompare API call allowing for appropriate error handling. In this function, we aim to extract CRYPTO_SYMBOL "BTC" in terms of FIAT_SYMBOL "USD" from BASE_URL API address published by CryptoCompare having obtained appropriate API_KEY. The function returns printed, on the console/screen, price of bitcoin, BTC, in terms of USD handling appropriate errors.

```
import requests

def fetch_btc_price():
  # Step 1: Input Parameters
  API_KEY = "your_api_key_here"  # Replace with your CryptoCompare API key if
needed
  BASE_URL = "https://min-api.cryptocompare.com/data/price"
  CRYPTO_SYMBOL = "BTC"
  FIAT_SYMBOL = "USD"

  # Step 2: Prepare API Call
  params = {
    "fsym": CRYPTO_SYMBOL,
    "tsyms": FIAT_SYMBOL
  }

  if API_KEY:  # If API key is required
    params["api_key"] = API_KEY

  # Step 3: Send HTTP Request
  try:
    response = requests.get(BASE_URL, params=params)

    # Step 4: Receive API Response
    if response.status_code == 200:
      # Step 5: Parse JSON Data
      data = response.json()
      btc_price = data.get(FIAT_SYMBOL)

      # Step 6: Store or Display Data
      if btc_price is not None:
        print(f"Bitcoin price in USD: ${btc_price}")
        # Optional: Store the price in a database or file
```

```
        else:
          print("Error: BTC to USD price not found in response.")
      else:
        # Handle Errors
        print(f"Error: Unable to fetch data. Status Code:
{response.status_code}")
        print(f"Response Message: {response.text}")
    except requests.RequestException as e:
      print(f"Exception occurred: {e}")

# Call the function
fetch_btc_price()
```

In the following two sections, we build on our knowledge and expand on the use of APIs covering structured time-series driven data as well as unstructured text driven data streams focused on digital asset markets.

3.3 Structured Data

Tabular Formats

Structured data in finance plays a pivotal role in **organizing and analyzing complex financial information**. By presenting data in a tabular format, financial analysts can efficiently *categorize, sort and manipulate large data sets* to uncover valuable insights. This scientific approach to data management enables professionals to identify trends, patterns, and anomalies that might otherwise remain hidden in unstructured data. Tools like **pandas**, a powerful Python library, have revolutionized the way financial data is processed, allowing for rapid calculations and visualizations. The structured nature of tabular data facilitates **machine learning applications** and **predictive modeling**, empowering financial institutions to make data-driven decisions with greater accuracy and confidence. As the volume of financial data continues to grow exponentially, the ability to leverage structured data effectively has become an indispensable skill for modern finance professionals seeking to gain a competitive edge in the market.

Pandas DataFrame

The **pandas DataFrame** is a powerful tool that revolutionizes the way we handle and analyze tabular data in scientific research. As a two-dimensional labeled data structure, it offers an *intuitive and efficient* approach to working with structured data. Scientists and researchers across various disciplines leverage pandas DataFrames to **organize, manipulate and derive insights** from complex data sets with ease. One of the key strengths of pandas DataFrame lies in its ability to seamlessly handle heterogeneous data types, making it invaluable for scientific applications where diverse data formats are common. Its rich set of built-in functions enables researchers to perform advanced statistical analyses, data cleaning and visualization tasks effortlessly.

A pandas DataFrame stores tabular data. Tabular data can be thought of as group of Series with the same shared index, with each series in the group comprising a column of data.

Consider the following data set cataloguing the properties of a series of rocks:

id	area	perimeter	shape	permeability
0	4990	2791.900	0.0903296	6.3
1	7002	3892.600	0.1486220	6.3
2	7558	3930.660	0.1833120	6.3
3	7352	3869.320	0.1170630	6.3
4	7943	3948.540	0.1224170	17.1

We can manually construct the DataFrame as follows:

```
import pandas as pd

df = pd.DataFrame({
    'area': pd.Series([4990, 7002, 7558, 7352, 7943]),
    'perimeter': pd.Series([2791.900, 3892.600, 3930.660, 3869.320, 3948.540]),
    'shape': pd.Series([0.0903296, 0.1486220, 0.1833120, 0.1170630, 0.1224170]),
    'permeability': pd.Series([6.3, 6.3, 6.3, 6.3, 17.1])
})

print(df)
```

This will also work. Pandas will automatically generate the series from a list of dictionaries for us:

```
import pandas as pd

df = pd.DataFrame([

    {'area':4990.0,'perimeter':2791.9, 'shape':0.0903296,'permeability':6.3},
    {'area':7002.0,'perimeter':3892.6, 'shape':0.148622, 'permeability':6.3},
    {'area':7558.0,'perimeter':3930.66,'shape':0.183312, 'permeability':6.3},
    {'area':7352.0,'perimeter':3869.32,'shape':0.117063, 'permeability':6.3},
    {'area':7943.0,'perimeter':3948.54,'shape':0.122417, 'permeability':17.1},
])

print(df)
```

Most operations that can be applied to series objects can also be applied to DataFrame objects – the result being the natural generalization from one to two dimensions.

```
import pandas as pd

df = pd.DataFrame([
  {'area':4990.0,'perimeter':2791.9, 'shape':0.0903296,'permeability':6.3},
  {'area':7002.0,'perimeter':3892.6, 'shape':0.148622, 'permeability':6.3},
  {'area':7558.0,'perimeter':3930.66,'shape':0.183312, 'permeability':6.3},
  {'area':7352.0,'perimeter':3869.32,'shape':0.117063, 'permeability':6.3},
  {'area':7943.0,'perimeter':3948.54,'shape':0.122417, 'permeability':17.1},
])

print(df + 50) # Adds 50 to every element in the DataFrame
```

In the context of our use case, we link previous section on APIs to pandas DataFrame build and deliver a tabular representation of downloaded cryptocurrency pairs. In the next Python snippet, we call "GET" APIs from CryptoCompare and deliver pandas DataFrames in tabular format:

```
import requests
import pandas as pd
```

```
import numpy as np

def fetch_crypto_prices(SYMBOL, API_KEY, LIMIT=2000):
    # Define CONSTANTS and VARIABLES
    if API_KEY.strip():  # Check if api_key is not empty or just whitespace
        headers = {'Apikey': API_KEY}  # The header with your API key
    else:
        headers = {}  # Empty headers if api_key is empty
    BASE_URL = f'https://min-api.cryptocompare.com/data/v2/histoday?fsym={SYMBOL}
&tsym=USD&limit={LIMIT}'

    # Send HTTP Request
    try:
        response = requests.get(BASE_URL, headers=headers)
        if response.status_code == 200:
            data = response.json()
        else:
            # Handle Errors
            print(f"Error: Unable to fetch data. Status Code:
{response.status_code}")
            print(f"Response Message: {response.text}")

    except requests.RequestException as e:
        print(f"Exception occurred: {e}")

    return data['Data']['Data']

def main(LIMIT = 2000,API_KEY=''):
    # Define a list of cryptocurrency pairs all in terms of USD
    crypto_pairs = ['BTC', 'ETH']

    # Create an empty DataFrame to store the data
    df = pd.DataFrame()
    # GET historical data for each pair
    for SYMBOL in crypto_pairs:
        print(f"GET data for {SYMBOL}...")
        data = pd.DataFrame( fetch_crypto_prices(SYMBOL,
                                                 API_KEY=API_KEY,
                                                 LIMIT=LIMIT) ) # Limiting to
30 days

        data ['date'] = pd.to_datetime(data ['time'], unit='s')
        data['sym'] = SYMBOL
        df = pd.concat([df,data], axis = 0)
    return df
```

In this example, we are interested in historical, daily Bitcoin "BTC" and Ethereum "ETH" digital asset prices (we can specify any cryptocurrency pairs). For this purpose we choose "histoday" specified APIs as provided by CryptoCompare endpoint. The resulting data are delivered in JSON format; however we process the data per digital asset and store and convert the JSON file into DataFrames at the point of the data extract. In addition, we have converted UNIX time stamp into human-readable format and added new column called "sym" to indicate each digital asset. This approach allows us to "stack" data sets "on top of each other" per digital asset symbol and per date.

Tabular format of the data extract (first ten rows) looks like this text, comma-delimited file:

sym,date,time,high,low,open,volumefrom,volumeto,close,conversionType,conversion Symbol BTC,2019-06-25,1561420800,11778.22,10992.37,11035.74,84123.73,953962631.15,11740.34,direct, BTC,2019-06-26,1561507200,13826.76,11679.1,11740.34,211449.88,2685872365.1,12913.28,direct, BTC,2019-06-27,1561593600,13314.05,10335.34,12913.28,202428.68,2345027203.81,11154.09,direct, BTC,2019-06-28,1561680000,12433.0,10772.75,11154.09,120700.97,1408438810.31,12355.06,direct, BTC,2019-06-29,1561766400,12362.9,11352.27,12355.06,81875.16,968516834.6,11884.1,direct, BTC,2019-06-30,1561852800,12200.02,10677.83,11884.1,80893.36,917158052.37,10769.05,direct, BTC,2019-07-01,1561939200,11207.0,10006.43,10769.05,115739.97,1225129699.57,10591.87,direct, BTC,2019-07-02,1562025600,10927.6,9678.1,10591.87,120994.95,1239524970.43,10844.13,direct, BTC,2019-07-03,1562112000,12009.59,10841.91,10844.13,115565.16,1313585829.89,11981.61,direct, BTC,2019-07-04,1562198400,12055.11,11067.68,11981.61,71141.03,831236841.56,11156.52,direct,

Next is a simple summary of data extracted from CryptoCompare APIs as it applies to BTC:

```
GET data for BTC...
<class 'pandas.core.frame.DataFrame'>
Index: 2001 entries, 0 to 2000
Data columns (total 11 columns):
 #   Column             Non-Null Count  Dtype
---  ------             --------------
 0   time               2001 non-null   int64
 1   high               2001 non-null   float64
 2   low                2001 non-null   float64
 3   open               2001 non-null   float64
 4   volumefrom         2001 non-null   float64
 5   volumeto           2001 non-null   float64
 6   close              2001 non-null   float64
 7   conversionType     2001 non-null   object
 8   conversionSymbol   2001 non-null   object
 9   date               2001 non-null   datetime64[ns]
 10  sym                2001 non-null   object
dtypes: datetime64[ns](1), float64(6), int64(1), object(3)
memory usage: 187.6+ KB
```

At this point, we have secured historical closing prices of BTC and ETH in tabular format. In the next section, we expand on graphical and visual data interpretation.

Graphical Formats

Structured data in finance is the backbone of modern financial analysis, transforming raw numbers into actionable insights. Imagine a vast sea of financial information, neatly organized into rows and columns, ready to reveal its secrets. This structured approach allows analysts to effortlessly sift through complex data sets, uncovering patterns and trends that might otherwise remain hidden. Visualizing this data brings it to life, with tools like interactive heat maps illuminating market correlations, and sleek line charts tracking stock performance over time. Picture a candlestick chart, each bar telling a story of market sentiment, or a mesmerizing tree map showcasing the composition of a diversified portfolio. These graphical representations don't just present data; they breathe life into it, enabling financial experts to spot anomalies, predict market movements and make informed decisions with confidence. By harnessing the power of structured data and compelling visualizations, finance professionals can navigate the complex world of markets and investments with unprecedented clarity and precision. In this section, we introduce a number of Python-based libraries used by FinTech professionals.

MatplotLib

Matplotlib is a plotting library that allows us to quickly generate plots from data [3.4]. It is inspired by Matlab, and many of the objects in its APIs are named similarly. `pyplot` is a convenient to use interface to `matplotlib`, containing support for many common plot types. `pyplot` is designed to be used interactively, that is, on a Python command line or in Jupyter notebook, thus its API has a lot of implicit elements. That is, `pyplot` is an object that only keeps track of one single "plot" at a time (though that plot may have many components). Keep this in mind when you are writing functions that call `pyplot` directly since `pyplot` will retain its state. To use `pyplot` you must import it. Note that `pyplot` is part of the `matplotlib` library, but as this is the only aspect of `matplotlib` we are using, we can use a more targeted import. We will be using the alias `plt` for the `pyplot` object. This versatile library is a must-have tool for scientists, engineers and data enthusiasts alike. With its intuitive interface and extensive feature set, matplotlib empowers users to create everything from simple line plots to complex 3D visualizations. Whether you're plotting experimental results, analyzing trends, or presenting complex data sets, matplotlib's flexibility shines through. It seamlessly integrates with NumPy and other scientific Python libraries, making it an indispensable part of the scientific Python ecosystem. From publication-quality figures to interactive plots, matplotlib opens up a world of possibilities for communicating your data-driven insights.

```
import matplotlib.pyplot as plt
```

Let's look at a simple scatter plot:

```
import matplotlib.pyplot as plt

x = [1,2,3,4,5,6,7]
y = [7,6,5,4,3,2,1]

plt.scatter(x, y)
plt.savefig('plot.jpg')
```

`plt.scatter` automatically creates a plot in the background. This is saved to a file when we call `plt.savefig`. The savefig method of pyplot saves the current plot to an image file. We can add an axis and title to this plot:

```
import matplotlib.pyplot as plt

x = [1,2,3,4,5,6,7]
y = [7,6,5,4,3,2,1]

plt.scatter(x, y)
plt.title('Chart title')
plt.xlabel('X')
plt.ylabel('Y')

plt.savefig('plot.png')
```

Note that the functions we called title, `xlabel` and `ylabel` are implicitly affecting the chart object created by pyplot, as per Figure 3.4. We can get direct access to the object implicitly created by pyplot by using `plt.gca()` and `plt.gcf()`. This retrieves the current axes and figure objects respectively. The figure object manages some parts of the chart such as the legend; however, the most important functionality lives in the axes object, which controls the x and y axes, title, and the actual contents of the plot.

Many of the visual aspects of pyplot's charts are customizable, including the following:

- The color used: e.g. `color='red'`. For most charts this applies to each series being plotted as a whole, but for scatter plots each data point can have its own color.
- The shape of data points: for example, `marker='x'` (other options include None, `'+'`, `'o'`. `'.'`, `','`, `'v'`, `'^'`, `'<'`, `'>'`, `'s'`, `'d'`, `'p'`, `'h'`)
- The line style (in line graphs): for example, `linestyle=':'` (other options include `'-'`, `'--'`, `'-.'`)

```
import matplotlib.pyplot as plt

x = [1, 2, 3, 4, 5, 6, 7]
y = [1, 1, 1, 2, 2, 2, 1]
z = [4, 5, 4, 5, 4, 5, 4]
w = [6, 8, 6, 8, 6, 8, 6]
```

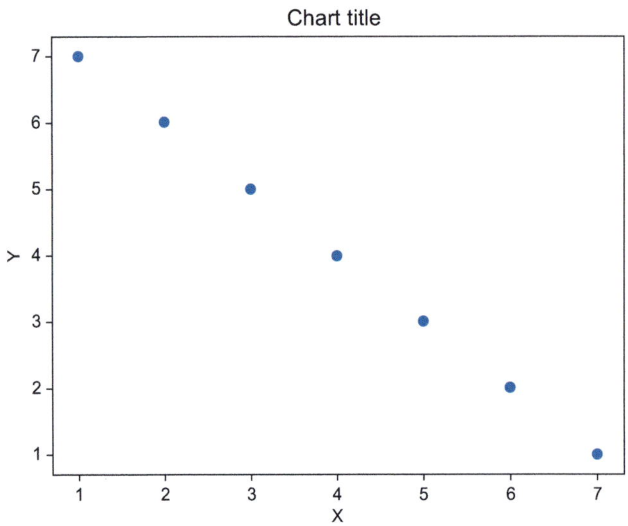

Figure 3.4 Simple Plot Function

```
plt.scatter(x, y) # Default: blue (for first series), dots
plt.scatter(x,z, marker='x', color='red') # Second series plotted will be red
crosses
plt.plot(x,w, linestyle='-.', marker='s', color='green') # Line plot with square
markers and dot-dashed lines
plt.savefig('plot.png')
```

Scatter plots have two additional parameters that can be useful for displaying more information about the data (i.e., more dimensions):

- `c`, e.g. `c = <sequence of values>`. This adds a dimension to the data that will be displayed by the color each point is given.
    - You can set the scale of colors used by matplotlib with the `cmap` parameter. Matplotlib provides quite a range of colormaps.
    - You can display the scale of colors used by calling the `colorbar()` method of `pyplot`
- `s`, for example, `s = <sequence of values>`. This adds a dimension to the data that will be displayed by the size each point is given.

```
import matplotlib.pyplot as plt

x = [1, 2, 3, 4, 5, 6, 7]
y = [1, 3, 4, 5, 7, 6, 5]
z = [5, 4, 3, 2, 1, 2, 3]
zz = [110, 80, 50, 70, 50, 80, 110]

plt.scatter(x, y, c=z, s=zz, cmap='plasma')
plt.colorbar()
plt.savefig('plot.png')
```

In Figure 3.5, chart properties are also customizable: `xlabel(), ylabel(), title()` takes a string and allows the setting of the x axis label, y axis label and the chart title. The `legend()` function automatically generates a legend when called.

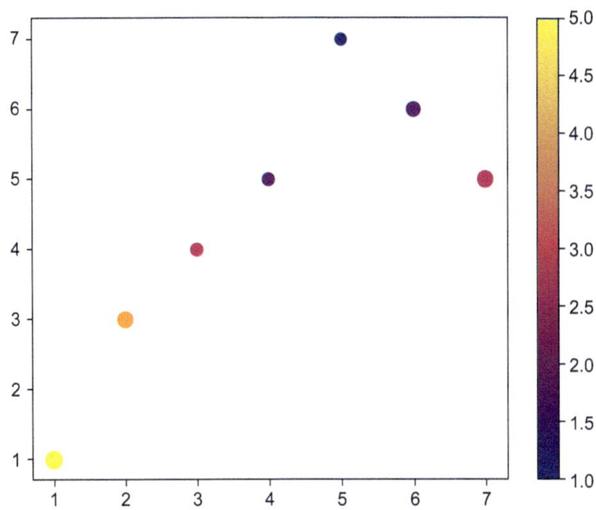

Figure 3.5 Cmap Color Schema

```
import matplotlib.pyplot as plt
import math

# Take 100 points between 0 and 2*pi
x = [ 2*math.pi*n/100 for n in range(0,100) ]
y = [ math.sin(n) for n in x ]
z = [ math.cos(n) for n in x ]

# Label the line in the plot
plt.plot(x, y, label='sin(x)')
plt.plot(x, z, label='cos(x)')

plt.xlabel('x')
plt.ylabel('f(x)')
plt.title('Functions')

# Create the legend
plt.legend()
plt.savefig('plot.png')
```

As per Figure 3.6, repeatedly calling plt.plot() will draw plots on top of each other. For charts such as scatter plots or line graphs, this is not a problem, but for bar charts it can be problematic:

```
import matplotlib.pyplot as plt

indices = ['A', 'B', 'C', 'D', 'E', 'F', 'G']
x = [1,2,3,4,5,6,7]
y = [7,6,5,4,3,2,1]
```

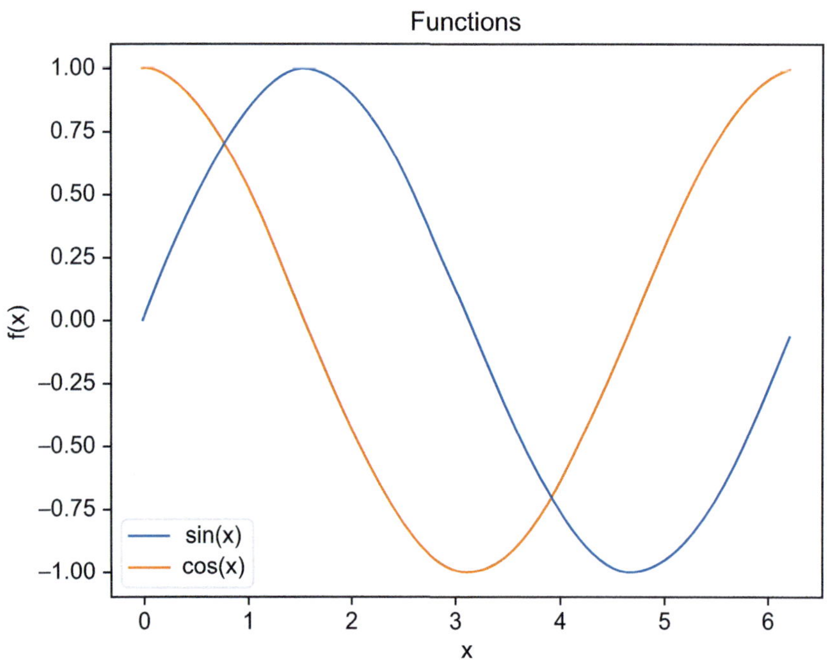

Figure 3.6 Legend

```
plt.bar(indices, x)
plt.bar(indices, y)
plt.savefig('bar.png')
```

Hence, you can plot multiple figures onto the same plot using `plt.subplot`

```
import matplotlib.pyplot as plt
import math

x = [ 2*math.pi*n/100 for n in range(0,100) ]
y = [ math.sin(n) for n in x ]
z = [ math.cos(n) for n in x ]
w = [ math.tan(n) for n in x ]
v = [ n * math.sin(n) for n in x ]

# Create a 2 by 2 subplot
# Select the 1st subplot
plt.subplot(2, 2, 1)
plt.plot(x, y, label='sin(x)')
plt.legend()

# Of the 2 by 2 subplots
# Select the second plot
plt.subplot(2, 2, 2)
plt.plot(x, z, label='cos(x)')
plt.legend()
plt.savefig('plot.png')

# Of the 2 by 2 subplots
# Select the third plot
plt.subplot(2, 2, 3)
plt.plot(x, w, label='tan(x)')
plt.legend()
plt.savefig('plot.png')

# Of the 2 by 2 subplots
# Select the fourth plot
plt.subplot(2, 2, 4)
plt.plot(x, v, label='x sin(x)')
plt.legend()
plt.savefig('plot.png')
```

Another variation shown in Figure 3.7 depicts capability to split visuals into various subplots. In further chapters we utilize other Python libraries in addition to MatplotLib, such as using direct plotting capabilities in pandas as well as Seaborn libraries.

Pandas

The **pandas** library is a powerhouse in the world of Python programming, revolutionizing the way data scientists and analysts work with structured data [3.5]. This open-source library provides high-performance, easy-to-use data structures and tools for data manipulation and analysis. At its core, pandas offers two primary data structures: Series for one-dimensional data and DataFrames for two-dimensional data, making it incredibly versatile for handling various data formats. With pandas, users can effortlessly load data from different sources (like CSV files or SQL databases), clean and preprocess it, and perform complex operations

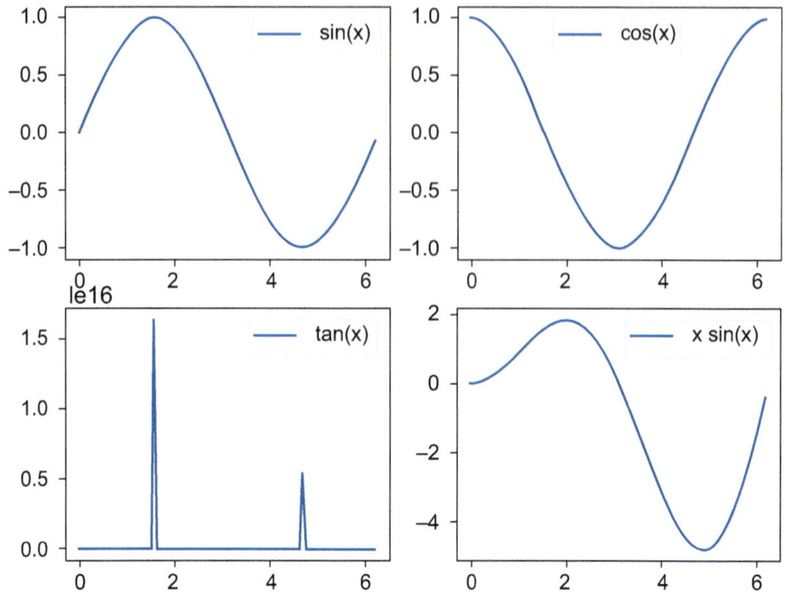

Figure 3.7 Subplots

with just a few lines of code. Its ability to handle missing data, merge data sets and conduct time series analysis makes it an indispensable tool in fields ranging from finance to scientific research. Whether you're a beginner looking to explore data analysis or a seasoned data scientist working on complex projects, pandas serves as a robust foundation for your data manipulation needs in Python.

Pandas `DataFrames` can be used to generate plots. The `plot()`, `boxplot()` and `hist()` functions allow us to get an overview of the data.

```
import pandas as pd
import matplotlib.pyplot as plt

df = pd.DataFrame([
  {'area':4990.0,'perimeter':2791.9, 'shape':0.0903296,'permeability':6.3},
  {'area':7002.0,'perimeter':3892.6, 'shape':0.148622, 'permeability':6.3},
  {'area':7558.0,'perimeter':3930.66,'shape':0.183312, 'permeability':6.3},
  {'area':7352.0,'perimeter':3869.32,'shape':0.117063, 'permeability':6.3},
  {'area':7943.0,'perimeter':3948.54,'shape':0.122417, 'permeability':17.1},
])

df.plot()
plt.savefig('plot.png')

df.boxplot()
plt.savefig('boxplot.png')

df.hist()
plt.savefig('hist.png')
```

Pandas will make calls to the default `matplotlib` context, and the plot can be manipulated like any matplotlib code. However, it does greatly simplify the process of plotting multiple series on the same axis.

```
import pandas as pd
import matplotlib.pyplot as plt

df = pd.DataFrame({
  'x': pd.Series([1,2,3,4,5,6,7]),
  'y': pd.Series([7,6,5,4,3,2,1])
})

df.plot(kind='bar')
plt.savefig('plot.png')
```

Because pandas makes calls to the default `matlibplot` context, a wide variety of plots are supported out of the box. We ask pandas to use a different type of plot by specifying the kind optional parameter.

```
import pandas as pd
import numpy as np
import matplotlib.pyplot as plt

df = pd.DataFrame([
    {'area':4990.0,'perimeter':2791.9, 'shape':0.0903296,'permeability':6.3},
    {'area':7002.0,'perimeter':3892.6, 'shape':0.148622, 'permeability':6.3},
    {'area':7558.0,'perimeter':3930.66,'shape':0.183312, 'permeability':6.3},
    {'area':7352.0,'perimeter':3869.32,'shape':0.117063, 'permeability':6.3},
    {'area':7943.0,'perimeter':3948.54,'shape':0.122417, 'permeability':17.1},
])

# Create a dense set of (random) data points to illustrate some of the plots
df_dense = pd.DataFrame(33*np.random.randn(1000, 2), columns=['a', 'b'])
df_dense['b'] = df_dense['b'] + np.arange(1000)

df.plot(kind='bar')
plt.savefig('bar.png')

df.plot(kind='bar', stacked=True)
plt.savefig('bar-stacked.png')

df.plot(kind='barh', stacked=True)
plt.savefig('barh-stacked.png')

# A histogram records the frequency of data points lying within certain
ranges
df_dense.plot(kind='hist', bins=50)
plt.savefig('hist.png')

df.plot(kind='box')
plt.savefig('box.png')

df.plot(kind='kde')
plt.savefig('kde.png')

df.plot(kind='area')
plt.savefig('area.png')

df.plot(kind='scatter', x='area', y='perimeter')
plt.savefig('scatter.png')

df_dense.plot(kind='scatter', x='a', y='b')
plt.savefig('dense-scatter.png')
```

```
# Hexbin records the number of points of a scatter plot that lie in a (hexago-
nal) region
df_dense.plot(kind='hexbin', x='a', y='b', gridsize=25)
plt.savefig('hexbin.png')

df.plot(kind='pie', subplots=True)
plt.savefig('pie.png')
```

As mentioned previously, plotting data using the `plot()` method of a `DataFrame` is especially useful when plotting multiple series on the same axis. With this usage in mind, pandas offers several practical plotting features that can assist multi-series analyses. We saw in the previous slide that you can add a color map to pyplot scatter plots to control the sequence of colors used in the "color dimension". The `plot()` method of a `DataFrame` also takes a `cmap` argument so that you can control the sequence of colors used across series.

```
import pandas as pd
import matplotlib.pyplot as plt

df = pd.DataFrame([
    {'area':4990.0,'perimeter':2791.9, 'shape':903.296,'permeability':6300},
    {'area':7002.0,'perimeter':3892.6, 'shape':1486.22, 'permeability':6300},
    {'area':7558.0,'perimeter':3930.66,'shape':1833.12, 'permeability':6300},
    {'area':7352.0,'perimeter':3869.32,'shape':1170.63, 'permeability':6300},
    {'area':7943.0,'perimeter':3948.54,'shape':1224.17, 'permeability':1710},
])

df.plot(kind='bar', cmap='plasma')
plt.savefig('plot.png')
```

In banking and finance, as you would expect, we are exposed to time-based observations. For example, on a daily basis, we observe market data, economic information and the flow of market news. In this section, our focus is on financial data series. Let us generate and process some random data and create a simple sandbox environment for financial-like driven data sets:

```
import pandas as pd
import numpy as np

#Now lets generate some random normal datapoints
a = np.random.standard_normal((9, 4))

#Now lets place "a" into Pandas DataFrames and name our columns
df = pd.DataFrame(a)
df.columns = ['No1', 'No2', 'No3', 'No4']

#Add some dates into the DataFrame index
dates = pd.date_range('2020-1-1', periods=9, freq='M')
df.index = dates

print(df)
```

Building on the previous steps, let's run some basic analytics on these numbers:

```
import pandas as pd
import numpy as np

#DATA GENERATION BLOCK
a = np.random.standard_normal((9, 4))
```

```
df = pd.DataFrame(a)
df.columns = ['No1', 'No2', 'No3', 'No4']

dates = pd.date_range('2020-1-1', periods=9, freq='M')
df.index = dates

#BASIC ANALYTICS
print(df.sum())
print(df.mean())
print(df.cumsum())
print(df.describe())
```

Let us continue with our previous example of randomly generated data points:

```
import pandas as pd
import numpy as np
import matplotlib.pyplot as plt

#DATA GENERATION BLOCK
a = 10*np.random.standard_normal((9, 4))
df = pd.DataFrame(a)
df.columns = ['No1', 'No2', 'No3', 'No4']
dates = pd.date_range('2020-1-1', periods=9, freq='M')
df.index = dates

#Calculate returns for No1 time series
ret_No1 = df['No1']/df['No1'].shift(1)
ret_No1.dropna(inplace=True)
plt.plot(ret_No1)
plt.savefig("plot1.png")
```

In the previous example, as shown in Figure 3.8, we generate a random sequence of numbers into four independent columns and provided base statistics and descriptive statistics sequences. Finally, we derived additional calculation in a form of "returns" and plotting the results using simple `plot()` function.

Let us introduce some basic ideas behind 3D graphics using Python by a simple simulation of financial time series, specifically as related to equity volatility measures. In this example, depicted in Figures 3.9a and 3.9b, we generate implied volatility measure for an asset with strikes from 50 to 150, to demonstrate base 3D capabilities.

```
import numpy as np
import matplotlib.pyplot as plt

strike = np.linspace(50, 150, 24)
ttm = np.linspace(0.5, 2.5, 24)
strike, ttm = np.meshgrid(strike, ttm)

#generate implied volatilities
iv = (strike - 100) ** 2 / (100 * strike) / ttm
fig, ax = plt.subplots(subplot_kw={"projection": "3d"})

surf = ax.plot_surface(strike, ttm, iv, rstride=2, cstride=2,
                       cmap=plt.cm.coolwarm, linewidth=0.5,
                       antialiased=True)

ax.set_xlabel('strike')
ax.set_ylabel('time-to-maturity')
ax.set_zlabel('implied volatility')
```

Figure 3.8 Time Series Returns

```
fig.colorbar(surf, shrink=0.5, aspect=5)
fig.savefig("plot.png")

fig = plt.figure(figsize=(8, 5))
ax = fig.add_subplot(111, projection='3d')
ax.view_init(30, 60)

ax.scatter(strike, ttm, iv, zdir='z', s=25,
           c='b', marker='^')

ax.set_xlabel('strike')
ax.set_ylabel('time-to-maturity')
ax.set_zlabel('implied volatility')
fig.savefig("plot1.png")
```

In addition to time-series techniques we conclude this exposition by providing an example of clustering. A cluster is a collection of objects with a set of features being associated with those objects. Usually, these features are similar in nature. The goal is to separate objects into specific and unique groups, called clusters, with similarities that are being maximized, intra-groups, and similarities that are being minimized, inter-groups. Clustering can be seen as a form of unsupervised learning, whereby we do not provide examples to assist the algorithm in solving and tasks, and we let the algorithm learn these features from the data available. It is

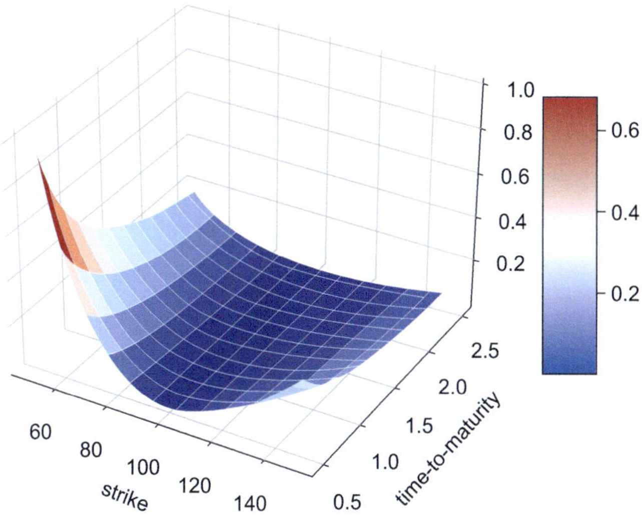

Figure 3.9a Clusters

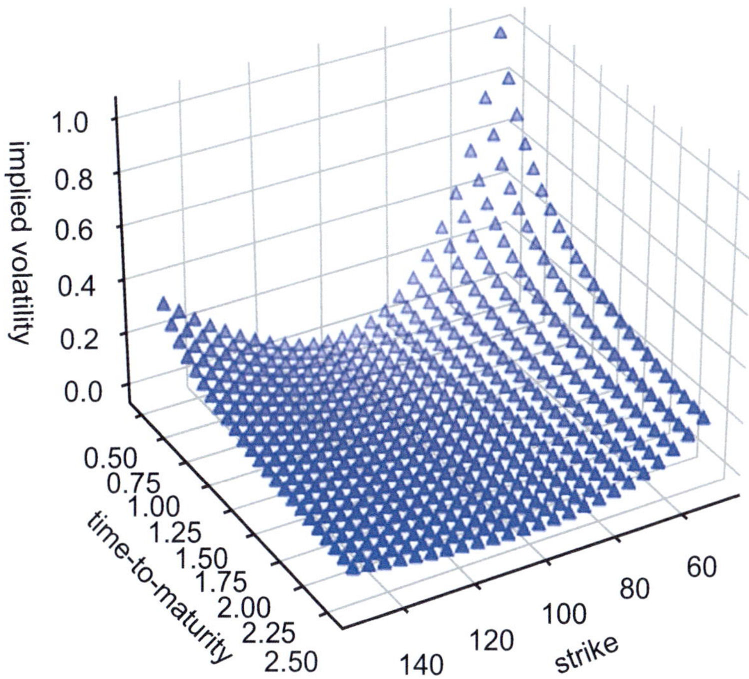

Figure 3.9b Cluster Examples

natural to observe clusters across financial data and more generally in banking and finance. Hence, it is important to understand data from a cluster-like perspective before further use of deeper analytical models across the data sets.

There are two main types of clusters

- **Partitional:** This technique creates a one-level partition of the objects.
- **Hierarchical:** This technique produces a nested sequence with a single all-inclusive cluster at the top.

K-Means attempts to split sample (rows) of X into a pre-determined number of clusters K. We use this form of cluster analysis across structured as well as unstructured data streams.

1. Initialize a random set of K centorids:

$$\left(u_k\right)_{k-1,\ldots,K}$$

2. Assign each sample Xn to one cluster, such that the within-cluster variance is minimized:

$$\sum_{n=1}^{N} min_k [\,|\, X_n - u_k \,|^2]$$

3. Update u based on the clusters from (2).
4. Repeat steps (2) and (3) until convergence.

```
import matplotlib.pyplot as mpl,matplotlib.cm as cm
from sklearn import datasets
from sklearn.cluster import KMeans

X,_=datasets.make_blobs(n_samples=10000,n_features=2,centers=3,random_state=0)

clusterer=KMeans(n_clusters=3).fit(X)
colors=cm.nipy_spectral(clusterer.labels_.astype(float)/3)
mpl.scatter(X[:,0],X[:,1],marker='.',s=30,lw=0,alpha=.5,c=colors,edgecolor='k')
mpl.savefig('kmeans.png',dpi=300)
```

The ability to understand clustered returns in time-series data settings or cluster or words in alternative textual data settings is critical in any FinTech applications. The previous example, Figure 3.10, showcase a simple KMeans sequence using standard *sklearn* Python library.

Seaborn

Pandas provides a `plot()` function that adds functionality to the `matplotlib.pyplot` plotting function – making it easier to handle a number of common tasks such as plotting multi-series plots. Seaborn, a powerful **Python data visualization library**, has revolutionized the way scientists and researchers present complex data [3.6]. Built on top of Matplotlib, Seaborn offers a high-level interface for creating *stunning statistical graphics* with minimal code. Its intuitive API allows users to effortlessly generate a wide array of plots, from simple scatter plots to intricate heat maps and violin plots. What sets Seaborn apart is its ability to seamlessly integrate with pandas DataFrames, making it an indispensable tool for exploratory data analysis in scientific research. By automatically applying aesthetically pleasing color palettes and styles, Seaborn elevates the visual appeal of graphs while maintaining their statistical integrity. The `seaborn` package enhances the pandas plotting environment, further

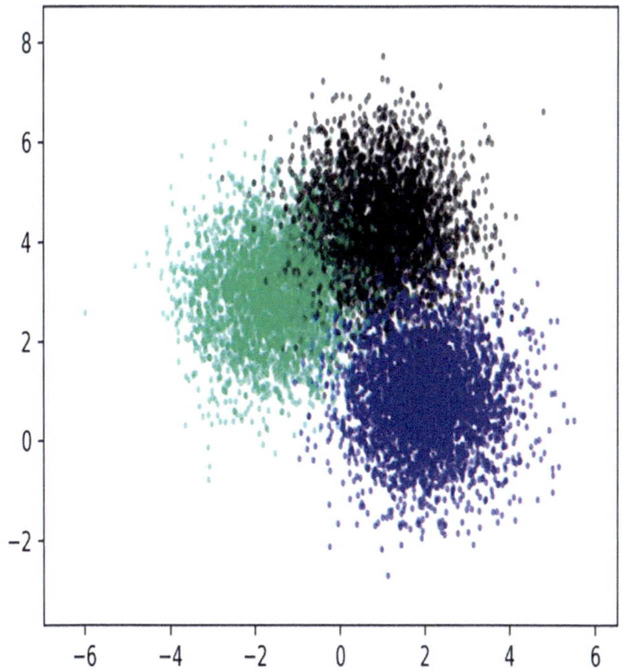

Figure 3.10 Advanced Clusters

simplifying some common tasks (particularly related to categorical data) as well as improving the overall presentation of plots.

Consider the following data set:

height	weight	gender
172	78	M
183	87	M
177	90	M
177	88	M
154	57	F
166	62	F
176	66	F
155	50	F

Suppose we would like to plot this data in a scatter plot with `'weight'` vs `'height'` and somehow identifying the genders. From earlier, we know that scatter plots can handle additional "dimensions" using colors and/or sizes. Unfortunately, trying something like: `df.plot(x='weight', y='height', c='gender')` results in an error because the c parameter is expecting a sequence of colors or numbers. One solution would be to extract the two sub-DataFrames corresponding to the two choices for "gender" and then plot them on the same axes.

```
import pandas as pd
import matplotlib.pyplot as plt
```

```
df = pd.DataFrame([
    {'height': 172, 'weight': 78, 'gender': 'M'},
    {'height': 183, 'weight': 87, 'gender': 'M'},
    {'height': 177, 'weight': 90, 'gender': 'M'},
    {'height': 177, 'weight': 88, 'gender': 'M'},
    {'height': 154, 'weight': 57, 'gender': 'F'},
    {'height': 166, 'weight': 62, 'gender': 'F'},
    {'height': 176, 'weight': 66, 'gender': 'F'},
    {'height': 155, 'weight': 50, 'gender': 'F'},
])

males = (df['gender'] == 'M')
females = (df['gender'] == 'F')
axes = df[males].plot(kind='scatter', x='weight', y='height', color='red')
df[females].plot(kind='scatter', x='weight', y='height', color='green', ax=axes)

plt.savefig('plot.png')
```

The seaborn package offers an extensive library of chart types, particularly well suited to dealing with categorical data. We will discuss a few of them. The `relplot()` function is the primary function for producing plots that highlight *relationships* between series: scatter plots and line plots. We have already seen its use for drawing scatter plots, the behavior is similar to the `plot()` method of a pandas DataFrame. When drawing line plots, however, relplot will *aggregate* points with the same x-coordinate and show their central tendency (i.e., *average value*) as well as a confidence interval for that estimation.

```
import seaborn as sns
import pandas as pd
import matplotlib.pyplot as plt

df = pd.DataFrame({
    'x': pd.Series([1, 1, 2, 2, 3, 3, 4, 4, 5, 5, 6, 6, 7, 7]),
    'y': pd.Series([1, 2, 2, 3, 3, 4, 3, 6, 5, 6, 6, 7, 7, 8])
})

df.plot(kind='line', x='x', y='y')
plt.savefig('pandas.png')

sns.relplot(kind='line', data=df, x='x', y='y')
plt.savefig('seaborn.png')
```

The `catplot()` function is the primary function for producing plots that display information about *categorical data*. In such plots, the x-axis ranges over the various categories a series contains (or, by default, all numerical series in the data), and the y-axis provides an indication of the value. A bar chart is the quintessential example of such a plot.

```
import pandas as pd
import matplotlib.pyplot as plt
import seaborn as sns
df = pd.DataFrame([
    {'height': 172, 'weight': 78, 'gender': 'M'},
    {'height': 183, 'weight': 87, 'gender': 'M'},
    {'height': 177, 'weight': 90, 'gender': 'M'},
    {'height': 177, 'weight': 88, 'gender': 'M'},
    {'height': 154, 'weight': 57, 'gender': 'F'},
    {'height': 166, 'weight': 62, 'gender': 'F'},
```

```
    {'height': 176, 'weight': 66, 'gender': 'F'},
    {'height': 155, 'weight': 50, 'gender': 'F'},
])

sns.catplot(kind='bar', data=df, x='gender', y='height')
plt.savefig('plot.png')
```

Like the line plot of `relplot()`, observations that fall into the same category are aggregated and the central tendency, with confidence intervals, are what is shown.

The `pairplot()` function of seaborn is similar to the `scatter_matrix()` function of `pandas.plotting` except that it makes use of some of the added functionality provided by the relplot() function of seaborn. For example, it is possible to add categorical dimensions using hue.

```
import pandas as pd
import matplotlib.pyplot as plt
import seaborn as sns

df = pd.DataFrame([
    {'area':4990.0,'perimeter':2791.9, 'shape':903.296,'permeability':'X'},
    {'area':7002.0,'perimeter':3892.6, 'shape':1486.22, 'permeability':'X'},
    {'area':7558.0,'perimeter':3930.66,'shape':1833.12, 'permeability':'X'},
    {'area':7352.0,'perimeter':3869.32,'shape':1170.63, 'permeability':'Y'},
    {'area':7943.0,'perimeter':3948.54,'shape':1224.17, 'permeability':'Y'},
    {'area':8885.0,'perimeter':4938.45,'shape':1124.78, 'permeability':'Y'}
])

sns.pairplot(data=df, hue='permeability')
plt.savefig('plot.png')
```

Cryptocurrency Visuals

To continue our discussion about structured data visualization we expand on the cryptocurrency use case. As in our previous example using APIs to extract tabular data interpretation we add here a simple graphical data analyses. In our `main()` function we add additional cryptocurrency tickers:

```
def main(LIMIT = 2000,API_KEY=''):
    # Define a list of cryptocurrency pairs all in terms of USD
    crypto_pairs = ['BTC', 'ETH', 'LTC', 'XRP', 'BCH', 'ADA', 'DOT', 'LINK', 'XLM',
'SOL']
```

One of the first visual tools to use is correlation matrix, depicting the snap in time of a relationship amongst all our digital assets. For this analysis we use `seaborn` library:

```
        # Correlation Analyses
        correlation_matrix = df.corr()

        # Plot the heatmap of the correlation matrix
        plt.figure(figsize=(12, 8))
        sns.heatmap(correlation_matrix, annot=True, cmap='coolwarm', vmin=-1,
vmax=1, cbar_kws={'label': 'Correlation'})

        # Increase font size of x and y ticks
        plt.xticks(fontsize=14)
        plt.yticks(fontsize=14)
```

```
# Increase font size of x and y labels
plt.xlabel('')
plt.ylabel('')

# Title
plt.title('Correlation Matrix Heatmap', fontsize=18)

# Save the figure
filename = 'correlation.png'
plt.savefig(os.path.join(exportpath, filename))
plt.show()
```

The previous graph depicted in Figure 3.11 shows how the variable behave +1 indicates positive relationship whereby −1 indicates these time series move in an opposite way to each other. Say, BTC vs ADA shows correlation equal to 0.63 indicating a positive price moves between BCT and ADA.

Expanding on the correlation analysis we add hierarchical clustering in Figure 3.12 driven by correlation (1-correlation) distance matrix:

```
# Clustering
# Compute the distance matrix using 1 - correlation
distance_matrix = 1 - correlation_matrix
# Perform hierarchical clustering using the linkage method
Z = linkage(distance_matrix, 'ward')

# Plot the dendrogram
plt.figure(figsize=(12, 8))
dendrogram(Z, labels=correlation_matrix.columns, leaf_rotation=90,
leaf_font_size=14)
```

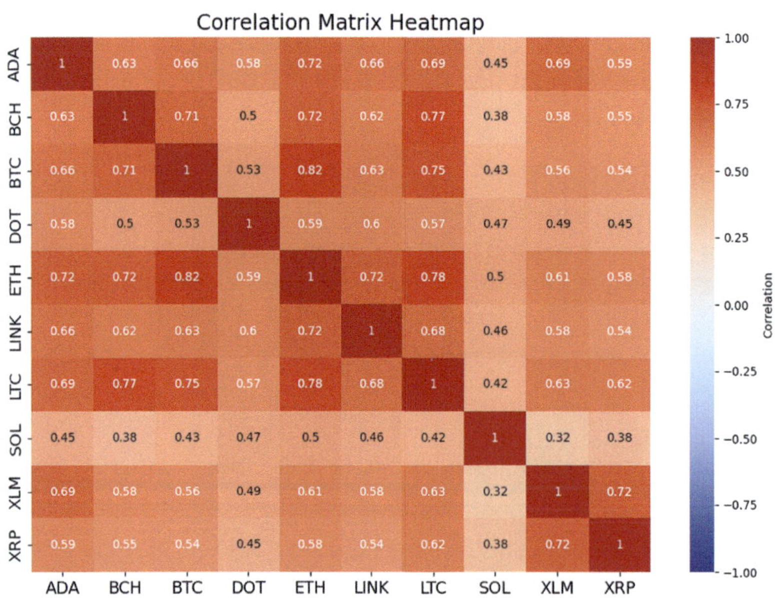

	ADA	BCH	BTC	DOT	ETH	LINK	LTC	SOL	XLM	XRP
ADA	1	0.63	0.66	0.58	0.72	0.66	0.69	0.45	0.69	0.59
BCH	0.63	1	0.71	0.5	0.72	0.62	0.77	0.38	0.58	0.55
BTC	0.66	0.71	1	0.53	0.82	0.63	0.75	0.43	0.56	0.54
DOT	0.58	0.5	0.53	1	0.59	0.6	0.57	0.47	0.49	0.45
ETH	0.72	0.72	0.82	0.59	1	0.72	0.78	0.5	0.61	0.58
LINK	0.66	0.62	0.63	0.6	0.72	1	0.68	0.46	0.58	0.54
LTC	0.69	0.77	0.75	0.57	0.78	0.68	1	0.42	0.63	0.62
SOL	0.45	0.38	0.43	0.47	0.5	0.46	0.42	1	0.32	0.38
XLM	0.69	0.58	0.56	0.49	0.61	0.58	0.63	0.32	1	0.72
XRP	0.59	0.55	0.54	0.45	0.58	0.54	0.62	0.38	0.72	1

Figure 3.11 Correlation Matrix

```
plt.title('Dendrogram : Clustering using Correlation', fontsize=18)
plt.xlabel('Stock', fontsize=16)
plt.ylabel('Distance', fontsize=16)

# Increase font size of x and y ticks
plt.xticks(fontsize=14)
plt.yticks(fontsize=14)

# Save the figure
filename = 'dendogram.png'
plt.savefig(os.path.join(exportpath, filename))
plt.show()
```

To continue with these basic visual data interpretations we add returns time-series, in Figure 3.14, and cumulative-return time series, in Figure 3.15, to the mix to understand dynamics within these selected digital assets:

```
# Time-series statistics (the first 6 digital assets)
plt.figure(figsize=(16, 20))
for i, stock in enumerate(df.columns[:6], 1):
    plt.subplot(3, 2, i)
    plt.plot(df.index, df[stock])
    plt.title(f'Time Series for {stock}', fontsize=14)
    plt.xlabel('Date', fontsize=14)

    plt.ylabel('Return', fontsize=14)
    plt.xticks(fontsize=14)
    plt.yticks(fontsize=14)
plt.tight_layout()
```

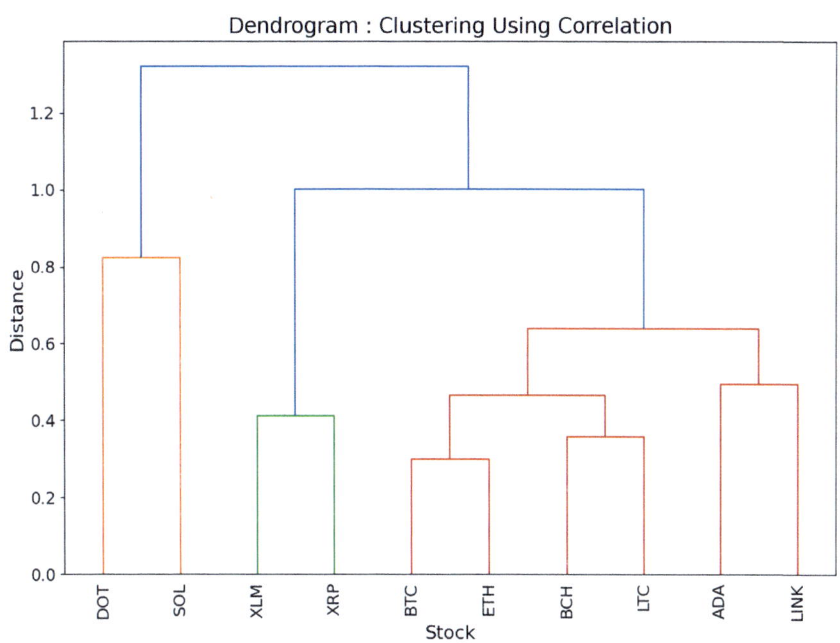

Figure 3.12 Clustering

```
# Save the figure
filename = 'time_series.png'
plt.savefig(os.path.join(exportpath, filename))
plt.show()

# Calculate rolling mean and standard deviation (window of 12 months)
rolling_stats = {}
for stock in df.columns:
```

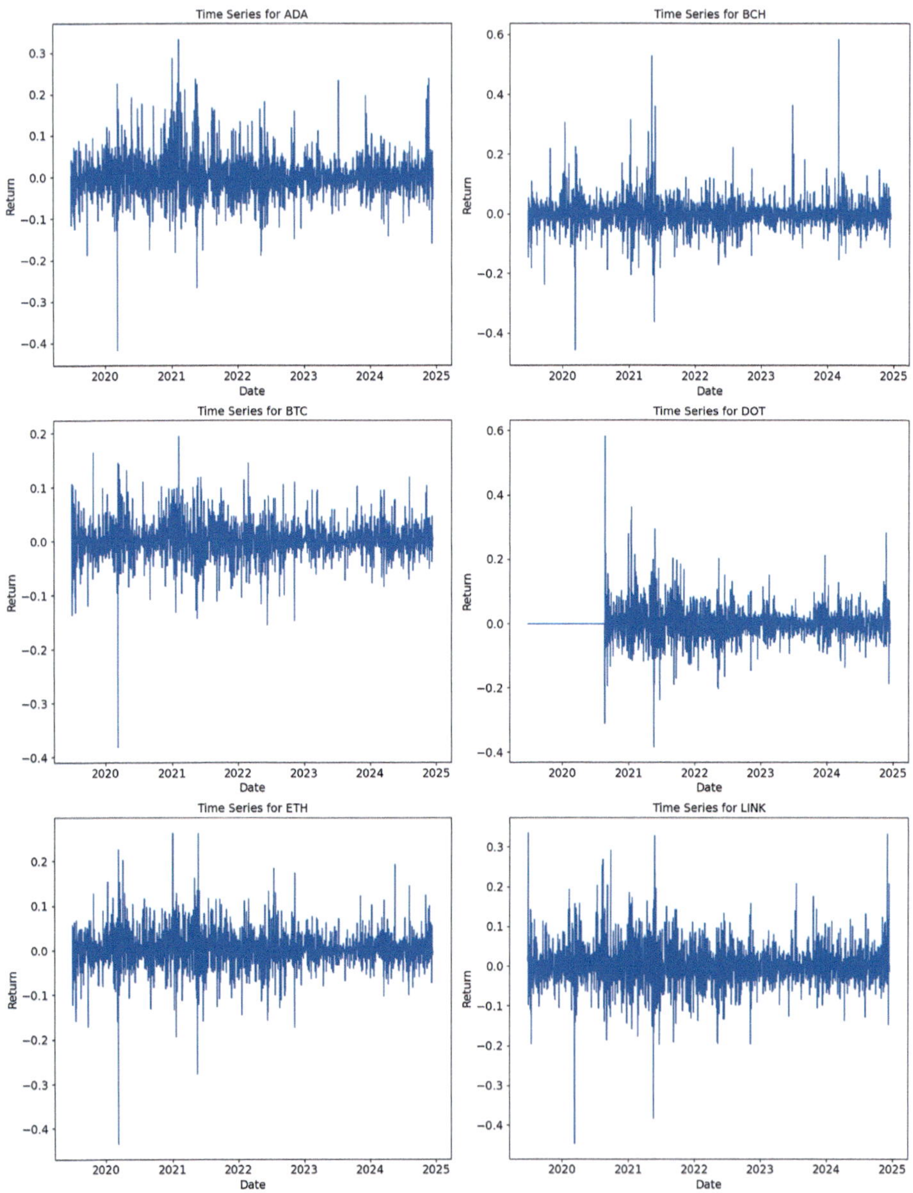

Figure 3.13 Returns

```
        rolling_stats[stock] = df[stock].rolling(window=21).agg(['mean',
'std'])
    # Plot rolling mean and standard deviation for each stock
    plt.figure(figsize=(16, 20))
    for i, stock in enumerate(df.columns[:6], 1):
        plt.subplot(3, 2, i)
        plt.plot(df.index, rolling_stats[stock]['mean'], label='Rolling Mean')
        plt.plot(df.index, rolling_stats[stock]['std'], label='Rolling Std')
        plt.title(f'Rolling Statistics for {stock}', fontsize=14)
        plt.xlabel('Date', fontsize=14)
        plt.ylabel('Return / Volatility', fontsize=14)
        plt.xticks(fontsize=14)
        plt.yticks(fontsize=14)
        plt.legend()
    plt.tight_layout()
    # Save the figure
    filename = 'time_series_rolling.png'
    plt.savefig(os.path.join(exportpath, filename))
    plt.show()
```

Last but not the least, in our journey we look at cumulative returns over time to gain insights as to how these specific digital assets performed for the past five years (time period covered from the APIs service). It is clear from the visual interpretation that COVID period dynamics differ from the other time frames. This could be an indication of potential investor's behavioral shifts. More on this in Chapter 9.

```
    # Calculate cumulative returns
    cumulative_returns = (1 + df).cumprod() - 1

    # Plot cumulative returns over time
    plt.figure(figsize=(10, 8))
    for column in cumulative_returns.columns:
        plt.plot(cumulative_returns.index, cumulative_returns[column],
label=column)

    # Customize the plot
    plt.title('Cumulative Returns Over Time', fontsize=16)
    plt.xlabel('Date', fontsize=14)
    plt.ylabel('Cumulative Return', fontsize=14)
    plt.legend(title='Stock', fontsize=14, title_fontsize=14)
    plt.xticks(rotation=45, fontsize=14)
    plt.yticks(fontsize=14)
    plt.tight_layout()

    # Save the figure
    filename = 'cumulative_return.png'
    plt.savefig(os.path.join(exportpath, filename))
    plt.show()
```

In this section, we covered base Python plotting capabilities as built into matplotlib, pandas and seaborn libraries as related to a powerful statistical analysis of digital assets. In the following section we introduce alternative data structures, predominately text driven and provide an exposition to valuable techniques that we use and apply in our further chapters.

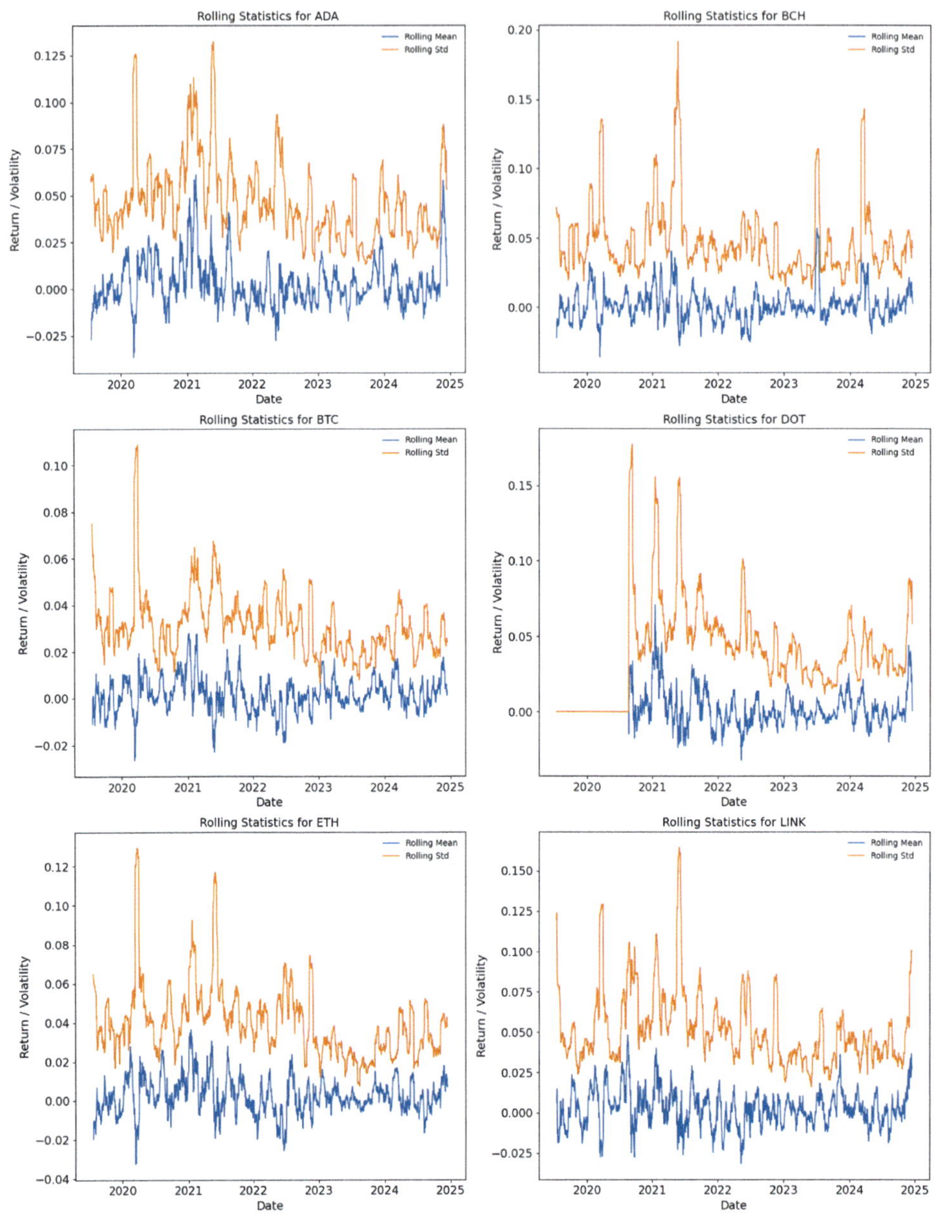

Figure 3.14 Rolling Returns

3.4 Unstructured Data

In the dynamic world of banking and finance, **unstructured data** has emerged as a goldmine of untapped insights. This vast sea of information includes customer emails, social media posts, call center transcripts and even handwritten loan applications. Unlike traditional structured data, these diverse sources offer a rich tapestry of customer sentiments, market

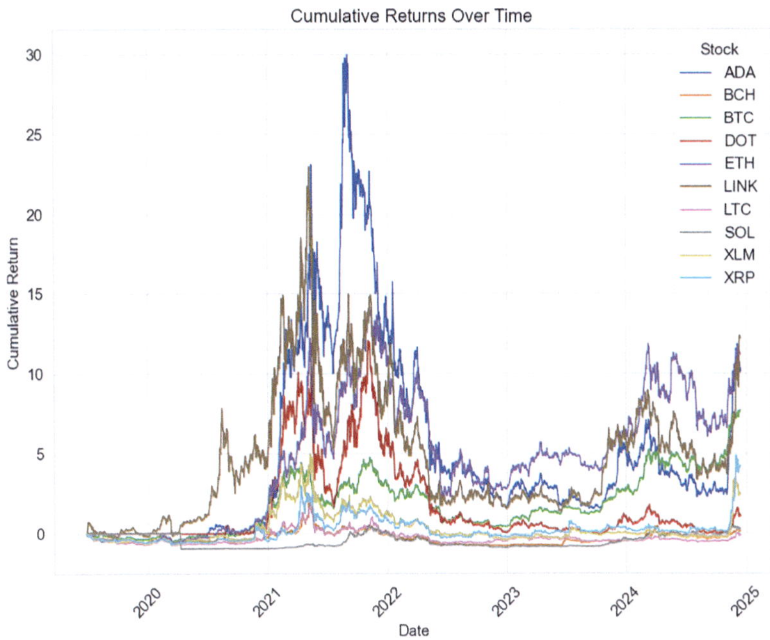

Figure 3.15 Cumulative Returns

trends, and potential risks. Financial institutions that harness the power of unstructured data analysis can uncover hidden patterns and make data-driven decisions with unprecedented accuracy. By employing advanced techniques such as natural language processing and machine learning, banks can transform seemingly chaotic information into actionable intelligence. This revolution in data analysis not only enhances risk management and fraud detection but also paves the way for personalized customer experiences and innovative financial products. As the financial landscape continues to evolve, the ability to derive meaningful insights from unstructured data will undoubtedly become a critical competitive advantage in the banking sector.

Clusters

To extend our discussion and exercises, we look deeper into the space of natural language processing. In short, can we develop an algorithm that is going to understand and COMPREHEND human language be it in any language format? Natural language processing is a branch of AI and machine learning space that is aimed to deliver on this possibility. There are several techniques currently used in NLP whereby syntactic analysis and semantic analysis are the two main modeling architectures. NLP algorithm is used to apply grammatical rules to a group of words and derive meaning from this selection – this is syntactic analysis approach. On the other hand, semantic analysis requires the algorithms to understand the meaning and interpretation of words and how sentences are structured. This is a more challenging approach.

PyTorch, a powerful open-source machine learning library, offers robust capabilities for visualizing and analyzing text data [3.7]. By leveraging PyTorch's tensor operations and neural network modules, data scientists can transform raw text into rich visual representations, unveiling hidden patterns and relationships within the language. These visualizations can range from simple word clouds to complex semantic networks, allowing researchers to derive valuable insights about linguistic structures, sentiment trends and thematic clusters. One particularly illuminating technique is the use of PyTorch to generate word embeddings and project them into a lower-dimensional space. This approach enables the creation of interactive scatter plots where semantically similar words cluster together, offering an intuitive way to explore the conceptual landscape of a text corpus. By applying dimensionality reduction algorithms like t-SNE or UMAP, analysts can further enhance these visualizations, making it easier to identify word associations and contextual relationships that might not be apparent from the raw text alone. Through these powerful visualization tools, PyTorch empowers researchers and practitioners to uncover nuanced insights from textual data, paving the way for more informed decision-making in fields ranging from natural language processing to content analysis and beyond.

In the next example, we extract Crypto related news using CryptoCompare APIs and snap text file for further processing and visualization. The code snippet uses the file and provides a basic text visual interpretation:

This is a brief snippet of text shown in Figure 3.16, extracted from the alternative data stream:

The following is a relevant Python code processing this text file. At a later chapter we return to these Python libraries in detail and dissect the underlying principles and techniques used. For the purposes of this exposition, we focus our attention on our new capabilities to gain a visual data interpretation.

```
import matplotlib.pyplot as plt
from wordcloud import WordCloud
```

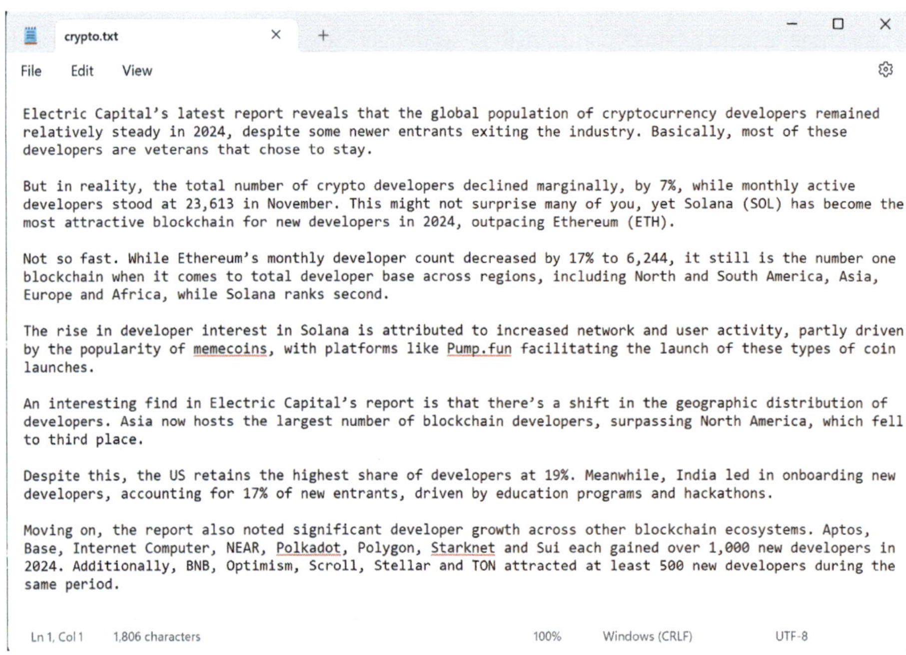
crypto.txt

File Edit View

Electric Capital's latest report reveals that the global population of cryptocurrency developers remained relatively steady in 2024, despite some newer entrants exiting the industry. Basically, most of these developers are veterans that chose to stay.

But in reality, the total number of crypto developers declined marginally, by 7%, while monthly active developers stood at 23,613 in November. This might not surprise many of you, yet Solana (SOL) has become the most attractive blockchain for new developers in 2024, outpacing Ethereum (ETH).

Not so fast. While Ethereum's monthly developer count decreased by 17% to 6,244, it still is the number one blockchain when it comes to total developer base across regions, including North and South America, Asia, Europe and Africa, while Solana ranks second.

The rise in developer interest in Solana is attributed to increased network and user activity, partly driven by the popularity of memecoins, with platforms like Pump.fun facilitating the launch of these types of coin launches.

An interesting find in Electric Capital's report is that there's a shift in the geographic distribution of developers. Asia now hosts the largest number of blockchain developers, surpassing North America, which fell to third place.

Despite this, the US retains the highest share of developers at 19%. Meanwhile, India led in onboarding new developers, accounting for 17% of new entrants, driven by education programs and hackathons.

Moving on, the report also noted significant developer growth across other blockchain ecosystems. Aptos, Base, Internet Computer, NEAR, Polkadot, Polygon, Starknet and Sui each gained over 1,000 new developers in 2024. Additionally, BNB, Optimism, Scroll, Stellar and TON attracted at least 500 new developers during the same period.

Ln 1, Col 1 1,806 characters 100% Windows (CRLF) UTF-8

Figure 3.16 Text Example

```
from collections import Counter
import re
from nltk.sentiment import SentimentIntensityAnalyzer
from nltk.tokenize import sent_tokenize, word_tokenize
import nltk

# Ensure you have the necessary NLTK data
nltk.download('vader_lexicon')
nltk.download('punkt')

# Load the text from the file
file_path = r'/crypto.txt'
with open(file_path, 'r') as file:
    text = file.read()

print(text)

# Text preprocessing
text_cleaned = re.sub(r'[^a-zA-Z\s]', '', text)  # Remove non-alphabetic
characters
words = word_tokenize(text_cleaned.lower())      # Tokenize and convert to
lowercase

# Word frequency count
word_counts = Counter(words)
common_words = word_counts.most_common(10)

# Sentiment Analysis
sia = SentimentIntensityAnalyzer()
sentences = sent_tokenize(text)
sentiments = [sia.polarity_scores(sentence)['compound'] for sentence in
sentences]

# Word Cloud Visualization
wordcloud = WordCloud(width=800, height=400, background_color='white').
generate_from_frequencies(word_counts)

# Plotting
plt.figure(figsize=(12, 6))

# Subplot 1: Word Cloud
plt.subplot(1, 2, 1)
plt.imshow(wordcloud, interpolation='bilinear')
plt.axis('off')
plt.title('Word Cloud of Text')

# Subplot 2: Sentiment Trend
plt.subplot(1, 2, 2)
plt.plot(sentiments, marker='o', linestyle='-', color='blue')
plt.axhline(0, color='red', linestyle='--', linewidth=1)
plt.title('Sentiment Analysis Trend')
plt.xlabel('Sentence Index')
plt.ylabel('Sentiment Score')
plt.tight_layout()
plt.show()

# Print common words
print("Most Common Words:", common_words)
```

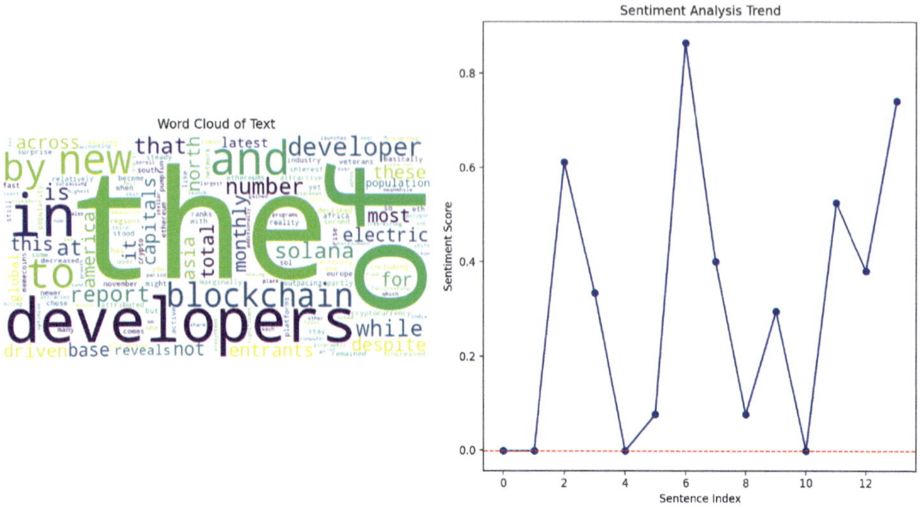

Figure 3.17 Text Clusters

The results show a visualization of the most frequent words, as depicted in Figure 3.17, with sizes proportional to frequency, sentiment trends as a line plot representing sentiment scores across sentences and a printed list of top ten words.

> Moving on, the report also noted significant developer growth across other blockchain ecosystems. Aptos, Base, Internet Computer, NEAR, Polkadot, Polygon, Starknet and Sui each gained over 1,000 new developers in 2024. Additionally, BNB, Optimism, Scroll, Stellar and TON attracted at least 500 new developers during the same period. Most Common Words: [('the', 14), ('of', 11), ('developers', 11), ('in', 10), ('and', 6), ('to', 5), ('new', 5), ('by', 4), ('blockchain', 4), ('developer', 4)].

By harnessing the power of natural language processing and machine learning, financial entities can now *decode vast amounts of unstructured data* with unprecedented efficiency. This technological leap forward enables banks to **gauge customer sentiment** with remarkable accuracy, allowing them to tailor services and address concerns proactively. Moreover, text analysis serves as a crystal ball for **market trend prediction**, empowering traders and analysts to stay ahead of the curve in volatile markets. Perhaps most crucially, it acts as a vigilant guardian against financial crimes, bolstering **fraud detection** capabilities and enhancing **risk assessment** processes. As financial landscapes grow increasingly complex, text analysis stands as an indispensable ally, transforming raw data into actionable insights that drive informed decision-making and foster innovation in the world of finance.

3.5 Visual Tools

TensorFlow

At its core, **TensorFlow** leverages tensor computations and dynamic computational graphs to optimize complex mathematical operations, allowing for efficient training of neural networks on massive data sets [3.8]. Its seamless integration with GPU acceleration unleashes the full potential of modern hardware, pushing the boundaries of what's possible in AI research and development. But TensorFlow isn't just about raw power – it's about accessibility and innovation. With its intuitive high-level APIs like Keras, even those new to machine learning can start building sophisticated models in no time.

Let us remain in the sentiment analytics space. The purpose of this session is to visualize complex unstructured data formats, within the FinTech data management sequence, for this purpose we use TensorFlow Embedding Projector results shown in Figure 3.18.

The **TensorFlow Embedding Projector** is a powerful data visualization tool that brings high-dimensional data to life. Imagine being able to explore complex relationships between words, images or any other data points in a visually intuitive way. At its base, the Embedding Projector takes abstract mathematical representations (embeddings) and projects them into a 3D space, allowing researchers and data scientists to *uncover hidden patterns* and *gain deeper insights* into their data.

One of the most exciting features of the Embedding Projector is its ability to let users interact with their data in real-time. You can rotate, zoom and even search for specific data points, making it feel like you're exploring a galaxy of information right at your fingertips. This interactivity is not just fun; it's incredibly valuable for tasks like understanding word relationships in natural language processing or visualizing similarities between images in computer vision projects.

The applications of the TensorFlow Embedding Projector are vast and growing. From improving recommendation systems to enhancing language models, this tool is helping push the boundaries of what's possible in machine learning. It's no exaggeration to say that the Embedding Projector is changing the way we understand and interact with complex data, making the abstract world of high-dimensional spaces more accessible than ever before.

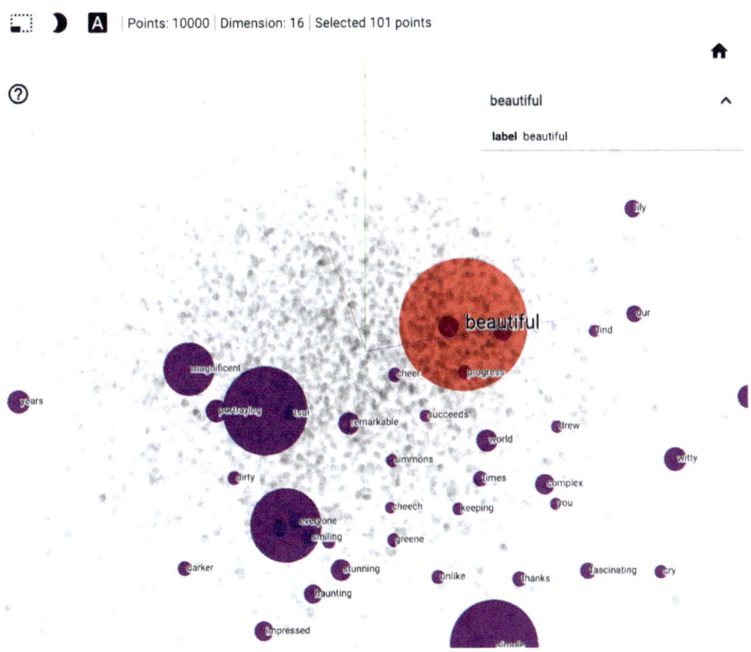

Figure 3.18 Embedding Editor

Following closely TensorFlow Tutorial we have previously concluded that machines cannot read text per se and hence we need some techniques to encode or convert text into numbers, numeric formats. One approach here is to encode each word using a unique number. Consider the sentence "The cat sat on the mat" you could assign 1 to "cat," 2 to "mat" and so on. You could then encode the sentence "The cat sat on the mat" as a dense vector like [5, 1, 4, 3, 5, 2]. This approach is efficient. Instead of a sparse vector, you now have a dense one. However, there is a more advanced form using word embedding.

> Word embeddings give us a way to use an efficient, dense representation in which similar words have a similar encoding. Importantly, you do not have to specify this encoding by hand. An embedding is a dense vector of floating point values (the length of the vector is a parameter you specify). Instead of specifying the values for the embedding manually, they are trainable parameters (weights learned by the model during training, in the same way a model learns weights for a dense layer). It is common to see word embeddings that are 8-dimensional (for small datasets), up to 1024-dimensions when working with large datasets. A higher dimensional embedding can capture fine-grained relationships between words, but takes more data to learn.
>
> Figure 3.19 is a diagram for a word embedding. Each word is represented as a four-dimensional vector of floating point values. Another way to think of an embedding is as "lookup table." After these weights have been learned, you can encode each word by looking up the dense vector it corresponds to in the table. The Embedding layer can be understood as a lookup table that maps from integer indices (which stand for specific words) to dense vectors (their embeddings). The dimensionality (or width) of the embedding is a parameter you can experiment with to see what works well for your problem, much in the same way you would experiment with the number of neurons in a Dense layer.

The following Python code snippet delivers two files we use to feed the TensorFlow Embedding Projector delivering 3D representation of text derived sentiment analytics. At further chapters we discuss the process and detailed approach to the visual results. For the purposes of this discussion it is sufficient to view the final outcome at this stage.

```
import io
import matplotlib.pyplot as plt
```

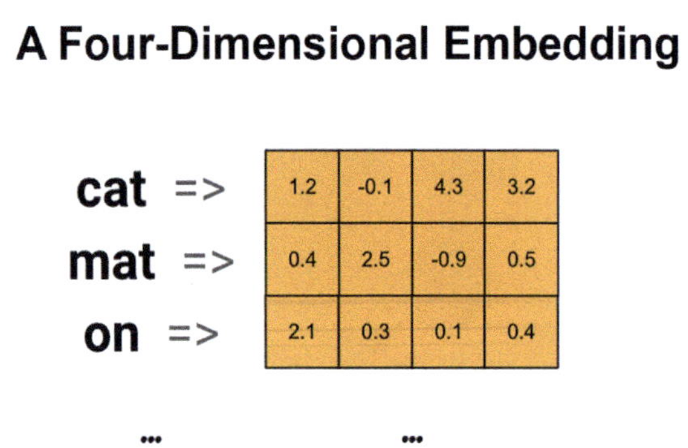

Figure 3.19 Embedding Editor Dimensions

```
import tensorflow as tf
from tensorflow import keras
from tensorflow.keras import layers
import tensorflow_datasets as tfds
tfds.disable_progress_bar()
'''
WORKSHOP TASKS:
Get familiar with IMDb database of movie reviews.
Run this script and extract 2 files
meta.tsv
vecs.tsv
Load these two files and analyse results within Embedding Projector

REFERENCES:
https://www.tensorflow.org/tutorials/text/word_embeddings
http://projector.tensorflow.org/
https://www.tensorflow.org/datasets/api_docs/python/tfds
https://ai.stanford.edu/~amaas/data/sentiment/
https://www.imdb.com/
'''

# Prepare and load database from IMDb reviews - sentiment analytics approach
to text
embedding_layer = layers.Embedding(1000, 5)
result = embedding_layer(tf.constant([1,2,3]))
result.numpy()
result = embedding_layer(tf.constant([[0,1,2],[3,4,5]]))
result.shape

(train_data, test_data), info = tfds.load(
    'imdb_reviews/subwords8k',
    split = (tfds.Split.TRAIN, tfds.Split.TEST),
    with_info=True, as_supervised=True)

encoder = info.features['text'].encoder
encoder.subwords[:20]

train_batches = train_data.shuffle(1000).padded_batch(10, ([-1],[]))
test_batches = test_data.shuffle(1000).padded_batch(10, ([-1],[]))

train_batch, train_labels = next(iter(train_batches))
train_batch.numpy()

embedding_dim=16

# Build sequential NN
model = keras.Sequential([
    layers.Embedding(encoder.vocab_size, embedding_dim),
    layers.GlobalAveragePooling1D(),
    layers.Dense(16, activation='relu'),
    layers.Dense(1)
])

model.summary()
model.compile(optimizer='adam',
              loss=tf.keras.losses.BinaryCrossentropy(from_logits=True),
              metrics=['accuracy'])
```

```
history = model.fit(
    train_batches,
    epochs=10,
    validation_data=test_batches, validation_steps=20)

history_dict = history.history
acc = history_dict['accuracy']
val_acc = history_dict['val_accuracy']
loss=history_dict['loss']
val_loss=history_dict['val_loss']

epochs = range(1, len(acc) + 1)

plt.figure(figsize=(12,9))
plt.plot(epochs, loss, 'bo', label='Training loss')
plt.plot(epochs, val_loss, 'b', label='Validation loss')
plt.title('Training and validation loss')
plt.xlabel('Epochs')
plt.ylabel('Loss')
plt.legend()
plt.show()

plt.figure(figsize=(12,9))
plt.plot(epochs, acc, 'bo', label='Training acc')
plt.plot(epochs, val_acc, 'b', label='Validation acc')
plt.title('Training and validation accuracy')
plt.xlabel('Epochs')
plt.ylabel('Accuracy')
plt.legend(loc='lower right')
plt.ylim((0.5,1))
plt.show()

e = model.layers[0]
weights = e.get_weights()[0]
print(weights.shape) # shape: (vocab_size, embedding_dim)

encoder = info.features['text'].encoder

out_v = io.open('vecs.tsv', 'w', encoding='utf-8')
out_m = io.open('meta.tsv', 'w', encoding='utf-8')

for num, word in enumerate(encoder.subwords):
    vec = weights[num+1] # skip 0, it's padding.
    out_m.write(word + "\n")

    out_v.write('\t'.join([str(x) for x in vec]) + "\n")
out_v.close()
out_m.close()
```

The previous code delivers 2x files vecs.tsv and meta.tsv. Now, open Embedding Projector as per Figure 3.20 and load these 2x files in as per Figure 3.21.

Figure 3.22 shows post processing utilizing "PCA" methodology we are likely going to see the following 3D spherical data interpretation of "positives" and "negatives" poles. The data we have used in our example using 50,000 movie reviews and this visual data interpretation can be used to showcase the most recent sentiment whether positive or negative and what sort of words are linked to this interpretation. For instance, when reading global news we

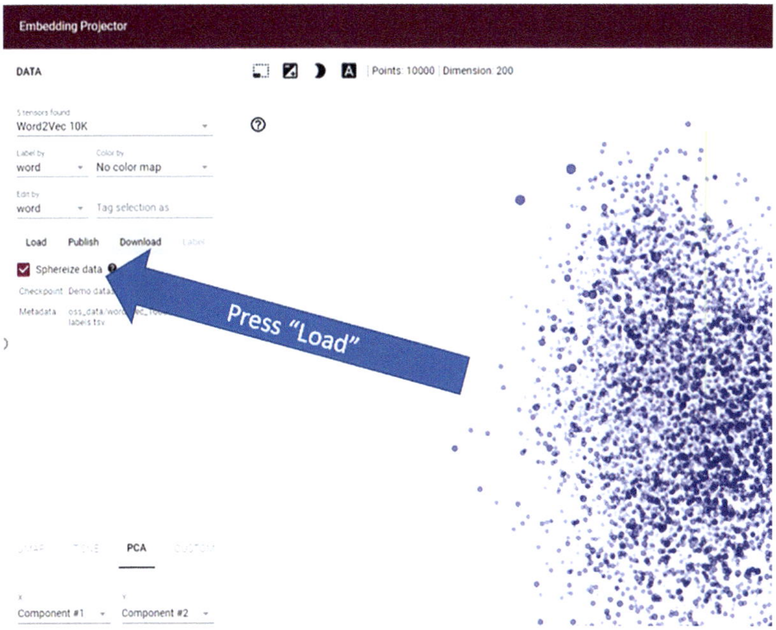

Figure 3.20 Embedding Example 1

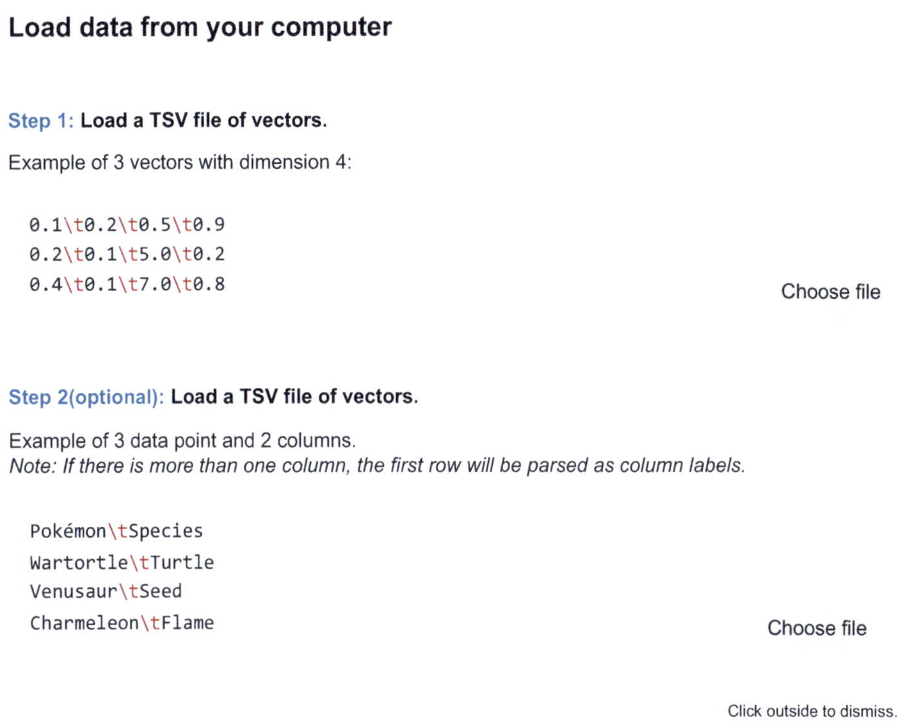

Figure 3.21 Embedding Example 2

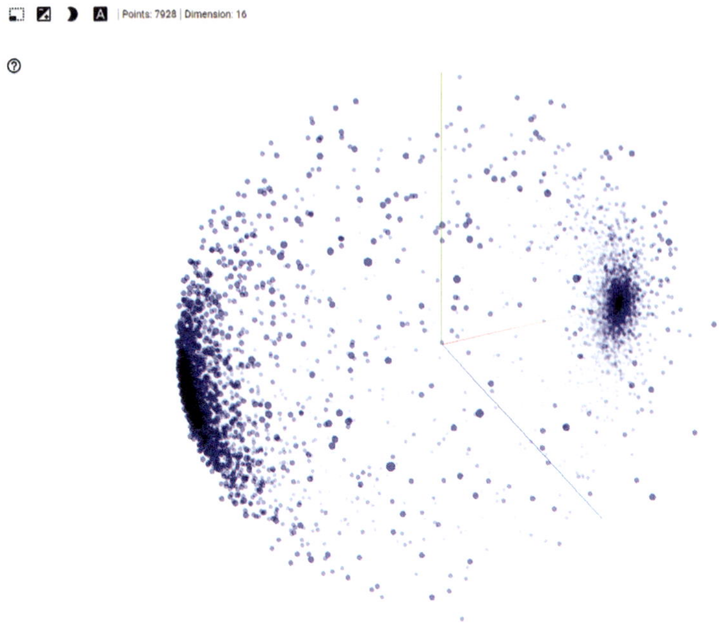

Figure 3.22 Embedding Example 3

can view the narrative per time period and can assess the most used words and hence news sentiment-like direction.

Why is this relevant to FinTech? In trading world this information can be used to adjust robo-advisory calculated portfolio weights – go long positive sentiment go short negative sentiment. In neo-bank space, this can be used to show this information to your clients to assist them in running their business more efficiently.

Figma

Figma, a cloud-based application design tool, revolutionizes collaborative creativity much like the interconnected neurons in our brains [3.9]. Just as neurons form intricate networks to process information, Figma enables designers to create complex visual systems with seamless collaboration. Its real-time editing feature mirrors the rapid synaptic connections in neural networks, allowing instant idea transmission and iteration. This parallel between Figma and neurobiology offers a profound insight: the power of interconnectedness in both digital and biological realms. By understanding this relationship, we can appreciate how tools like Figma not only facilitate design but also emulate nature's most sophisticated information processing system, inspiring us to create more intuitive and responsive digital experiences. Figma, a powerful design tool, is revolutionizing the way banks and financial institutions visualize data and create user-centric experiences. By utilizing Figma's prototyping capabilities, banks can test and iterate on new features, such as personalized investment recommendations, before full implementation. We utilize and introduce Figma design studios in later chapters while building pro-forma FinTech applications.

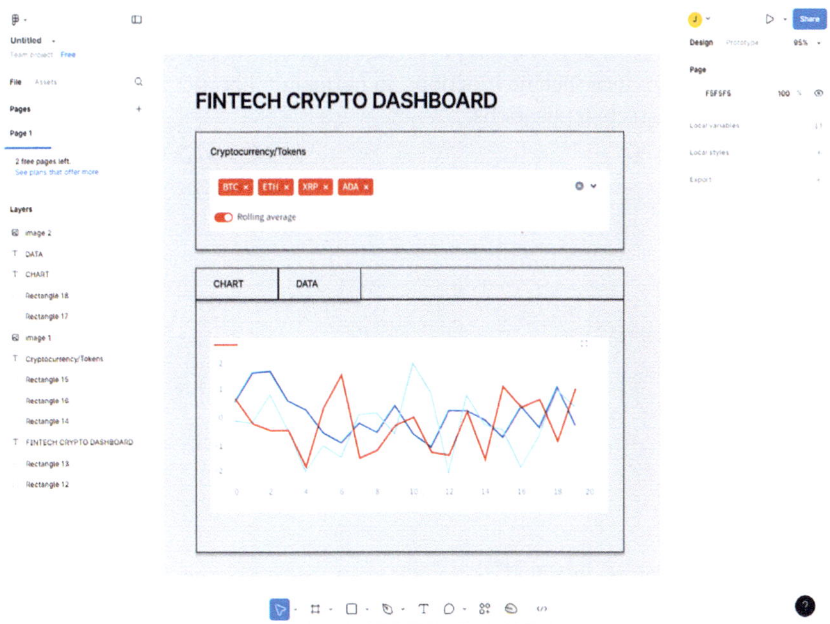

Figure 3.23 Figma Crypto Dashboard

Based on our previous "Cryptocurrency Visuals" section, we derive a simple customer journey utilizing Figma Toolbox. The user wishes to design a simple dashboard showing a selection of cryptocurrencies of the user's choice providing a simple graphical representation of daily returns driven by closing prices. In addition, the user wants to have the ability to select Rolling average calculation. The results are shown on the same screen in two tabs, one dedicated to graphical results, the other dedicated to tabular results.

This Figma design created using Figma Toolbox depicts the aforementioned simple use case, as shown in Figure 3.23. The focus is on the shape, sketch and flow in terms of inputs and outputs. What are the predefined input parameters and what the user expects to receive in return. In the following section we utilize Streamlit to build this simple "sketch" into a base FinTech app prototype.

Streamlit

Imagine turning complex data into beautiful, interactive visualizations with just a few lines of Python code. That is the magic of **Streamlit**, a revolutionary open-source library that's transforming how data scientists and analysts share their findings [3.10]. With Streamlit, you can effortlessly create web apps for your data projects, allowing you to showcase and derive insights in real time. Streamlit's intuitive interface makes it a breeze to build everything from simple data displays to sophisticated machine learning models. Want to plot a graph? Just use `st.line_chart()`. Need to upload a file? `st.file_uploader()` has got you covered. The library's real power lies in its ability to turn your Python scripts into interactive web apps instantly, enabling you to focus on the data, not the web development. Imagine creating a dashboard that updates as new data flows in, or an interactive model that users can tweak with sliders and buttons. That is the kind of engaging, insightful experience Streamlit delivers. We utilize and introduce specific functions and Streamlit libraries in later chapters while building pro-forma FinTech applications.

```
import streamlit as st

st.title("Streamlit for FinTech...")
st.markdown(
    """
    This is a sandbox for you to try Streamlit and have FinTech fun.

    **There's :rainbow[so much] you can build!**

    Imagine turning complex data into beautiful, interactive visualizations
with just a few lines of Python code.
    That's the magic of **Streamlit**, a revolutionary open-source library
that's transforming how data scientists and analysts share their findings
    """
)
if st.button("Welcome on Board!!!"):
    st.balloons()
```

The previous Python snippet runs base Streamlit app delivering website in this format, as shown in Figure 3.24:

To expand on our previous crypto example "Cryptocurrency Visuals" we utilize previous Figma drawings and app sketch to build a simple dashboard to showcase few capabilities and library tools from Streamlit. In the next example we start with a direct API call function extracting crypto data from CryptoCompare for specified crypto symbols,

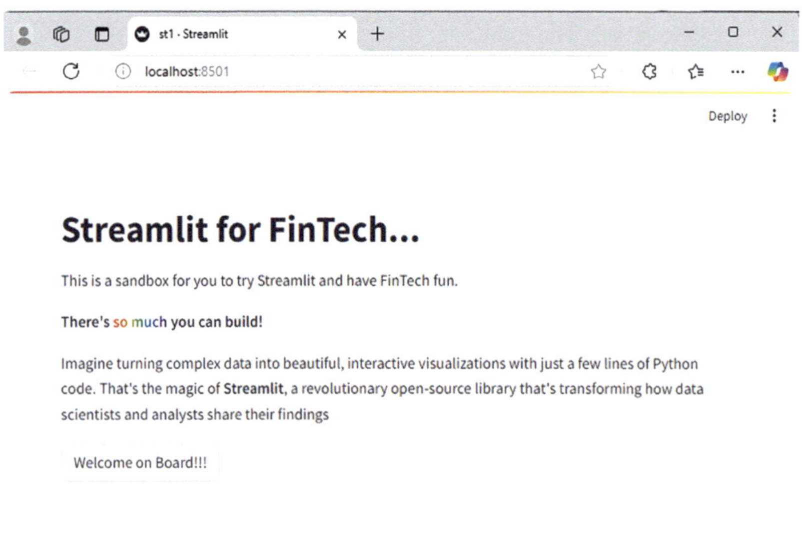

Figure 3.24 Streamlit for FinTech

starting with BTC, ETH, XRP and ADA. Secondly, we process extracted data to select "close" price and calculate crude data frequency percentage change called "returns" as seen here:

```
import requests
import streamlit as st
import pandas as pd

st.write("FINTECH CRYPTO DASHBOARD")

all_crypto = ['BTC','ETH','XRP','ADA']

def etl_crypto_data(symbol, api_key, limit=1000):
    if api_key.strip():  # Check if api_key is not empty or just whitespace
        headers = {'Apikey': api_key}  # The header with your API key
    else:
        headers = {}  # Empty headers if api_key is empty

    url = f'https://min-api.cryptocompare.com/data/v2/histoday?fsym={symbol}&tsym=
USD&limit={limit}'
    response = requests.get(url, headers=headers)
    data = response.json()
    return data['Data']['Data']

def feature_crypto_data(all_crypto,api_key='', limit=1000):
    df = pd.DataFrame()
    # Fetch historical data for each pair
    for symbol in all_crypto:
        data = pd.DataFrame(etl_crypto_data(symbol,api_key=api_key,
                                            limit=limit) )
        data ['date'] = pd.to_datetime(data ['time'], unit='s')
        data.drop(['time'], inplace = True, axis = 1)
        data['sym'] = symbol
        data['returns'] = data['close'].pct_change()
        df = pd.concat([df,data], axis = 0)
    return df.pivot(index='date', columns='sym', values='returns')

with st.container(border=True):
    users = st.multiselect("Cryptocurrency/Tokens", all_crypto,
default=all_crypto)
    rolling_average = st.toggle("Rolling average")

data = feature_crypto_data(all_crypto,api_key='', limit=1000)
if rolling_average:
    data = data.rolling(5).mean().dropna()

tab1, tab2 = st.tabs(["Chart", "Dataframe"])
tab1.line_chart(data, height=550)
tab2.dataframe(data, height=550, use_container_width=True)
```

As seen from the code snippet, Streamlit is fully integrated into the "business" logic of the data flow resulting in this simple dashboard view, as shown in Figure 3.25:

The previous simple dashboard depicting a selection of cryptocurrencies and processing up-to-date dynamic price extracts and return calculations, is running locally on your local host http://localhost:8501/, however this simple yet powerful FinTech app can easily be deployed and hosted on a secured cloud service of your choice.

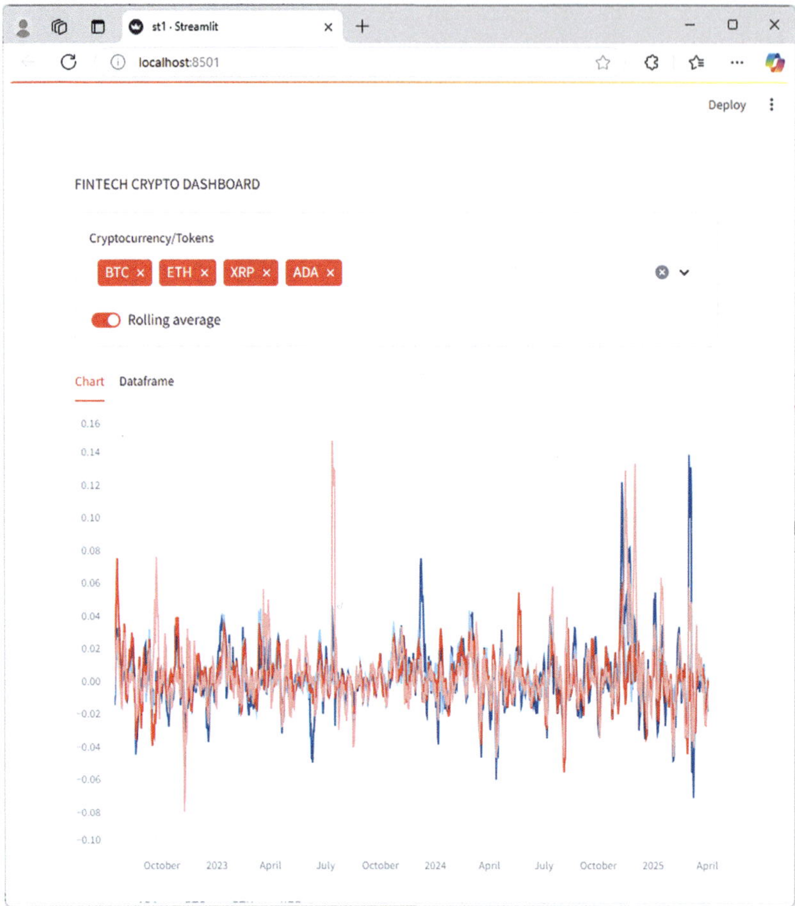

Figure 3.25 Crypto Dashboard

3.6 Case Study: Simply Wall St

To enrich our journey through data visualization, starting with API, moving into base tabular and graphical Python libraries as used for structured as well as unstructured data streams, we analyze visually driven FinTech product developed and delivered by Simply Wall St [3.11]. In this case study we analyze equity data streams, as opposed to previous cryptocurrency data streams, with the intention of aligning our discussion with DDF concept and stepping through the notion of data stations delivering on final FinTech product. The product here is visual in nature. Simply Wall St's FinTech product visualization turns complex wholesale financial information into applicable retail based information. The company offers visual tools and infographics to help users understand the fundamentals of companies. Hence, the entire product is driven by design and visual interpretation of complex data streams. This innovative platform has changed how people work with financial data. Investment decisions are now more available and accessible than before. Simply Wall St uses advanced data visualization tools and interactive features that set a new standard for financial analysis, as shown in Figure 3.26. This case study will explore these features in detail.

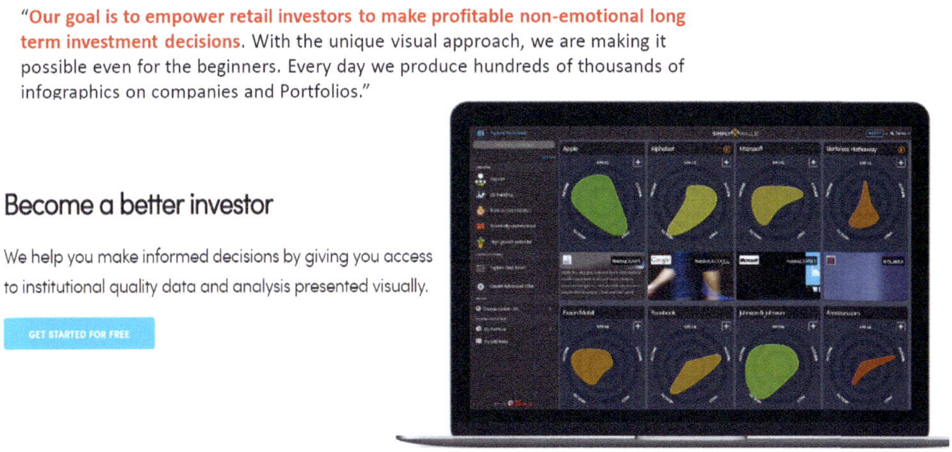

Figure 3.26 Simply Wall St Digital Product

Snowflake Analysis

Simply Wall St reshaped the scene with its breakthrough approach to financial data visualization. The platform undertook the task to change how people invest by helping them follow long-term investing principles. Their groundbreaking concept emphasized visualizing fundamental company data – using Snowflake visualization system – instead of showing it in traditional text-based formats. The Snowflake visualization system represents a new way to analyze companies through five key criteria:

- Valuation
- Future growth
- Past performance
- Financial health
- Dividend performance

This system's strength comes from its scoring approach. Each criterion goes through six individual checks, and successful checks earn a score of 1. The Snowflake's shape and color give users a quick visual summary of where a company stands. In short, the strength is derived from visual interpretation of complex data streams as per the following Figure 3.27.

In the context of the DDF, Simply Wall St collects financial data from various sources, such as **S&P Global Market Intelligence** including official company filings, news flows and market data streams. Then, uses algorithms and machine learning to analyze and visualize data providing detailed reports, stock analysis and portfolio management tools. Implementation tools include, snowflake analysis, portfolio analysis and insider trading data information.

Stage 1: ETL (Extract, Transform, Load)

Simply Wall St acquires and **extracts** complex institutional data streams from sources like company filings, stock exchanges, financial news, and market data providers. Then integrity checks are performed to ensure accuracy and the data is cleaned and **transformed** into a standardized format. Relevant data points such as earnings, revenue, P/E ratios, and insider trading

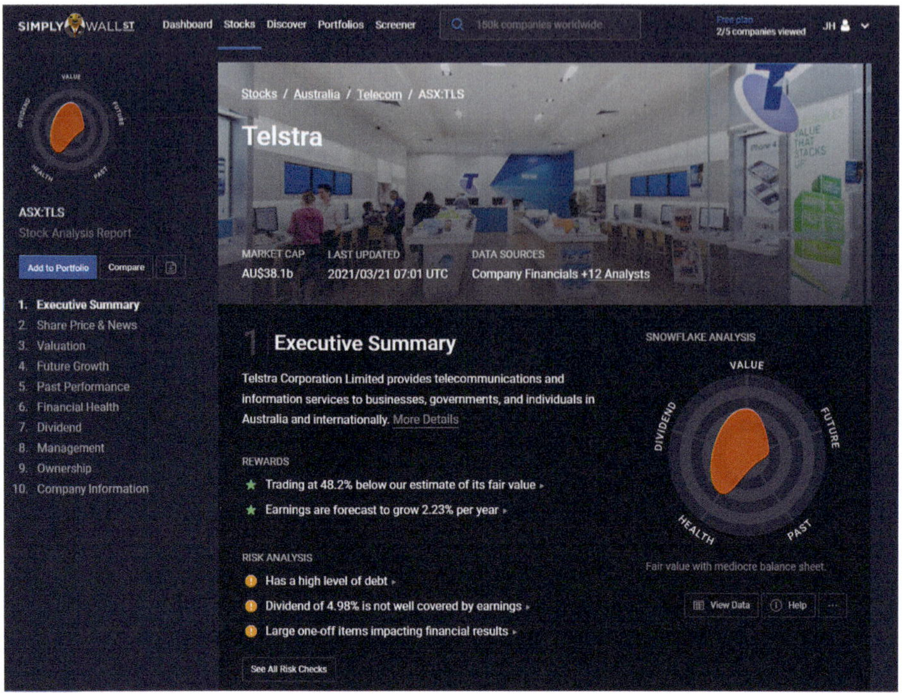

Figure 3.27 Simply Wall St Equity Example

activities are identified and extracted. The cleaned and transformed data is **loaded** into Simply Wall St's cloud based and secured databases, ready for further analysis and visualization.

Stage 2: Feature Engineering

Simply Wall St identifies key data features relevant to stock analysis such as earnings, revenue, P/E ratios, dividends, and insider trading activities. From the raw data obtained in Stage 1, new variables are created. For example, growth rates, valuation metrics, and risk factors are derived from basic financial data. The selected and engineered features are aligned with the business objectives, derivation of Snowflake Analytics, ensuring the data is relevant for generating accurate and insightful stock analysis.

Stage 3: Model Design

Simply Wall St utilizes advanced analytics to design models that transform raw data into actionable insights. The models generate visual representations like snowflake graphs, which summarize a company's strengths and weaknesses in an easily understandable format. This stage is critical as it forms the core analytical framework that helps customers make informed stock purchase decisions.

Stage 4: Implementation

In the final implementation stage, Simply Wall St packages the results from the model design into an easy-to-use product for customers. This includes interactive reports, infographics, and user-friendly dashboards hosted in digital domains easily accessible via mobile devices. The product is delivered to customers via the Simply Wall St platform, providing them with the tools to make informed investment decisions. Customer feedback is collected and analyzed to continually improve the product. Insights from feedback are passed back to all stations in the data factory to refine data acquisition, feature engineering, and model design.

Overall, Simply Wall St has changed how we perceive, consume and use complex financial data. Their platform makes complex investment decisions clearer and more available to millions of users. Simply Wall St's Snowflake visualization system and strong technical architecture prove that financial analysis can be straightforward and clear. The platform's growth and user numbers are remarkable. More than 7 million investors trust the platform and spend over 3 minutes per visit. Simply Wall St shows that well-laid-out visualization tools reshape how people work with financial data.

3.7 Case Study: altFINS

altFINS' trading platform's foundation rests on its powerful Crypto Screener that reshapes the scene for traders finding profitable opportunities [3.12]. This tool automatically scans over 3,000 cryptocurrencies using 26 different chart patterns and more than 120 technical indicators, unlike the old manual scanning methods. The platform stands out with its AI-powered pattern recognition engine. Traders can now work with statistically confirmed signals instead of guesswork while spotting potential breakouts. altFINS' engine identifies altcoins trading in profitable formation patterns. The platform detected 18 altcoins in Channel Down patterns and 12 in Falling Wedge patterns, as an example. These patterns prove valuable since historical data shows Channel Down breakouts have a 73% success rate, while Falling Wedge breakouts achieve 64% success.

The platform offers over 100 preset and dynamic market scans that instantly spot coins that are the following:

- In an uptrend with increasing momentum
- Breaking out of time-tested patterns
- Reaching overbought or oversold conditions (perfect for timing entries and exits)

Traders and potential investors can build custom screens using combinations of technical indicators like Moving Averages, MACD, RSI, and various chart patterns on top of that. This customization helps target opportunities that match specific trading strategies precisely.

altFINS provides expert-curated trade setups for over 65 popular cryptocurrencies, complete with entry levels, price targets, and stop-loss recommendations as depicted in Figure 3.28. The platform's detailed approach suits experienced traders and beginners who want to develop their skills in cryptocurrencies of all types. The platform automates the tedious process of scanning thousands of assets. Traders never miss potential opportunities whatever the market conditions.

Trading becomes easier with altFINS's convenient features. You can input quantities as percentages and use "Best" price options for limit orders that fill automatically with current bid/ask prices. Traders no longer need to switch between analysis tools and exchange platforms. The platform's unified trading environment stands out as its strength. It merges with 12 major exchanges through secure API integrations, including Binance, Bitfinex, Kraken, Coinbase and others. The platform's DEX aggregator pulls liquidity from more than 100 decentralized exchanges. This gives traders exceptional market access. altFINS provides detailed tracking of your entire crypto ecosystem:

- A single dashboard shows holdings across multiple exchanges
- Performance metrics display gains/losses and asset allocation
- Screener results can focus on coins in your portfolio

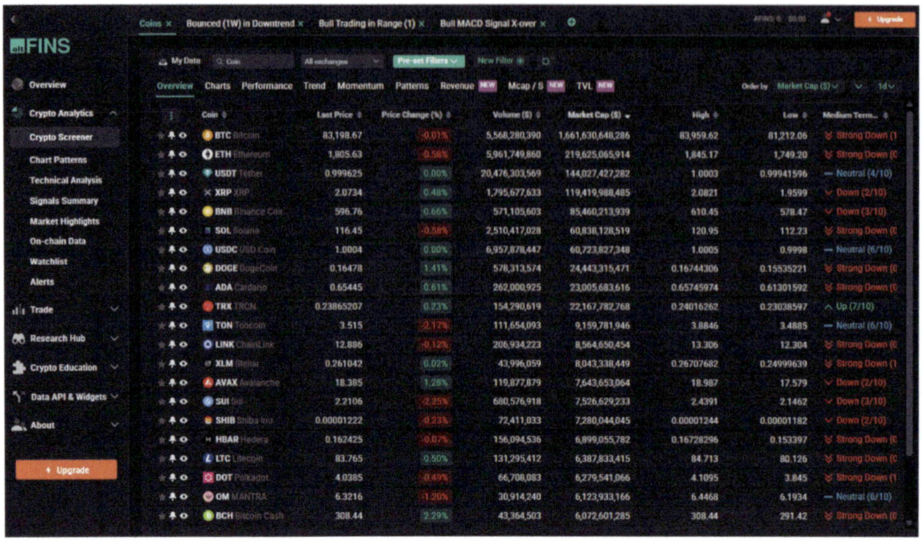

Figure 3.28 altFINS Crypto Filter

The alert system boosts portfolio management with custom notifications for the following:

- Price levels when assets hit specific targets
- Percentage changes that catch big movements
- Technical indicator conditions through filter alerts
- Chart and candlestick patterns (supporting 36 popular patterns)

These alerts work with your portfolio, watchlist or both. You receive them through push notifications, email and website alerts. This multi-channel delivery will give a clear view of critical market movements.

Furthermore, altFINS' "Coin Picks" are the foundations of its research offerings – detailed reports on cryptocurrencies that could grow ten times. These analytical reports review projects based on several significant factors: user adoption metrics, unique value propositions, tokenomics structures, competitive positioning, ecosystem development and regulatory considerations. Past Coin Picks featured projects like Solana and Polygon, which later saw substantial market growth. Traders who want to learn will find altFINS' educational resources valuable. The content explains technical analysis basics, trading strategies, and platform-specific tutorials. New traders can build confidence, while experienced ones gain fresh views on market analysis. The Research Hub combines vital insights from respected industry sources and serves as a central point for market intelligence. The platform's news features track over 40 trusted sources, so traders can stay updated about changes that might affect their positions.

On-chain data analytics adds another layer to research tools. Traders can track asset movements, understand user behavior, and measure fundamental metrics like Total Value Locked (TVL). As per Figure 3.29, technical indicators remain useful, but on-chain insights reveal deeper blockchain activity that could influence prices.

In the context of the DDF, altFINS collects crypto data in structured and unstructured format from various collated sources. Then, uses large language models, AI-based algorithms

Figure 3.29 altFINS On-Chain Crypto Data

and other deep learning methodologies to analyze and visualize data providing detailed reports, crypto analysis and portfolio management tools.

Stage 1: ETL (Extract, Transform, Load)

altFINS acquires and **extracts** complex crypto market as well as on-chain data streams from sources like token/project filings, crypto news and other market data providers. Then integrity checks are performed to ensure accuracy and the data is cleaned and **transformed** into a standardized format. Relevant data points such as project earnings, revenue and on-chain activities are identified and extracted. The cleaned and transformed data is **loaded** into altFINS cloud based and secured databases, ready for further analysis and visualization.

Stage 2: Feature Engineering

altFINS identifies key data features relevant to crypto analysis. From the raw data obtained in Stage 1, new variables are created. For example, technical analysis, chart patterns, signals, trading analytics and risk factors are derived. The selected and engineered features are aligned with the business objectives, ensuring the data is relevant for generating accurate and insightful crypto analysis and trading signals.

Stage 3: Model Design

altFINS utilizes advanced AI driven analytics to design models that transform raw data into actionable insights. The models generate visual representations like signal graphs, which summarize a crypto's strengths and weaknesses in an easily understandable format. This stage is critical as it forms the core analytical framework that helps customers make informed crypto purchase decisions.

Stage 4: Implementation

In the final implementation stage, altFINS packages the results from the model design into an easy-to-use product for customers. This includes interactive reports, infographics, and user-friendly dashboards hosted in digital domains easily accessible via mobile devices. The product is delivered to customers via the altFINS platform, providing them with the tools to make informed investment decisions. Customer feedback is collected and analyzed to continually improve the product. Insights from customer feedback interaction with altFINS assistants are passed back to all stations in the data factory to refine data acquisition, feature engineering, and model design, similar to our previous case study covered in this chapter.

3.8 Summary

This chapter explores data visualization as a transformative tool in banking and finance, building on foundational concepts of data structures, algorithms, and the digital data factory (DDF). It emphasizes how data visualization turns raw numbers into actionable insights, enabling professionals at all levels to interact with complex financial data more effectively.

The role of data visualization is to transform complex data sets into digestible insights for both experts and non-experts. Structured data form the backbone of financial reporting and analytics, whereas unstructured data adds depth through analysis of sources like social media sentiments, news articles, videos or sound coverage. Tools have evolved to include dynamic dashboards, heat maps, network diagrams and even augmented reality displays. These tools enhance decision-making by shortening reaction times to market changes, improve risk assessments and overall democratizing access to financial insights. This Chapter is aimed to enhance reader's understanding of data visualization in finance, introduce Python visualization libraries and tools and present a FinTech case study showcasing practical implementation. Skills developed in this chapter form an invaluable toolset to be used in the following chapters.

Data visualization is revolutionizing the finance industry by making complex data accessible, actionable and impactful for stakeholders. By combining structured and unstructured data with cutting-edge tools like Streamlit and Figma, financial institutions can unlock deeper insights, improve decision-making, and democratize access to financial information.

3.9 Exercises

Exercise 3.1

Use CryptoCompare APIs to extract JSON files with latest crypto news in English. Then, use Co-Pilot, or any chatbot of your choice, to describe, analyze and visualize a given data set as per our previous examples. Provide a concise summary of the results. Focus on the accuracy of the results!

Exercise 3.2

Use CryptoCompare APIs to extract BTC, ETH, XRP, ADA recent traded prices and volumes. Then, use Figma to design a sketch of your Crypto Dashboard. Lastly, use Streamlit, following Python code snippet in this chapter and build a simple, dynamic app showcasing summary price and volume sequence of your selected crypto assets. Focus on the accuracy of the results!

Figure 3.30 altFINS BTC Graphical Interpretation to be used by Co-Pilot analysis (upload into AI chatbot and follow up with prompt)

Exercise 3.3

Use the given picture reference related to BTC. Then, use Co-Pilot, or any chatbot of your choice, to request detailed analytics based on this picture shown in Figure 3.30.

Design a prompt for the AI Co-Pilot. Describe and analyze results from the Co-Pilot. Focus on the accuracy of the results!

3.10 Further Reading

- Dickerson, A., & Hric, J. (2024). FINS5545 Financial Market Data Literacy Course Notes, UNSW Business School.
- Gamma, E., Helm, R., Johnson, R., & Vlissides, J. (1995). Design Patterns, Addison Wesley.
- Kleppmann, M. (2017). Designing Data-Intensive Applications, O'Reilly.

3.11 References

[3.1] CryptoCompare: https://www.cryptocompare.com/
[3.2] CryptoCompare API: https://min-api.cryptocompare.com/documentation
[3.3] API GET Example: https://min-api.cryptocompare.com/data/price?fsym=ETH&tsyms=BTC,USD,EUR
[3.4] MatplotLib: https://matplotlib.org/
[3.5] Pandas: https://pandas.pydata.org/
[3.6] Seaborn: https://seaborn.pydata.org/
[3.7] PyTorch: https://pytorch.org/
[3.8] Tensorflow: https://www.tensorflow.org/
[3.9] Figma: https://www.figma.com/
[3.10] Streamlit: https://streamlit.io/
[3.11] Simply Wall St: https://simplywall.st/
[3.12] altFINS: https://altfins.com/

Chapter 4

Data Modeling in FinTech

DOI: 10.4324/9781003477747-5

4.1 Introduction

The purpose of this chapter is to implement the digital data factory (DDF) concept and apply relevant tools and Python libraries covered in the previous chapters to a practical use case. Data modeling plays a **critical role** in the realm of data science, serving as the foundation for effective analysis and decision-making. In today's data-driven landscape, the importance of robust data models cannot be overstated. These models provide a structured framework for organizing, interpreting, and leveraging vast amounts of information, enabling data scientists to extract meaningful insights and patterns. The advent of *artificial intelligence* (AI) models, particularly large language models (LLMs), has further revolutionized the field. LLMs, with their ability to process and generate human-like text, have become invaluable tools in enhancing data modeling techniques. By integrating LLMs into the data modeling process, data scientists can now uncover hidden relationships, generate predictive analytics and automate complex data interpretation tasks with unprecedented accuracy and efficiency. This synergy between traditional data modeling and cutting-edge AI technologies is propelling the field of data science forward, opening new avenues for innovation and driving transformative changes across industries.

In this chapter we connect this traditional data modeling and cutting-edge AI technologies implementing DDF concepts. Given the inherent complex nature of FinTech applications and services, AI tools such as chatbot and Co-Pilot and AI Agent are not in position to deliver on the entire FinTech solution or the entire product yet. Hence, the notion of introducing a logical sequence of steps, "stations." We break down the data modeling and application development process into these "pockets of similar tasks" and narrow down the purpose to use AI Agents. As a result, we introduce the reader to new cutting-edge techniques to use AI tools in this context, following the notion of DDF data flows. At every step, station, of our data modeling process we introduce the reader to pseudocode language to be used to "talk" to the AI agents. This approach adds clarity to prompt engineering and delivers more accurate results while working closely with prediction-based AI tools.

Learning Outcome

At the end of this chapter the reader will be able to do the following:

- Apply digital data factory (DDF) concept to a practical use case
- Apply and understand complex Python data structures
- Utilize prediction analytics in practice
- Apply visualization tools, Streamlit and Figma
- Implement FinTech DDF solution: IoT Carbon Footprint

4.2 Data Structures

This chapter introduces you to some of the most useful built-in data structures provided by Python: lists, tuples, sets and dictionaries. As programming languages have developed, agglomeration structures such as these have proven to be the cornerstone to working with data, and Python has some of the most powerful techniques for manipulating these data structures among modern programming languages. A data structure is the means by which a program stores pieces of information (i.e., data) in a systematic way (i.e., structured) so that it can be handled and processed during the program's execution. We have already seen some basic (low-level) data structures with the basic data types (e.g., ints, floats, booleans, strings, etc) – these are structured representations of small pieces of information. As programmers, however, we typically consider data structures at a conceptually higher level: using the basic data types as the fundamental units of data and considering structures built up from these, for example, sequences of ints.

Data Structures Primer

It is constructive to start with a brief revision of base data structures as used in Python. This is to allow us to dive deeper into more complex structures used in complex neural networks, for instance. Feel free to jump to the next section, for those readers with base knowledge of Python data structures.

List

A list is an ordered container of objects, possibly empty. The objects can be of any type, and they need not all be of the same type. Each is called an item of the list. You can specify a list using a list literal, which is a sequence of expressions, each of which refers to an object, separated by commas, and surrounded by square brackets. For example:

```
[2, 4, 6, 8]
['cat', 'mouse', 'cat', 'mouse']
[1, 3.14, 'a', True]
[] (the empty list)
```

Note that the same object can be included more than once in a list. We can use Python's `len()` function to find the number of items in a list:

```
print(len([1, 2, 3])) # 3 items
print(len(['12', '45'])) # 2 items
print(len([1, 3.14, 'hello', True])) # 4 items
print(len([])) # 0 items
```

Each item in a list has a unique index, starting from 0. So the first item has index 0, the second item has index 1, and so on. You can refer to the items in a list by using the indexing operator []:

```
x = ['a', 'b', 'c', 'd', 'e']
print(x[-1])
print(x[-2])
```

Indexes can also be negative. The last item has index −1, the second last item has index −2, and so on.

You can also use the indexing operator to get a *slice of a list*. The syntax for slicing is `list[begin:end]`, where `begin` is the start index and `end` is the end index. The `end` index is non-inclusive.

```
x = ['a', 'b', 'c', 'd', 'e']
print(x[0:3]) # Prints items from index 0 to less than 3
```

Notice that `x[0:3]` returns items with index 0 to 2, rather than 0 to 3 as you might expect – this can be very confusing! You can also use negative indices when slicing:

```
x = ['a', 'b', 'c', 'd', 'e']
print(x[1:-1])
```

If you don't specify a start index, then it is assumed to be zero. If you don't specify an end index, then it is assumed to be the length of the list (an invalid index, but as it is excluded – this is fine and is the way to include the last element of the list). If you don't specify either, then the whole list is returned.

```
x = ['a', 'b', 'c', 'd', 'e']
print(x[:3])
print(x[1:])
print(x[:])
```

Python allows you to add a third parameter to the slice to control the step. This parameter allows you to easily extract every nth element from the list. The syntax for slicing with a step is list[begin:end:step], where step is an integer.

```
x = ['a', 'b', 'c', 'd', 'e']
print(x[::2]) # Every second element
print(x[::3]) # Every third element
print(x[::-1]) # Every element in reverse
print(x[::-2]) # Every second element in reverse
```

You can check whether a list contains a certain value by using the in keyword:

```
x = ['a', 'b', 'c', 'd', 'e']
x[0] = 'z'
print(x)
```

You can add an item to the end of a list by using the `append()` method:

```
x = ['a', 'b', 'c', 'd', 'e']
x.append('f')
print(x)
```

You can insert an item at a specified index by using the `insert()` method:

```
x = ['a', 'b', 'c', 'd', 'e']
x.insert(2, 'x')
print(x)
```

You can extend a list with the items from another list by using the `extend()` method:

```
x = ['a', 'b', 'c', 'd', 'e']
y = ['x', 'y', 'z']
x.extend(y)
print(x)
```

You can join two lists by using the + operator:

```
x = ['a', 'b', 'c', 'd', 'e']
y = ['f', 'g', 'h']
print(x + y)
```

You can remove an item by index by using the `pop()` method, if `pop()` isn't given an index, then the last index will be removed, the removed element will be returned:

```
x = ['a', 'b', 'c', 'd', 'e']
```

```
print(x.pop(2))
print(x)
print(x.pop())
print(x)
```

You can remove any item by its index with the `del` keyword:

```
x = ['a', 'b', 'c', 'd', 'e']
del x[1]
print(x)
```

You can remove the first item with a given value by using the `remove()` method:

```
x = ['a', 'b', 'c', 'd', 'e', 'c']
x.remove('c')
print(x)
```

You can remove all items from a list by using the clear() method:

```
x = ['a', 'b', 'c', 'd', 'e']
x.clear()
print(x)
```

You can use the `count()` method to find the number of times a specified value appears in a list:

```
x = [1, 3, 7, 8, 7, 5, 4, 6, 8, 5]
print(x.count(7))
```

You can use the `index()` method to find the index of the first occurrence of a value. If the value is not found, then Python raises an error.

```
x = [1, 3, 7, 8, 7, 5, 4, 6, 8, 5]
print(x.index(7))
```

`sum()` computes the sum of a list:

```
print(sum([1, 3, 7, 8, 7, 5, 4, 6, 8, 5]))
```

`all()` returns True if all items evaluate to `True` using the `bool()` function.

```
print(all([True, True, True]))
print(all(['a', 'a', 'a']))
print(all(['', 'a', 'b']))
```

You can sort the elements of a list by using the sort() method, which orders the items by comparing their values using the < operator.

```
x = [1, 5, 4, 2, 3]
x.sort()
print(x)
```

```
x = ['c', 'a', 'e', 'b', 'd']
x.sort()
print(x)
```

```
x = [1, 5, 4, 2, 3]
x.sort(reverse=True)
print(x)
```

Suppose you have a list of words and you want to sort them by length. If you use the sort() method, then you will get the wrong result – it will sort them alphabetically. What you need to do is sort using a function that returns, for each item in the list, a value that you would like to sort the item by. In this case, we want to sort by length, so we can use the len() function.

```
x = ['dog', 'chicken', 'mouse', 'horse', 'goat', 'donkey']
x.sort(key=len)
print(x)
```

It is very common to loop through the items in a list one by one. You could access each element using its index – and use a `while` statement to go through the whole list:

```
vowels = ['a', 'e', 'i', 'o', 'u']
i = 0
while i < len(vowels):
  print(vowels[i])
  i += 1
```

But it is better to use a `for` loop, which is custom-made for this kind of thing:

```
vowels = ['a', 'e', 'i', 'o', 'u']
for v in vowels:
  print(v)
```

`break` and `continue` can also be used inside for loops.

```
vowels = ['a', 'e', 'i', 'o', 'u']

print('Everything before o:')
for v in vowels:
  if v == 'o':
    break
  print(v)

print('Everything except o:')
for v in vowels:
  if v == 'o':
    continue
  print(v)
```

Sometimes when we loop through a list, we need to use the index of an item as well as its value. We can do this by using the enumerate() function.

```
vowels = ['a', 'e', 'i', 'o', 'u']
for i, v in enumerate(vowels):
  print('The vowel at index', i, 'is', v)
```

The items in a list can be of any type. In particular, they can be lists. So it's possible to create lists of lists. They behave just like any other list.

```
numbers = [[1,2,3],[3,4,5],[6,7,8]]
print(len(numbers))
print(numbers[0])

numbers.reverse()
print(numbers)
```

Notice that numbers has length 3 because it contains just three items (each of which also happens to be a list of items). Notice that `numbers[0]` is the first of the three items, which happens to be a list. Notice that the reverse() method reverses the order of the three items but doesn't do anything to the items themselves. Since `numbers[0]` is a list, we can do all of the usual lists things with it:

```
numbers = [[1,2,3],[3,4,5],[5,6,7]]
print(len(numbers[0]))
print(numbers[0][0])
numbers[0].reverse()
print(numbers[0])
```

When we have a list of lists we might end up using nested for loops. Suppose that we want to add up all of the numbers that appear in numbers. We can do this as follows:

```
numbers = [[1,2,3],[3,4,5],[5,6,7]]
total = 0
for i in numbers:
  for j in i:
    total += j
print(total)
```

Tuples

A tuple is a list that is *immutable*, which means that it cannot be modified. Tuple literals are like list literals, except you use round brackets rather than square brackets:

```
(2, 4, 6, 8)
('cat', 'mouse', dog')
(1, 3.14, 'a', True)
() (the empty tuple)
```

Tuples can be viewed as multidimensional literals, for example, a two-dimensional point `(1,3)`, a name-surname pairing: `('John', 'Smith')`, or a day-month-year triple representing a `date (26,1,2020)`. The immutability of tuples binds the individual components tightly together – it is not possible for a program to alter one component separately from the others, and the order of the elements is important: `('John', 'Smith')` and `('Smith', 'John')` are fundamentally different objects. So it is more sensible to view a tuple as a single, complex object, rather than as a collection of smaller objects. This makes tuples ideal for representing data where there is a strong connection between the components and where it should be difficult for a programmer to alter one aspect independently of the others. While a list can almost always be used where a tuple can be, by using tuples in the appropriate setting, you are signalling to anyone reviewing your code that the *guarantee of immutability* of the object is important.

You can mostly work with tuples just like you work with lists: Use `len()` to find the number of items

```
x = ('a', 'b', 'c', 'd', 'e')
y = (1, 1, 2, 3)
print(len(x))
print(len(y))
```

Use `in` to check for an item and `count` to count the number of occurrences of an item

```
y = (1, 1, 2, 3, 5, 8)
print(4 in y)
print(y.count(1))
```

Join two tuples with +

```
x = (1, 2, 3)
y = (4, 5, 6)
z = x + y # Note this will give a tuple
print(z)
```

Use `sum`, `all`, and `any` to combine items of the appropriate type.

```
y = (1, 1, 2, 3)
z = (True, False, True)
print(sum(y))
print(all(z))
print(any(z))
```

But because tuples are **immutable** there are various things that you **cannot do**: Change the elements of the tuple:

```
x = (0, 2, 3)
x[0] = 1
```

Add items to the tuple:

```
x = (1, 2, 3)
x.append(4)
```

Remove elements from the tuple:

```
x = (1, 2, 3)
x.remove(2)
```

Sort the tuple:

```
x = (1, 3, 2)
x.sort()
```

Sets

A set is an unordered container of unique objects (i.e., the same object cannot be included more than once). Set literals are like list literals, except you use curly brackets rather than square brackets:

```
{2, 4, 6, 8}
{'cat', 'mouse', dog'}
{1, 3.14, 'a', True}
{} (the empty set)
```

Just as with tuples, a list can often be used where a set is being used, raising the question, "what are the advantages of using sets rather than lists?" Besides the set operations union, intersection, and difference available only to sets, the primary reason to use the set structure over the list structure is that it guarantees the uniqueness of elements and unordered storage. While there may be some theoretical efficiency to be gained in terms of how Python stores sets rather than lists, the primary reason for using the set structure from a programming perspective should be to signal to anyone reviewing your code that these properties are important.

The items in a set are unordered, which means that they have no index. If you try to refer to an item in a set by using square brackets notation, you will get an error:

```
x = {'cat', 'mouse', 'dog'}
print(x[0]) # Error
```

Because they are not ordered, you can't be sure what order Python will list them in (try running the following snippet multiple times):

```
vowels = {'a', 'e', 'i', 'o', 'u'}
print(vowels)
```

('Smith', 'John')('Smith', 'John')('Smith', 'John')('Smith', 'John')('Smith', 'John')

The items are also unique, which means that the same object cannot be included more than once in the set. If you try to include the same object more than once Python will ignore all but the first:

```
x = {'cat', 'mouse', 'dog', 'cat', 'cat'}
print(x)
```

You can use Python's `len()` function to get the number of items in a set:

```
print(len({'a', 'e', 'i', 'o', 'u'}))
print(len({}))
```

You can use the in keyword word to check whether an item is in a set:

```
names = {'John', 'Bob', 'Alice'}
print('John' in names)
print('Eve' in names)
```

You can add a single item to a set by using the set's `add()` method

```
vowels = set()
vowels.add('a')
vowels.add('e')
vowels.add('e') # No error, just not added
print(vowels)
```

You can remove items from a set using the set's `remove()` or `discard()` methods. If the item is not in the set, then using `remove()` will cause an error, but using `discard()` will not

```
vowels = {'a', 'e', 'i', 'o', 'u'}
vowels.remove('a')
print(vowels)
vowels.discard('f') # No error
print(vowels)
vowels.remove('f') # Error
```

You can remove all items from a set by using the set's `clear()` method:

```
vowels = {'a', 'e', 'i', 'o', 'u'}
vowels.clear()
print(vowels)
```

The union of two sets is the set of items that belong to either or both sets:

You can get the union of two sets using either the | operator or the `union()` method:

```
evens = {2, 4, 6, 8}
primes = {2, 3, 5, 7}
```

```
print(evens | primes)
print(evens.union(primes))
print(primes.union(evens))

print(evens & primes)
print(evens.intersection(primes))
print(primes.intersection(evens))

print(evens - primes)
print(evens.difference(primes))
print(primes - evens)
print(primes.difference(evens))
```

Dictionaries

A dictionary is an unordered collection of key-value pairs. e.g. `{'name': 'John', 'age': 54}`. It represents a mapping from a set of keys to a set of values. While lists, tuples and sets represent collections of objects, dictionaries represent a *relationship* between two collections: a set of keys and a set of values. The relationship is a many-one relationship – multiple keys can be related to the same value, but a single key can only be related to at most one value. This is not too much of a restriction. A reasonably simple way to overcome this if there is a need to map a key to multiple values is to use a list (or set) of items as the value in the key-value pairs.

A situation that commonly arises, particularly when naively programming with data, is an abundance of lists that all need to align on their indices: for example, the third item in list x corresponds to the third item in list y. If you find yourself in this situation, then you should be working with dictionaries. Dictionaries are a robust and safe way of managing relationships between data items.

It may appear that lists can be viewed as dictionaries where the list indices are the keys, however, there are some notable differences – particularly after items have been removed. In the case of lists, the indices of the items appearing after a removed item will all be changed, whereas for a dictionary the keys are not affected when an item is removed. Each effect has its benefits: from a list perspective, the "next available key" is easy to find, resulting in minimal overhead for adding new items; whereas from a dictionary point of view, there is the stability between the item and the index it is assigned, as well as a (partial) record of the deletions that have occurred.

Dictionary literals are presented in curly braces like set literals, with key-value pairs separated by commas, and each key and value separated with a colon.

```
scores = {
  'Alice': 0,
  'Bob': 1,
  'Eve': 2,
  'Mallory': 3,
}
print(scores)
```

A key and a value can be any object. Keys do not all have to be the same type, and neither do values; however it is good programming practice to keep the types consistent.

```
dictionary = {
  1: 'one',
  'two': 2, # Mixing key types is not good practice as it can lead to confusion
  3: 3
}
```

```
print(dictionary)
```

In a dictionary, values can be duplicated, but keys must be unique. If multiple items with the same key are given, then only the latest value is stored.

```
scores = {
  'Alice': 1,
  'Bob': 1
}
print(scores)
scores = {
  'Alice': 0,
  'Alice': 1
}
print(scores)
```

Items can be retrieved from the dictionary using the indexing operator. Note that indices of a dictionary are key values, which are not necessarily integers.

```
scores = {
  'Alice': 0,
  'Bob': 1,
  'Eve': 2,
  'Mallory': 3,
}
print(scores['Alice'])
```

Updating an item in a dictionary is the same as updating an item in a list.

```
scores = {
  'Alice': 0,
  'Bob': 1,
  'Eve': 2,
  'Mallory': 3,
}
scores['Bob'] = 900
scores['Alice'] += 1
print(scores)
```

The `del` keyword works the same on dictionaries as it does on lists.

```
scores = {
  'Alice': 0,
  'Bob': 1,
  'Eve': 2,
  'Mallory': 3,
}
del scores['Bob']
print(scores)
```

Iterating a dictionary directly yields only the keys.

```
scores = {
  'Alice': 0,
  'Bob': 1,
  'Eve': 2,
```

```
  'Mallory': 3,
}
for key in scores:
  print(key)
```

Fortunately, Python dictionaries provide an easy access function, **items()**, to get the items as well:

```
scores = {
  'Alice': 0,
  'Bob': 1,
  'Eve': 2,
  'Mallory': 3,
}
for key, value in scores.items():
  print(key, value)
```

NumPy

One of the most critical data structures is an array [4.1]. *Arrays* generally structure other (fundamental) objects in rows and columns – in a sense representing the true notion of STRUCTURED DATA format – well-defined observations, objects, in rows and/or columns.

A one-dimensional array then represents a vector of, in general numbers, in a single row or column. However, an array can represent an `i x j matrix` of elements. This concept generalizes to `i x j x k cubes` of elements in three dimensions. Here, Python library *NumPy* is designed to handle specialized data structures such as arrays in convenient and efficient ways.

First, we look at arrays by using standard Python libraries – lists. A simple list can be seen as a one-dimensional array, and since lists can contain other objects, we can combine lists of lists and select elements as per the following:

```
v = [0.5, 0.75, 1.0, 1.5, 2.0]  # vector of numbers
m = [v, v, v]  # matrix of numbers
print(m)
print(m[1])
print(m[1][0])
```

This allows for a more generic form of nesting:

```
v1 = [0.5, 1.5]
v2 = [1, 2]
m = [v1, v2]
c = [m, m]  # cube of numbers
print(c)
```

Important Note: combining objects as previous works with reference pointers to the original objects:

```
v = [0.5, 0.75, 1.0, 1.5, 2.0]
m = [v, v, v]
print(m)

#Now chnage the value of the FIRST element of the v object and see what
#happens to the m object!

v[0] = 'Python'
print(m)
```

In short, by changing elements of the original v object we have affected the elements of the generated m object! To avoid this we can use **"deepcopy"** module here:

```
from copy import deepcopy
v = [0.5, 0.75, 1.0, 1.5, 2.0]
m = 3*[deepcopy(v),]
print(m)

#Now change first element of v
v[0] = 'Python'
print(m)
```

Now, we look to use *numpy.ndarray* instances

```
import numpy as np
a = np.array([0, 0.5, 1.0, 1.5, 2.0])
print(type(a))
print(a[:2])  # indexing as with list objects in 1 dimension
print(a.sum())  # sum of all elements
print(a.std())  # standard deviation
print(a.cumsum())  # running cumulative sum
print(a * 2)
print(a ** 2)
print(np.sqrt(a))
```

There is a spectrum of predefined actions you can execute on top of NumPy derived arrays as per previous example.

```
import numpy as np
a = np.array([0, 0.5, 1.0, 1.5, 2.0])
b = np.array([a, a * 2])
print(b)
print(b[0])  # first row
print(b[0, 2])  # third element of first row
print(b.sum())
print(b.sum(axis=0)) # sum along axis 0, i.e. column-wise sum
print(b.sum(axis=1)) # sum along axis 1, i.e. row-wise sum
```

Another critical feature of numpy.arrays is the ability to create structured arrays, that is, similar function to the initialization of SQL tables. First, we define "format" as dt and then use data to use dtype=dt to project predefined data structure:

```
import numpy as np
dt = np.dtype([('Name', 'S10'), ('Age', 'i4'),
               ('Height', 'f'), ('Children/Pets', 'i4', 2)])
s = np.array([('Smith', 45, 1.83, (0, 1)),
              ('Jones', 53, 1.72, (2, 2))], dtype=dt)
print(s)
print(s['Name'])
print(s['Height'].mean())
print(s[1]['Age'])
```

Vectorization of code is a critical strategy when you are looking to simplify and make your code run faster, which is basically all the time! The basic idea is not to iterate across objects but use one operation to cover all the bases. For example, use matrix calculations as opposed to element iterations code sequences. One core reason why NumPy arrays are efficient is this notion of vectorization. For instance, we can add two NumPy arrays element-wise as follows:

```
import numpy as np
r = np.random.standard_normal((4, 3))
s = np.random.standard_normal((4, 3))
print(r+s)
```

NumPy allows for *broadcasting*, to combine objects of different shape within a single operation used across neural networks for example:

```
import numpy as np
r = np.random.standard_normal((4, 3))
s = np.random.standard_normal(4)
print(r + s)
```

This is not going to work, hence:

```
import numpy as np
r = np.random.standard_normal((4, 3))
s = np.random.standard_normal(4)
print(r.transpose() + s)
print(np.shape(r))
print(np.shape(s))
print(np.shape(r.T))
```

Here we expand on our previous basic algorithm of Pricing European Call Option. NumPy allows for powerful vectorization and broadcasting capabilities. For example, assume we have a vector of 100 numbers:

$$\vec{v} = \begin{pmatrix} 1 \\ 2 \\ \cdots \\ 100 \end{pmatrix}$$

Scalar multiplication of this vector should yield the following:

$$\vec{u} = 2.\vec{v} = \begin{pmatrix} 2 \\ 4 \\ \cdots \\ 200 \end{pmatrix}$$

Let's have a look at simple Python *list* vs *numpy.array* interpretation:

```
v = [*range(1,6)]
print(v)
print(2*v)
#now setup numpy array
import numpy as np
```

```
v = np.arange(1,6)
print(v)
print(2*v)
```

Numpy.arrays deliver as expected, as opposed to a simple Python list that simply returns the original array two times. This feature is important when dealing with complex systems such as neural networks or Monte Carlos Simulations. Let's extend on the previous algorithm from Chapter 1. Now:

```
#
# Monte Carlo valuation of European call options with NumPy
# mcs_vector_numpy.py
# Reference: YH, Ch.3 pp.64
#
import math
import numpy as np
from time import time

np.random.seed(20000)
tick = time()

# Parameters
S0 = 100.; K = 105.; T = 1.0; r = -0.01; sigma = 0.38
M = 50; dt = T / M; I = 100000 * 2

# Simulating I paths with M time steps
S = np.zeros((M + 1, I))
S[0] = S0
for t in range(1, M + 1):
  z = np.random.standard_normal(I)  # pseudorandom numbers
  z -= z.mean()  # corrects 1st moment
  z /= z.std()  # corrects 2nd moment
  S[t] = S[t - 1] * np.exp((r - 0.5 * sigma ** 2) * dt
                           + sigma * math.sqrt(dt) * z)
  # vectorized operation per time step over all paths

# Calculating the Monte Carlo estimator
C0 = math.exp(-r * T) * np.sum(np.maximum(S[-1] - K, 0)) / I

# Results output
tock = time() - tick
print("European Option Value %7.3f" % C0)
print("Duration in Seconds   %7.3f" % tock)
```

In this section, we covered basic Python data structures and critical techniques we need to build on our next phase. In the following section we are ready to discuss an application of DDF into a hypothetical data driven use case.

4.3 Workshop: Internet of Things Carbon Footprint Data Use Case

The **Internet of Things (IoT)** is revolutionizing the way we interact with technology in our daily lives. This innovative concept refers to the vast network of interconnected devices that collect, share and analyze data without human intervention. From *smart homes* to *industrial automation*, IoT is transforming various sectors by enabling real-time monitoring and decision-making. This technology connects everyday devices to the internet, allowing them to collect and share data. In apartments and houses, IoT applications are transforming energy management and environmental awareness. **Smart thermostats** learn our preferences and adjust temperatures automatically, while **energy meters** provide real-time data on electricity consumption. **Home automation systems** integrate these devices, offering centralized control and monitoring. These IoT solutions not only enhance comfort but also play a crucial role in measuring and reducing our environmental impact. By analyzing data from connected devices, homeowners can now easily calculate their **carbon footprint**, gaining insights into their energy usage patterns and identifying areas for improvement. This seamless integration of IoT in residential settings empowers individuals to make informed decisions about their energy consumption, ultimately contributing to a more sustainable future.

Sandbox IoT Use Case

In this Sandbox IoT use case, we deliver an outline of our FinTech digital product within the DDF concept discussed in the previous chapters. The product here is designed to deliver accurate energy consumption predictions to our customers allowing our customers to understand their energy usage and carbon footprint and relevant cost structure – adding value in a form of financial insights. We simulate data factory (DDF) processing by stepping through each station in turn. The focus in this exercise is on the data management sequence in terms of how we are processing and passing data across the stations and what techniques we are utilizing in order to add value to our product or service offering. In this use case, as FinTech specialist you sit in between Technology Team and Product Design Team.

> Your task is to design conceptual solution to IoT Home Automation FinTech Application delivering visual insights to your customers. You step through each Station in turn. The focus in this exercise is on the data management sequence in terms of how you passing data across the stations and what techniques you are utilizing in order to add value to your FinTech product.

The structured data steams consist of electricity consumption in "kW" of home utilities (e.g., fridge, dishwasher, heaters) and external weather conditions (e.g., temperature, humidity) in minute-by-minute intervals for a duration of 365 days for an hypothetical home as depicted in Figure 4.1.

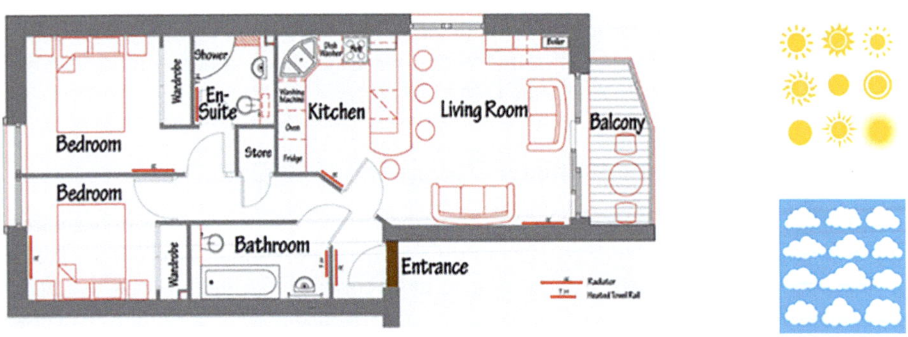

Figure 4.1 Hypothetical Home Setup

The result and delivery from this exercise is in a form of Python scripts and data sequences and final FinTech application design using Figma and Streamlit libraries. The intention is to deliver these components to your Technology Team and Product Design Team for further evaluation and final development.

DDF

From a practical standpoint, we look at data management from the perspective of the digital data factory floor. Figure 4.2 depicts applied DDF to our use case.

Inside the secured walls of the data factory floor we operate four distinct workstations. In the following sections we "sit" within each of these workstations and cover the Python solutions as applied to this use case.

- Station #1: Data Lake / ETL (Extract, Transform, Load)
- Station #2: Prompt and Feature Engineering
- Station #3: Model Design
- Station #4: Implementation

These stations are interconnected by internal data streams. In our case, we utilize pandas DataFrames to pass data in between stations. The notion behind this concept is to break down the inherent complexity of FinTech application design and provide logical sequence to internal data streams with the ability to operate and use chatbot/Co-Pilot solutions to assist within each station.

Figure 4.3 shows the requirement to iterate continuously across the DDF stations. Starting from data harvest in station 1. Data Lake, cleansing and loading data into different formats and passing downstream into station 2. Prompt and Feature Engineering for further processing and feature extractions. Then, moving along into station 3. AI Model applying selected and filtered features to solve the task at hand and, finally processing results and data streams

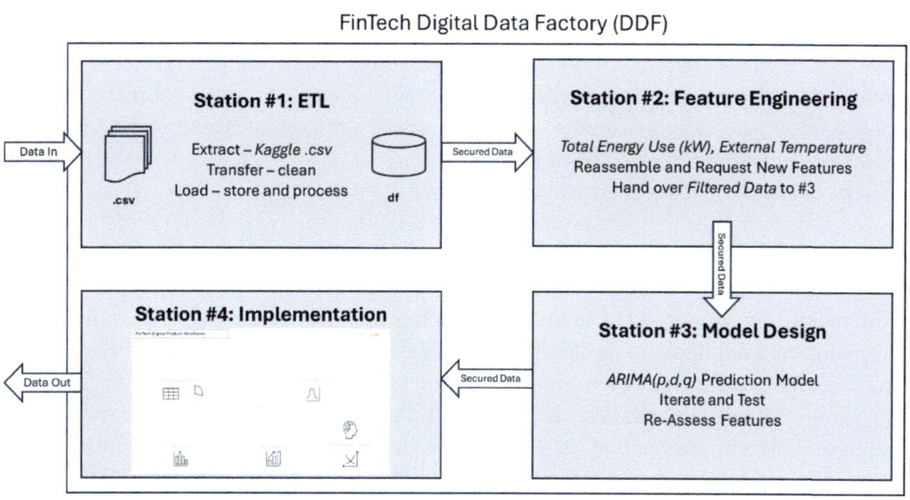

Figure 4.2 Applied DDF

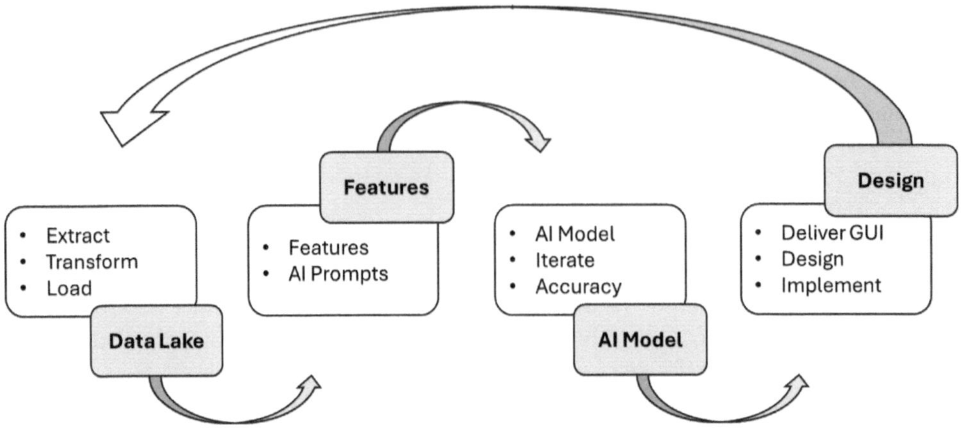

Figure 4.3 Applied DDF Iteration Cycle

in station 4. Design and implementing final dashboards or application design. The cycle is built for flexibility and repetitions allowing for a feedback loop to pass back into the starting point, station 1. Data Lake for next iteration to proceed. In the following section, we step through applied DDF and simulate our first iteration.

4.4 Station 1: Data Lake

In this station, we load already collected data points – provided to us in .csv structured format. In a real-world example, we would be looking into Hadoop-like .json text formats per sensor per room per weather station accessed via API connections hosted inside a secured cloud environment. Unlike traditional data warehouses, data lakes offer a *flexible and scalable repository* for storing vast amounts of structured and unstructured data from diverse sources. In the fast-paced world of financial technology, data lakes enable firms to **consolidate customer information, transaction records, market data, and regulatory compliance details** into a single, accessible ecosystem. This centralized approach facilitates real-time analytics, machine learning applications, and predictive modeling, empowering FinTech organizations to **make data-driven decisions swiftly**. By leveraging data lakes, financial institutions can enhance fraud detection, personalize customer experiences, optimize risk management, and streamline regulatory reporting processes.

Authenticity of the data is critical at this stage.

Pandas

In the rapidly evolving world of financial technology, **pandas** has emerged as an indispensable tool for data manipulation and analysis. This open-source Python library offers a robust framework for handling complex financial data sets with ease and efficiency. Pandas excels in processing time-series data, a crucial aspect in FinTech applications such as stock market analysis and algorithmic trading. Its **DataFrame** structure allows for seamless integration of diverse data sources, from CSV files to SQL databases, enabling FinTech professionals to consolidate and analyze vast amounts of financial information. With built-in functions for calculating moving averages, correlations and other financial metrics, pandas streamlines the process of deriving actionable insights from raw data. Moreover, its compatibility with other Python libraries like NumPy and Matplotlib makes it an integral part of the FinTech data science ecosystem, empowering developers and analysts to build sophisticated financial models and visualizations.

To use pandas, you have to import the library, typically providing an alias `pd`:

```
import pandas as pd
```

The core concept of pandas is the DataFrame. It is a table-like object containing the data. It has rows and columns that can be individually retrieved and manipulated. The typical workflow with pandas is as follows:

1. Load data into a DataFrame.
2. Work with the DataFrame to get data in the correct format, that is, ensuring the columns are properly labelled and with the correct datatype set.
3. Manipulate the DataFrame to find the information you want.
4. (Optional) Export reformatted data.

Examples of some core functions used in data handling and processing under pandas DataFrames, in this book we operate mostly with CSV, SQL, JSON formats.

Format	Input	Output	Comment
CSV	`read_csv()`	to_csv	text file
XLS	`read_excel()`	to_excel	s/s
HDF	`read_hdf()`	to_hdf	HDF5 db
SQL	`read_sql()`	to_sql	SQL tables
JSON	`read_json()`	to_json	JavaScript Object
MSGPACK	`read_msgpack()`	to_msgpack	Portable library
HTML	`read_html()`	to_html	HTML code
GBQ	`read_gbq()`	to_gbq	Google Big Query
DTA	`read_stata()`	to_stata	Formats 104, 105
Any	`read_clipboard`	to_clipboard	From HTML
Any	`read_pickle`	to_pickle	Structured Python Object

Before we look at the DataFrame, we begin by looking at the `Series`. The DataFrame can be thought of as a two-dimensional version of the Series. The Series is a one-dimensional labelled array. They are based on NumPy arrays and can only contain values of the same type. Here, the Series constructor is called.

```
import pandas as pd

s = pd.Series([1,2,3,4,5,6])
print(s)

s = pd.Series([0.2, 0.3, 0.4, 0.5, 0.6])
print(s)
```

An index can be added to provide a label to the values of the `Series`.

```
import pandas as pd

s = pd.Series([1,2,3,4], index=['a','b','c','d'])
print(s)
```

The index is expected to be the same length as the Series itself.

A Series with an index can also be created from a dictionary:

```
import pandas as pd

s = pd.Series({'a': 1, 'b': 2, 'c': 3, 'd': 4, 'e': 5})
print(s)
```

If we have provided an index, we can use the index:

```
import pandas as pd

s = pd.Series([1,2,3,4], index=['a','b','c','d'])
print(s['c'])
```

We can also use a list to extract multiple values:

```
import pandas as pd

s = pd.Series([1,2,3,4], index=['a','b','c','d'])
print(s[['c', 'a']])
```

You can apply most numeric operations, such as addition and multiplication, to Series objects to obtain new Series objects. When combining Series objects, they are always aligned using the index.

```
import pandas as pd

s1 = pd.Series({'a': 1, 'b': 2, 'c': 3, 'd': 4, 'e': 5})
s2 = pd.Series({'e': 10, 'a': 20, 'b': 30, 'c': 40, 'd': 50})
s3 = pd.Series({'a': 100, 'b': 200, 'c': 300, 'd': 400, 'f': 600})

print(s1 + s2) # Add items in s1 to their counterparts in s2
print(s1 * s2) # Multiply items in s1 to their counterparts in s2
print(s1 + s3) # Python will match all that it can, assiging NaN (not a number)
to unmatched items

print(3 + s1) # Add 3 to all elements in s1
print(3 * s1) # Multiply all elements of s1 by 3
```

In the resulting series `s1 + s2`, the value of `'a'` is the same as `s1['a'] + s2['a']`. Operators like ==, !=, <, <=, >, >= can also be applied to Series objects to obtain a Series of booleans. However, to combine Series of booleans, you use the operators &, |, and ~ instead of and, or, and not (respectively).

```
import pandas as pd

s1 = pd.Series([1, 2, 3, 4, 5])
s2 = pd.Series([3, 1, 2, 5, 4])

print(s1 < s2)
print(s1 >= 3)

print((s1 < s2) | ~(s1 >= 3))
```

A pandas `DataFrame` stores tabular data. Tabular data can be thought of as group of `Series` with the same shared index, with each `Series` in the group comprising a column of data. We can manually construct the DataFrame as follows:

```
import pandas as pd

df = pd.DataFrame({
  'area': pd.Series([4990, 7002, 7558, 7352, 7943]),
  'perimeter': pd.Series([2791.900, 3892.600, 3930.660, 3869.320, 3948.540]),
  'shape': pd.Series([0.0903296, 0.1486220, 0.1833120, 0.1170630, 0.1224170]),
  'permeability': pd.Series([6.3, 6.3, 6.3, 6.3, 17.1])
})

print(df)
```

This will also work; pandas will automatically generate the Series from a list of dictionaries for us:

```
import pandas as pd

df = pd.DataFrame([
  {'area':4990.0,'perimeter':2791.9, 'shape':0.0903296,'permeability':6.3},
  {'area':7002.0,'perimeter':3892.6, 'shape':0.148622, 'permeability':6.3},
  {'area':7558.0,'perimeter':3930.66,'shape':0.183312, 'permeability':6.3},
  {'area':7352.0,'perimeter':3869.32,'shape':0.117063, 'permeability':6.3},
  {'area':7943.0,'perimeter':3948.54,'shape':0.122417, 'permeability':17.1},
])

print(df)
```

Most operations that can be applied to `Series` objects can also be applied to `DataFrame` objects – the result being the natural generalization from one to two dimensions.

```
import pandas as pd

df = pd.DataFrame([
  {'area':4990.0,'perimeter':2791.9, 'shape':0.0903296,'permeability':6.3},
  {'area':7002.0,'perimeter':3892.6, 'shape':0.148622, 'permeability':6.3},
  {'area':7558.0,'perimeter':3930.66,'shape':0.183312, 'permeability':6.3},
  {'area':7352.0,'perimeter':3869.32,'shape':0.117063, 'permeability':6.3},
  {'area':7943.0,'perimeter':3948.54,'shape':0.122417, 'permeability':17.1},
])

print(df + 50) # Adds 50 to every element in the DataFrame
```

Extract, Transfer, Load (ETL)

In this station we aim to utilize **pandas** and **NumPy** libraries to demonstrate structured data handling and data controls. Specifically focusing on the following:

- Data Load
- Data Cleansing and Formatting
  - Columns formatting
  - Dates formatting
  - Cleansing/duplicate controls
  - Hand-over to Station 2. in `df` format

The data can be downloaded from Kaggle [4.2]. Given we are provided with extracted (E) and transformed (T) data stream in a form of `.csv` our first tasks is to load (L) the data set into our computational environment. As the first step post data access and download, we set the file to read-only. Basically, this is to ensure that the original data source is set to be the source of truth. The following Python snippet contains worked example relevant to station 1.

> This CSV file contains the readings with a time span of 1 minute of house appliances in kW from a smart meter and weather conditions of that particular region. This CSV file contains the readings with a time span of 1 minute OF 350 DAYS of house appliances in kW from a smart meter and weather conditions of that particular region.

In short, energy data (Kw) from house appliances and weather information. The following appliances are connected to and data retrieved via a smart IoT sensors: Dishwasher, Furnace, Home office, Fridge, Wine cellar, Garage door, Kitchen, Barn, Well, Microwave, Living room, Solar power generation, etc. Also, weather data are provided in equal time intervals: Cloud cover, Temperature, Humidity, Wind speed, etc. Based on this data set we can analyze relationship between energy consumption by appliances over time, detect anomalous usage of appliances or explore the relationship between weather conditions and energy generated by solar power. Assuming we know exact sequence of steps at this moment to proceed we prepare a simple pseudocode version:

```
FUNCTION Station1_loadData(etl_path, export_path):
    # Stage 1: Extract, Transform, Load (ETL)
    # Purpose: Load, cleanse, and prepare data for next processing stage

    # LOAD VARIATION #1: Load CSV data from internal file system
    LOAD data FROM CSV file located at etl_path INTO DataFrame df

    # Display information about the data
    CALCULATE number of rows (nRow) and columns (nCol) IN df
    PRINT number of rows and columns
    PRINT first 5 rows, last 5 rows
    PRINT column information and data types

    # CLEANSING: Prepare data for Station #2
    # Remove last row containing an error
    REMOVE last row FROM df

    # Handle missing or invalid values
    REPLACE infinities (positive/negative) WITH NaN IN df
    DROP rows containing NaN values FROM df

    # Clean column names
    RENAME columns BY REMOVING '[kW]' FROM their names IN df

    # Convert and process time column
    CONVERT 'time' column TO datetime format USING Unix timestamp
    SET datetime index BASED on starting date '2016-01-01 05:00' WITH minute
frequency
```

```
    # Add day-of-week information
    ADD new column 'day_of_week' BASED on day name FROM 'time' column

    # Set 'time' as index and remove duplicates
    SET 'time' column AS index IN df
    REMOVE duplicate timestamps, KEEPING last occurrence

    # Handle errors in 'cloudCover' column
    CONVERT 'cloudCover' column TO numeric, REPLACING errors WITH NaN
    BACKFILL missing values IN 'cloudCover'

    # Analyze categorical columns
    DISPLAY head of 'icon' and 'summary' columns
    CALCULATE value counts and percentage distributions FOR 'icon' column

    # Correlation analysis
    FILTER numeric columns FROM df INTO numeric_df
    COMPUTE correlation matrix FOR numeric_df
    PLOT heatmap of correlation matrix

    # Aggregate and visualize data
    PLOT daily and weekly resampled mean of 'use' column
    PLOT bar charts FOR energy usage grouped BY 'summary' and 'icon'

    # Export cleansed data
    EXPORT df TO CSV file located at export_path

    RETURN df
END FUNCTION
```

Followed by the actual Python code:

```
import pandas as pd
import numpy as np
from datetime import datetime
import matplotlib.pyplot as plt
import seaborn as sns
import kagglehub

# Download latest version
# path = kagglehub.dataset_download("taranvee/
smart-home-dataset-with-weather-information")

etl_path = r'HomeC.csv'
export_path = r'DDF_Station_1.csv'
def Station1_loadData(etl_path, export_path):
    """
    Stage 1: Extract, Transform, Load (ETL)
    Process data load post extract and transfer phases
    :return: df cleansed dataset
    """

    ## LOAD VARIATION #1: Direct file from your internal file system
    # This file is read-only and can NOT be changed as this is the original
source of truth
```

```
    # Load the CSV file into a DataFrame
    df = pd.read_csv(etl_path, delimiter=',', low_memory=False)

    # Display basic information about the DataFrame
    nRow, nCol = df.shape
    print(f'There are {nRow} rows and {nCol} columns')
    print(df.head(5))
    print(df.tail(5))
    print(df.info())
    # Inspect columns
    print(df.columns)
    # Data types #
    print(df.dtypes)

    ## CLEANSING: Clean dataset to be ready for handover to Station #2
    # Remove the last row as it has a "/" error
    df = df.iloc[:-1]

    # Check for NaN / Infs etc.
    df = df.replace([np.Inf, -np.Inf], np.NaN)
    df = df.dropna()

    # Rename columns by removing '[kW]'
    df.columns = [col.replace(' [kW]', '') for col in df.columns]

    # Convert the 'time' column to datetime format
    df['time'] = pd.to_datetime(df['time'].astype(int), unit='s')
    df['time'] = pd.DatetimeIndex(pd.date_range('2016-01-01 05:00',
periods=len(df),  freq='min'))

    # Set the day of the week
    df['day_of_week'] = df.reset_index()['time'].dt.day_name()

    # Set the index
    df = df.set_index(['time'])

    # Remove duplicate timestamps and keep only the last value
    df = df[~df.index.duplicated(keep='last')]

    # Fix errors in 'cloudCover' column
    df['cloudCover'] = pd.to_numeric(df['cloudCover'], errors='coerce')
    df['cloudCover'] = df['cloudCover'].bfill()

    # Inspect icon and summary which are "objects"
    df['icon'].head()
    df['summary'].head()

    # Value counts
    df['icon'].value_counts()
    df['icon'].value_counts(normalize = True) * 100

    # Inspect correlations
    numeric_df = df.select_dtypes(include=['float64', 'int64'])
    correlation_matrix = numeric_df.corr()

    # Plot correlation matrix
    plt.figure(figsize=(10, 8))
    sns.set(font_scale=1.2)
    sns.heatmap(correlation_matrix, annot=False, cmap='coolwarm', fmt=".2f",
linewidths=0.5)
```

```
    plt.title('Correlation Matrix')
    plt.xticks(rotation=90)
    plt.yticks(rotation=0)
    plt.tight_layout()
    plt.show()

    # Re-sample to daily
    df['use'].resample('D').mean().plot(title="Daily kW Usage", legend=True)
    plt.show()
    df['use'].resample('W').mean().plot(title="Weekly kW Usage", legend=True)
    plt.show()

    # Plot energy usage by weather summary
    df.groupby('summary')['Living room'].mean().sort_values().plot(kind='bar',
title="Living Room Usage by Weather", legend=True)
    plt.show()
    df.groupby('summary')['House overall'].mean().sort_values().plot(kind='bar',
title="House Usage by Weather", legend=True)
    plt.show()

    # Plot energy usage by icon
    df.groupby('icon')['Living room'].mean().sort_values().plot(kind='bar',
title="Living Room Usage by Icon", legend=True)
    plt.show()
    df.groupby('icon')['House overall'].mean().sort_values().plot(kind='bar',
title="House Usage by Icon", legend=True)
    plt.show()

    # Export cleaned data to CSV file
    # Stage 1 Complete
    df.to_csv(export_path)

    return df
```

The input parameters passed into the Python function `Station1_loadData(etl_path, export_path)` relate to source of truth, data extracted from the source, and storage in a form of `.csv` file post cleansing and transfer. The output from this function is in a form of pandas DataFrames `df` to be passed down stream into *Station 2. Prompt and Feature Engineering*. There are two components in this station, (i) data load and (ii) data cleansing. We start with data load and visual data display as follows:

```
    ## LOAD VARIATION #1: Direct file from your internal file system
    # This file is read-only and can NOT be changed as this is the original
source of truth
    # Load the CSV file into a DataFrame
    df = pd.read_csv(etl_path, delimiter=',', low_memory=False)

    # Display basic information about the DataFrame
    nRow, nCol = df.shape
    print(f'There are {nRow} rows and {nCol} columns')
    print(df.head(5))
    print(df.tail(5))
    print(df.info())
    # Inspect columns
    print(df.columns)
    # Data types #
    print(df.dtypes)
```

We use inbuild pandas function to load `.csv` file format directly into DataFrames using `pd.read_csv()` function, resulting in visual structured data interpretation containing 503,911 rows and 32 columns:

```
[5 rows x 32 columns]
<class 'pandas.core.frame.DataFrame'>
RangeIndex: 503911 entries, 0 to 503910
Data columns (total 32 columns):
 #   Column                Non-Null Count   Dtype
---  ------                --------------   -----
 0   time                  503911 non-null  object
 1   use [kW]              503910 non-null  float64
 2   gen [kW]              503910 non-null  float64
 3   House overall [kW]    503910 non-null  float64
 4   Dishwasher [kW]       503910 non-null  float64
 5   Furnace 1 [kW]        503910 non-null  float64
 6   Furnace 2 [kW]        503910 non-null  float64
 7   Home office [kW]      503910 non-null  float64
 8   Fridge [kW]           503910 non-null  float64
 9   Wine cellar [kW]      503910 non-null  float64
 10  Garage door [kW]      503910 non-null  float64
 11  Kitchen 12 [kW]       503910 non-null  float64
 12  Kitchen 14 [kW]       503910 non-null  float64
 13  Kitchen 38 [kW]       503910 non-null  float64
 14  Barn [kW]             503910 non-null  float64
 15  Well [kW]             503910 non-null  float64
 16  Microwave [kW]        503910 non-null  float64
 17  Living room [kW]      503910 non-null  float64
 18  Solar [kW]            503910 non-null  float64
 19  temperature           503910 non-null  float64
 20  icon                  503910 non-null  object
 21  humidity              503910 non-null  float64
 22  visibility            503910 non-null  float64
 23  summary               503910 non-null  object
 24  apparentTemperature   503910 non-null  float64
 25  pressure              503910 non-null  float64
 26  windSpeed             503910 non-null  float64
 27  cloudCover            503910 non-null  object
 28  windBearing           503910 non-null  float64
 29  precipIntensity       503910 non-null  float64
 30  dewPoint              503910 non-null  float64
 31  precipProbability     503910 non-null  float64
```

The next phase is to cleanse the data. Note, this is not the original data set. The steps we execute at this point are conducted on loaded data into our computing environment (in memory in this case). We check for NaN/Infs data observations using `df = df.replace([np.Inf, -np.Inf], np.NaN)` and `df = df.dropna()`. Then, by observing visual column usage we lighted up the data source by dropping naming conventions "kW" by using `df.columns = [col.replace(' [kW]', '') for col in df.columns]`. Next step is to secure the "time" sequence. We know that the observations are in time sequence, time-series. Hence, we need to ensure our "time" measure is accurate and correct in depicting passing time. We convert "time" column into `datetime` format by `df['time'] = pd.to_datetime(df['time'].astype(int), unit='s')` and set the initial time observation `df['time'] = pd.DatetimeIndex(pd.

`date_range('2016-01-01 05:00', periods=len(df), freq='min'))` and conclude by setting the `df` index to `df = df.set_index(['time'])` converting the entire DataFrame into time-series observations. Post completing additional cleansing exercises we are in a position to explore simple visual and graphical data interpretation.

From a graphical perspective, we start with correlation matrix:

```
    # Inspect correlations
    numeric_df = df.select_dtypes(include=['float64', 'int64'])
    correlation_matrix = numeric_df.corr()

    # Plot correlation matrix
    plt.figure(figsize=(10, 8))
    sns.set(font_scale=1.2)
    sns.heatmap(correlation_matrix, annot=False, cmap='coolwarm', fmt=".2f",
linewidths=0.5)
    plt.title('Correlation Matrix')
    plt.xticks(rotation=90)
    plt.yticks(rotation=0)
    plt.tight_layout()
    plt.show()
```

Resulting in the following graph:

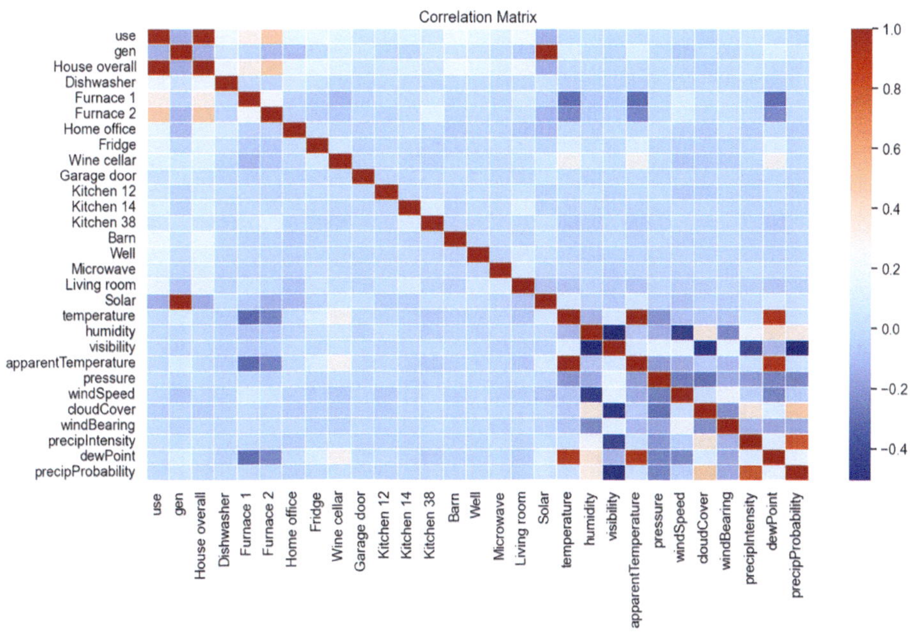

Figure 4.4 Station 1 Correlation

Form the previous correlation matrix in Figure 4.4, it appears we observe patterns in the observations as related to specific home utilities, overall electricity consumption and weather patterns. These initial "insights" will become invaluable during our features selection in station 2. To ensure we observe clean dataframes, we add three additional views, namely, (i) daily electricity usage in Figure 4.5, (ii) overall house usage by weather type, in Figure 4.6 and (iii) overall house usage by weather icon (identifier), in Figure 4.7.

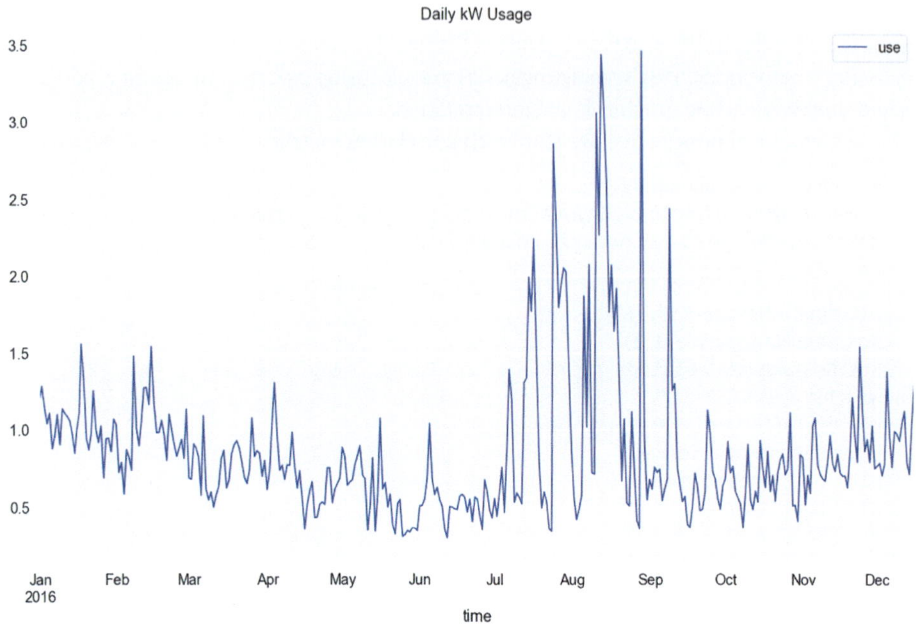

Figure 4.5 Station 1 Daily Observation

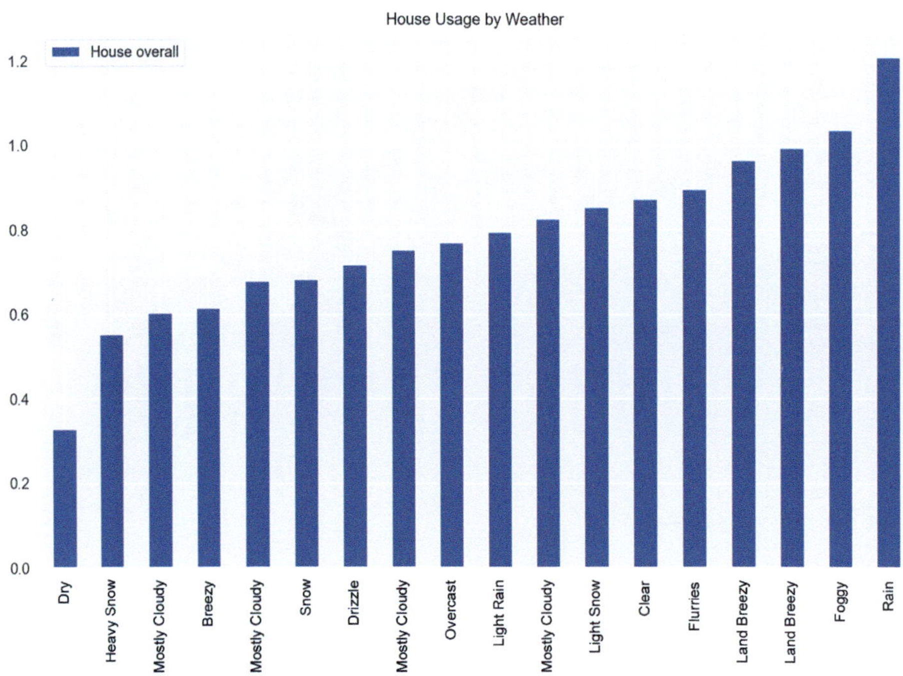

Figure 4.6 Station 1 Weather Type

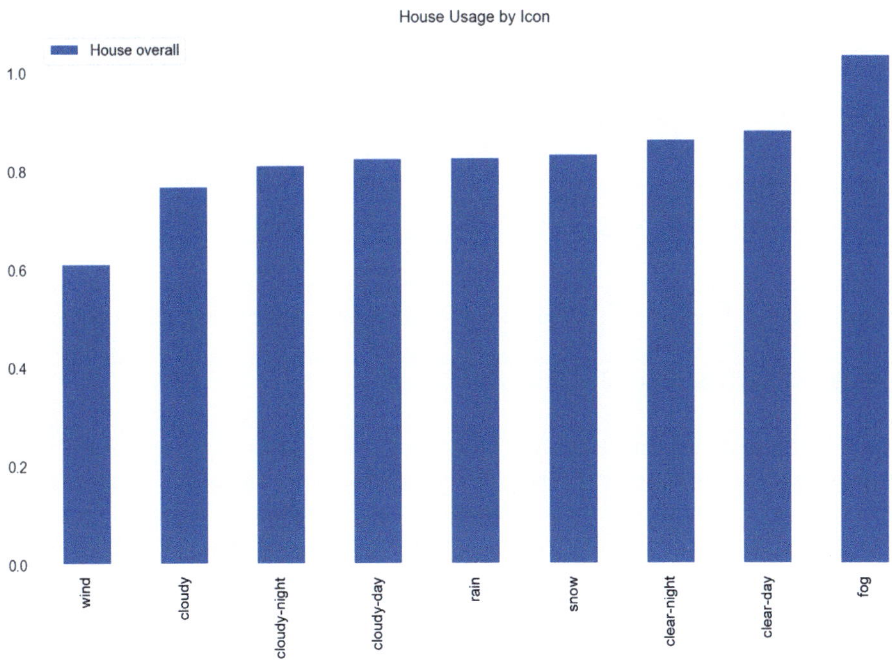

Figure 4.7 Station 1 Weather Icon

Based on the preliminary observations we can see the pattern of electricity consumption and possible correlation to weather conditions. We pursue these "features" further in station 2. We have started by loading pre-specified data from Kaggle data source in a form of `.csv` file, post extract, transfer and load actions our final result from station 1 is in a form of cleansed DataFrame data structure `df`.

4.5 Station 2: Prompt and Feature Engineering

In this station, we expand on the cleaned data streams and start building and preparing model features. Here, you need to understand the business use case in detail. **Prompt engineering** and **feature engineering** are two crucial techniques that significantly enhance the performance of machine learning models in data science. *Prompt engineering* involves crafting effective input prompts to guide AI models, particularly large language models, towards generating desired outputs. This technique is essential for optimizing model responses and improving task-specific performance. On the other hand, *feature engineering* focuses on selecting, transforming, and creating relevant features from raw data to improve model accuracy and efficiency. By carefully extracting and manipulating data attributes, data scientists can uncover hidden patterns and relationships that algorithms might otherwise miss. Both prompt and feature engineering require creativity, domain knowledge, and iterative experimentation to achieve optimal results, making them indispensable skills for data scientists aiming to develop robust and high-performing machine learning solutions.

Feature Selection

The aim of this station is to filter and select and/or generate and create relevant features for further processing to be passed down to *Station 3. Model Design*. Specifically focusing on:

- Aggregation
- Core feature identification
- Hand over features to *Station 3. Model Design*

The input into this station is in a form of DataFrames generated from station 1. The output from this station is in a form of DataFrames to be handed over to Station 3. Model Design.

Utility of the data is critical at this stage.

The task here is to provide model features in the overall dataframes (df) as well as specialized formatting required for neural networks via TensorFlows data structures. Caveat, it is constructive to note that we do cover neural networks implementation at this point in this chapter, however, we cover the theoretical and mathematical interpretation in the later chapters for further exposition. From computational perspective we focus our attention on ARIMA modeling framework only. Assuming we know exact sequence of steps at this moment to proceed, we prepare a simple pseudocode version:

```
FUNCTION Station2_featureEngineering(file_path, export_path, freq="D"):
    # Stage 2: Feature Engineering
    # Purpose: Process cleaned data and extract relevant features for modeling

    # Load data
    LOAD data FROM CSV file located at file_path INTO DataFrame df
    CONVERT 'time' column TO datetime format

    # Aggregate and clean columns
    CREATE new column 'Furnace' BY summing 'Furnace 1' and 'Furnace 2'
    CREATE new column 'Kitchen' BY summing 'Kitchen 12', 'Kitchen 14', and
'Kitchen 38'
    DROP columns ['Furnace 1', 'Furnace 2', 'Kitchen 12', 'Kitchen 14', 'Kitchen
38', 'icon', 'summary']

    # Setup energy core features
    RENAME 'use' AS 'use_House'
    RENAME 'gen' AS 'gen_Sol'
    DROP columns ['use', 'House overall', 'gen', 'Solar', 'apparentTemperature']
    SET 'time' AS index

    # Calculate rolling statistics
    CALCULATE 24-hour rolling standard deviation, skew, and kurtosis FOR
'use_House'
    STORE results AS new columns ['use_House_vol', 'use_House_skw',
'use_House_kur']

    # Select features for modeling
    SELECT relevant columns INTO DataFrame df2, including:
```

```
        - 'use_House', 'gen_Sol' (dependent variables)
        - Appliance usage (e.g., 'Dishwasher', 'Home office', etc.)
        - Weather features (e.g., 'temperature', 'humidity', etc.)
        - Rolling statistics (e.g., 'use_House_vol', 'use_House_skw',
'use_House_kur')

    # Resample data based on specified frequency (freq)
    IF freq IS "D":
        RESAMPLE df2 DAILY AND CALCULATE mean
        CALCULATE energy usage shocks relative to rolling mean OVER 3, 7, and
14 days
        DROP rows WITH NaN values
    ELSE IF freq IS "h":
        RESAMPLE df2 HOURLY AND CALCULATE mean
        CALCULATE energy usage shocks relative to rolling mean OVER 3, 7, and
14 days (in hours)
        DROP rows WITH NaN values

    # Export processed data
    EXPORT df2 TO CSV file located at export_path

    RETURN df2
END FUNCTION
```

With Python representation:

```
import pandas as pd

def Station2_featureEngineering(file_path, export_path, freq="D"):
    """
    Receive cleaned data from Station #1 process all relevant features
    :param df: input clean data streams
    :return: df: return relevant features
    """
    df = pd.read_csv(file_path,low_memory=False)
    df['time'] = pd.to_datetime(df['time'])

    # There are multiple columns in Furnance and Kitchen.
    # Aggregate them into new column by summing them up.
    df['Furnace'] = df[['Furnace 1','Furnace 2']].sum(axis=1)
    df['Kitchen'] = df[['Kitchen 12','Kitchen 14','Kitchen 38']].sum(axis=1)
    df.drop(['Furnace 1','Furnace 2','Kitchen 12','Kitchen 14',
             'Kitchen 38','icon','summary'], axis=1, inplace=True)

    # Setup energy core features
    df['use_House'] = df['use']
    df['gen_Sol'] = df['gen']
    df.drop(['use','House overall','gen','Solar','apparentTemperature'],
            axis=1, inplace=True)

    df = df.set_index(['time'])
```

```
    # Volatility/Skew and Kurtosis of energy usage #
    df['use_House_vol'] = df.rolling(window = (1*60*24))['use_House'].std()
    df['use_House_skw'] = df.rolling(window = (1*60*24))['use_House'].skew()
    df['use_House_kur'] = df.rolling(window = (1*60*24))['use_House'].kurt()

    # Output features relevant to Stage 3 Model Design#
    df2 = df[['use_House', 'gen_Sol', # Left-hand-side variables
                'Dishwasher', 'Home office', 'Fridge', 'Wine cellar', 'Garage door',
                'Barn', 'Well', 'Microwave', 'Living room',
                'temperature', 'humidity', # Right-hand-side variables
                'visibility', 'pressure', 'windSpeed',
                'cloudCover', 'windBearing', 'precipIntensity', 'dewPoint',
                'precipProbability',
                # Vol / Skew / Kurtosis
                'use_House_vol', 'use_House_skw', 'use_House_kur'
                ]]

    # Use resampling frequency for further analysis
    if freq == "D":
        df2 = df2.resample("D").mean()

        # Shocks/deviation to the energy usage relative to the mean #
        # 3-Day
        df2['use_House_shock_3d'] = df2['use_House']-df2['use_House'].
rolling(window=3).mean()
        # 7-Day
        df2['use_House_shock_7d'] = df2['use_House']-df2['use_House'].
rolling(window=7).mean()
        # 14-Day
        df2['use_House_shock_14d'] = df2['use_House']-df2['use_House'].
rolling(window=14).mean()
        # Drop NaN
        df2 = df2.dropna()

    elif freq == "h":
        df2 = df2.resample("h").mean()

        # Shocks/deviation to the energy usage relative to the mean #
        # 3-Day
        df2['use_House_shock_3d'] = df2['use_House']-df2['use_House'].rolling(win
dow=3*24).mean()
        # 7-Day
        df2['use_House_shock_7d'] = df2['use_House']-df2['use_House'].rolling(win
dow=7*24).mean()
        # 14-Day
        df2['use_House_shock_14d'] = df2['use_House']-df2['use_House'].rolling(win
dow=14*24).mean()
        # Drop NaN
        df2 = df2.dropna()

    # Export cleaned feature data to CSV file
    # Stage 2 Complete delivers df files to be passed to Station 3
    df2.to_csv(export_path)

    return df2
```

We initiate station 2 with loading `df` from station 1 and aggregating number of selected and related features:

```
# There are multiple columns in Furnance and Kitchen.
# Aggregate them into new column by summing them up.
df['Furnace'] = df[['Furnace 1','Furnace 2']].sum(axis=1)
df['Kitchen'] = df[['Kitchen 12','Kitchen 14','Kitchen 38']].sum(axis=1)
df.drop(['Furnace 1','Furnace 2','Kitchen 12','Kitchen 14',
         'Kitchen 38','icon','summary'], axis=1, inplace=True)
```

and coordinating core features to be passed down to our model design station:

```
# Setup energy core features
df['use_House'] = df['use']
df['gen_Sol'] = df['gen']
df.drop(['use','House overall','gen','Solar','apparentTemperature'],
        axis=1, inplace=True)

df = df.set_index(['time'])
```

We complete filtering exercise driven by business requirements. At this stage we are not engaging high-frequency analytics and are more concerned with "hourly" and "daily" data sets. Hence, as part of the filtering process, we specify resampling frequency, `D for daily and h for hourly`:

```
# Use resampling frequency for further analysis
```

Overall, final delivery of this station is in a form of DataFrames containing core features to be analyzed and used in station 3.

```
# Output features relevant to Stage 3 Model Design#
df2 = df[['use_House', 'gen_Sol', # Left-hand-side variables
                'Dishwasher', 'Home office', 'Fridge', 'Wine cellar', 'Garage
door',
                'Barn', 'Well', 'Microwave', 'Living room',
                'temperature', 'humidity', # Right-hand-side variables
                'visibility', 'pressure', 'windSpeed',
                'cloudCover', 'windBearing', 'precipIntensity', 'dewPoint',
                'precipProbability',
                # Vol / Skew / Kurtosis
                'use_House_vol', 'use_House_skw', 'use_House_kur'
                ]]
```

Feature engineering stands as a cornerstone in the realm of data science, playing a pivotal role in transforming raw data into meaningful insights. This process involves selecting, manipulating, and creating features that best represent the underlying patterns in data, significantly enhancing the performance and accuracy of machine learning models. By distilling complex information into more digestible forms, feature engineering not only improves model efficiency but also unveils hidden relationships within data sets that might otherwise remain obscured. Ultimately, the art and science of feature engineering empower data scientists to extract maximum value from their data, driving more informed decision-making and unlocking the true potential of predictive analytics.

Prompt Selection

Prompt engineering, or as we refer to prompt selection, has become a pivotal aspect, especially when it comes to feature selection from tabular data. By leveraging advanced techniques such as LLM prompting, feature importance, dimensionality reduction, and correlation analysis, data scientists and AI researchers can significantly enhance their analytical capabilities.

LLM prompting involves utilizing large language models to generate relevant prompts that guide the feature selection process. This technique can uncover hidden patterns and insights that might be overlooked by traditional methods. **Feature importance** is another critical technique, which ranks features based on their predictive power, allowing analysts to focus on the most impactful variables.

Dimensionality reduction techniques, such as PCA (principal component analysis), help in simplifying complex data sets by reducing the number of variables while preserving essential information. This not only improves computational efficiency but also enhances the clarity of the analysis. **Correlation analysis** is employed to identify and quantify the relationships between different features, ensuring that redundant or highly correlated features are appropriately managed, as highlighted in Station #1.

By integrating these techniques, FinTech operators, data scientists and business analysts can achieve more accurate and efficient feature selection, leading to better model performance and more reliable insights. Prompt selection is not a science; it depends on the aspect of the exercise as well as LLM model used to derive the results. This evolving nature of prompt selection drives us to recommend the use of pseudocoding sequence in the prompt design to be able to narrow down the scope of the utility returned from LLM Co-pilot.

In this case, we look at our IoT use case. Using ChatGPT to prompt slimmed versions of our Station #1 data source (selected first 1,000 rows of data "HomeC.csv") we start with "Analyze and provide main data features from the above excel file", as show in the prompt in Figures 4.7(i) and 4.7(ii).

While on the case, let us be more specific regarding the task and refocus our prompt to be more specific, namely, "Provide feature engineering for ML applications like energy prediction?" within the same prompt, with the following results:

As per the aforementioned results, the LLM model response seems robust in aggregate, and this is seen as our first step towards being able to communicate with Co-Pilots in order to provide enhanced analytical capabilities for our FinTech operations. The caveat in utilizing Co-Pilots is to remain, always check and confirm the accuracy of the results.

4.6 Station 3: Model Design

Predictive analytics and AI model design are revolutionizing the FinTech industry, offering unprecedented insights into financial trends and customer behavior. By leveraging vast amounts of data, financial institutions can now forecast market movements, assess credit risks and personalize services with remarkable accuracy. AI models, particularly machine learning algorithms, analyze historical data to identify patterns and make data-driven predictions, enabling more informed decision-making in areas such as fraud detection, investment strategies, and customer retention. For instance, these technologies can predict a customer's likelihood of defaulting on a loan or detect unusual transaction patterns that may indicate fraudulent activity. As FinTech companies continue to innovate, the integration of predictive analytics and AI is not just enhancing operational efficiency but also creating new products

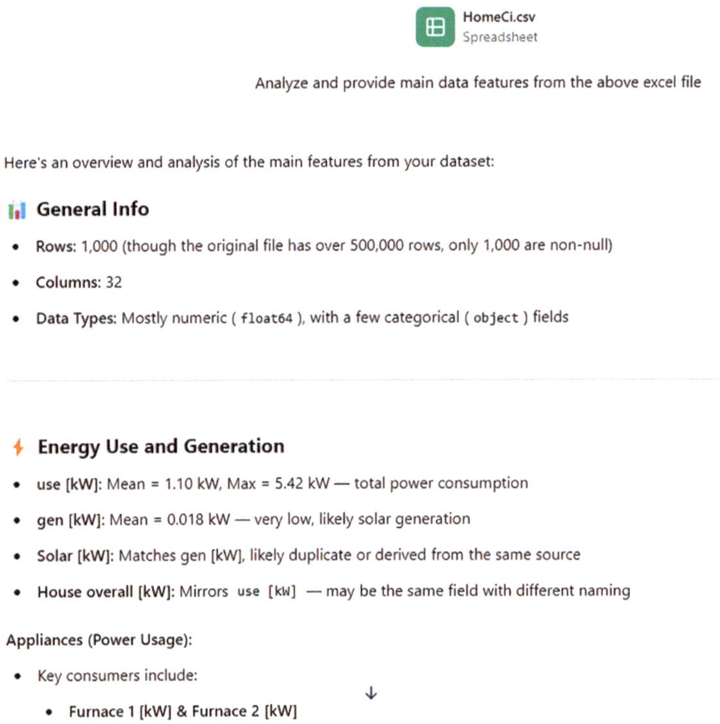

Figure 4.7(i) LLM Prompt

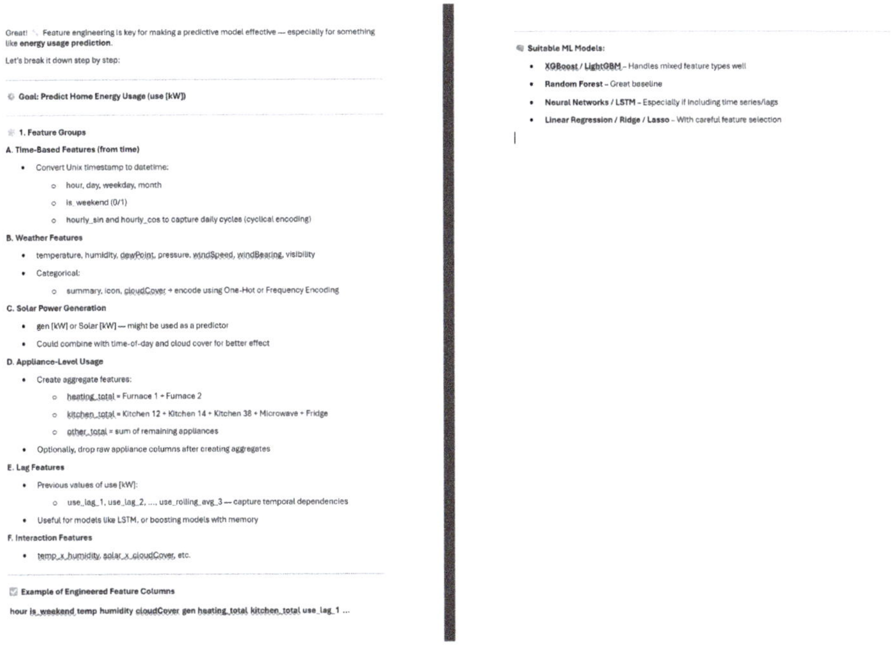

Figure 4.7(ii) LLM Prompt Results

and services, fundamentally transforming how financial services are delivered and consumed in the digital age.

Autoregressive Integrated Moving Average (ARIMA)

The autoregressive integrated moving average (ARIMA) model is one of the most frequently used modeling methodologies when dealing with time-series data streams. This versatile model combines three key components: **autoregression** (AR), which uses past values to predict future ones; **integration** (I), which differentiates the data to make it stationary; and **moving average** (MA), which incorporates the dependency between an observation and residual errors from past observations. ARIMA is particularly effective in capturing complex patterns in data, making it invaluable in fields such as economics, finance and weather forecasting. Its ability to handle both seasonal and non-seasonal data sets it apart from simpler forecasting methods. By adjusting the parameters of each component, analysts can fine-tune the model to fit various types of time series data, from stock prices to sales figures. This flexibility and accuracy have cemented ARIMA's position as a cornerstone in modern time series analysis and predictive modeling.

ARIMA belongs to a group of standard statistical models dedicated to time series analytics and forecasting:

- Autoregressive (AR) defines model variables using past or lagged observations
- Integrated (I) defines differencing of time series to make time-series stationary
- Moving average (MA) defines the dependency between an observation and a model residual error

$$y'_t = c + \varphi_1 y'_{t-1} + \ldots + \varphi_p y'_{t-p} + \theta_1 \epsilon_{t-1} + \ldots + \theta_q \epsilon_{t-q} + \epsilon_t$$

where y'_t is the differenced time series, c the intercept, $\varphi_1 y'_{t-1} + \ldots + \varphi_p y'_{t-p}$ is the lagged values and $\theta_1 \epsilon_{t-1} + \ldots + \theta_q \epsilon_{t-q} + \epsilon_t$ is the lagged errors. Few examples here:

$$ARIMA(2,0,1) = y_t = a_1 y_{t-1} + a_2 y_{t-2} + b_1 \epsilon_{t-1}$$

$$ARIMA(3,0,1) = y_t = a_1 y_{t-1} + a_2 y_{t-2} + a_3 y_{t-3} + b_1 \epsilon_{t-1}$$

$$ARIMA(1,1,0) = \delta y_t = a_1 \delta y_{t-1} + \epsilon_t, where, \delta y_t = y_t - y_{t-1}$$

$$ARIMA(2,1,0) = \delta y_t = a_1 \delta y_{t-1} + a_2 \delta y_{t-2} + \epsilon_t, where, \delta y_t = y_t - y_{t-1}$$

Then the question becomes how do we implement this modeling framework in our **DDF Station 3: Model Design**. To be able to model `AR+I+MA` components we explicitly specify each component via input model parameters in a standard format defined as `ARIMA(p, d, q)` whereby the parameters `p, d, q` are integers as per the following:

- (p) the number of lag observations, lag order
- (d) the number of times that observations are differenced, degree of differencing
- (q) the number depicting the size of the moving average windows, order of moving averages.

The magic of this model is that if you do have stationary and univariate data sequence, the model performs relatively well in terms of model prediction and relevant accuracy. Hence, this is a rather powerful model and can be used in various settings – the FinTech space is full of time-series observations. Given the generic model structure AR+I+MA and generic computational speed, this is indeed a useful tool. However, as is usually the case in real-world scenarios, we do not have stationary and univariate data streams and hence as in the application of modeling frameworks caution is in order. Hence, the advances in neural networks–like models are proving mode adept in FinTech areas. In our use case, we utilize `ARIMA(p, d, q)` model structure. In summary, as per the following, ARIMA can be split into long term (AR filter) + stochastic trend (Integration filter) + short term (MA filter) + error (white noise) effects, and in order to actually implement ARIMA in a production environment, deep study of **DATA** is absolutely critical! Once again leading us to conclude that it is the **DATA MANAGEMENT** that matters most.

Predictive Analytics

In simple terms, can we add tools or insights to our FinTech product or services that allow our clients to forecast or predict more accurate outcomes in the near future? In this station, your task is to prepare prediction models to be used in the overall solution. You have your dataframes (df) prepared (daily and hourly) and handed over from Station 2 focusing on the following:

- Model delivery
- Model accuracy
- Optimization
- Computational Speed
- Clarity of results; dataframes

Clarity and parsimony of the resulting data is critical at this stage.

The humble task here is to provide an accurate depiction of real-world conditions and to design a predictive model delivering consistently accurate predictions.

Basic Assessment

To start with, from business perspective, it is logical to assume a relationship between the energy consumption and external temperature across time. We look at temperature and overall energy consumption using Seaborn library, delivering clear and distinct patterns:

```
# ****** GRAPHICS (BASICS) ******
# Let's investigate time-series plots #
# Set the style for seaborn
sns.set(style='whitegrid', context='notebook')
# Temperature over time #
plt.figure(figsize=(12, 6))
plt.title("Temperature Over Time", fontsize=16)
sns.lineplot(x='time', y='temperature', data=df, label="Temperature")
plt.xlabel('Date', fontsize=16)
```

```
plt.ylabel('Temperature in Fahrenheit', fontsize=16)
plt.legend(loc="upper right", fontsize=14)
plt.xticks(fontsize=16)
plt.yticks(fontsize=16)
plt.grid(True)

# Save/Show the plot
# plt.savefig(os.path.join(export_path, 'temperature.png'))
plt.show()

# Energy use over time #
plt.figure(figsize=(12, 6))
plt.title("Energy Usage [kW] Over Time", fontsize=16)
sns.lineplot(x='time', y='use_House', data=df, label='Energy Usage [kW]')
plt.xlabel('Date', fontsize=16)
plt.ylabel('Energy Usage [kW]', fontsize=16)
plt.legend(loc="upper right", fontsize=14)
plt.xticks(fontsize=16)
plt.yticks(fontsize=16)
plt.grid(True)

# Save/Show the plot
# plt.savefig(os.path.join(export_path, 'energy_usage.png'))
plt.show()
```

Given the distinct patterns between these two features, as shown in Figures 4.8 and 4.9, we run a simple regression with added polynomial terms. **Polynomial ordinary least squares regression** plays a crucial role in the realm of data science, offering a powerful tool for modeling complex relationships between variables. This advanced technique extends the capabilities of simple linear regression by allowing for *curved relationships*, making it invaluable

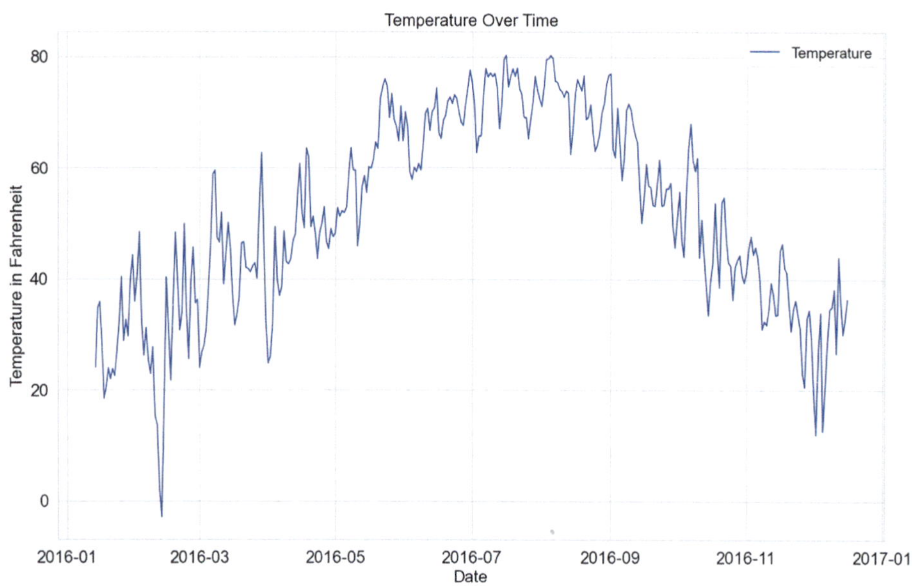

Figure 4.8 Temperature

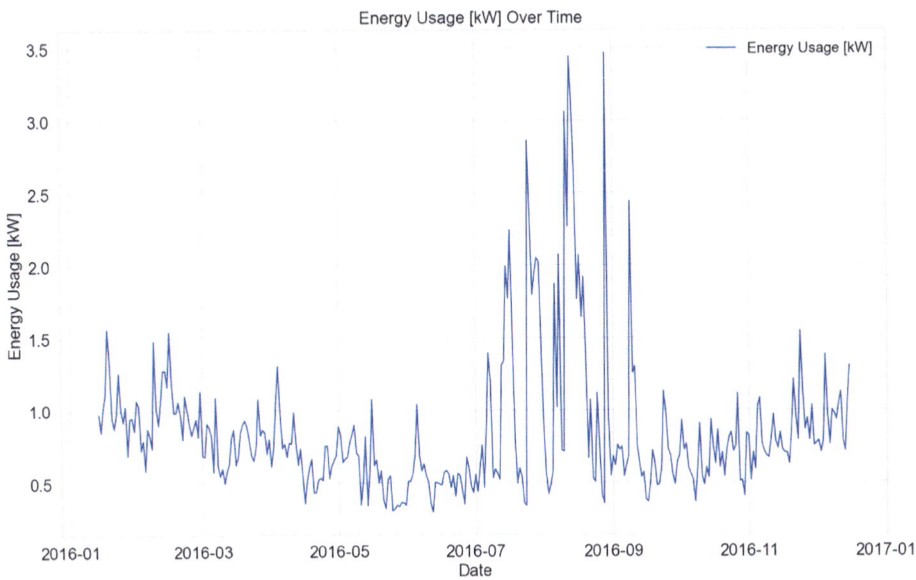

Figure 4.9 Overall Energy

for analyzing real-world phenomena that don't follow strictly linear patterns. In data science applications, polynomial regression shines when dealing with data sets that exhibit nonlinear trends, enabling analysts to **capture intricate patterns** and make more accurate predictions. Its importance lies in its ability to balance model complexity with interpretability, providing insights into how different factors interact across various scales. By employing polynomial terms, data scientists can uncover hidden relationships in their data, leading to more robust models and deeper understanding of underlying processes. This versatility makes polynomial ordinary least squares regression an **essential tool** in a data scientist's toolkit, applicable across diverse fields from economics to environmental science, where understanding nuanced relationships is key to driving informed decision-making and innovation.

```
# ****** GRAPHICS (ADVANCED)      ******
# ****** SCATTER PLOT             ******
# ****** With OLS Line            ******

from sklearn.linear_model import LinearRegression
from sklearn.preprocessing import PolynomialFeatures

# Define the data
X = df[['temperature']].values
y = df[['use_House']].values

# Function to perform and plot linear or polynomial regression
def lin_regplot(X, y, degree=1, save_path=None):
    plt.figure(figsize=(10, 6))

    # Create polynomial features if degree > 1
    if degree > 1:
        poly = PolynomialFeatures(degree)
        X_poly = poly.fit_transform(X)
    else:
        X_poly = X
```

```
    # Fit the model
    slr = LinearRegression()
    slr.fit(X_poly, y)
    y_pred = slr.predict(X_poly)

    # Print the regression parameters
    if degree == 1:
        print('ML Slope: %.3f' % slr.coef_[0][0])
        print('ML Intercept: %.3f' % slr.intercept_[0])
    else:
        print(f'Polynomial Coefficients: {slr.coef_}')
        print(f'Intercept: {slr.intercept_}')

    # Plotting
    sns.scatterplot(x=X.flatten(), y=y.flatten(), s=50, label='Actual Data')
    # Sort the values for a smoother line plot
    sorted_idx = np.argsort(X.flatten())
    X_sorted = X.flatten()[sorted_idx]

    y_pred_sorted = y_pred.flatten()[sorted_idx]

    plt.plot(X_sorted, y_pred_sorted, color='red', linewidth=2, label=f'{degree}-
degree Regression Line')
    plt.title('Temperature vs. Energy Use', fontsize=16)
    plt.xlabel('Temperature (F)', fontsize=14)
    plt.ylabel('Energy Use (kW)', fontsize=14)
    plt.legend()
    plt.grid(True)
    plt.tight_layout()

    # Save the plot if save_path is provided
    if save_path:
        plt.savefig(os.path.join(save_path, 'ols_regression_advanced.png'))

    # Show the plot
    plt.show()
```

From the visual data interpretation seen in Figure 4.10, it is clear that the relationship between energy consumption and external temperature is complex in nature, and any predictive modeling framework needs to incorporate additional features and techniques to account for the "missing" explanatory power.

Part I: Anomaly Detection

From a business perspective, we proceed by applying anomaly detection technique to overall energy consumption, seeking to detect potential breaches in overutilizing the energy consumption at any given time. This can be applied to any home device or IoT sensor. Anomaly detection in data science is a critical process that identifies data points, events, or observations that deviate significantly from the expected pattern in a data set. This powerful technique plays a crucial role in various fields, from fraud detection in financial services to fault diagnosis in industrial systems. Data scientists employ a range of methods to spot anomalies, including statistical approaches, machine learning algorithms, and deep learning models.

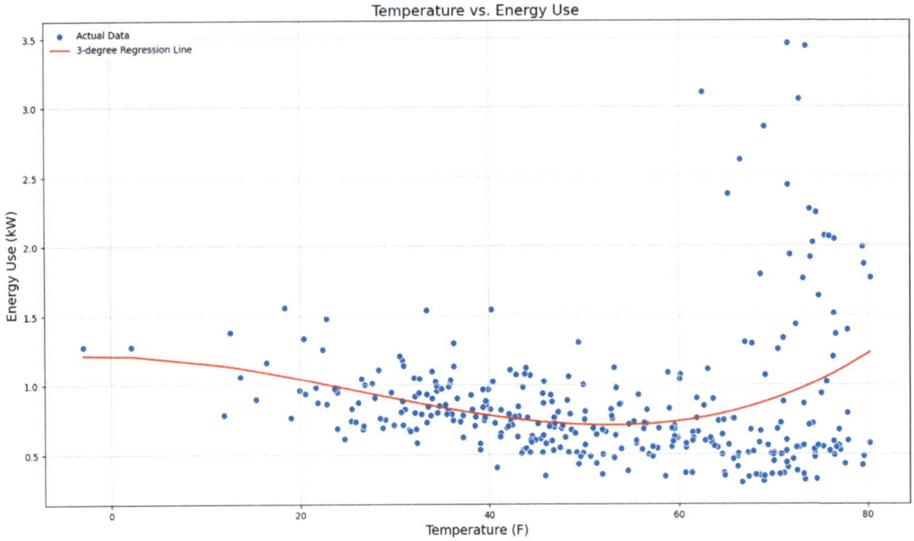

Figure 4.10 External Temperature

These tools can uncover both point anomalies (individual instances) and contextual anomalies (instances anomalous in a specific context). By flagging unusual patterns, anomaly detection helps organizations preemptively address potential issues, optimize processes, and gain valuable insights from their data. As the volume and complexity of data continue to grow, the importance of robust anomaly detection techniques in extracting meaningful information and ensuring data quality cannot be overstated.

```
    @staticmethod
    def mean_absolute_percentage_error(y_true, y_pred):
        """Calculate Mean Absolute Percentage Error"""
        return np.mean(np.abs((y_true - y_pred) / y_true)) * 100

    @staticmethod
    def plotMovingAverage(series, window, plot_intervals=False, scale=1.96,
plot_anomalies=False, filepath=None):
        """
        Plot moving average with optional confidence intervals and anomalies

        :param series: dataframe with timeseries
        :param window: rolling window size
        :param plot_intervals: show confidence intervals
        :param scale: scale for confidence intervals
        :param plot_anomalies: show anomalies
        :param filepath: path to save the plot as a file
        """
        rolling_mean = series.rolling(window=window).mean()

        plt.figure(figsize=(12, 6))
        plt.title(f"Moving average with window size = {window}", fontsize=16)
        plt.plot(rolling_mean, "g", label="Rolling mean trend")
```

```
    # Plot confidence intervals for smoothed values
    if plot_intervals:
        mae = mean_absolute_error(series[window:], rolling_mean[window:])
        deviation = np.std(series[window:] - rolling_mean[window:])
        lower_bond = rolling_mean - (mae + scale * deviation)
        upper_bond = rolling_mean + (mae + scale * deviation)
        plt.plot(upper_bond, "r--", label="Upper Bond / Lower Bond")
        plt.plot(lower_bond, "r--")

        # Having the intervals, find abnormal values
        if plot_anomalies:
            anomalies = series[(series < lower_bond) | (series >
upper_bond)]
            plt.plot(anomalies, "ro", markersize=10)

    plt.plot(series[window:], label="Actual values")
    plt.xlabel('Date', fontsize=16)
    plt.ylabel('Energy Usage [kW]', fontsize=16)
    plt.legend(loc="upper right", fontsize=14)
    plt.xticks(fontsize=16, rotation=45)
    plt.yticks(fontsize=16)
    plt.grid(True)
    # Adjust layout to make room for the rotated x-axis labels
    plt.tight_layout()
    plt.subplots_adjust(bottom=0.2)

    # Save the plot if filepath is provided
    if filepath:
        plt.savefig(filepath)

    plt.show()
```

The anomaly detection technique computes and plots rolling mean using specified window. Then computes mean absolute error (MAE) and standard deviation, calculates upper and lower bounds based on the following:

- lower_bound = rolling_mean – (MAE + scale * deviation)
- upper_bound = rolling_mean – (MAE + scale * deviation)

Then plots bounds as dashed lines and identifies points outside this prespecified confidence interval as depicted in Figure 4.11.

In case of 90% confidence interval the bands are narrow, we are less certain on energy spikes. In other words, we are 90% certain that energy use remains within these bands based on a historical rolling 30-day average.

Part II: ARIMA(p,d,q) Model

Finally, we are in a position to run our ARIMA model to predict the future energy consumption for the entire house/apartment. This is the model we deliver as part of our FinTech application. Delivering predictive pattern into the future to inform our customer about expected energy consumption, relevant costs and carbon footprint profile.

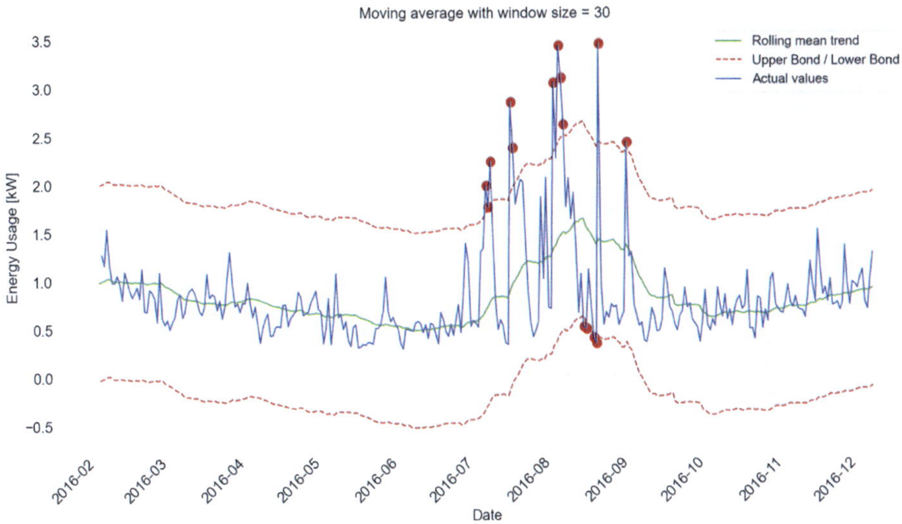

Figure 4.11 Anomaly Detection

```
@staticmethod
    def ARIMAts(data, tt_ratio, idx, filepath=None, plot_all=False):
        """
        Apply ARIMA model for time series prediction

        :param data: dataframe with timeseries data
        :param tt_ratio: train-test split ratio
        :param idx: index for the timeseries data
        :param filepath: path to save the plot as a file
        :param plot_all: plot entire data with train-test split indication
        :return: dataframe with actual and predicted values
        """
        X = data.iloc[:, 0].values
        size = int(len(X) * tt_ratio)
        train, test = X[:size], X[size:]
        history = list(train)
        predictions = []
        for t in range(len(test)):
            model = ARIMA(history, order=(1, 0, 1))
            model_fit = model.fit()
            yhat = model_fit.forecast()[0]
            predictions.append(yhat)
            history.append(test[t])
            print(f'progress: {round(100 * (t / len(test)))}%\t predicted={yhat:.
6f}, expected={test[t]:.6f}', end="\r")

        error = mean_squared_error(test, predictions)
        print(f'\n Test MSE: {error:.3f}')

        # Handle Output
        dfpred = pd.DataFrame(predictions, index=idx[size:], columns=['Predict
ion'])
```

```
        dfact = pd.DataFrame(X, index=idx, columns=['Actual'])
        dfout = dfact.merge(dfpred, how="left", left_index=True,
right_index=True)
        dfp = dfout if plot_all else dfout.dropna()

        # Plotting
        plt.figure(figsize=(12, 6))
        plt.title("ARIMA Model Predictions", fontsize=16)
        plt.plot(dfp.index, dfp['Actual'], color='blue', linewidth=2,
label="Original Data")
        plt.plot(dfp.index, dfp['Prediction'], color='green', linewidth=3,
label="Predicted Data")
        if plot_all:
            plt.axvline(x=dfact.index[size - 1], linewidth=5, color='red')
        plt.xlabel('Date', fontsize=16)
        plt.ylabel('Energy Usage [kW]', fontsize=16)
        plt.legend(loc="upper right", fontsize=14)
        plt.xticks(fontsize=16, rotation=45)
        plt.yticks(fontsize=16)
        plt.grid(True)
        # Adjust layout to make room for the rotated x-axis labels
        plt.tight_layout()
        plt.subplots_adjust(bottom=0.2)

        # Save the plot if filepath is provided
        if filepath:
            plt.savefig(filepath)

        plt.show()

        return dfout
```

ARIMA(1,0,1) is fitted to the energy consumption time-series delivering decent model fit, 9.48% out-of-sample R2, as shown in Figure 4.12.

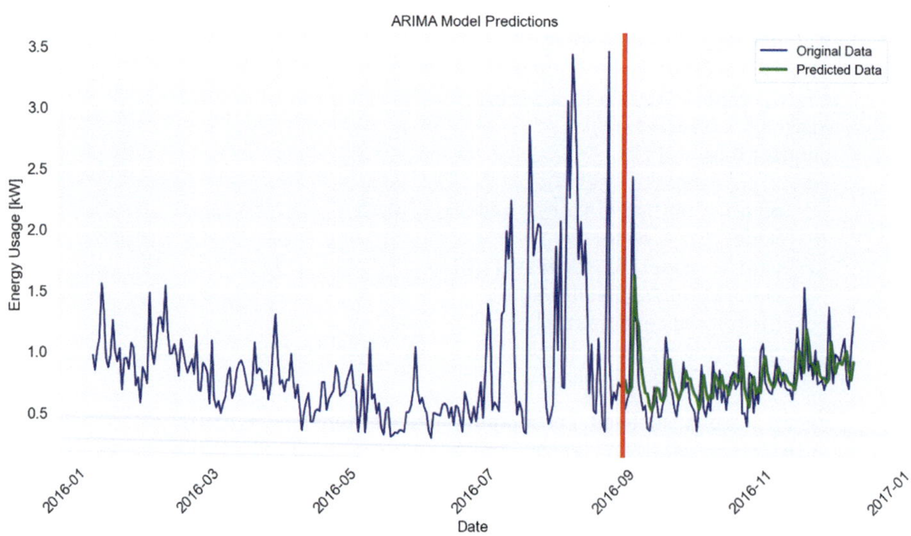

Figure 4.12 ARIMA Predictions

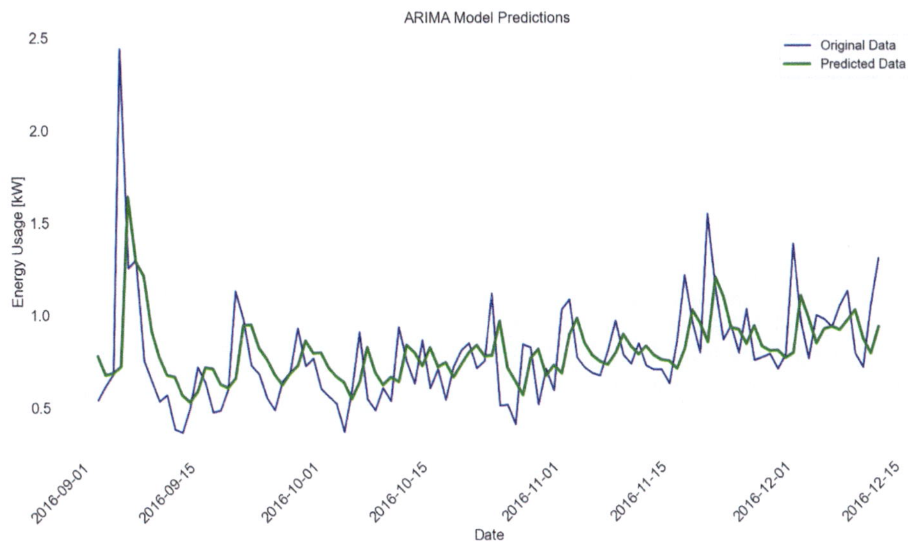

Figure 4.13 ARIMA Hourly

At first glance the predictions (green line) seem to be close to the original data (blue). The following graph in Figure 4.13 depicts hourly data set, out-of-sample only.

Part III: Long-Short Term Memory Neural Networks

Long Short-Term Memory (LSTM) networks have revolutionized the field of data science by addressing the vanishing gradient problem in traditional recurrent neural networks. These sophisticated neural network architectures, designed with a unique cell state and gating mechanism, excel at processing and predicting time series data with long-term dependencies. LSTMs achieve this by selectively remembering or forgetting information over extended sequences, making them invaluable for tasks such as natural language processing, speech recognition, and financial forecasting. In the realm of data science, LSTMs have proven particularly effective for analyzing complex temporal patterns in large data sets, enabling more accurate predictions and insights in fields ranging from stock market analysis to climate modeling. Their ability to capture long-range dependencies in data has made LSTMs an indispensable tool for data scientists tackling sequential data challenges in an increasingly dynamic and data-rich world. We cover LSTM network in the later chapters.

LSTM model requires substantially more data points and observations to be able to deliver on consistent and accurate results. We use hourly data with an excellent out-of-sample 39.43% R2 result showing python script and model fit in Figure 4.14.

```
    @staticmethod
    def LSTM_RNN_Advanced(x_train, x_test, y_train, y_test, index,
filepath=None):
        """
        Build and train an advanced LSTM model with batch normalization and
regularization

        :param x_train: training data features
        :param x_test: test data features
```

```
        :param y_train: training data labels
        :param y_test: test data labels
        :param index: index for the test data
        :param filepath: path to save the plot as a file
        :return: dataframe with actual and predicted values
        """
        model = Sequential()
        model.add(LSTM(units=32, return_sequences=True, input_shape=(x_train.
shape[1], 1)))
        model.add(BatchNormalization())
        model.add(LSTM(units=16))
        model.add(BatchNormalization())
        model.add(Dense(units=1, kernel_regularizer=l1_l2(l1=0.01, l2=0.01)))
# Add L1L2 regularization
        model.compile(optimizer='adam', loss='mean_squared_error')
        model.summary()
        model.fit(x_train, y_train, epochs=64, batch_size=128)

        predictions = model.predict(x_test)
        df = pd.DataFrame(predictions, index=index, columns=['LSTM Predicted
Usage'])
        df['Actual Usage'] = y_test

        # Plotting
        plt.figure(figsize=(12, 6))
        plt.title("LSTM Model Predictions -- Advanced", fontsize=16)
        plt.plot(df['Actual Usage'], color='blue', label='Original Usage')
        plt.plot(df['LSTM Predicted Usage'], color='red', label='Predicted Usage')
        plt.xlabel('Date', fontsize=16)
        plt.ylabel('Energy Usage [kW]', fontsize=16)
        plt.legend(loc="upper right", fontsize=14)
        plt.xticks(fontsize=16, rotation=45)
        plt.yticks(fontsize=16)
        plt.grid(True)
        # Adjust layout to make room for the rotated x-axis labels
        plt.tight_layout()
        plt.subplots_adjust(bottom=0.2)

        # Save the plot if filepath is provided
        if filepath:
            plt.savefig(filepath)

        plt.show()

        return df
```

We discuss LSTM from theoretical standpoint in later chapters. Briefly we utilize sequential model 64 epochs Adam optimizer with mean square error benchmark, in this case. More on the LSTM model design later.

4.7 Station 4: Implementation

Software design and implementation play a crucial role in the rapidly evolving FinTech industry. In this sector, where financial services meet cutting-edge technology, robust software architecture is paramount to ensure security, scalability, and regulatory compliance. Fintech

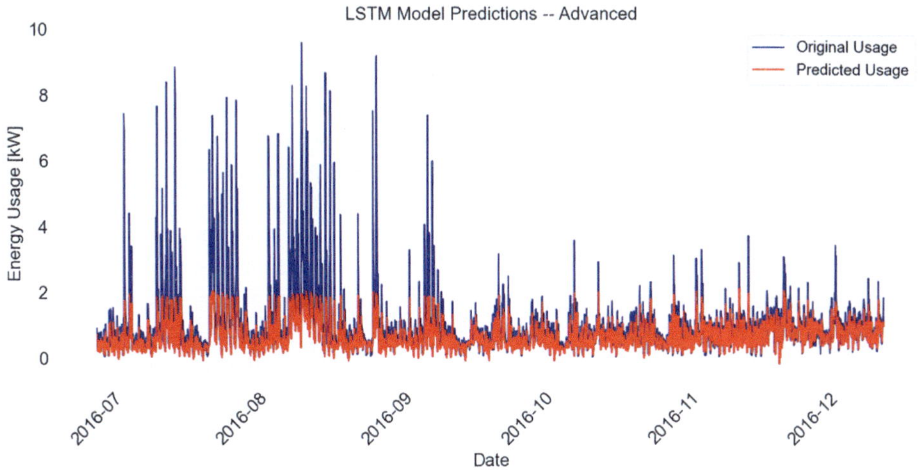

Figure 4.14 LSTM Hourly

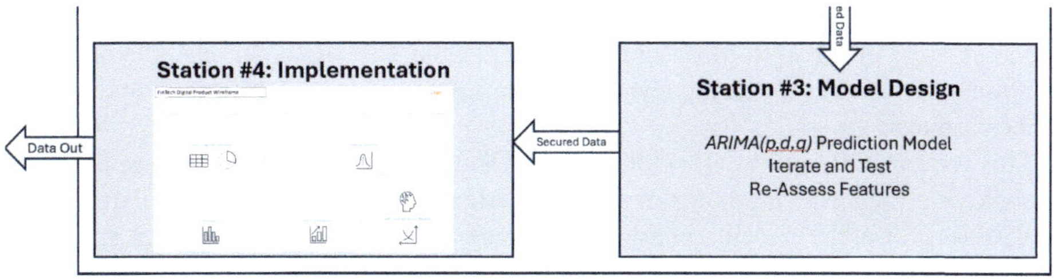

Figure 4.15 Implementation Station 4

applications often require real-time processing capabilities, integration with legacy banking systems, and the ability to handle large volumes of sensitive data. Implementing these designs presents unique challenges, such as maintaining data integrity across distributed systems and ensuring seamless user experiences across multiple platforms. Moreover, FinTech software must be adaptable to ever-changing financial regulations and market conditions. As the industry continues to disrupt traditional banking, effective software design and implementation remain key drivers of innovation and success in the FinTech landscape.

As per Figure 4.15, station 4. Implementation forms a "glue" to our solution. It is here that we bring all the results together and focus on customer journey. Items and results that matter and are of relevance to our customers.

We have started our data science and FinTech journey in *Station 1. Data Lake*, processed vast amount of data and filtered and required features in *Station 2. Prompt and Feature Engineering*. Then, we invested considerable amount of time on understanding the nature of the business and building modeling frameworks to handle the solutions in *Station 3. Model Design*. Lastly, in this final station we deliver on our first FinTech application design. The intention is to deliver wireframes and Python scripts to our Technology Teams and Product Design Teams. Ultimately, this is the space where we meet customer's journey and requirements.

FIGMA

As mentioned in Chapter 3, FIGMA, traditionally known as a collaborative interface design tool, has found a surprising ally in the realm of data science. This versatile platform is revolutionizing how data scientists approach visualization and collaboration. By leveraging FIGMA's intuitive design capabilities, data professionals can create stunning, interactive dashboards and infographics that bring complex data to life. Further to FIGMA use, **wireframes** play a crucial role in the data science workflow, serving as low-fidelity visual representations of data-driven interfaces and dashboards. These skeletal blueprints allow data scientists to **map out the structure and functionality** of their analytical tools before diving into full-scale development. By utilizing wireframes, data professionals can effectively communicate complex data relationships and user interactions, ensuring that stakeholders have a clear understanding of the proposed solution. Wireframes in data science often incorporate placeholders for key elements such as charts, graphs, and interactive components, enabling teams to **iterate quickly on design concepts** without the overhead of detailed data visualization. This approach not only streamlines the development process but also helps in identifying potential usability issues early on, ultimately leading to more intuitive and user-friendly data products. As data science projects become increasingly complex, wireframes serve as an invaluable tool for bridging the gap between raw data insights and actionable, user-centric analytics platforms.

In our use case, a simple drawing with a pen and paper would be sufficient to depict the necessary steps of the customer's journey. Next, Figure 4.16 shows an example of a simple wireframe dashboard showcasing few critical summary data to be highlighted and delivered to the customer:

This version adds results derived from our DDF. Hence, implementation stage is designed to implement the FinTech product or service offering directly to the customer. Part III of this book uses real-world FinTech scenarios to showcase several variations of design studios and implementation steps.

FIGMA, on the other hand, allows for advanced design generation and team collaboration as seen in Figure 4.17. As a result and as opposed to a simple wireframe sketch, FIGMA

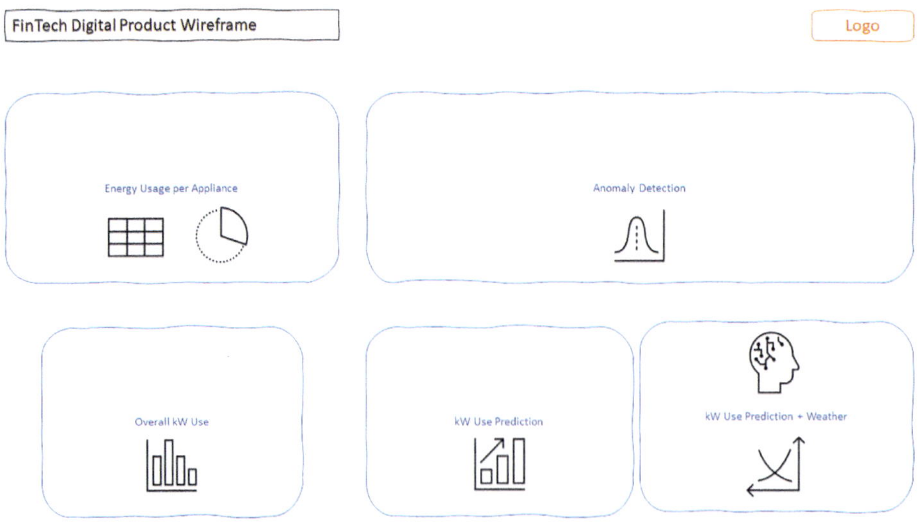

Figure 4.16 Empty Wireframes

Figure 4.17 Filled Wireframes in FIGMA Digital Device

allows for dynamic features to be incorporate in the design. In actual fact, it is possible to design the entire visual interpretation of the FinTech solution within web as well as app-based replication.

Streamlit

At this stage, we do not wish to build the entire IoT solution prototype. The purpose is to provide base and core background techniques to enhance your capabilities to be able to do so. Later chapters of this book demonstrate Streamlit in more realistic scenarios, such as use of Robo-Advisory platforms. The next Python snippet showcases an expansion of our previous Station #1 code flow and adds the capabilities of Streamlit into the mix.

```
import streamlit as st
import pandas as pd
import numpy as np

etl_path = r'HomeC.csv'
export_path = r'DDF_Station_1.csv'

def Station1_loadData(etl_path, export_path):
    """
    Stage 1: Extract, Transform, Load (ETL)
    Process data load post extract and transfer phases
    :return: df cleansed dataset
    """

    ## LOAD VARIATION #1: Direct file from your internal file system
```

```
    # This file is read-only and can NOT be changed as this is the original
source of truth
    # Load the CSV file into a DataFrame
    df = pd.read_csv(etl_path, delimiter=',', low_memory=False)

    ## CLEANSING: Clean dataset to be ready for handover to Station #2
    # Remove the last row as it has a "/" error
    df = df.iloc[:-1]

    # Check for NaN / Infs etc.
    df = df.replace([np.Inf, -np.Inf], np.NaN)
    df = df.dropna()

    # Rename columns by removing '[kW]'
    df.columns = [col.replace(' [kW]', '') for col in df.columns]

    # Convert the 'time' column to datetime format
    df['time'] = pd.to_datetime(df['time'].astype(int), unit='s')
    df['time'] = pd.DatetimeIndex(pd.date_range('2016-01-01 05:00',
periods=len(df),  freq='min'))

    # Set the day of the week
    df['day_of_week'] = df.reset_index()['time'].dt.day_name()

    # Set the index
    df = df.set_index(['time'])

    # Remove duplicate timestamps and keep only the last value
    df = df[~df.index.duplicated(keep='last')]

    # Fix errors in 'cloudCover' column
    df['cloudCover'] = pd.to_numeric(df['cloudCover'], errors='coerce')
    df['cloudCover'] = df['cloudCover'].bfill()

    # Export cleaned data to CSV file
    # Stage 1 Complete
    df.to_csv(export_path)

    return df

st.write("IoT App: Station #1 Data ETL Sandbox")
st.subheader("Visual Interpretation of Station #1 ETL utilizing basic plot
Streamlit function."
             "With Streamlit, you can effortlessly create web apps for your data
projects, "
             "allowing you to showcase and derive insights in real-time.
Streamlit's intuitive i"
             "nterface makes it a breeze to build everything from simple data
displays to "
             "sophisticated machine learning models.")

######## Execute the functions    ########
######## Station 1                ########
file_path   = r'HomeC.csv' # Add your file path here
export_path = r'kaggle_raw_stage_1.csv' # Add your file path here

# execute station 1 sequence
df = Station1_loadData(etl_path, export_path)

# resample base enegry usage data to daily frequency
```

```
dfD = df['use'].resample('D').mean()

# prepare a simple non-interactive chart and data view using Streamlit
line_chart()
tab1, tab2 = st.tabs(["Energy Usage", "Dataframe"])
tab1.line_chart(dfD, height=550)
tab2.dataframe(dfD, height=550, use_container_width=True)
```

This code, once executed, delivers on a simple web based application, as shown in Figure 4.18:

The screen delivered, IoT Dashboard Station #1, is a light version as this is not interactive in a form of data inputs and data outputs. This is to showcase a simple non-interactive use of Streamlit. The code snippet comprises of two components, (i) Station #1 code function encapsulating the DDF concept of ETL and (ii) actual web app control components with executable code sequence.

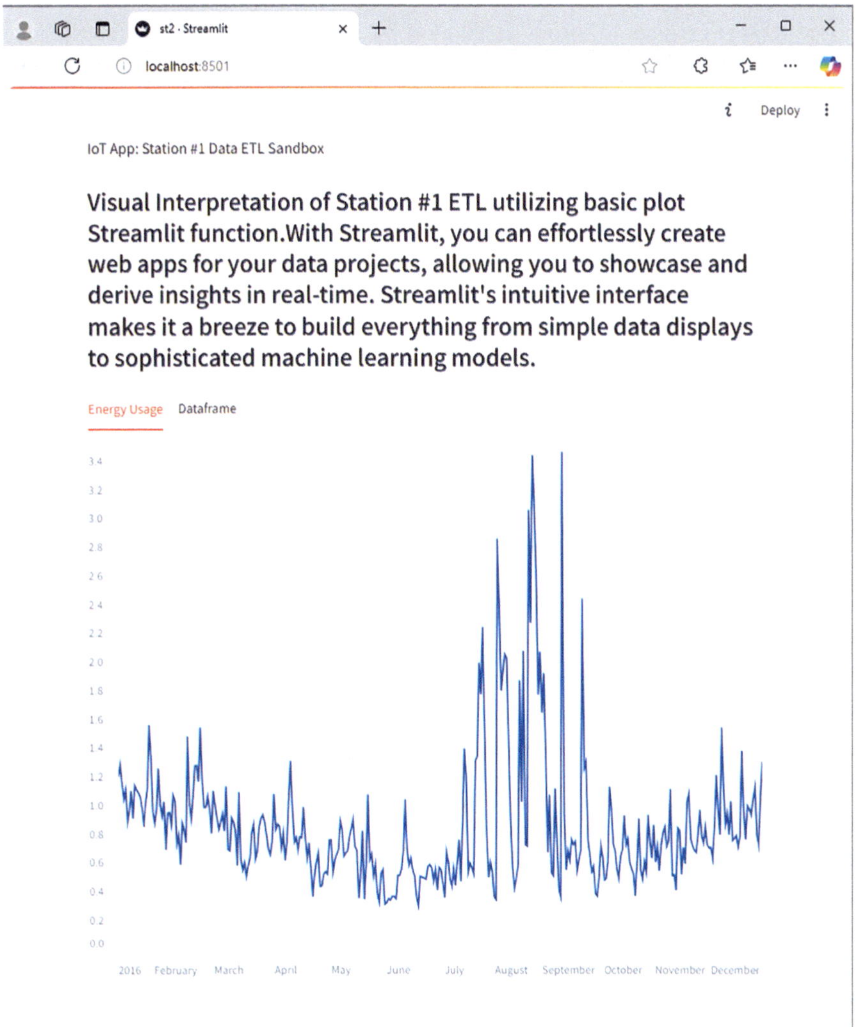

Figure 4.18 IoT App Streamlit Light Version

```
######## Execute the functions    ########
######## Station 1                ########
file_path   = r'HomeC.csv' # Add your file path here
export_path = r'kaggle_raw_stage_1.csv' # Add your file path here

# execute station 1 sequence

df = Station1_loadData(etl_path, export_path)

# resample base enegry usage data to daily frequency
dfD = df['use'].resample('D').mean()

# prepare a simple non-interactive chart and data view using Streamlit
line_chart()
tab1, tab2 = st.tabs(["Energy Usage", "Dataframe"])
tab1.line_chart(dfD, height=550)
tab2.dataframe(dfD, height=550, use_container_width=True)
```

The code snippet extracts "d'" from the Station #1 and then we control extract of a feature "use" directly to pass downstream to be exposed to Streamlit library and eventually exposed on a screen to the user. In later chapters we connect all DDF stations and utilize LLM internal capabilities to expedite and build powerful components to our FinTech solutions.

4.8 Summary

This chapter dives into the implementation of the **digital data factory (DDF)** concept, emphasizing the crucial role of data modeling in data science for effective analysis and decision-making. It highlights how robust data models provide a structured framework for interpreting vast amounts of information, crucial in today's data-driven landscape. The advent of artificial intelligence (AI) models, especially large language models (LLMs), has revolutionized data modeling by enabling the extraction of meaningful insights and automation of complex tasks. The chapter particularly focuses on the synergy between traditional data modeling and cutting-edge AI technologies, showcasing its application in FinTech. By breaking down the data modeling and application development process into logical "stations," it introduces readers to new techniques for using AI tools, enhancing clarity and accuracy in prompt engineering.

The chapter utilizes revolutionary concept of the **Internet of Things (IoT)**, which is transforming our interaction with technology by connecting everyday devices to the internet. This vast network of interconnected devices enables real-time monitoring and decision-making across various sectors, from *smart homes* to *industrial automation*. In residential settings, IoT applications like **smart thermostats**, **energy meters** and **home automation systems** are enhancing comfort and environmental awareness by providing real-time data on energy consumption and enabling centralized control. A specific use case in the FinTech sector is highlighted, where IoT data is used to deliver hypothetical energy consumption predictions, helping users understand their energy usage, carbon footprint, and cost structure. This integration empowers individuals to make informed decisions, contributing to a more sustainable future.

Furthermore, this chapter concludes Section I of the book, delivering base concepts as encapsulated in the digital data factory (DDF) and FinTech toolkit in terms of Python code snippets, methodologies and steps necessary to form a concise solution to a complex problems faced by FinTech operators. The following Section II of the book introduces the reader to theoretical modeling frameworks used by finance and FinTech practitioners. The emphasis is placed on the practical nature of these new techniques. We elevate the critical importance of data governance and AI ethics as core components in any FinTech solution.

4.9 Exercises

Exercise 4.1

Based on the Streamlit application introduced in this chapter, add interactive components to Station #1 to the IoT App.

- Add data input button
- Add refresh button
- Add toggle button to select "M" monthly and "D" daily frequency

Exercise 4.2

Based on the Streamlit application introduced in this chapter, add interactive components to Station #1 to the IoT App.

- Add additional tab "Correlation"
- Add the results of this Python code to the tab

Exercise 4.3

Based on the Streamlit application introduced in this chapter, add interactive components to Station #1 to the IoT App. Use AI Co-Pilot of your choice and upload abbreviated "HomeC.csv" file (limited to 1,000 rows of data). Prompt the Co-Pilot to extract 'col["use"]' as per our Station #1 exercise, then prompt the Co-Pilot to return Streamlit version of Python code. Compare and contract Co-Pilot results. Focus on accuracy!

4.10 Further Reading

- Dickerson, A., & Hric, J. (2024). FINS5545 Financial Market Data Literacy Course Notes, UNSW Business School.
- Gamma, E., Helm, R., Johnson, R., & Vlissides, J. (1995). Design Patterns, Addison Wesley.
- Kleppmann, M. (2017). Designing Data-Intensive Applications, O'Reilly.

4.11 References

[4.1] NumPy: https://numpy.org/
[4.2] Kaggle: https://www.kaggle.com/datasets/taranvee/smart-home-dataset-with-weather-information

SECTION 2

Advanced Tools for Finance and FinTech

Chapter 5

Bitcoin and Tokenization

5.1 Introduction

This chapter kicks off the Section 2 of this book, which covers theoretical and mathematical interpretation of ML and AI modeling frameworks. This second section introduces fundamental supervised and unsupervised learning algorithms that can add value in finance and banking applications. In the context of the DDF concept, this section focuses on *DDF Model Selection* phase. However, in this chapter we introduce state-of-the-art tokenization approach and then, in the proceeding chapters, various unsupervised learning techniques to extract high-quality signals and information from key source of alternative data, limited to text data format throughout the rest of the book.

DOI: 10.4324/9781003477747-7

This chapter starts with the introduction to **blockchain**, technology with a potential utility across finance and banking use cases. Then, we proceed and discuss **bitcoin** and further the notion of tokenization within the **decentralized finance (DeFi)** framework. Then, we expose the reader to practical examples of utilizing smart contracts from programmatic perspective. We use **Ethereum** platform with its own Solidity language to build a smart contract application using Python scripting sequences. The focus of this chapter is on the process of asset tokenization in order to build a foundational understanding to be applied at a later stage of the book. Finally, we provide a number of contra-arguments relevant to exposing deficiencies in blockchain-based technologies to be aware of from a practitioner's standpoint.

Learning Outcomes

- Introduce blockchain technology
- Outline the concepts behind decentralization
- Explain CeFi and DeFi
- Understand how smart contracts can fit into FinTech solution
- Overview alternative assets and tokenization
- Explore relevant legal repercussions and dilemmas

5.2 Blockchain

A blockchain is a shared database or digital ledger that records information across a computer network. The system does not keep data in one place. Instead, it shares similar copies of this ledger with multiple participants, called nodes. The name "blockchain" comes from its data structure – information gets grouped into "blocks" linked together in a "chain" through cryptographic techniques. Each new block has a cryptographic hash (a unique string of numbers and letters) of the previous block [5.1]. This creates a continuous, connected sequence depicted in Figure 5.1.

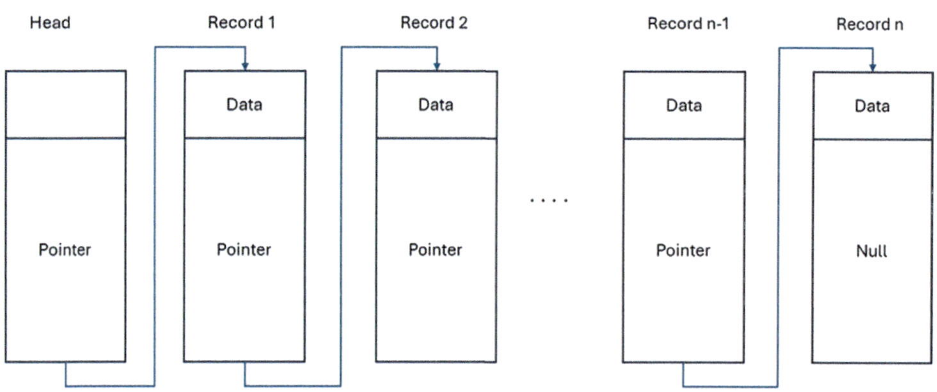

Figure 5.1 Hash Pointer

Blockchain's revolutionary aspect lies in its operation. The network's computers must verify and approve any new information through consensus. This verified data becomes permanent and almost impossible to change with three core features:

1. **Decentralized** – no single authority controls the entire system
2. **Distributed** – multiple copies exist across the computer network
3. **Immutable** – once recorded, information is practically impossible to change

This setup creates a system where participants trust the data without needing to trust each other. The system makes secure transactions possible between parties without an intermediary like a bank or government to verify their exchange.

The main difference between blockchain and traditional databases lies in their structure and control methods. Traditional databases have a central authority (usually an administrator) that manages, updates and secures all information. Two businesses rarely share a single database because it raises trust issues – the database's controller could change records without the other party's knowledge. Blockchain changes this setup completely. Each participant keeps their own copy of the entire record history. The network spots and fixes any inconsistencies automatically when someone tries to change information. Here are the key architectural differences:

- **Control** – Traditional databases use a centralized client/server model where one entity has full control. Blockchain uses a peer-to-peer network that distributes control among all participants.
- **Data structure** – Databases organize information in tables with rows and columns. Blockchain arranges data in chronologically ordered blocks connected through cryptographic hashes.
- **Security** – Traditional databases can add encryption, but it is optional. Blockchain builds in cryptography from the start, making it naturally more secure.
- **Modification capability** – Authorized database users can edit or delete existing data. Blockchain only allows new information, previous records stay unchanged, creating a permanent history.

Blockchain creates trust through technology rather than institutions. Companies using blockchain do not need to trust each other; they can trust the system itself. The blockchain immediately shows who tried to make unauthorized changes if either party attempts to alter records. This unchangeable and transparent nature makes blockchain valuable for applications needing high security, verifiable histories, or coordination between parties who might not completely trust each other.

How Blockchain Works

From the DDF perspective, for a FinTech practitioner, is it important to understand the details behind this design. In the first phase *DDF Extract, Transfer and Load* we deal with the initial data harvest, data processing and data storing. This is the source of truth. Blockchain is yet another form of processing data structures and delivering added functionality ultimately delivering on final FinTech product. In this sense, blockchain is a digital record-keeping that happens in four steps:

1. **Record transactions as blocks.** A blockchain transaction starts when it broadcasts to all computers (nodes) in the network. These transactions hold vital information like the sender's identity, digital signature, public key and the amount of data moving across. The transactions don't go straight into the blockchain. They sit in a temporary space called a memory pool or "mempool." The system groups these transactions into what we call a block as they pile up over time. The block can hold about 4MB of transactions, gets sealed and moves to the next step once it fills up with verified transactions.
2. **Link blocks using cryptography.** The system creates a unique identifier for each block after it fills with data. This happens through a cryptographic hash function that turns the block's contents into a fixed-length string of characters – the hash. The smart part of blockchain's design shows up in the block connections. Every new block carries the previous block's hash in its header. This creates an unbreakable chain. Any changes to a block's content would change its hash value and clash with the next block's reference. In short, if someone tampers with block #30's data, its hash changes. So block #31, which holds block #30's hash, spots this mismatch right away. This cryptographic linking makes the blockchain highly resistant to tampering and forms the foundations of its security.
3. **Achieve consensus through network validation.** The blockchain network needs to agree on valid transactions and the next block to add. This agreement process, called consensus, sits at the heart of blockchain operation. Blockchain networks use consensus algorithms to reach agreement without central control. The system works like this: Miners (specialized super-computers) compete to solve a complex math puzzle. They search for a specific hash value by adjusting a "nonce" number. The first miner to find a solution below a target value wins the right to add the block.
4. **Other nodes check if the solution works.** This process makes sure everyone agrees on the same blockchain version, which stops fraud and double-spending. On top of that, some blockchains use different methods like Proof of Stake (PoS), where validators get picked based on their token holdings.
5. **Finalize and distribute the ledger.** The new block joins the blockchain permanently after everyone agrees and verifies it. Several things happen at this point. The winning miner or validator gets cryptocurrency as a reward – *this creates new coins in many blockchain systems.* Then the updated blockchain goes out to all network nodes so everyone has the same ledger copy. The transaction wraps up, but networks often wait for more blocks as extra proof. Bitcoin usually needs six confirmations (about an hour) before a transaction settles fully. Once recorded, nobody can change the transaction. They would need to control over 51% of the network's computing power to even try.

5.3 Bitcoin

Bitcoin's trip started on August 18, 2008, when someone registered the *bitcoin.org* domain. The real story began on October 31, 2008. A mysterious person called Satoshi Nakamoto wrote a game-changing whitepaper, "*Bitcoin: A Peer-to-Peer Electronic Cash System.*" This nine-page document showed how to create digital money without banks [5.2]. Bitcoin's operational framework rests on blockchain technology. This public ledger records all confirmed transactions. Bitcoin differs from traditional financial systems because it operates on a decentralized network where miners compete to solve complex mathematical puzzles.

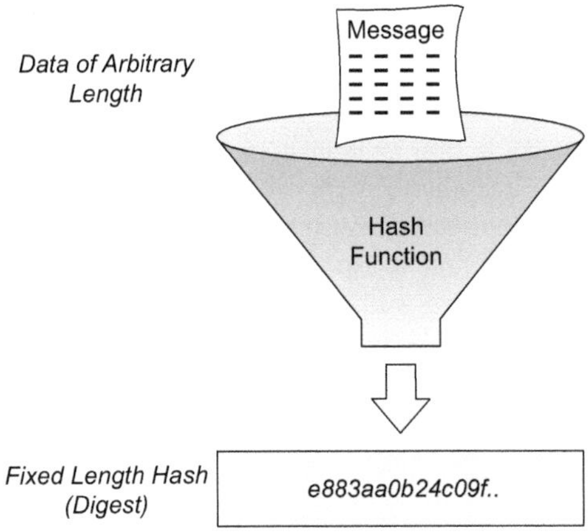

Figure 5.2 Hash Generator

How Bitcoin Works

As per our previous discussion about blockchain mechanism, Bitcoin mining acts as a distributed consensus system that validates pending transactions and adds them to the blockchain. Miners solve cryptographic puzzles with specialized hardware through the SHA-256 hashing algorithm, as shown in Figure 5.2. The process demands computational resources, and the Bitcoin network currently hashes at approximately 569.29 exahashes per second as of May 2024 [5.3].

Miners start by gathering pending transactions from the mempool to create new blocks. Each block stores transaction data in a 4MB file. The process continues as miners adjust a "nonce" number until they discover a hash value below the network's difficulty target. The target adjusts every 2016 blocks to keep an average block time of ten minutes. Miners broadcast their solutions to the network after finding a valid hash. The network adds the new block to the blockchain after validation, and miners receive 3.125 bitcoins plus transaction fees. The block reward drops by half about every four years, with the latest halving happening in April 2024. The Proof-of-Work consensus mechanism protects network security by making attacks too expensive. A theoretical risk called a "51% attack" might happen if someone controlled more than half of the network's mining power. This makes such attempts financially unfeasible for larger networks.

Proof of work is driven by miners (super-computers) competing to solve an intentionally difficult puzzle (imagine a physical gold mine operation that is rather complex and costly investment for a mining company to execute) [5.4]. In order to create a block, the miner that proposes that block is required to find a number (nonce), as described previously, that when concatenated with the previous hash, and the list of transactions that comprise that block and take the hash of this whole string, then that hash output should be a number less some target:

$$h(nonce \| previoushash \| text \| text \| \ldots \| text) < target$$

Bitcoin maintains security, decentralization and immutability without central authority through this elegant system of cryptographic puzzles and economic incentives. Bitcoin's value comes from its lack of supply (there will only ever be 21 million coins) and how many people want to buy it. There is no inherent intrinsic value of Bitcoin per se. Unlike regular money, no government backs Bitcoin – it becomes valuable as more people use it and find it useful. Professional investors now look at it as a way to spread risk and protect against inflation. Bitcoin stands as a challenge to traditional banking. People who support it see it as "digital gold" that gives financial power back to regular people instead of central banks.

Bitcoin will change without doubt, especially as miners approach the last coins around 2140. Whether it ends up as digital gold, a payment system or a revolutionary idea, Bitcoin has changed how we think about money in today's digital world.

5.4 Decentralization

The notion of decentralization is at the core of blockchain technology. Traditional systems keep data in one place under one authority's control. Blockchain does things differently – it spreads similar copies of its ledger across many computers in a network. This makes the system tough to tamper with. The network of computers must verify new transactions instead of a central authority. This process, called consensus, lets everyone agree on what's in the ledger without needing middlemen like banks or governments.

Decentralized finance (DeFi) represents a new peer-to-peer financial system that uses blockchain and cryptocurrencies. Users can make direct transactions without traditional intermediaries. DeFi creates an open financial sector that runs on software built on public blockchains, with Ethereum leading the way.

The core principles that define DeFi include the following:

- **Decentralization** – The system runs without central control. Network participants share power, which encourages security and democratic decision-making.
- **Transparency** – The blockchain makes all transactions and smart contract code public. Anyone can verify and audit transactions.
- **Permissionless access** – You can participate with just an internet connection and compatible wallet, whatever your location or traditional banking status.
- **Trustless transactions** – Blockchain technology guarantees security so parties can transact without mutual trust.

Smart contracts are the foundations of DeFi. These self-executing codes automate financial arrangements and enforce agreement terms without middlemen. This automation recreates traditional financial instruments in an open, decentralized space.

How DeFi Is Different From Traditional Finance

Traditional finance depends on centralized institutions like banks as gatekeepers. DeFi works through peer-to-peer networks that remove these middlemen. So transactions that took days in traditional systems now finish in minutes.

Traditional finance requires users to trust institutions with their funds and transactions. DeFi gives users direct control over their assets through smart contracts. This change enables complete financial autonomy and helps solve problems that traditional banks don't deal very well with.

DeFi makes financial services available to more people by removing barriers. Traditional banks might deny services based on various factors. DeFi platforms work without restrictions and are available to anyone with internet access.

DeFi removes fees that banks and other financial institutions typically charge. On top of that, it lets parties negotiate interest rates directly and lend cryptocurrency through DeFi networks.

Based on the Auer et al. (2023) paper, DeFi can be defined as follows:

> Definition 1 Decentralized Finance (DeFi) is a competitive, contestable, composable and non-custodial financial ecosystem built on technology that does not require a central organization to operate and that has no safety net. It consists of financial protocols – implemented as "smart contracts" – running on a network of computers to automatically manage financial transactions. Implemented on top of DLT, it does not require banks or other traditional centralized intermediaries. The underlying ecosystem is competitive as novel intermediaries – miners or validators – compete to process and settle transactions. Users can choose from different financial protocols; these are contestable as anyone can become an intermediary or deploy a protocol or even start a new ledger; composable as complex services can be assembled from basic protocols; and non-custodial as users can keep direct custody of their assets when accessing financial services. DeFi does not come with any safety net as it lacks protection from criminal conduct or investor fraud and erroneous transactions cannot be undone.

According to the authors, DeFi represents a transformative shift in financial services, utilizing distributed ledger technologies to deliver functions such as lending, investing, and cryptoasset exchange – *all without traditional centralized intermediaries*. These services are executed through a variety of DeFi protocols, which operate as collections of **smart contracts** – automated software programs that replicate conventional financial logic [5.5].

Rather than engaging directly with counterparties, users interact with these smart contracts, which aggregate resources from multiple participants while allowing individuals to retain control over their funds.

What Is Decentralized Finance vs Centralized Finance

Centralized finance (CeFi) includes traditional banking, stock markets, bond markets, and similar institutions under central authorities. DeFi moves trust from institutions to code and foundational technology.

CeFi builds trust through government oversight and legal frameworks. DeFi creates trust through transparent blockchain technology and permanent transaction records. CeFi uses private records of intermediaries. DeFi records all contracts and transactions on public blockchains.

CeFi institutions must follow **strict** know-your-customer (KYC) regulations. DeFi allows relative anonymity. In spite of that, DeFi transactions remain traceable even without personal names. CeFi works through trusted third parties that control financial activities. DeFi utilizes smart contracts and blockchain to automate processes. This basic difference creates a system where users trust the code instead of institutions.

DeFi Crypto Wallets and User Access

Users need special crypto wallets to use DeFi applications. Unlike banks that hold your money, DeFi wallets let you control your funds directly.

DeFi wallets come in two main types:

1. **Self-custody wallets**: You control everything through private keys or seed phrases and connect straight to DeFi protocols.
2. **Custodial wallets**: Exchanges manage these wallets and keep control of the private keys.

Your journey into what is DeFi in crypto starts with a self-custody wallet. These non-custodial wallets open the door to the DeFi ecosystem and let you

- Link to dApps through browser extensions or mobile apps
- Confirm transactions from your wallet
- Keep full control of your assets with private keys
- Use your funds on different devices with your recovery phrase

Users work with DeFi through decentralized applications (dApps). You don't need to create accounts like traditional banking apps – just connect your wallet. After a quick approval, you can start using lending platforms, decentralized exchanges or yield farming protocols. Your wallet serves as both your DeFi identity and security system. You do not need usernames or passwords, but your assets stay safe. We do not venture further into DeFi protocols in this chapter. Before using some practical coding examples or tokenization processes, it is constructive to expose stable coins.

Stable Coins

Based on Ma et al. (2023) study, the authors explore the **economic design and risks** of fiat-backed stablecoins, particularly focusing on **USDT (Tether)** and **USDC (Circle)**. Despite price stability mechanisms via arbitrage, stablecoins remain **vulnerable to runs**, especially if users lose confidence in their redeemability. Like ETFs, most investors trade stablecoins in secondary markets, while only a few arbitrageurs can redeem them directly with issuers at $1 [5.6].

- **Price stability vs. run risk tradeoff**: More efficient arbitrage narrows price fluctuations but increases the chance of investor panic and mass redemptions.
- **Arbitrage concentration** varies: USDT has fewer, more dominant arbitrageurs, leading to larger price deviations; USDC has a more competitive structure and lower price volatility.
- **Reserve asset quality matters**: More illiquid reserves (e.g., corporate bonds) raise redemption risks during stress events.
- **Regulatory classification constraints**: Stablecoins don't pay dividends to avoid being classified as securities, but doing so could reduce run risk and enhance price stability.

The authors develop a model showing that **panic-driven runs are possible** and that **design choices like arbitrage efficiency and dividend policies** critically influence stability.

Empirical data confirms non-trivial run probabilities for both USDT and USDC, though these risks have declined over time.

The stablecoin ecosystem has grown into four distinct categories. Each category uses different ways to keep prices stable in the volatile cryptocurrency market.

Fiat-Backed: USDT, USDC and TrueUSD

Fiat-backed stablecoins now dominate the digital world. They make up about 87% of all stablecoins in circulation. These digital tokens keep their value through a simple 1:1 backing with traditional currencies like the US dollar. The system works by holding one dollar in reserve for every stablecoin issued.

Tether (USDT) stands at the top with over $94.80 billion in market value. Its backing comes from USD reserves (83.89%), secured loans (5.36%), precious metals (3.95%), Bitcoin (3.81%), and other investments (2.97%) [5.7]. USD Coin (USDC), the second-largest stablecoin, matches its value with US dollar assets and releases detailed monthly checks by Deloitte. TrueUSD (TUSD) goes a step further with daily attestations that prove their reserves match the tokens in circulation.

People widely adopt fiat-backed stablecoins because they

- Work reliably over long periods
- Provide high liquidity across platforms
- Run on simple mechanisms
- Follow regulatory compliance and audits

Crypto-Backed: DAI and Wrapped BTC

Crypto-backed stablecoins use other cryptocurrencies as collateral through blockchain smart contracts. These stablecoins need extra collateral to handle market swings, unlike their fiat-backed cousins.

DAI, from MakerDAO, shows how a decentralized stablecoin can stay close to the US dollar's value. DAI doesn't rely on just one cryptocurrency. It uses many types of collateral including Ethereum, Bitcoin and others. Smart contracts called Maker collateral vaults lock these assets and make sure the collateral value stays higher than the DAI issued.

Wrapped Bitcoin (WBTC) offers another approach to crypto-backed stablecoins. It matches Bitcoin's value exactly on the Ethereum blockchain. This lets Bitcoin work with Ethereum-based apps while keeping Bitcoin's price.

Commodity-Backed: Gold-Pegged Tokens

Commodity-backed stablecoins get their value from physical assets, usually gold. Each token lets you own a specific amount of the commodity, which stays in secure vaults with regular audits.

Pax Gold (PAXG) leads this category. One token equals one troy ounce of gold kept in London Bullion Market Association vaults. They release monthly reports where auditors check the reserves. Tether Gold (XAUT) works similarly and lets holders exchange tokens for real gold. They currently have about 246,524.33 fine troy ounces backing their tokens.

Algorithmic: TerraUSD and USDD

Algorithmic stablecoins keep their value through smart contracts instead of using assets as backing. They use computer programs to control supply based on demand, similar to central banks.

TerraUSD (UST) became a warning story in this space. Once the third-largest stablecoin, it relied on its partner token LUNA to stay at one dollar. May 2022 saw UST crash from $1 to 10 cents. LUNA fell from $182.73 to almost nothing, and $68.80 billion in market value disappeared. USDD, Tron's algorithmic stablecoin, faced similar problems. It lost its dollar peg on June 13, 2022, showing the risks these automatic stabilizing systems carry.

5.5 Smart Contracts

From tokenization perspective, smart contracts are in our focus. Smart contracts are different from regular digital documents. They work as self-executing programs that take action automatically when certain conditions are met on a blockchain network. Once deployed, they run without human input and create a trustless environment where parties don't need to know each other. In short, smart contracts are computer programs that live on a blockchain and run predefined actions based on coded rules.

These digital agreements run by themselves on decentralized systems. They remove the need for middlemen like lawyers, banks or escrow agents. The code becomes unchangeable after deployment on networks like Ethereum. This unchangeable nature will give all participants confidence that the contract runs exactly as programmed. Basically, smart contracts turn trust from human relationships into mathematical certainty through code. They connect applications with the blockchain ledger and turn business logic into actual operations.

The code in smart contracts follows simple "if/when . . . then" statements. These statements are the foundations of how they work:

1. **Contract Creation**: Users decide how blockchain will show their transactions and agree on rules. Developers code these rules using special languages like Solidity (for Ethereum) [5.8].
2. **Deployment**: Someone uploads the smart contract to blockchain through a transaction. The code goes into the data field. The contract starts working after verification and becomes permanent.
3. **Monitoring Conditions**: The active contract watches the blockchain for specific trigger events or conditions.
4. **Automatic Execution**: Network computers (nodes) run the contract's actions when conditions are right. To cite an instance, see how funds go to vendors after payment, or ownership changes on specific dates.
5. **Recording Results**: The blockchain records results right away. This creates a permanent record that authorized parties can see.

Smart contracts do not run on just one server. Every node in the network runs them, which makes tampering or censorship nowhere near possible. Smart contracts have their limits though. They work best with clear, measurable conditions rather than agreements that need interpretation or have planned gray areas.

Ethereum

Bitcoin brought blockchain technology to life in 2008, but smart contracts only became practical when Ethereum launched in 2015. Ethereum's creator, Vitalik Buterin, saw Bitcoin's protocol as a "weak version" of original smart contract vision. He responded by building a stronger version using the Solidity programming language [5.9].

Ethereum set itself apart from Bitcoin by creating a platform that focused on smart contract functionality. Bitcoin had limited scripting abilities, while Ethereum offered a Turing-complete programming environment where developers could create complex, self-executing agreements.

This layered architecture opened new possibilities for businesses. Developers found it easier to create smart contracts that were faster, more transparent, and more secure. Smart contracts soon became the core of decentralized applications (dApps), decentralized autonomous organizations (DAOs) and the entire decentralized finance (DeFi) ecosystem.

Smart contracts' technical journey spans from Bitcoin's simple scripting language to Ethereum's sophisticated Solidity. Bitcoin added basic programmability through its Script language, which was intentionally limited to ensure security. The language avoided looping and wasn't Turing-complete.

Bitcoin Script defined conditions for spending blockchain assets and let users sign transactions to update the distributed ledger. Its simple design aimed to block security attacks and protect Bitcoin's core security principles.

Solidity's Turing-complete nature lets developers write programs that manipulate and change data. These programs run on a global, decentralized computer called the Ethereum Virtual Machine (EVM) [5.10].

Bitcoin Script and Ethereum smart contracts differ in several key ways:

1. Bitcoin scripts don't maintain state and keep all information in locking and unlocking scripts, while Ethereum smart contracts have persistent contract storage.
2. Bitcoin scripts work only for specific transactions and might disappear during pruning, but Ethereum smart contract code stays on the blockchain until someone destroys it.
3. Ethereum's Turing-completeness allows loops and recursion, which enables much more complex applications.

This progress led developers to create token standards like **ERC-20** for *fungible tokens* and **ERC-721** for *non-fungible tokens*. These standards now form the foundations of today's thriving blockchain ecosystem.

Smart contracts in blockchain technology fall into three main categories. Each category serves different functions but shares the basic features of automation and trustless execution.

Smart Legal Contracts With Digital Signatures

Smart legal contracts blend traditional legal agreements with blockchain technology. These contracts create legally binding relationships between parties through digital signatures and execute automatically when conditions are met. They differ from regular smart contracts that just run code because they carry legal weight and bring serious risks for non-compliance.

The real value of these contracts lies in their automatic execution while staying legally enforceable. To cite an instance, Home Depot employs smart legal contracts with vendors to track shipments and receipts. This system allows "a settlement with every single transaction versus waiting six, nine, 12 months down the road."

The biggest problem with smart legal contracts comes from their unchangeable nature – they **cannot be altered** once deployed. This feature clashes with traditional contract law that lets parties change agreements after signing. Notwithstanding that, their public visibility on blockchain means anyone can see them after deployment, which raises privacy concerns for financial institutions.

These contracts continue to spread across manufacturing, cryptocurrency, and real estate industries. They streamline processes that used to involve extensive paperwork.

Decentralized Autonomous Organizations (DAOs)

DAOs offer a revolutionary way of collective governance powered by smart contracts. These organizations run without central leadership. Community members who own specific tokens get voting rights to govern the organization.

The core features of DAOs include:

- **Decentralized governance** through community-driven decision making
- **Token-based voting systems** where proposals need majority approval
- **Open-source transparency** with rules and operations recorded on blockchain
- **Self-execution** of decisions through smart contract automation

DAOs work as blockchain-governed entities with shared goals that the community controls. The blockchain-based rules embedded in the contract's code control how the organization works and spends money, instead of executives or presidents.

VitaDAO shows this concept in action. It funds longevity research without needing grant applications or patent registrations. Each VitaDAO project receives an Intellectual Property Non-Fungible Token (IP-NFT). This system lets DAO members handle research submissions, distribute funds, and find study patients.

DAOs face risks from cyberattacks because their open-source code makes them vulnerable to reverse engineering.

Application Logic Contracts for IoT and APIs

Application Logic Contracts (ALC) go beyond human agreements to help devices and systems communicate. These contracts use application-based code that stays in sync with other blockchain contracts.

ALCs work with Internet of Things (IoT) devices to connect the internet with the physical world and prove information shared between devices. Smart ATMs use sensors to tell operators about needed maintenance. Smartwatches enable **contactless digital payments** that talk directly to banks.

Beam Technologies' smart toothbrush shows this idea at work. The toothbrush connects with their dental insurance company. It collects dental hygiene data and sends it to Beam Dental. Users might get lower premium rates based on how often and how long they brush.

ALCs excel at automated data transfer that triggers responses. They make use of blockchain as a secure way to exchange data between devices and systems.

Right now, ALCs mostly work under single managing programs that only communicate through the same blockchain server. This limits device connectivity. Many sectors still have room to grow using this traceable data approach.

Digital Data Factory (DDF)

In the context of our DDF platform, next, we break down Python script demonstrating Ethereum smart contract capabilities from programmatic perspective. In this exposition we setup a "simple" smart contract to include basic function:

1. Storage of a number value
2. Owner tracking
3. Set, get and increment function
4. Event emission for state changes

To run this script in its entirety, the reader is required to install dependencies such as *pip install web3 eth-account*, start a local blockchain like *Ganache* or connect to a *testnet*, update correct links within the following script sequences and run as provided. To operate blockchain FinTech platform on Ethereum, advanced programming skills are in order, such as an experience with Solidity language.

Smart contract in Python:

```
#!/usr/bin/env python3
"""
Ethereum Smart Contract Demo
Demonstrates deploying and interacting with a simple smart contract using Web3.
py
"""

from web3 import Web3
import json
from eth_account import Account
import os

# Simple smart contract in Solidity (for reference)
CONTRACT_SOURCE = '''
pragma solidity ^0.8.0;

contract SimpleStorage {
    uint256 private storedData;
    address public owner;

    event DataStored(uint256 indexed value, address indexed by);

    constructor() {
        owner = msg.sender;
    }

    function set(uint256 x) public {
        storedData = x;
        emit DataStored(x, msg.sender);
    }
```

```
    function get() public view returns (uint256) {
        return storedData;
    }

    function increment() public {
        storedData += 1;
        emit DataStored(storedData, msg.sender);
    }
}
'''

# Pre-compiled contract bytecode and ABI (you would normally compile with
solc)
CONTRACT_BYTECODE="0x608060405234801561001057600080fd5b50600080546001600160a01b0
3191633179055610 1db806100326000396000f3fe608060405234801561001057600080fd5
b50600436106100575760003560e01c80632a1afcd91461005c57806360fe47b11461007657806
36d4ce63c1461009157806378e979251461009957806 38da5cb5b146100a1575b600080fd5b61
00646100b6565b60405190815260200160405180910390f35b61008961008436600461018 05
65b6100bc565b005b61006461010756 5b610089610110565b600054610064600160016 0a01
b031681565b60015490565b60018190556040518190339 07f69404c0a482e0b62b5ed
cf4c7612c156040eaadefe41ad801c6ea1fd43e3e8e590600090a350565b60015490565
b60018054600090815260209190915260409020805460010190556001546040513391 7f6940
4c0a482e0b62b5edcf4c7612c156040eaadefe41ad801c6ea1fd43e3e8e591a2565b600060
20828403121561019257600080fd5b503591905056fea2646970667358221220a8c65b3
f6c45a5c8b3e7b8a4d8e7f1234567890abcdef1234567890abcdef123464736f6c63430008120033"

CONTRACT_ABI = [
    {
        "inputs": [],
        "stateMutability": "nonpayable",
        "type": "constructor"
    },
    {
        "anonymous": False,
        "inputs": [
            {"indexed": True, "internalType": "uint256", "name": "value", "type":
"uint256"},
            {"indexed": True, "internalType": "address", "name": "by", "type":
"address"}
        ],
        "name": "DataStored",
        "type": "event"
    },
    {
        "inputs": [],
        "name": "get",
        "outputs": [{"internalType": "uint256", "name": "", "type": "uint256"}],
        "stateMutability": "view",
        "type": "function"
    },
    {
        "inputs": [],
        "name": "increment",
        "outputs": [],
```

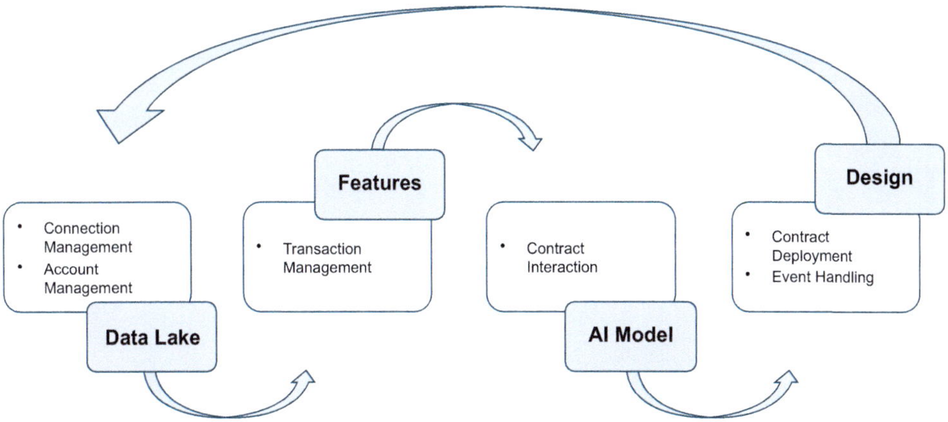

Figure 5.3 Applied DDF Concept Relevant to BlockChain Scenario

```
            "stateMutability": "nonpayable",
            "type": "function"
        },
        {
            "inputs": [],
            "name": "owner",
            "outputs": [{"internalType": "address", "name": "", "type": "address"}],
            "stateMutability": "view",
            "type": "function"
        },
        {
            "inputs": [{"internalType": "uint256", "name": "x", "type": "uint256"}],
            "name": "set",
            "outputs": [],
            "stateMutability": "nonpayable",
            "type": "function"
        }
]
```

The DDF is represented as the blockchain platform, in this case hosted on Ethereum, broken down into functionality as per Figure 5.3.

Data lake comprises from connection and account management, equivalent to standard on cloud functionality. Features are represented within transaction management functionality. Model design is driven by contact interaction, and design is defined in contract deployment and event handling. Hence, the DDF factory floor is represented within the Ethereum ecosystem.

Data Lake

In this first phase, we initialize connection to Ethereum node (or your test environment as a start). Account and connection management is the core functionality at this stage. This step is represented within our new *class EthereumContractDemo*. Secured, and potentially off-the-grid, storage is strongly recommended to track private login details such as *private_key*.

```python
class EthereumContractDemo:
    def __init__(self, rpc_url="http://127.0.0.1:8545"):
        """Initialize connection to Ethereum node"""
        self.w3 = Web3(Web3.HTTPProvider(rpc_url))
        self.account = None
        self.contract = None

        # Check connection
        if not self.w3.is_connected():
            print("⚠️  Warning: Not connected to Ethereum node")
            print("   This demo requires a local blockchain (like Ganache) or testnet")
            return

        print(f"✅ Connected to Ethereum node")
        print(f"   Chain ID: {self.w3.eth.chain_id}")
        print(f"   Latest block: {self.w3.eth.block_number}")

    def create_account(self):
        """Create or load an Ethereum account"""
        # In production, load from secure storage
        private_key = os.getenv('PRIVATE_KEY')

        if private_key:
            self.account = Account.from_key(private_key)
            print(f"✅ Loaded account: {self.account.address}")
        else:
            # Create new account for demo
            self.account = Account.create()
            print(f"✅ Created new account: {self.account.address}")
            print(f"   Private key: {self.account.key.hex()}")
            print("   ⚠️  Store this private key securely!")

        # Check balance
        balance = self.w3.eth.get_balance(self.account.address)
        balance_eth = self.w3.from_wei(balance, 'ether')
        print(f"   Balance: {balance_eth} ETH")

        if balance_eth < 0.01:
            print("   ⚠️  Low balance - you may need test ETH to deploy contracts")
```

Features

In our simple hypothetical example, we enter and increment an amount hosted on a public Ethereum network as a smart contract, feature consists of transaction management steps.

```python
    def send_transaction(self, contract_function):
        """Helper to send a contract transaction"""
        try:
            transaction = contract_function.build_transaction({
                'from': self.account.address,
                'nonce': self.w3.eth.get_transaction_count(self.account.address),
                'gas': 100000,
                'gasPrice': self.w3.eth.gas_price,
            })
```

```
            signed_txn = self.w3.eth.account.sign_transaction(transaction, self.
account.key)
            tx_hash = self.w3.eth.send_raw_transaction(signed_txn.
rawTransaction)
            return tx_hash

        except Exception as e:
            print(f"❌ Transaction error: {e}")
            return None

    def wait_for_transaction(self, tx_hash):
        """Wait for transaction confirmation and show receipt"""
        try:
            receipt = self.w3.eth.wait_for_transaction_receipt(tx_hash)
            if receipt.status == 1:
                print(f"    ✅ Transaction confirmed: {tx_hash.hex()}")
                return receipt
            else:
                print(f"    ❌ Transaction failed: {tx_hash.hex()}")
                return None
        except Exception as e:
            print(f"❌ Transaction wait error: {e}")
            return None
```

Features here are operational in nature. In case of, say, real estate tokenization, feature consists of various forms of processing transactions, such as rental income, bills flows etc.

Model

This stage defines value creation, in our example, number and numeric incremental functionality. The following function demonstrates various contract interactions, the brains of the smart contract. In this instance, we can read initial stored number, set a new value, or execute an increment to previously observed number. These interactions, driven by our manual coordination in this case, will get reflected on the public blockchain as executed and specified by us and shared and viewed by all participants instantaneously.

```
    def interact_with_contract(self):
        """Demonstrate various contract interactions"""
        if not self.contract:
            print("❌ No contract deployed")
            return

        print("\n🔄 Interacting with Smart Contract...")

        try:
            # Read contract owner
            owner = self.contract.functions.owner().call()
            print(f"   Contract owner: {owner}")

            # Read initial stored value
            initial_value = self.contract.functions.get().call()
            print(f"   Initial stored value: {initial_value}")

            # Set a new value
            print("   Setting value to 42...")
```

```
            tx_hash = self.send_transaction(self.contract.functions.set(42))
            if tx_hash:
                self.wait_for_transaction(tx_hash)

                # Read updated value
                new_value = self.contract.functions.get().call()
                print(f"    New stored value: {new_value}")

            # Increment the value
            print("    Incrementing value...")
            tx_hash = self.send_transaction(self.contract.functions.
increment())
            if tx_hash:
                self.wait_for_transaction(tx_hash)

                # Read final value
                final_value = self.contract.functions.get().call()
                print(f"    Final stored value: {final_value}")

        except Exception as e:
            print(f"✗ Interaction error: {e}")
```

To glue the process together, last phase, *Design*, deals with smart contract deployment and event handling.

Design

In this implementation phase, we create contract instance, build relevant transactions, sign and send transactions and confirm eventual deployment, as per this code snippet:

```
    def deploy_contract(self):
        """Deploy the smart contract"""
        if not self.w3.is_connected() or not self.account:
            print("✗ Cannot deploy: No connection or account")
            return False

        print("\n📝 Deploying Smart Contract...")

        try:
            # Create contract instance
            contract = self.w3.eth.contract(abi=CONTRACT_ABI,
bytecode=CONTRACT_BYTECODE)

            # Build transaction
            transaction = contract.constructor().build_transaction({
                'from': self.account.address,
                'nonce':
self.w3.eth.get_transaction_count(self.account.address),
                'gas': 2000000,
                'gasPrice': self.w3.eth.gas_price,
            })
            # Sign and send transaction
            signed_txn = self.w3.eth.account.sign_transaction(transaction,
self.account.key)
            tx_hash =
self.w3.eth.send_raw_transaction(signed_txn.rawTransaction)
```

```
            print(f"   Transaction hash: {tx_hash.hex()}")
            print("   Waiting for confirmation...")

            # Wait for transaction receipt
            tx_receipt = self.w3.eth.wait_for_transaction_receipt(tx_hash)

            if tx_receipt.status == 1:
                self.contract = self.w3.eth.contract(
                    address=tx_receipt.contractAddress,
                    abi=CONTRACT_ABI

                )
                print(f"✅ Contract deployed at:
{tx_receipt.contractAddress}")
                print(f"   Gas used: {tx_receipt.gasUsed:,}")
                return True
            else:
                print("❌ Contract deployment failed")
                return False

        except Exception as e:
            print(f"❌ Deployment error: {e}")
            return False
```

It is at this phase, client interaction plays an important role. Hence, event handling is represented through a *listener* function:

```
    def listen_to_events(self):
        """Demonstrate event listening"""
        if not self.contract:
            print("❌ No contract deployed")
            return

        print("\n👂 Listening for Contract Events...")

        try:
            # Get past events
            event_filter =
self.contract.events.DataStored.create_filter(fromBlock='latest')
            print("   Watching for DataStored events...")
            print("   (This would run continuously in a real application)")

            # In a real app, you'd run this in a loop:
            # for event in event_filter.get_new_entries():
            #     print(f"   📡 Event: Value {event.args.value} stored by
{event.args.by}")
        except Exception as e:
            print(f"❌ Event listening error: {e}")
```

This post-deployment, implementation functionality is designed to be executed continuously in real-world FinTech applications, such as real estate tokenization platform. In "Chapter 11, FinTech Application: PropTech," we expose a practical example of tokenization of a real estate and there we expand on the DDF concept further.

In the previous exposition, we have shown a simple smart contract programmatic example. The core notion is to demonstrate the potential in such application. The expediency of execution and controls, the storage capabilities and computations and blockchain tracking are highlighted here.

5.6 Tokenization

Tokenization involves converting the ownership of a real-world asset, such as real estate, into digital tokens on a blockchain. Each token represents a share of the property, allowing for fractional ownership. In the context of real estate, ERC-20 fungible tokens on the Ethereum blockchain are commonly used. These tokens are identical and interchangeable, making them ideal for representing ownership shares.

There are various methods of tokenizing real estate, each with its unique advantages:

1. **Full Property Tokenization**: The entire property is tokenized, and tokens are sold to multiple investors. This method allows for shared ownership and reduces entry barriers for small investors.
2. **Partial Property Tokenization**: Only a portion of the property is tokenized. This can be useful for raising capital without selling the entire property.
3. **Debt Tokenization**: Instead of equity, the debt associated with a property is tokenized. Investors can buy tokens representing a share of the property's mortgage.

In the realm of property tokenization, compliance with real estate regulations and KYC/AML requirements is paramount. Ensuring that all participants are verified and that transactions adhere to legal standards is crucial for maintaining trust and legitimacy in the market. Ethereum, with its robust infrastructure and smart contract capabilities, is the preferred blockchain platform for implementing ERC-20 tokens in real estate. Smart contracts automate and enforce the terms of agreements, ensuring seamless and secure transactions [5.11].

> The ERC-20 introduces a standard for Fungible Tokens, in other words, they have a property that makes each Token be exactly the same (in type and value) as another Token. For example, an ERC-20 Token acts just like the ETH, meaning that 1 Token is and will always be equal to all the other Tokens.

In this flow we show a simple example of Solidity based fungible token (ERC-20) representing ownership shares of a property that mints all initial supply of tokens named "RET" to the contract creator (admin).

```
// SPDX-License-Identifier: MIT
pragma solidity ^0.8.0;

import "@openzeppelin/contracts/token/ERC20/ERC20.sol";

contract RealEstateToken is ERC20 {
    address public admin;

    constructor(uint256 initialSupply) ERC20("RealEstateToken", "RET") {
        admin = msg.sender;
        _mint(admin, initialSupply);
    }
}
```

Once deployed, the contract creator issues and transfers to another account minted X number of tokens.

```
from brownie import RealEstateToken, accounts
```

```
def main():
    admin = accounts[0]
    initial_supply = 1_000_000 * 10**18  # 1 million tokens with 18 decimals

    # Deploy contract
    token = RealEstateToken.deploy(initial_supply, {'from': admin})
    print(f"Contract deployed at {token.address}")

    # Transfer some tokens to another account
    recipient = accounts[1]
    tx = token.transfer(recipient, 100_000 * 10**18, {'from': admin})
    tx.wait(1)
    print(f"Transferred 100,000 RET to {recipient.address}")
```

Further functionality such as whitelisting or KYC checks and web front end can be in-build. Tokenization, particularly through ERC-20 tokens on the Ethereum blockchain, holds a potential to revolutionize the real estate market. By enhancing liquidity, transparency, and accessibility, tokenization can democratize property investment and streamline transactions. However, it is essential to address regulatory and technical challenges to fully realize its benefits. As we continue to innovate and adapt, tokenization could become a cornerstone of modern real estate investment.

5.7 Deficiencies and Legal Dilemmas

Blockchain technology shows great promise but faces substantial hurdles that hold back its widespread adoption. These challenges need ongoing solutions as the technology evolves.

The biggest problem blockchain faces is **scalability**. Bitcoin's network processes just seven to ten transactions per second (TPS), which is nowhere near what systems like Visa can handle with thousands of TPS. The root cause lies in Bitcoin's architecture – its 1MB block size and ten-minute block time put hard limits on throughput. Network congestion drives up fees and slows down confirmations during busy periods. This creates what experts call the "blockchain trilemma" – trying to scale up without giving up security and decentralization.

Proof-of-Work (PoW) systems need **massive computing power that burns through energy**. The carbon footprint is huge, especially when miners rely on nonrenewable energy. Some positive changes are happening; still, the environmental effects raise serious concerns.

The borderless, decentralized nature of blockchain makes **regulation** challenging. Laws for cryptocurrencies, token offerings and smart contracts vary across countries. It also proves challenging to follow KYC/AML rules while keeping blockchain's privacy features intact. Based on Aquilina et al., despite being designed for payments, cryptocurrencies largely failed in this original purpose – the paper notes that surveys show only small percentages of households use crypto for goods and services. Instead, cryptocurrencies became vehicles for speculation, with price volatility attracting waves of investors seeking high returns [5.12].

Based on Arner et.al. (2023), the dramatic collapse of crypto firms like **FTX** reveals systemic weaknesses in the crypto ecosystem that closely resemble the failures of traditional finance. Despite being marketed as decentralized and transparent alternatives to conventional systems, cryptocurrencies have evolved into **"financialized" structures** riddled with **market failures** such as centralization, conflicts of interest, opacity and regulatory gaps [XY]. Crypto originally sought to avoid the flaws of traditional finance, but in practice, it **replicates many of them**, including irrational investor behavior, manipulation and poor governance. Crypto has adopted centralized intermediaries and recreated traditional financial products (e.g., exchanges, derivatives), leading to similar systemic risks. This trend undermines the very premise of decentralization and innovation. The **collapse of FTX** exemplifies how crypto has mirrored traditional finance's structural risks rather than eliminating them. Without robust regulation and governance, crypto markets risk repeating the mistakes of the past. To survive and mature, the crypto ecosystem must be brought within a **clear, coordinated and risk-sensitive regulatory perimeter** [5.13].

Interesting secondary effect of this lack of regulation is observed in the data quality, specifically when dealing with cryptocurrency markets. Schwenkler et al. (2025) analyze data from leading vendors and document pervasive mislabeling, measurement errors and discrepancies in reported market metrics [5.14]. This is yet another potential for regulatory bodies to step in and require new approach to data dissemination and official distribution.

Lastly, blockchains are secure from within, but they have weak points – **the 51% attack risk** stands out. These attacks happen when bad actors take control of most of a network's processing power. This lets them reverse transactions and potentially spend coins twice. Bitcoin's size makes it safer, but smaller cryptocurrencies face much higher risks.

On the other hand, smart contracts offer groundbreaking capabilities with clear advantages and drawbacks that affect their real-life use. However, smart contracts clash with data protection rules, especially the GDPR. The same immutability that makes them secure goes against the right to erasure (Article 17) and right to rectification (Article 16) required by European data protection law. This creates a tough compliance issue – personal data on a blockchain can't be changed or deleted as regulations demand. Even storing encrypted personal data hashes on-chain might still fall under GDPR rules if someone can trace them back to people. Developers suggest keeping personal data off-chain and storing only references on the blockchain as a possible "fix."

In addition, Ethereum struggles with scalability issues that limit smart contract performance. The network processes only 15–40 transactions per second, which creates bottlenecks during busy times. Network congestion, higher gas fees, and slower transaction confirmations result from this limitation. Complex smart contracts need more computing power, which makes these scalability problems worse. Layer 2 solutions like Arbitrum try to help by processing transactions off-chain, but they bring new challenges, including long waiting times when moving assets back to Ethereum's main network.

Furthermore, the DeFi landscape goes beyond simple transactions. Users can access collateralized borrowing without credit checks through lending platforms. DEXs enable peer-to-peer trading through liquidity pools instead of order books. Yield farming protocols let users maximize returns by providing liquidity. Flash loans create new financial possibilities through uncollateralized lending. These features are beyond the topics covered in this book.

These innovations bring great potential, but major challenges exist. Security vulnerabilities have led to billions in lost funds through exploits. Market manipulation tactics like sandwich attacks and wash trading damage trust. Price volatility creates substantial risks for new users.

New DeFi users should approach with caution. They can alleviate risks by choosing self-custody wallets from reputable developers, starting small, disconnecting after sessions, and researching projects before investing. Security audits add extra protection for careful participants.

5.8 Summary

This chapter lays the **foundational knowledge** for understanding blockchain, Bitcoin, decentralization, and DeFi. It explains how these technologies disrupt traditional finance and how AI and machine learning techniques can fit or be added into the DDF flow, specifically within the DDF Model Selection stage. It sets the stage for practical applications, especially in **tokenization and alternative data modeling**, covered later in the book. An example of a simple smart contract implementation in Python is offered to highlight the flow and relevance to previously studied DDF concept. In addition, this chapter outlines the importance of understanding the capabilities as well as deficiencies of new technologies, introduction of blockchain and tokenization, as applicable to finance and banking domain.

Furthermore, this chapter initiates Section 2 of the book, delivering base concepts as encapsulated in the digital data factory (DDF) and FinTech toolkit in terms of Python code snippets, methodologies and steps necessary to form a concise solution to a complex problem faced by FinTech practitioners. Tokenization is likely to remain on the radars of most finance and banking practitioners.

5.9 Concept Questions and Answers

Q1: What role does consensus play in maintaining the security and integrity of a blockchain network?

A1: Consensus is a fundamental mechanism that ensures all participants (nodes) in a blockchain network agree on the current state of the distributed ledger. It prevents fraudulent transactions, double spending and network splits. In decentralized systems, consensus protocols – such as Proof of Work (PoW) or Proof of Stake (PoS) – validate and approve new blocks without needing a centralized authority. Every new transaction or block must be agreed upon by the majority of the network. This shared agreement forms the basis of blockchain's trustless environment, where cryptographic and algorithmic validation replaces institutional trust.

Q2: Explain how Bitcoin's Proof-of-Work mechanism contributes to decentralization and security.

A2: Proof-of-Work (PoW) underpins Bitcoin's decentralized architecture by allowing anyone with computing resources to participate in block creation (mining). In PoW, miners solve complex cryptographic puzzles to validate transactions and create new blocks. This process requires significant computational effort, which deters malicious actors because altering any part of the blockchain would require redoing the PoW for all subsequent blocks and gaining majority (51%) control of network power – an economically and technically prohibitive task. Therefore, PoW decentralizes validation and ensures the integrity and immutability of the ledger.

Q3: In the context of DeFi, what does "trustless" mean, and how is it achieved?

A3: In decentralized finance (DeFi), "trustless" refers to a system where transactions and financial agreements do not require trust between parties or reliance on intermediaries. This is achieved through smart contracts – self-executing programs that run on public blockchains like Ethereum. These contracts automatically enforce predefined rules and conditions, removing the need for human involvement or institutional oversight. For instance, a DeFi lending contract can lock collateral, disburse loans, and collect repayments automatically, based solely on code, thus enabling peer-to-peer financial interactions without trust dependencies.

Q4: How does blockchain structure differ fundamentally from traditional databases in terms of data modification and control?

A4: Traditional databases are centrally controlled, allowing authorized users to read, modify, or delete data. They typically use a client-server model and store data in tabular formats. In contrast, blockchain is a peer-to-peer, append-only system. It stores data in linked blocks that are cryptographically secured. Each block references the hash of the previous one, forming an immutable chain. Once data is recorded on the blockchain, it cannot be altered without consensus and re-mining all subsequent blocks, which is computationally infeasible. This structure decentralizes control and ensures tamper resistance and transparency.

Q5: What economic and cryptographic principles underlie the value and security of Bitcoin?

A5: Bitcoin's value and security are rooted in both economic scarcity and cryptographic integrity. Scarcity: There is a hard-coded limit of 21 million Bitcoins, making it deflationary and resistant to inflationary monetary policies. This mimics precious metals like gold, hence the term "digital gold." Cryptography: SHA-256 hashing ensures that transaction data and block links are tamper-proof. Game Theory and Incentives: Miners are rewarded for honest behavior through block rewards and transaction fees. Attempts to subvert the system are economically irrational due to the cost of hardware, energy and the risk of devaluation. This combination creates a secure, decentralized currency system without needing trust in any single party.

Q6: Define "tokenization" in the context of financial assets and blockchain technology.

A6: Tokenization is the process of converting ownership of physical or digital assets into blockchain-based tokens. These tokens represent fractional or full ownership of the underlying asset and can be traded on blockchain platforms. In finance, tokenized assets can include real estate, art, stocks, or commodities. Blockchain's immutability and transparency ensure that ownership records are secure and tamper-proof. Tokenization enhances liquidity, accessibility and efficiency by enabling 24/7 global trading, removing intermediaries and reducing settlement times.

Q7: How do fiat-backed stablecoins like USDT maintain their peg to the US dollar?

A7: Fiat-backed stablecoins such as USDT (Tether) and USDC (USD Coin) maintain a 1:1 peg to the US dollar by holding equivalent cash or cash-equivalent reserves. For every stablecoin issued, the issuer claims to hold one dollar in reserve. These coins remain stable due to arbitrage mechanisms: if the stablecoin trades below $1, traders buy it and redeem it with the issuer for $1, driving the price up; if it trades above, they sell to lock in profit, bringing the price down. Regular audits, transparency, and redemption mechanisms contribute to maintaining the peg.

Q8: What distinguishes CeFi from DeFi in terms of user identity and regulatory compliance?

A8: Centralized Finance (CeFi) platforms – like traditional banks or exchanges – are subject to regulatory compliance and must implement Know-Your-Customer (KYC) and Anti-Money Laundering (AML) checks. Users are required to verify their identities before accessing services. In contrast, DeFi operates on permissionless public blockchains where users interact with applications using non-custodial crypto wallets (e.g., MetaMask) without revealing personal identity. While DeFi offers pseudonymity, all transactions remain publicly visible and traceable on the blockchain, creating transparency despite the lack of formal identification.

Q9: Why is decentralization considered a core feature of DeFi, and what advantages does it offer?

A9: Decentralization in DeFi means no single entity controls the network. This architecture offers: Resilience: no central point of failure, Censorship resistance: no authority can block users, Global inclusion: anyone with internet access can participate, User autonomy: users retain custody of their assets. Decentralization shifts trust from intermediaries to transparent, verifiable code, reducing costs and democratizing access to financial services. It also enables composability, allowing different protocols to interoperate like financial "LEGO bricks" in building complex services.

Q10: How does the DDF model integrate blockchain in the ETL (Extract, Transfer, Load) phase?

A10: In the digital data factory (DDF) framework, the ETL phase involves collecting, transforming and storing raw data. Blockchain can serve as both a source of raw data (e.g., transaction logs, smart contract interactions) and a verifiable storage mechanism. Due to its immutability, blockchain ensures data integrity from the outset. For FinTech applications, integrating blockchain in ETL enables secure and traceable data pipelines, especially useful when building AI/ML models that rely on accurate historical data, such as in fraud detection, credit scoring or asset tokenization.

5.10 Further Reading

- Dickerson, A., & Hric, J. (2024). FINS5545 Financial Market Data Literacy Course Notes, UNSW Business School.
- Harvey, C. R., Ramachandran, A., & Santoro, J. (2021). DeFi and the Future of Finance, John Wiley & Sons.
- Hric, J. (2024). FINS5548 Financial Technology, UNSW Business School.

5.11 References

[5.1] Bacon, J., Michels, J.D., Millard, C., & Singh, J. (2017). Blockchain Demystified, Queen Mary UoL, School of Law, Legal Studies Research Paper No. 268/2017

[5.2] Satoshi Nakamoto. (2008). "Bitcoin: A Peer-to-Peer Electronic Cash System", Unknown.

[5.3] Hash Generator Example: https://passwords-generator.org/sha256-hash-generator

[5.4] Bitcoin and Cryptocurrency Technologies: https://bitcoinbook.cs.princeton.edu/

[5.5] Auer, R., Haslhofer, B., Kitzler, S., Saggese, P., & Vicor, F. (2023). The Technology of Decentralized Finance (DeFi), BIS Working Papers No. 1066.

[5.6] Ma, Y., Zeng, Y., & Zhang, A. (2023). Stablecoins Runs and the Cetralization of Arbitrage, SSRN.

[5.7] Tether: https://tether.to/en/

[5.8] Solidity: https://soliditylang.org/

[5.9] Ethereum: https://ethereum.org/en/

[5.10] Ethereum White Paper: https://ethereum.org/en/whitepaper/

[5.11] ERC-20: https://ethereum.org/en/developers/docs/standards/tokens/erc-20/

[5.12] Aquilina, M., Cornelli, G., Frost, J., & Gambacorta, L. (2025). Cryptocurrencies and Decentralized Finance: Functions and Financial Stability Implications, BIS Papers No.156.

[5.13] Arner, D.W., Zetzsche, D.A., Buckley, R.P., & Kirkwood, J. (2023). The Financialization of Crypto: Lessons from FTX and the Crypto Winter of 2022–2023, SSRN.

[5.14] Schwenkler, G., Shah, A., & Yang, D. (2025). Aggregate Confusion in Crypto Market Data, SSRN.

Chapter 6

Machine Learning Tools for Finance and FinTech

DOI: 10.4324/9781003477747-8

6.1 Introduction

Machine learning has become essential in finance and FinTech, offering powerful tools for analysis, automation and decision-making across various applications. ML models analyze vast data sets to assess creditworthiness, detect fraud and quantify risks more accurately than traditional methods. Banks use ensemble methods and neural networks to evaluate loan applications and portfolio risks. Sophisticated algorithms execute trades based on market patterns, news sentiment and technical indicators. Techniques include reinforcement learning for strategy optimization and deep learning for price prediction. Real-time transaction monitoring uses anomaly detection algorithms to identify suspicious patterns. Machine learning adapts to evolving fraud tactics better than rule-based systems. Automated investment platforms use ML to create personalized portfolios, rebalance investments, and provide financial advice based on individual risk profiles and goals, amongst other use cases.

The field continues evolving rapidly, with explainable AI becoming crucial for regulatory compliance promising to revolutionize complex financial modeling. In this chapter we discuss machine learning applications in finance and how these applications differ significantly from other domains due to several unique characteristics of financial markets and data, such as data non-stationarity, signal-to-noise or adversarial environment.

Traditional ML includes random forests, support vector machines and gradient boosting for structured financial data. **Deep learning** powers natural language processing for news analysis, document processing and customer service chatbots. **Time series analysis** uses LSTM networks and ARIMA models for forecasting market movements and economic indicators.

In the previous chapter, we looked at tokenization within the context of digital data factory (DDF) concept. In this chapter, we place the reader squarely into the *DDF Model selection* section and expose recent developments in ML and AI techniques as applied to finance and banking arena. We start with a simple **ordinary least square (OLS)** model and proceed to exposing, LASSO regression, decision tree model and random forest modeling framework, concluding with the exposition of **recurrent neural network (RNN)** architecture from conceptual, mathematical and programmatic standpoints. Recurrent neural networks (RNNs) are widely used in finance due to their ability to process sequential data and capture temporal dependencies. The sequential nature of financial data, in quantitative as well as qualitative formats, makes RNNs particularly valuable tool, as they can remember previous states and use that information to make predictions about future conditions.

In the following Chapter 7 and Chapter 8, we dive deeper into the intricacies of **long-short term memory recurrent neural network (LSTM RNN)** to provide the reader with core mathematical and conceptual formulations necessary for sentiment analytics and **large language model (LLMs)** utilization.

Learning Outcomes

At the end of this chapter the reader will be able to do the following:

- Comprehend requirements needed to select a prediction model
- Outline theoretical concepts behind core prediction models
- Explain base neural network design
- Understand how neural network functions
- Overview recurrent neural network model
- Explore relevant model assumptions and hyperparameters

6.2 Basic Predictive Models

Digital Data Factory (DDF)

As discussed in "Chapter 2: Data Management for FinTech," DDF model design workstation is responsible for analytics and model design. Authenticity and utilization given the collection of available data as combined with the business problem at hand forms the core brains of this station. Your job here is to consume Station #2 prompts and features and build a sustainable modeling framework to deliver business-critical and actionable results. Your results are being passed on the last Station #4 for final implementation.

As per Figure 6.1, a model design workstation is an important component of the DDF concept utilizing the field of predictive analytics. It is responsible for creating models that can accurately forecast future outcomes. The success of these models is resulting in the clarity and parsimony of the results. We submerge the user into the workings of model design in this section. We use a hypothetical data example, Boston Real Estate from Kaggle [6.1]. The data contains 506 observations and 14 variables. In this exercise, we focus on predicting property value (MV) based on a number of rooms (RM) variable only. Our next focus is to design and

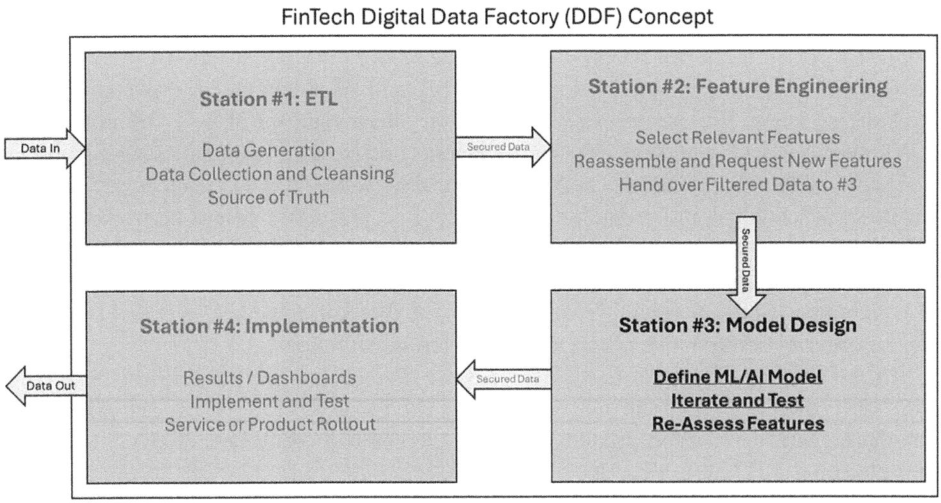

Figure 6.1 DDF Model Design/Selection, Station #3

select an appropriate model to predict a value of a property given the size variable. The focus is on theoretical model selection, Python representation and a measure of accuracy, in short, how do we select a model to, ultimately, proceed into our DDF Station #4 Implementation. We start with a simple ordinary least square regression and end our exposition introducing long-short term memory neural networks.

Ordinary Least Square Regression

Ordinary least squares (OLS) is a fundamental concept in statistical modeling and data analysis. It is a method used to estimate the parameters in a linear regression model, ensuring the best fit for the observed data. The **key assumptions** of OLS include linearity, independence, homoscedasticity and normality of errors. These assumptions ensure the validity and reliability of the model. Violations of these assumptions can lead to biased or inefficient estimates, making it essential to check these conditions before applying OLS.

The **estimation method** of OLS involves minimizing the sum of the squared differences between the observed and predicted values. This method provides the best linear unbiased estimates (BLUE) of the regression coefficients, making it a preferred choice in many analytical scenarios.

Applications of OLS are widespread across various fields such as economics, finance, social sciences and engineering. For instance, in economics, OLS is used to estimate the relationship between consumer spending and income, while in finance, it helps in modeling asset returns.

However, OLS is not without its **limitations**. It is sensitive to outliers and can be significantly affected by multicollinearity among the predictors. Moreover, if the assumptions of OLS are violated, the estimates may not be reliable. Advanced techniques or robust methods may be required to address these issues. From a practical standpoint, FinTech operators tend to use OLS technique as the worst case model selection. In short, in most real-world instances, OLS assumptions do not hold, and hence the OLS results, coefficients and predictions are inaccurate and cannot be relied on [6.2].

Simple Linear Regression Model

For predicting property value (MV) based on number of rooms (RM), we use the linear model:

$$Y = \beta_0 + \beta_1 X + \varepsilon$$

Where:

- Y = Property value (MV) – dependent variable
- X = Number of rooms (RM) – independent variable
- β_0 = y-intercept (property value when rooms = 0)
- β_1 = slope (change in property value per additional room)
- ε = error term (residuals)

Parameter Estimation

The OLS method minimizes the sum of squared residuals:

$$SSE = \Sigma(y_i - \hat{y}_i)^2 = \Sigma(y_i - \beta_0 - \beta_1 x_i)^2$$

Analytical Solutions

Slope (β_1):

$$\beta_1 = \Sigma(x_i - \bar{x})(y_i - \bar{y}) / \Sigma(x_i - \bar{x})^2 = [n \cdot \Sigma(x_i y_i) - \Sigma(x_i) \cdot \Sigma(y_i)] / [n \cdot \Sigma(x_i^2) - (\Sigma(x_i))^2]$$

Intercept (β_0):

$$\beta_0 = \bar{y} - \beta_1 \cdot \bar{x}$$

Where $\bar{x}$ and $\bar{y}$ are sample means.

Model Evaluation Metrics

1. **R-squared (Coefficient of Determination):**

$$R^2 = 1 - SSE / SST = 1 - \Sigma(y_i - \hat{y}_i)^2 / \Sigma(y_i - \bar{y})^2$$

2. **Mean Squared Error (MSE):**

$$MSE = SSE / (n - 2) = \Sigma(y_i - \hat{y}_i)^2 / (n - 2)$$

3. **Standard Error of Estimate:**

$$SE = \sqrt{MSE} = \sqrt{[\Sigma(y_i - \hat{y}_i)^2 / (n - 2)]}$$

Overall, *OLS* (β_0, β_1) are the core model coefficients and *mean square error* (*MSE*) is the model measure of accuracy. These output model parameters independently define the model at hand. We do use these parameters going forward when compared to other models to make a model design decision and a selection. The lower the measure of MSE, given all else equal, the more accurate the model predictions.

Python Implementation

Now let us continue with a comprehensive Python implementation:

```
import numpy as np
import pandas as pd
import matplotlib.pyplot as plt
from sklearn.linear_model import LinearRegression
from sklearn.metrics import r2_score, mean_squared_error
```

```
import seaborn as sns

# Load the data
data = pd.read_csv('boston.csv')
X = data['RM'].values  # Number of rooms
y = data['MV'].values  # Property values

print("Boston Housing Data Analysis")
print("="*40)
print(f"Dataset size: {len(X)} observations")
print(f"RM (rooms) - Mean: {X.mean():.3f}, Std: {X.std():.3f}")
print(f"MV (value) - Mean: {y.mean():.3f}, Std: {y.std():.3f}")
```

As a start, we load relevant libraries and load our data sample, *Boston.csv*. Next we isolate core variables, *RM* and *MV*. and view basic array *mean()* and *std()* for each.

To proceed in the model design process, we build manual OLS implementation as follows:

```
# Manual calculation of regression coefficients
n = len(X)
x_mean = np.mean(X)
y_mean = np.mean(y)

# Calculate slope (β₁) and intercept (β₀)
numerator = np.sum((X - x_mean) * (y - y_mean))
denominator = np.sum((X - x_mean) ** 2)
beta_1 = numerator / denominator
beta_0 = y_mean - beta_1 * x_mean

print(f"\nManual OLS Calculations:")
print(f"β₁ (slope): {beta_1:.4f}")
print(f"β₀ (intercept): {beta_0:.4f}")
print(f"Equation: MV = {beta_0:.4f} + {beta_1:.4f} × RM")

# Predictions using manual coefficients
y_pred_manual = beta_0 + beta_1 * X

# Calculate R-squared manually
ss_res = np.sum((y - y_pred_manual) ** 2)
ss_tot = np.sum((y - y_mean) ** 2)
r_squared_manual = 1 - (ss_res / ss_tot)

# Calculate other metrics
mse_manual = ss_res / (n - 2)
rmse_manual = np.sqrt(mse_manual)

print(f"\nManual Model Evaluation:")
print(f"R² = {r_squared_manual:.4f}")
print(f"MSE = {mse_manual:.4f}")
print(f"RMSE = {rmse_manual:.4f}")
```

Hereabove, we implement OLS analytical solution and model evaluation metrics to run across our test data set. It is advisable, when designing and selecting appropriate models for FinTech solutions to chalk the results against any available parametric or simulation-driven implementation.

```
# Verify with scikit-learn
X_sklearn = X.reshape(-1, 1)  # sklearn expects 2D array
model = LinearRegression()
```

```
model.fit(X_sklearn, y)
y_pred_sklearn = model.predict(X_sklearn)

print(f"\nScikit-learn Verification:")
print(f"β₁ (slope): {model.coef_[0]:.4f}")
print(f"β₀ (intercept): {model.intercept_:.4f}")
print(f"R² = {r2_score(y, y_pred_sklearn):.4f}")
print(f"MSE = {mean_squared_error(y, y_pred_sklearn):.4f}")
```

In addition to the previous step, we need to explore any model assumption and test for model robustness.

```
# Statistical Analysis
correlation = np.corrcoef(X, y)[0, 1]
print(f"\nStatistical Insights:")
print(f"Correlation coefficient: {correlation:.4f}")
print(f"For each additional room, property value increases by ${beta_1*1000:.
0f}")
print(f"Model explains {r_squared_manual*100:.1f}% of variance in property
values")

# Residual Analysis
residuals = y - y_pred_manual
print(f"\nResidual Analysis:")
print(f"Mean residual: {np.mean(residuals):.6f} (should be ~0)")
print(f"Std of residuals: {np.std(residuals):.4f}")
```

Results shown here:

```
Boston Housing Data Analysis
==================================================
Dataset size: 506 observations
RM (rooms) - Mean: 6.285, Std: 0.702
MV (value) - Mean: 22.533, Std: 9.188

Manual OLS Calculations:
β₁ (slope): 9.1021
β₀ (intercept): -34.6706
Equation: MV = -34.6706 + 9.1021 × RM

Manual Model Evaluation:
R² = 0.4835
MSE = 43.7736
RMSE = 6.6162

Scikit-learn Verification:
β₁ (slope): 9.1021
β₀ (intercept): -34.6706
R² = 0.4835
MSE = 43.6006
```

Based on the results, we can state that there is a positive relationship between property size and property value as depicted in the slop of the model, positive 9.1021. This manually derived slope results is confirmed by using a pre-build OLS model from an external library *scikit-learn*. Finally, it is recommended to run visual confirmation in 2D or 3D is available of any model design/selection processes.

```
# Create comprehensive visualization
```

```
fig, ((ax1, ax2), (ax3, ax4)) = plt.subplots(2, 2, figsize=(15, 12))

# 1. Scatter plot with regression line
ax1.scatter(X, y, alpha=0.6, color='blue', s=30)
ax1.plot(X, y_pred_manual, color='red', linewidth=2, label=f'y = {beta_0:.2f}
+ {beta_1:.2f}x')
ax1.set_xlabel('Number of Rooms (RM)')
ax1.set_ylabel('Property Value (MV)')
ax1.set_title(f'Linear Regression: Property Value vs Rooms\nR² =
{r_squared_manual:.4f}')
ax1.legend()
ax1.grid(True, alpha=0.3)

# 2. Residual plot
ax2.scatter(y_pred_manual, residuals, alpha=0.6, color='green', s=30)
ax2.axhline(y=0, color='red', linestyle='--', linewidth=2)
ax2.set_xlabel('Predicted Values')
ax2.set_ylabel('Residuals')
ax2.set_title('Residual Plot\n(Check for homoscedasticity)')
ax2.grid(True, alpha=0.3)

# 3. Q-Q plot for residual normality
from scipy import stats
stats.probplot(residuals, dist="norm", plot=ax3)
ax3.set_title('Q-Q Plot of Residuals\n(Check for normality)')
ax3.grid(True, alpha=0.3)

# 4. Distribution of residuals
ax4.hist(residuals, bins=30, alpha=0.7, color='purple', edgecolor='black')
ax4.axvline(x=0, color='red', linestyle='--', linewidth=2)
ax4.set_xlabel('Residuals')
ax4.set_ylabel('Frequency')
ax4.set_title('Distribution of Residuals')
ax4.grid(True, alpha=0.3)

plt.tight_layout()
plt.show()
```

In Figure 6.2 we can see a strong positive relationship between the size of the property and the value, as expected. We tend to observe non-normality and skewness in the residuals. As the last step in this process, we use the model to predict results. In this case we are interested to see a value of a property given a new input variable, number of rooms representing size of this new property.

```
# Prediction examples
print(f"\nPrediction Examples:")
test_rooms = [4, 6, 8, 10]
for rooms in test_rooms:
    predicted_value = beta_0 + beta_1 * rooms
    print(f"  {rooms} rooms → Predicted value: ${predicted_value:.2f}k")

# Model assumptions check
print(f"\nModel Assumptions Check:")
print(f"1. Linearity: Check scatter plot - should show linear relationship")
print(f"2. Independence: Assumed (depends on data collection)")
```

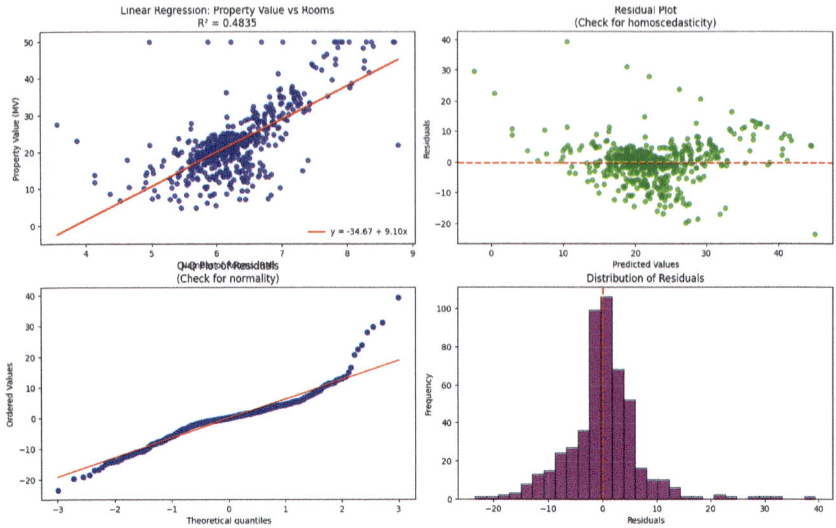

Figure 6.2 OLS Basic Statistics

```
print(f"3. Homoscedasticity: Check residual plot - should show constant
variance")
print(f"4. Normality of residuals: Check Q-Q plot and histogram")

# Summary statistics
print(f"\nSummary Statistics:")
print(f"Min rooms: {X.min():.1f}, Max rooms: {X.max():.1f}")
print(f"Min value: ${y.min():.1f}k, Max value: ${y.max():.1f}k")
print(f"Standard error of regression: {rmse_manual:.4f}")
```

Results as shown here:

```
Prediction Examples:
  4 rooms → Predicted value: $1.74k
  6 rooms → Predicted value: $19.94k
  8 rooms → Predicted value: $38.15k
  10 rooms → Predicted value: $56.35k

Model Assumptions Check:
1. Linearity: Check scatter plot - should show linear relationship
2. Independence: Assumed (depends on data collection)
3. Homoscedasticity: Check residual plot - should show constant variance
4. Normality of residuals: Check Q-Q plot and histogram

Summary Statistics:
Min rooms: 3.6, Max rooms: 8.8
Min value: $5.0k, Max value: $50.0k
Standard error of regression: 6.6162

Statistical Insights:
Correlation coefficient: 0.6954
For each additional room, property value increases by $9102
Model explains 48.4% of variance in property values
```

```
Residual Analysis:
Mean residual: -0.000000 (should be ~0)
Std of residuals: 6.6031
```

In summary, there appears to be a strong positive correlation *(R=0.69)* between rooms and property value. Each additional room increases property value by approx. *$9,102* and the OLS model explains about *48%* of the variance in property values. The final model is defined as *MV = −34.67 + 9.10(RM)*. There is a number of items we need to highlight here, the *MSE = 43.77*, is this high or low as relative to ideal error *MSE* = 0 and is there a reason for beta_0 to be −34.67? Is the model explaining the entirety of the relationship? Based on these observations, we need to investigate further.

LASSO Regression

Let us introduce more advanced method of regression type of modeling. LASSO (least absolute shrinkage and selection operator) is a regularized linear regression technique that performs both variable selection and regularization to enhance prediction accuracy and interpretability. We introduce LASSO using only one feature in this case focusing on *MSE* measure [6.3].

For a linear regression problem with

- **X**: Design matrix (n × p) where n = samples, p = features
- **y**: Response vector (n × 1)
- β: Coefficient vector (p × 1)

In the case of standard linear regression (OLS), the ordinary least squares solution minimizes:

$$\mathrm{RSS}(\beta) = \| y - X\beta \|^2 = \Sigma_i \left(y_i - \Sigma_j x_{ij}\beta_j\right)^2$$

LASSO Objective Function

LASSO adds an L1 penalty term:

$$L(\beta) = \| y - X\beta \|^2 + » \| \beta \|_1 = \Sigma_i \left(y_i - \Sigma_j x_{ij}\beta_j\right)^2 + »\Sigma_j \left|\beta_j\right|$$

Where:

- $\lambda \geq 0$: Regularization parameter controlling shrinkage strength
- $\|\beta\|_1 = \Sigma_j \left|\beta_j\right|$: L1 norm (sum of absolute values)

Key Properties

1. **Shrinkage**: As λ increases, coefficients shrink toward zero
2. **Sparsity**: L1 penalty can set coefficients exactly to zero
3. **Variable Selection**: Automatically selects relevant features
4. **Bias-Variance Tradeoff**: Introduces bias to reduce variance

LASSO regularization, also known as L1 regularization, is a technique used in linear regression to prevent overfitting and enhance model interpretability by shrinking some coefficients to zero, basically running in-build automatic feature selection. This is achieved by adding a penalty term to the loss function, which is based on the absolute values of the coefficients. The strength of the penalty is controlled by a **hyperparameter (often denoted as lambda or alpha)**. A higher lambda value leads to a stronger penalty and more coefficients being shrunk to zero. LASSO regression minimizes this combined objective function to find the optimal coefficients. The core logic is that penalty term helps to reduce the complexity of the model, making it less prone to overfitting on the training data set. Similar techniques are used in neural networks, hence we introduce the approach here.

Optimization

LASSO optimization is a convex problem but not differentiable due to the L1 penalty. Common algorithms include the following:

- **Coordinate Descent**: Iteratively optimize one coefficient at a time
- **LARS (Least Angle Regression)**: Efficient path algorithm
- **Proximal Gradient Methods**: Handle non-smooth penalty

Cross-Validation for λ Selection

The optimal λ is typically chosen using k-fold cross-validation:

$$CV(\lambda)=(1/k)\Sigma_i MSE\_i(\lambda)$$

Where MSE_i(λ) is the mean squared error on fold i.

Python Implementation

As per previous OLS regression section, we load relevant data, our *Boston.csv* sample and expand on basic descriptive statistics.

```
# Create visualizations
fig, axes = plt.subplots(2, 2, figsize=(12, 10))

# Distribution of RM (number of rooms)
axes[0,0].hist(data['RM'], bins=30, alpha=0.7, color='skyblue', edgecolor='black')
axes[0,0].set_title('Distribution of RM (Number of Rooms)')
axes[0,0].set_xlabel('Number of Rooms')
axes[0,0].set_ylabel('Frequency')

# Distribution of MV (median value)
axes[0,1].hist(data['MV'], bins=30, alpha=0.7, color='lightcoral',
edgecolor='black')
axes[0,1].set_title('Distribution of MV (Median Value)')
axes[0,1].set_xlabel('Median Value ($1000s)')
axes[0,1].set_ylabel('Frequency')
```

```
# Scatter plot: RM vs MV
axes[1,0].scatter(data['RM'], data['MV'], alpha=0.6, color='green')
axes[1,0].set_title('RM vs MV Relationship')
axes[1,0].set_xlabel('Number of Rooms (RM)')
axes[1,0].set_ylabel('Median Value (MV)')

# Correlation heatmap
correlation = data.corr()
sns.heatmap(correlation, annot=True, cmap='coolwarm', center=0, ax=axes[1,1])
axes[1,1].set_title('Correlation Matrix')

plt.tight_layout()
plt.show()

print(f"Correlation between RM and MV: {data['RM'].corr(data['MV']):.4f}")
```

Resulting in a graphical data interpretation, Figure 6.3 showing variables distribution and a strong positive relationship between RM and MV.

Before implementing LASSO from a library *from sklearn.linear_model import Lasso, LassoCV* we split the data into two components (i) TRAIN and (ii) TEST using ***from** sklearn.model_selection **import** train_test_split, cross_val_score*, as shown in Figure 6.4. This is a critical component in ML/AI model implementation. We train our model on a selection of data (say 80% from the total data distribution) and then apply trained model using test (say 20% from the total data distribution). This is done to measure accuracy and to ensure trained data is stable and not showing overfitting. In addition, we do execute standardization of X matrix (our example contains single data array).

```
# Prepare the data
X = data[['RM']].values  # Features (number of rooms)
y = data['MV'].values     # Target (median value)
```

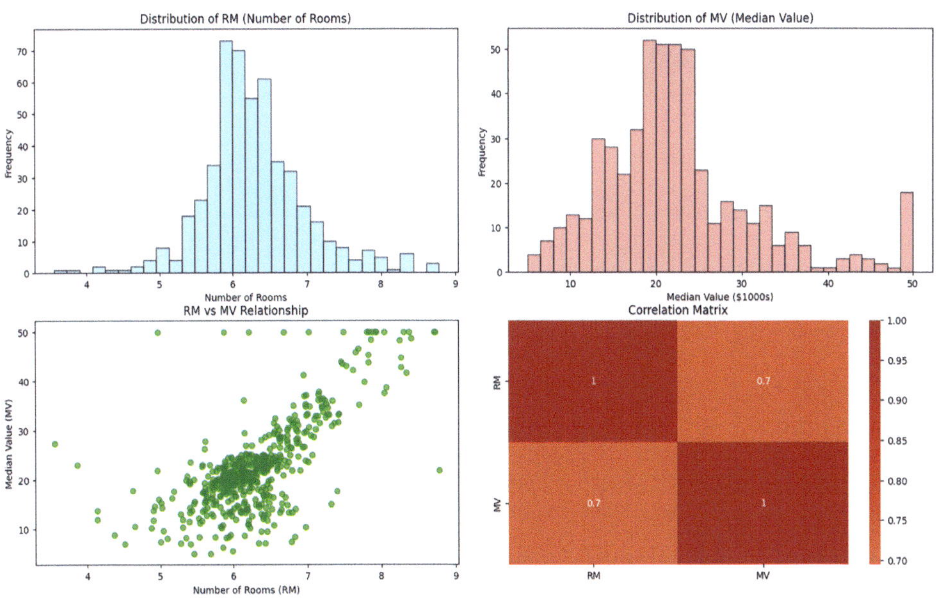

Figure 6.3 LASSSO Basic Statistics

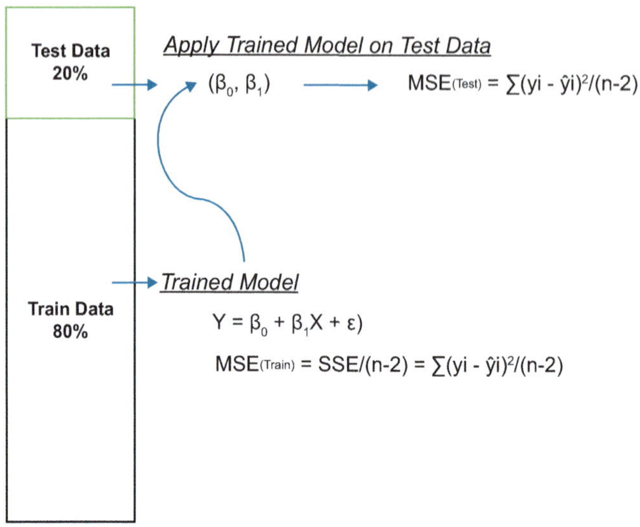

Figure 6.4 Split Data Set Into TRAIN and TEST

```
print(f"Feature matrix X shape: {X.shape}")
print(f"Target vector y shape: {y.shape}")

# Split the data
X_train, X_test, y_train, y_test = train_test_split(
    X, y, test_size=0.2, random_state=42
)

print(f"Training set: {X_train.shape[0]} samples")
print(f"Test set: {X_test.shape[0]} samples")

# Standardize features (important for regularization)
scaler = StandardScaler()
X_train_scaled = scaler.fit_transform(X_train)
X_test_scaled = scaler.transform(X_test)

# Use LassoCV to find optimal lambda
lasso_cv = LassoCV(
  alphas=np.logspace(-4, 1, 100),  # Range of lambda values
  cv=5,                             # 5-fold cross-validation
  random_state=42,
  max_iter=10000
)

# Fit the model
lasso_cv.fit(X_train_scaled, y_train)
print(f"Optimal lambda (alpha): {lasso_cv.alpha_:.6f}")
print(f"Number of non-zero coefficients: {np.sum(lasso_cv.coef_ != 0)}")
print(f"LASSO coefficient: {lasso_cv.coef_[0]:.6f}")
print(f"LASSO intercept: {lasso_cv.intercept_:.6f}")
```

Previously, we split the data set to train/test components and trained model on train data set. Let us compare the results to OLS, should be looking similar as our data contain only one feature, RM.

```
from sklearn.linear_model import LinearRegression

# Fit standard linear regression (OLS)
ols = LinearRegression()
ols.fit(X_train_scaled, y_train)

# Make predictions
y_pred_ols = ols.predict(X_test_scaled)
y_pred_lasso = lasso_cv.predict(X_test_scaled)

# Calculate metrics
mse_ols = mean_squared_error(y_test, y_pred_ols)
mse_lasso = mean_squared_error(y_test, y_pred_lasso)
r2_ols = r2_score(y_test, y_pred_ols)
r2_lasso = r2_score(y_test, y_pred_lasso)

print("Model Comparison:")
print(f"{'Metric':<15} {'OLS':<10} {'LASSO':<10}")
print("-" * 35)
print(f"{'MSE':<15} {mse_ols:<10.4f} {mse_lasso:<10.4f}")
print(f"{'R²':<15} {r2_ols:<10.4f} {r2_lasso:<10.4f}")
print(f"{'Coefficient':<15} {ols.coef_[0]:<10.4f} {lasso_cv.coef_[0]:<10.4f}")
```

From the results we observe LASSO performs slightly "better" by showing lower *MSE* error relative to *OLS MSE*.

```
Optimal lambda (alpha): 0.107227
LASSO coefficient: 6.516729
LASSO intercept: 22.796535

Model Comparison:
Metric          OLS        LASSO
-----------------------------------
MSE             46.1448    45.9719
R²              0.3708     0.3731
Coefficient     6.6240     6.5167
```

Given the importance of regularization, let us explore further with visual interpretation depicted in Figures 6.5 and 6.6:

```
# Create regularization path
alphas = np.logspace(-4, 1, 100)
coefficients = []

for alpha in alphas:
    lasso = Lasso(alpha=alpha, max_iter=10000)
    lasso.fit(X_train_scaled, y_train)
    coefficients.append(lasso.coef_[0])

# Plot regularization path
plt.figure(figsize=(10, 6))
plt.plot(alphas, coefficients, 'b-', linewidth=2)
plt.axvline(x=lasso_cv.alpha_, color='red', linestyle='--',
            label=f'Optimal λ = {lasso_cv.alpha_:.6f}')
plt.axhline(y=0, color='black', linestyle='-', alpha=0.3)
plt.xlabel('Regularization Parameter (λ)')
plt.ylabel('Coefficient Value')
plt.title('LASSO Regularization Path')
```

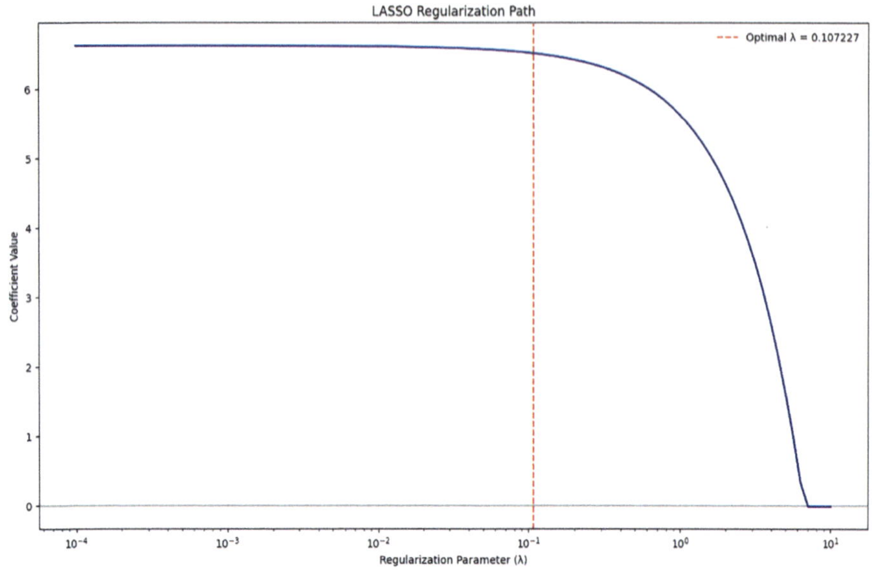

Figure 6.5 LASSO Regularization Path

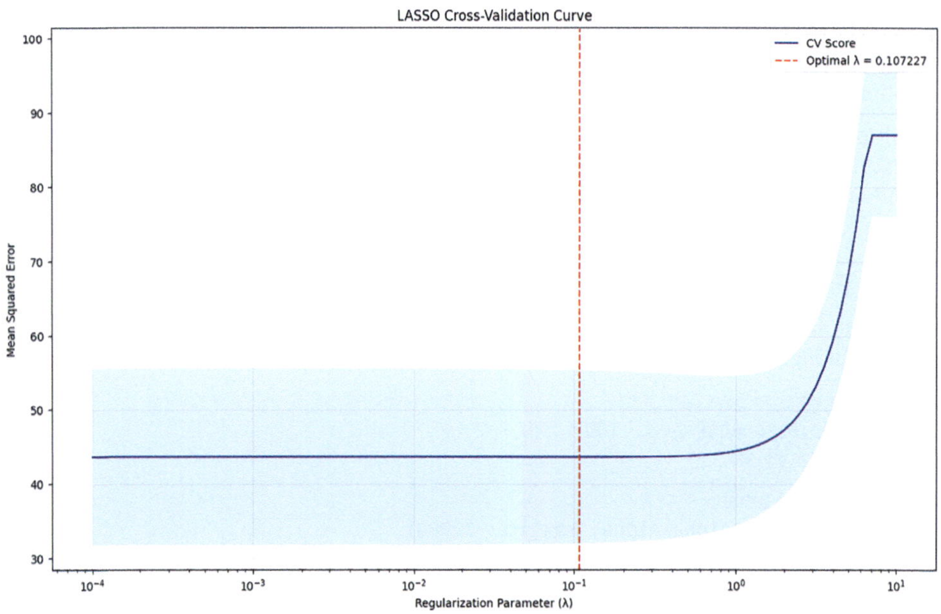

Figure 6.6 LASSO Cross-Validation Curve

```
plt.xscale('log')
plt.grid(True, alpha=0.3)
plt.legend()
plt.show()

# Plot cross-validation curve
plt.figure(figsize=(10, 6))
```

```
plt.plot(lasso_cv.alphas_, lasso_cv.mse_path_.mean(axis=1), 'b-', label='CV Score')
plt.fill_between(lasso_cv.alphas_,
                 lasso_cv.mse_path_.mean(axis=1) -
lasso_cv.mse_path_.std(axis=1),
                 lasso_cv.mse_path_.mean(axis=1) +
lasso_cv.mse_path_.std(axis=1),
                   alpha=0.2)
plt.axvline(x=lasso_cv.alpha_, color='red', linestyle='--',
            label=f'Optimal λ = {lasso_cv.alpha_:.6f}')
plt.xlabel('Regularization Parameter (λ)')
plt.ylabel('Mean Squared Error')
plt.title('LASSO Cross-Validation Curve')
plt.xscale('log')
plt.legend()
plt.grid(True, alpha=0.3)
plt.show()
```

Finally, we show prediction visualization for both OLS and LASSO approaches, in Figure 6.7, using our data set.

```
# Create prediction plot
plt.figure(figsize=(12, 5))

# Plot 1: OLS predictions
plt.subplot(1, 2, 1)
plt.scatter(y_test, y_pred_ols, alpha=0.7, color='blue')
plt.plot([y_test.min(), y_test.max()], [y_test.min(), y_test.max()], 'r--', lw=2)
plt.xlabel('Actual Values')
plt.ylabel('Predicted Values')
plt.title(f'OLS Predictions (R² = {r2_ols:.4f})')
plt.grid(True, alpha=0.3)

# Plot 2: LASSO predictions
plt.subplot(1, 2, 2)
plt.scatter(y_test, y_pred_lasso, alpha=0.7, color='green')
plt.plot([y_test.min(), y_test.max()], [y_test.min(), y_test.max()], 'r--', lw=2)
plt.xlabel('Actual Values')
plt.ylabel('Predicted Values')
plt.title(f'LASSO Predictions (R² = {r2_lasso:.4f})')
plt.grid(True, alpha=0.3)

plt.tight_layout()
plt.show()
```

Overall, the aim is to find more accurate model. The measure of accuracy we use is *MSE*. Based on this exercise we conclude that LASSO is slightly more accurate to OLS.

Decision Tree

Based on the previous OLS and LASSO discussion, we have concluded that *MSE* measure is the most appropriate approach in deciding which model is "better," or stated differently, which model is more accurate. Given we use MSE, logical extension is to ask whether there is a model based on MSE measure to use. A decision tree, *from sklearn.tree import DecisionTreeRegressor*, is a hierarchical model that makes predictions by learning simple decision rules from data

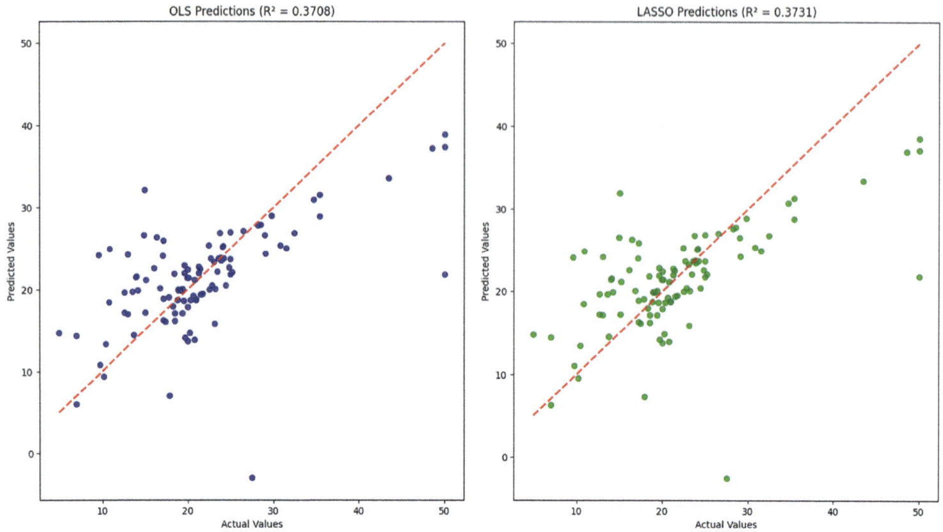

Figure 6.7 Prediction Visualization

features. For regression tasks (predicting continuous values like house prices), the tree splits the data into regions and predicts the mean value within each region [6.4].

Impurity Measures

For regression trees, we use mean squared error (MSE) as the impurity measure:

$$MSE = (1/n) \times \Sigma(yi - \hat{y})^2$$

Where

- n = number of samples in the node
- yi = actual value for sample i
- ŷ = predicted value (mean of all samples in the node)

Information Gain

The best split is chosen by maximizing the reduction in impurity:

$$\text{Information Gain} = \text{MSE\_parent} - \Sigma(\text{ni}/\text{n} \times \text{MSE\_child\_i})$$

Where

- MSE_parent = impurity of parent node
- ni = number of samples in child node i
- n = total number of samples in parent node

Split Selection

For a continuous feature like RM (number of rooms), we evaluate splits of the form:

- Left child: RM ≤ threshold
- Right child: RM > threshold

The algorithm tests all possible thresholds and selects the one with maximum information gain.
Tree structure each internal node contains:

- Feature: Which variable to split on (e.g., RM)
- Threshold: The split value (e.g., RM ≤ 6.5)
- Left/Right children: Resulting branches

Each leaf node contains:

- Prediction: Mean target value of samples in that region
- Sample count: Number of training samples

Python Implementation

Decision tree algorithm is driven by a search for lowest *MSE* in our case within one feature RM. Each split reduces the total MSE by partitioning data into more homogeneous groups using greedy approach, selecting the best split at each node within considering any future splits. Deeper trees have lower bias by higher variance leading to potential overfitting. In extreme case, decision tree can explain and predict 100% of the data variance in train data sequence slitted into miniscule groups. However, this model, heavily overfitted, fails when implemented using test data set. We do split data into train and test setting as per LASSO example in the previous section.

```
# Create and train decision tree models with different depths
depths = [2, 3, 5, 10]
models = {}
results = {}

for depth in depths:
    # Create model
    dt = DecisionTreeRegressor(
        max_depth=depth,
        random_state=42,
        min_samples_split=5,
        min_samples_leaf=2
    )

    # Train model
    dt.fit(X_train, y_train)

    # Make predictions
    y_pred_train = dt.predict(X_train)
    y_pred_test = dt.predict(X_test)
```

```
    # Calculate metrics
    train_mse = mean_squared_error(y_train, y_pred_train)
    test_mse = mean_squared_error(y_test, y_pred_test)
    train_r2 = r2_score(y_train, y_pred_train)
    test_r2 = r2_score(y_test, y_pred_test)

    models[depth] = dt
    results[depth] = {
        'train_mse': train_mse,
        'test_mse': test_mse,
        'train_r2': train_r2,
        'test_r2': test_r2
    }

    print(f"\nDepth {depth}:")
    print(f"  Train MSE: {train_mse:.3f}")
    print(f"  Test MSE: {test_mse:.3f}")
    print(f"  Train R²: {train_r2:.3f}")
    print(f"  Test R²: {test_r2:.3f}")
```

Decision tree with depth 3 is the choice in this case as we achieve the lowest *test MSE* measure. As compared to OLS and LASSO this is the "best" model choice now.

```
Training set size: 404
Test set size: 102

Depth 2:
  Train MSE: 35.023
  Test MSE: 37.568
  Train R²: 0.597
  Test R²: 0.488

Depth 3:
  Train MSE: 32.624
  Test MSE: 35.842
  Train R²: 0.624
  Test R²: 0.511

Depth 5:
  Train MSE: 29.165
  Test MSE: 38.746
  Train R²: 0.664
  Test R²: 0.472

Depth 10:
  Train MSE: 19.435
  Test MSE: 44.834
  Train R²: 0.776
  Test R²: 0.389
```

Visual interpretation shown in Figure 6.8 shows the model step-wise form, as opposed to a linear form derived using OLS and LASSO previously and also the exploding overfitting danger post reaching depth 3.

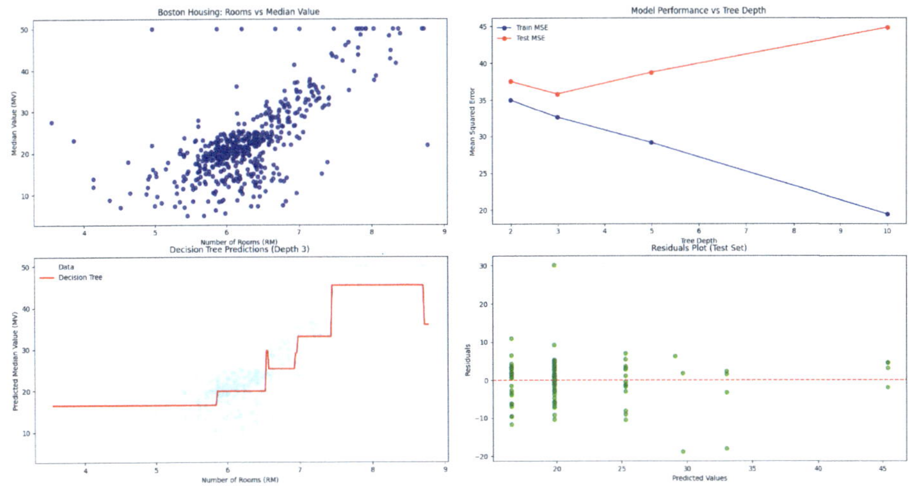

Figure 6.8 Decision Tree Visualization

The sign here is ever-increasing accuracy in train and equivalent decreasing accuracy using trained model in test data space, as reflected by observing train vs test MSE increasing deviation given enhanced model depth. At this stage, we have founds the best model choice in our hypothetical example. Is there yet better way to model decision trees then?

Random Forest

Before we proceed to our final destination in this chapter, neural networks, we add one more layer of complexity to our previous model exposition. Random forest is an ensemble method built on decision trees. For regression, a decision tree partitions the feature space into regions and predicts the mean target value within each region. Theoretically, we should find previous decision tree as per our previous model example using one feature, RM.

Random forest is a powerful and versatile machine learning algorithm widely used in scientific analysis. It operates by constructing multiple decision trees during training and outputting the mode of the classes (classification) or mean prediction (regression) of the individual trees. The random forest algorithm assumes that the individual trees are uncorrelated. By combining these uncorrelated trees, the overall model can achieve better accuracy and robustness. It also assumes that the data set features are randomly sampled with replacement, ensuring diverse trees. The estimation method in random forest involves the bootstrap aggregating technique, also known as bagging. Each decision tree is trained on a random subset of the data, and the final prediction is made by averaging the predictions of all trees. This method reduces overfitting and improves the model's generalization [6.5].

Random Forest Algorithm

Random forest combines multiple decision trees using bootstrap Aggregating (Bagging):

- Create B bootstrap samples from original data set

- Each sample has same size as original, with replacement
- Reduces variance: Var(average) = Var(individual)/B

Random feature selection:

- At each split, randomly select m features from total p features
- Typically m = √p for classification, m = p/3 for regression
- Reduces correlation between trees

Final Prediction

ŷ_RF = (1/B) * Σ(ŷ_i) for regression
Bias-Variance Decomposition:
$E[(y - \hat{y})^2] = Bias^2 + Variance + Irreducible\ Error$

Random Forest

- Bias: Similar to individual trees (high bias if trees are shallow)
- Variance: Significantly reduced through averaging
- Overfitting: Reduced due to randomness and averaging

Generalization Error:

$$E[\text{Error}] \leq \rho^{*}(\text{Var\_tree}/B) + \text{Bias}^2$$

Where $\bar{\rho}$ is average correlation between trees.

Despite its advantages, random forest has limitations. It can be computationally intensive and memory-consuming, especially with large data sets. The algorithm may also struggle with data sets containing noisy data or irrelevant features. Additionally, interpretability can be an issue, as the model's decision-making process is not as transparent as simpler algorithms.

Python Implementation

The following code snippet shows bootstrap mechanism in *class SimpleRandomForest* calling in decision tree, hence the computational overhead of random forest.

```
# Random Forest Implementation
class SimpleRandomForest:

    def __init__(self, n_estimators=100, max_depth=3, min_samples_split=2,
random_state=42):

        self.n_estimators = n_estimators
        self.max_depth = max_depth
        self.min_samples_split = min_samples_split
        self.random_state = random_state
        self.trees = []
        self.feature_indices = []

    def _bootstrap_sample(self, X, y, random_state):
        """Create bootstrap sample"""
```

```
        np.random.seed(random_state)
        n_samples = X.shape[0]
        indices = np.random.choice(n_samples, n_samples, replace=True)
        return X[indices], y[indices]

    def fit(self, X, y):
        """Train the random forest"""
        np.random.seed(self.random_state)

        for i in range(self.n_estimators):
            # Bootstrap sampling
            X_bootstrap, y_bootstrap = self._bootstrap_sample(X, y, i)

            # Train individual tree
            tree = SimpleDecisionTree(
                max_depth=self.max_depth,
                min_samples_split=self.min_samples_split
            )
            tree.fit(X_bootstrap, y_bootstrap)

            self.trees.append(tree)

    def predict(self, X):
        """Make predictions using all trees"""
        predictions = np.array([tree.predict(X) for tree in self.trees])
        return np.mean(predictions, axis=0)
```

When running across our data set, we get the following results, $MSE = 34.84$:

```
Loading Boston Housing Data...
Training set size: 404
Test set size: 102

1. Single Decision Tree:
   MSE: 35.84
   R²: 0.511

2. Simple Random Forest (Custom Implementation):
   MSE: 34.68
   R²: 0.527

3. Scikit-learn Random Forest:
   MSE: 34.29
   R²: 0.532
```

With visual interpretation as shown in Figure 6.9:

To summarize, in this section we exposed the reader to four core and basic machine learning models as used by FinTech practitioners, namely, (i) OLS, (ii) LASSO, (iii) decision tree and (iv) random forest. We have demonstrated the critical importance of utilizing train versus test data set split and observing strict implementation of relevant models focusing on one specific measure, *MSE*. Based on our results, and driven by our controlled hypothetical example, using RM and MV variables we conclude that random forest should be the model of choice, with the following results:

Model	MSE
LASSO	45.97
Decision Tree	35.84
Random Forest	34.68

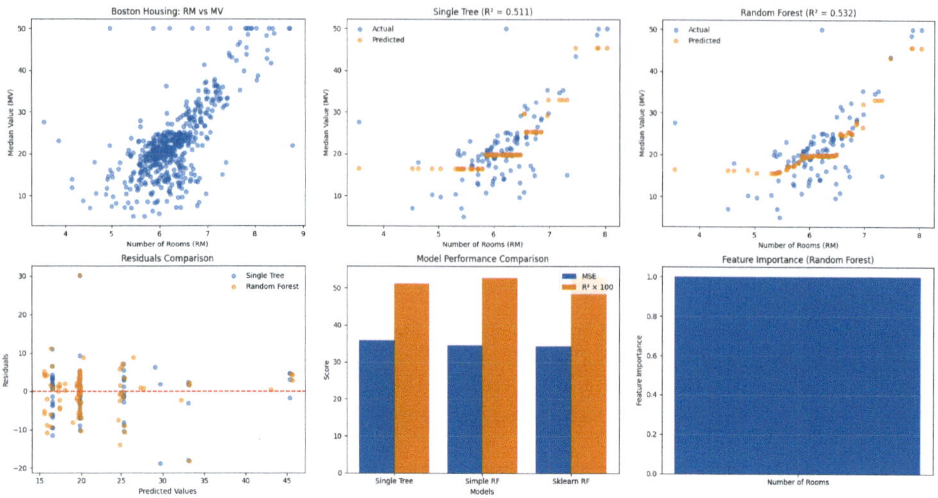

Figure 6.9 Random Forest Visualization

OLS MSE is driven by the entire data set, hence we have excluded this measure. The previous results are based on test data implementation, hence we have trained our models on trained data then executed across test data sets and observed *MSE* measures. In short, in this hypothetical example, we recommend to select random forest to proceed to DDF implementation stage.

6.3 Why Machine Learning in Finance Is Different

Expanding on our previous discussion about algorithms in "Chapter 1: Data Science for FinTech," machine learning in finance presents unique challenges that distinguish it from implementations in other scientific domains, as outlined in López de Prado's "Advances in Financial Machine Learning." Financial data suffers from fundamental structural problems rarely encountered in other sciences. Unlike controlled laboratory experiments or natural phenomena with clear patterns, financial data is characterized by extremely low signal-to-noise ratios. The underlying patterns are often buried beneath layers of market noise, making feature extraction and model training exceptionally difficult. Additionally, financial data sets frequently contain survivorship bias, look-ahead bias and data snooping issues that can lead to misleading results.

Financial markets undergo constant structural changes due to evolving regulations, technological advances, market participant behavior and macroeconomic shifts. This creates a nonstationary environment where historical relationships may suddenly break down. Unlike physics or biology where fundamental laws remain constant, financial markets exhibit regime changes that can render previously successful models obsolete overnight.

Financial time series represent a single path realization of a complex stochastic process. Unlike other sciences where experiments can be repeated under controlled conditions, financial markets provide only one historical trajectory. This creates severe limitations for backtesting and model validation, as researchers cannot truly replicate market conditions or generate independent samples for testing.

Traditional supervised learning relies on clear, objective labels, but financial outcomes are often ambiguous. Determining what constitutes a "profitable" trade or a "good" investment decision involves subjective choices about time horizons, risk adjustments and benchmark selections. López de Prado introduces sophisticated labeling methods like triple-barrier labeling to address these challenges, but the fundamental ambiguity remains.

Financial features must account for the complex, multidimensional nature of market data. Simple technical indicators often fail to capture the underlying market dynamics. Features must be carefully constructed to avoid look-ahead bias while incorporating market microstructure effects, volatility clustering and cross-asset relationships that don't exist in other domains.

Perhaps most importantly, financial markets represent an adversarial environment where participants actively work to exploit any discoverable patterns. As soon as a profitable strategy becomes known, it tends to be arbitraged away, unlike natural phenomena that remain constant regardless of human knowledge. This creates an arms race where successful models must continuously evolve or become obsolete.

Financial ML must integrate risk management from the outset, considering position sizing, portfolio construction and drawdown control. Unlike other applications where model accuracy is the primary concern, financial models must balance expected returns against potential losses, incorporating concepts like maximum drawdown, Sharpe ratios, and tail risk.

6.4 Machine Learning

Machine learning is a subset of artificial intelligence that enables computer systems to automatically learn, improve and make decisions from data without being explicitly programmed for every specific task. Instead of following pre-written instructions, these systems identify patterns in data and use those patterns to make predictions or decisions about new, unseen information.

The core concept revolves around training algorithms on data sets so they can recognize relationships, trends and structures within the data. Once trained, these models can generalize their learning to make accurate predictions or classifications on new data they haven't encountered before.

Machine learning operates through several main approaches. Supervised learning uses labeled training data where the algorithm learns from input-output pairs to predict outcomes for new inputs. Common examples include email spam detection, image recognition and medical diagnosis. Unsupervised learning finds hidden patterns in data without labeled examples, such as customer segmentation, anomaly detection or recommendation systems. Reinforcement learning involves agents learning through trial and error by receiving rewards or penalties for their actions, commonly used in game playing, robotics and autonomous systems.

Machine learning applications span virtually every industry. In healthcare, it assists with medical imaging analysis and drug discovery. In technology, it powers search engines, recommendation systems and virtual assistants. Transportation benefits through autonomous vehicles and route optimization. Finance uses it for fraud detection and algorithmic trading. Entertainment platforms employ it for content recommendation and personalization.

As indicated previously, finance and banking domain involves additional layers of not directly observed attributes or changing conditions. Hence, even though we have selected random forest as our primary model for our FinTech solution, this is not likely static choice, and the model conditions are likely going to evolve.

6.5 Deep Learning

The learning process typically involves feeding large amounts of data into mathematical models that adjust their internal parameters to minimize prediction errors. These models range from simple linear regression to complex neural networks with millions of parameters. Deep learning, a subset of machine learning, uses artificial neural networks with multiple layers to learn hierarchical representations of data, proving particularly effective for tasks involving images, speech and natural language.

Artificial Neural Networks

Artificial intelligence is the field of computer science focused on creating systems that can perform tasks typically requiring human intelligence. These systems are designed to perceive their environment, process information, reason about problems, learn from experience and make decisions to achieve specific goals. The field includes several core areas of study and application. Machine learning represents one major branch where systems improve their performance through experience with data. Natural language processing enables computers to understand, interpret and generate human language. Computer vision allows machines to interpret and analyze visual information from images and videos. Robotics combines AI with physical systems to create machines that can interact with and manipulate the physical world.

AI systems operate along a spectrum of capabilities. Narrow AI or weak AI focuses on specific, well-defined tasks like playing chess, recognizing faces or translating languages. These systems excel in their particular domain but cannot transfer their intelligence to other areas. General AI or strong AI represents the theoretical goal of creating machines with human-level intelligence across all cognitive tasks, though this remains largely unrealized.

Artificial neural networks (ANN) can be viewed as a collection of sophisticated algorithms attempting to replicate the functionality of our human brain, specifically neural network structures. ANNs can learn any approximation of a functional format $y = f(x)$. This approach is useful in, say, pattern recognition, data classification, picture recognition, voice recognition or time series modeling among other purposes.

Network Layers

From a simple perspective, the most common type of artificial neural network consists of three groups, or layers, of units as can be seen in Figure 6.10. A layer of "input" units is connected to a layer of "hidden" units, which is connected to a layer of "output" units.

- **Input units:** The activity of the input units represents the raw information that is fed into the network. This is also called the input layer.
- **Hidden units:** The activity of each hidden unit is determined by the activities of the input units and the weights on the connections between the input and the hidden units. This is also called the hidden layer.
- **Output units:** The behavior of the output units depends on the activity of the hidden units and the weights between the hidden and output units. This is also called the output layer.

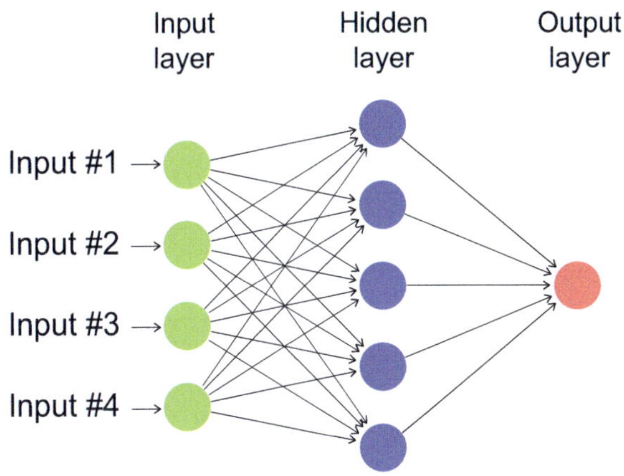

Figure 6.10 Network Layers

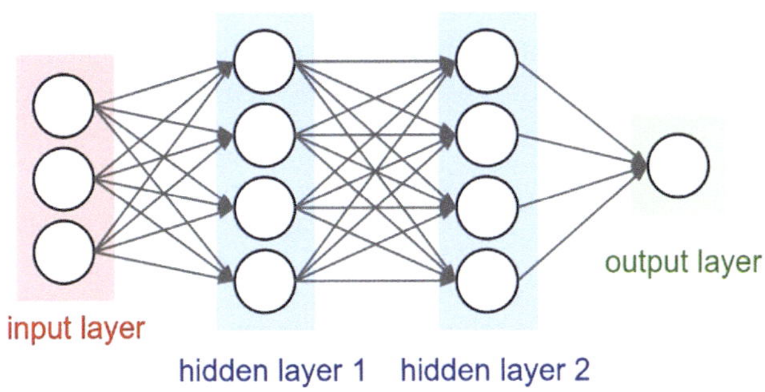

Figure 6.11 Network Layers Flow

As opposed to standard regression analytics, here you have the ability to "learn" hidden dynamics within your input data by applying recursive pattern and applying weights applicable to various hidden layers. Before diving deeper into recurrent neural network design, let us define some critical concepts.

Now, we look into the neural network (NN), the way this network "learns" the true dynamics as derived from the data is via hidden layers. Once each hidden layer the network learns new feature space by first computing linear transformations and then applying nonlinear function which will be defined as the new input to the next layer. Hence, we look at the neural network as a process, information flow like process, flowing through hidden layers into the final output layer as per Figure 6.11.

Say for a three-layer NN the functional format would look like $f(x) = f3(f2(f1(x)))$. As an example and each layer we learn a different representation of the presented data, say, a picture we can start by identifying edges, then contour and then dive deeper into the more complex feature of that picture resulting in final object identification.

Single Neuron

From a computational perspective, one core unit is called a neuron or node or unit in equivalent terms. Basically, imagine a node taking in some inputs, processing such input and then

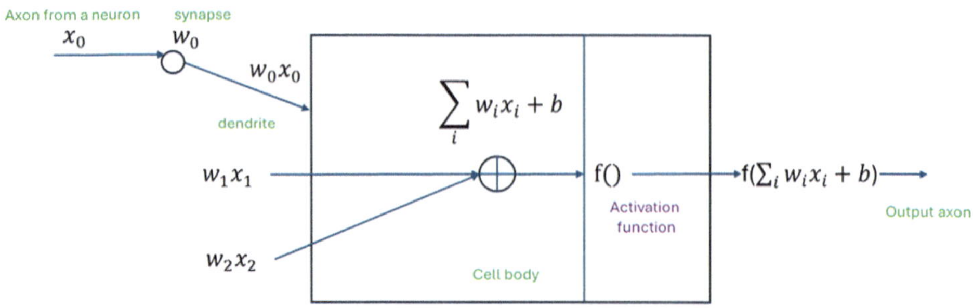

Figure 6.12 Single Neuron

delivering an output. Each input has an associated **weight (w)**, which is assigned on the basis of its relative importance to other inputs [6.6]. The node applies a function f (defined in the next section) to the weighted sum of its inputs:

The previous network shown in Figure 6.12 takes numerical inputs **X1** and **X2** and has weights **w1** and **w2** associated with those inputs. Additionally, there is another input **1** with weight **b** (called the **Bias**). Another critical component of neural networks as seen previously is called "activation function."

Activation Function

Activation functions serve as the mathematical gateways that determine whether and how strongly a neuron should be activated in a neural network. They transform the weighted sum of inputs into an output signal, introducing nonlinearity that enables neural networks to model complex patterns and solve sophisticated problems.

Without activation functions, neural networks would simply perform linear transformations regardless of their depth, essentially reducing to basic linear regression. The nonlinear properties of activation functions allow networks to approximate any continuous function, capture intricate relationships in data and learn complex decision boundaries that separate different classes or predict continuous values.

The activation function introduces a form of nonlinearity to the Y outcome variable. There are several activation functional forms for instance, as shown in Figure 6.13:

Sigmoid

The sigmoid function was historically popular, mapping inputs to values between 0 and 1 using the formula 1/(1 + e^(-x)). This creates a smooth S-shaped curve that naturally represents probabilities. However, sigmoid functions suffer from vanishing gradient problems in deep networks, where gradients become extremely small during backpropagation, making it difficult to train deeper layers effectively.

This function takes in a value as an input and sets the output to fit in between 0 and 1 levels, mostly used to depict probability results, as such in Figure 6.14:

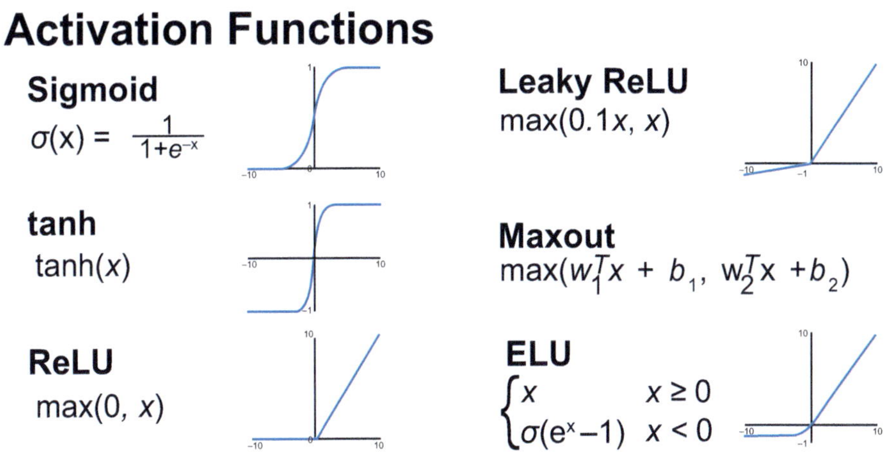

Figure 6.13 Activation Functions

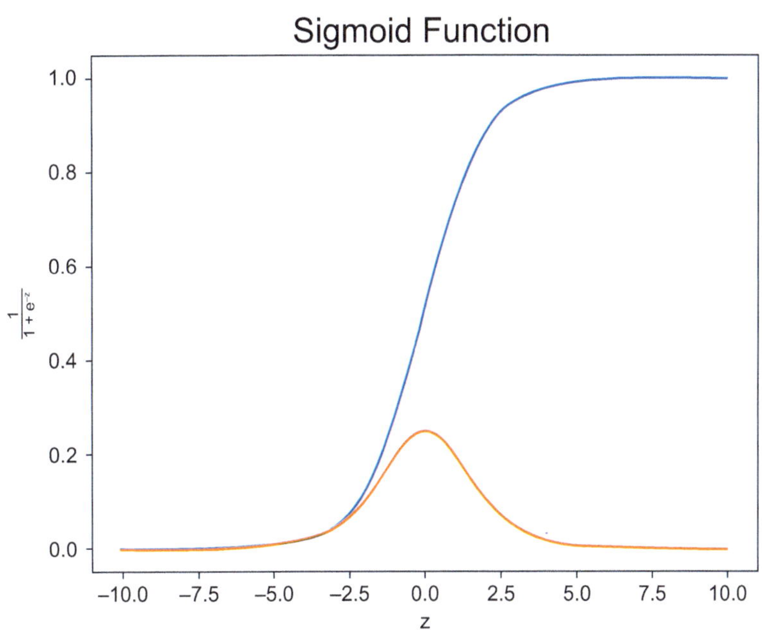

Figure 6.14 Sigmoid Function

```
import numpy as np
import matplotlib.pyplot as plt

# Define fuctional format
def sigmoid(Z):
    A = 1 / (1 + np.exp(-Z))
    return A, Z
```

```
# Plot activation functions
z = np.linspace(-10, 10, 100)

# Computes post-activation
A_sigmoid, z= sigmoid(z)

# Plot sigmoid
plt.plot(z, A_sigmoid, label="Function")
plt.plot(z, A_sigmoid * (1 - A_sigmoid))
plt.xlabel("z")
plt.ylabel(r"$\frac{1}{1 + e^{-z}}$")
plt.title("Sigmoid Function", fontsize=16)
plt.savefig("plot.png")
```

Another variation of the previous section is Softmax version of that looks at various levels of classification given probability levels between 0 and 1. This is relevant to problems related to classifying objects into categories as opposed to having binary solutions as either true or false.

Tanh

The hyperbolic tangent (tanh) function addresses some sigmoid limitations by mapping inputs to values between −1 and 1, providing zero-centered outputs that can help with convergence during training. Like sigmoid, it still experiences vanishing gradients in very deep networks but often performs better than sigmoid for hidden layers.

The hyperbolic tangent function is used as an alternative activation function here defined as defining output within −1 and 1, as shown in Figure 6.15.

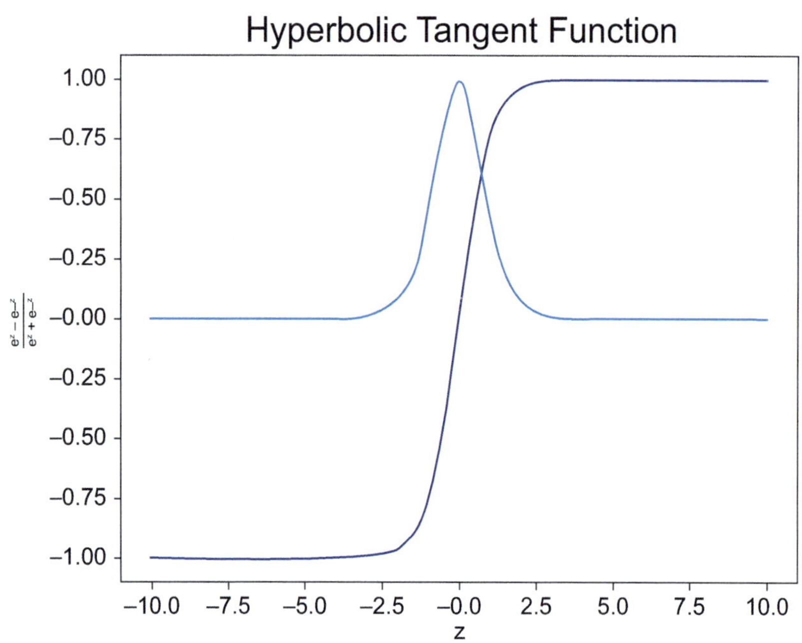

Figure 6.15 Tanh Function

```
import numpy as np
import matplotlib.pyplot as plt
def tanh(Z):
    A = np.tanh(Z)
    return A, Z

# Plot the activation function
z = np.linspace(-10, 10, 100)
# Computes post-activation outputs
A_tanh, z = tanh(z)

# Plot tanh
plt.plot(z, A_tanh, 'b', label = "Function")
plt.plot(z, 1 - np.square(A_tanh))
plt.xlabel("z")
plt.ylabel(r"$\frac{e^z - e^{-z}}{e^z + e^{-z}}$")
plt.title("Hyperbolic Tangent Function", fontsize=16)
plt.savefig("plot.png")
```

One last activation function we look at via Python is called ReLU, rectified linear unit. ReLU forms the base of all neural networks as it is usually used as a default activation function in most applications.

ReLU

Rectified linear unit (ReLU) has become the most widely used activation function due to its simplicity and effectiveness. ReLU outputs the input directly if positive, otherwise zero (max(0,x)). This function accelerates training by avoiding vanishing gradients for positive inputs, provides computational efficiency, and introduces sparsity by zeroing out negative values. However, ReLU can suffer from "dying ReLU" problems where neurons become permanently inactive.

ReLU function is defined as follows and shown in Figure 6.16:

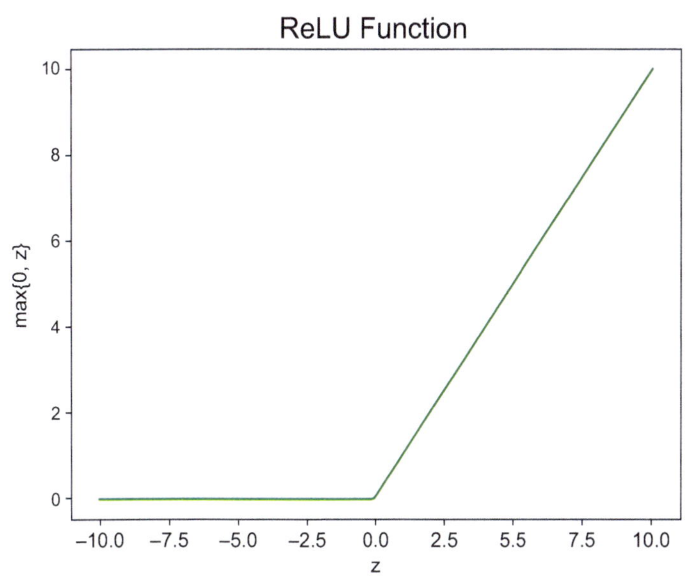

Figure 6.16 ReLU Function

```
import numpy as np
import matplotlib.pyplot as plt

def relu(Z):
    A = np.maximum(0, Z)
    return A, Z

# Plot the activation function
z = np.linspace(-10, 10, 100)

# Computes post-activation outputs
A_relu, z = relu(z)

# plot relu
plt.plot(z, A_relu, 'g')
plt.xlabel("z")
plt.ylabel(r"$max\{0, z\}$")
plt.title("ReLU Function", fontsize=16)
plt.savefig("plot.png")
```

The choice of activation function significantly impacts network performance, training speed and the ability to learn complex patterns. Hidden layers typically use functions like ReLU or its variants for their training efficiency, while output layers use functions matched to the specific task – sigmoid for binary classification, softmax for multi-class problems or linear activations for regression tasks.

In order to complete the basics of neural network mechanics, we need to comprehend the importance of forward versus backward propagation. This is as opposed to a simple linear regression where we run optimization as one instance of finding a solution to our simple regression model. However, before understanding the implications of forward and backward propagation, let us look at the theoretical approach to logistic regression.

Logistic Regression

Logistic regression serves as a fundamental machine learning technique in finance, particularly valuable for binary classification problems where outcomes fall into distinct categories. Here are key examples of its application across various financial domains.

Credit risk assessment represents one of the most common applications. Banks and lending institutions use logistic regression to predict whether a loan applicant will default or successfully repay their debt. The model analyzes factors such as credit score, debt-to-income ratio, employment history, loan amount and payment history to output a probability score between 0 and 1, where values closer to 1 indicate higher default risk. This probability helps lenders make informed decisions about loan approvals and interest rate pricing.

Fraud detection relies heavily on logistic regression to identify potentially fraudulent transactions. The model examines transaction characteristics including amount, location, time of day, merchant type and user spending patterns. When a transaction exhibits unusual patterns compared to historical behavior, the model assigns a high probability of fraud, triggering additional security measures or transaction blocking.

Stock price direction prediction applies logistic regression to forecast whether stock prices will move up or down. Traders input technical indicators such as moving averages, trading volume, price momentum and market sentiment scores. The model outputs binary predictions about price direction, though this application requires careful consideration of market efficiency and the limitations of historical pattern prediction.

Insurance claim classification helps insurance companies predict claim likelihood and severity. The model analyzes policyholder characteristics, coverage details, risk factors and historical claim patterns to classify policies as high-risk or low-risk, informing underwriting decisions and premium pricing strategies.

Regulatory compliance monitoring uses logistic regression to flag potentially suspicious activities requiring regulatory reporting. Financial institutions monitor transaction patterns, account relationships and customer behavior to identify activities that may violate anti-money laundering regulations or other compliance requirements

We have an input variable X , say, an image, and we want to know the probability that the image belongs to a class 1, say, a car. For a given X , the output then will be in terms of real values:

$$y = w^T X + b$$

However, because we are looking to find out the probability defined in the spectrum of a range between 0 and 1. Hence we apply the sigmoid function to the output:

$$\hat{y} = \sigma\left(w^T X + b\right)$$

where:

$$\sigma(z) = \frac{1}{1 + e^{-z}}$$

Hence, if z is very large, then $exp(-z)$ will be close to 0 and therefore the output will be 1. Contrary, if z is very small, $exp(-z)$ will be very large and hence the output will be 0.

Logistic Regression Cost Function

To train the parameters w and b of the logistic regression, we need some sort of a cost function that is going to define the parameters w and b such that at least one of the training sets, the outputs of the y predictions will be close to the actual values. Here we can define this function to be such:

$$\vartheta(\hat{y}, y) = \frac{1}{2}(\hat{y} - y)^2$$

The issue here is non-convexity, hence for gradient descent we redefine the previous function for logistic regression creating convexity such that:

$$\vartheta(\hat{y}, y) = -\left(y\log\hat{y} + (1 - y)\log(1 - \hat{y})\right)$$

Here the loss function is defined for a single training sample. However, we need to look at the entire training sample to define the cost function for a logistic regression:

$$J(w,b) = \frac{1}{m}\sum_{i-1}^{m}\vartheta\left(\hat{y}^i, y^i\right)$$

In short, here we need to make sure that the cost function is as small as possible. For this to be achieved, we need to optimize parameters w and b.

Gradient Descent

Gradient descent is a technique that is used to learn parameters w and b by optimizing given function, as previous. The function is convex, and hence we expect one global minima and that's the core reason for choosing the previous functional format. Let's investigate what is needed to run gradient descent:

1. Initialise w and b – we can set these vectors to 0
2. Take a step in the steepest downhill direction
3. Repeat step 2 until global optimum is achieved, defined as derivative being set to zero

Then the new, updated, equations for gradient descent will be:

$$w \cong w - \alpha\frac{\delta J(w,b)}{\delta w}$$

$$b \cong b - \alpha\frac{\delta J(w,b)}{\delta b}$$

Here, a is the learning rate, you will hear about later on, that controls how big a step we want to take after each iteration.

So in summary, let us step through logistics regression gradient descent now. The equations are as follows:

$$z = w^T X + b$$

$$\hat{y} = a = \sigma(z)$$

$$\vartheta(a,y) = -(y\log(a) + (1-y)\log(1-a))$$

Now, say for two features x1 and x2 the computational graph for computing the loss will be defined as follows in Figure 6.17:

This is what we call **forward propagation**, to calculate the first iteration of the loss function $L(a,y)$. Kind of equivalent to your standard regression methodology. However, this is not enough to find the optimized $w1$, $w1$ and b parameters. So now we do need to find derivatives of these parameters with respect to the entire function and update their parameters at each iteration in order to find the "optimal" results. This is what is called **backward propagation** as we go back in time to get to the "new" parameter sets only to start again moving forward.

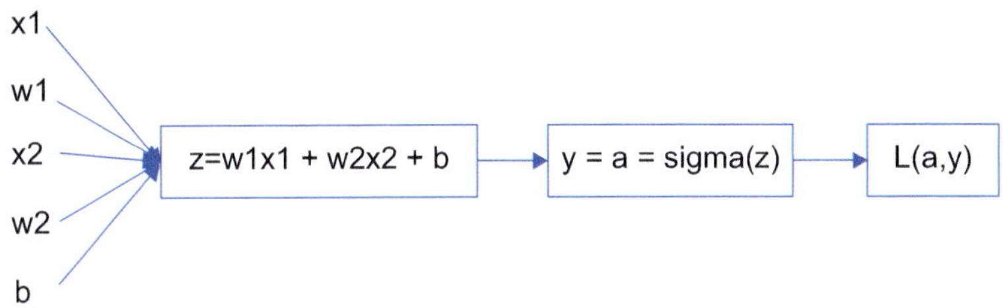

Figure 6.17 Loss Function Computation

Basically, we need to follow these steps:

1. Calculate da defined as $da = dL/da = (-y/a) + (1-y)/(1-a)$
2. Calculate dz defined as $dz = (dL/da)(da/dz) = [(-y/a) + (1-y)/(1-a)]^{*}[a(1-a)] = a - y$
3. Calculate $dw1$ defined as $dw = [(dL/da)(da/dz)]^{*}dz/dw1 = (a-y)^{*}dz/dw1$
4. Similar to $w1$ and b

Finally, the weights are updated following this first pass of the iteration for a single training set as such:

$$w_1 = w_1 - \alpha dw_1$$

$$w_2 = w_2 - \alpha dw_2$$

$$b = b - \alpha db$$

Because we are dealing with multiple training sets, we do need to look at how we calculate the previous set in this case, hence:

$$J(w,b) = \frac{1}{m}\sum_{i-1}^{m} L\left(a^{(i)}, y\right)$$

$$a^{(i)} = \hat{y}^{(i)} = \sigma\left(z^{(i)}\right) = \sigma\left(w^{T}x^{(i)} + b\right)$$

And the derivatives w.r.t. the parameters can be written as:

$$\frac{\delta}{\delta w_i} J(w,b) = \frac{1}{m}\sum_{i-1}^{m} \frac{\delta}{\delta w_i} L\left(a^{(i)} y^{(i)}\right)$$

Here is a simple, non-vectorized and rather "inefficient" way to calculate the forward and backward propagation steps in Python:

```
#Source: Andrew Ng, 2019

J = 0; dw1 = 0; dw2 =0; db = 0;
w1 = 0; w2 = 0; b=0;
for i = 1 to m

    # Forward pass
    z(i) = W1*x1(i) + W2*x2(i) + b
    a(i) = Sigmoid(z(i))
    J += (Y(i)*log(a(i)) + (1-Y(i))*log(1-a(i)))

    # Backward pass
    dz(i) = a(i) - Y(i)
    dw1 += dz(i) * x1(i)
    dw2 += dz(i) * x2(i)
    db  += dz(i)
J /= m
dw1/= m
dw2/= m
db/= m
# Gradient descent
w1 = w1 - alpha * dw1
w2 = w2 - alpha * dw2
b = b - alpha * db
```

Recurrent Neural Network (RNN)

In this final section we look at recurrent neural networks (RNNs). A traditional NN cannot by default persist with memory or cannot remember items from the past necessarily. Hence a new form of NN was created to account for sequential data streams. RNN are networks with loops, allowing information to be maintained, stared and reused as needed.

Basically, a recurrent neural network (RNN) is a type of neural network architecture specifically designed to process sequential data by maintaining memory of previous inputs through internal feedback loops. Unlike traditional feedforward networks that process inputs independently, RNNs have connections that create cycles, allowing information to persist and influence future predictions.

The fundamental characteristic of RNNs lies in their ability to use hidden states that act as memory. At each time step, the network processes the current input along with the hidden state from the previous time step, creating a form of temporal memory that captures information about what the network has seen in the sequence so far. This hidden state is updated at each step and passed forward, creating a chain of dependencies across time.

The basic RNN architecture consists of an input layer, a hidden layer with recurrent connections and an output layer. The hidden layer maintains a state vector that gets updated based on both the current input and the previous hidden state. This update typically involves applying weights to both the input and previous hidden state, combining them, and passing the result through an activation function like tanh or ReLU.

For example, the previous picture in Figure 6.18 depicts RNN and contains A cell that looks at some input x(t) and outputs value h(t). A loop allows information to be passed from one step of the network to the next, unfolded here:

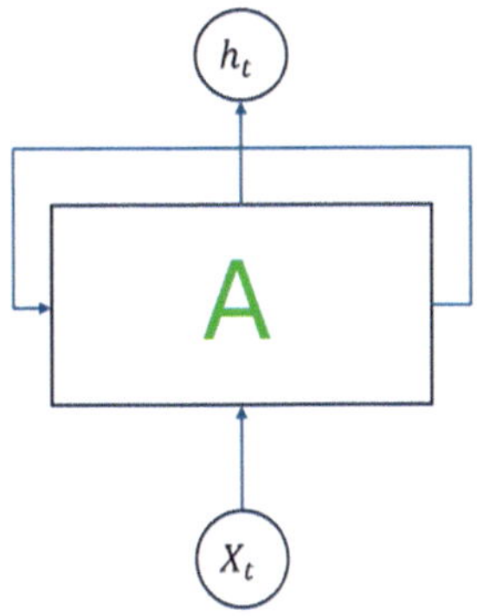

Figure 6.18 RNN A Cell

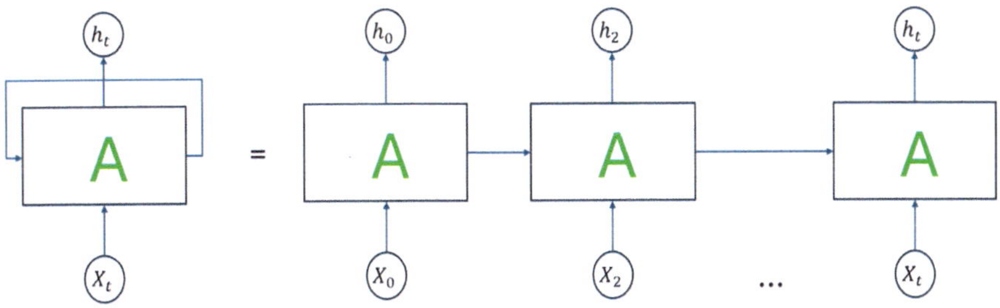

Figure 6.19 RNN Chain

Due to this chain feature, as shown in Figure 6.19, these networks are adept at dealing with sequence data streams, such as being generated by finance and banking operators on a daily basis. In addition to sequences, these networks can actually be rather useful when dealing with lists, a.k.a. statements, text paragraphs. At a later stage of the book, we explore this world further [6.7].

In short, RNNs excel in applications involving sequential data. **Language modeling** uses RNNs to predict the next word in a sentence by learning patterns in text sequences. **Machine translation** employs encoder-decoder architectures where one RNN encodes the source language sequence and another decodes it into the target language. **Speech recognition** leverages RNNs to convert audio sequences into text by learning temporal patterns in speech signals. **Time series forecasting** applications use RNNs to predict future values based on historical sequences, making them valuable for financial prediction, weather forecasting and demand planning. **Sentiment analysis** employs RNNs to classify the emotional tone of text by processing word sequences and understanding context.

Python Implementation

To build up our conceptual understanding of neural networks, let us first look at a simple example using *math.sin()* function that is predefined and well-behaved. We should be able to build a model that is going to predict the next step/result with relatively high accuracy. As opposed to analyzing a relationship among various features we focus on a sequence, predicting next observation.

As a start, we generate 100 sequences of randomly initiated sine waves to prepare training data set for our RNN architecture, as shown in Figure 6.20.

```
# Example: Sine wave prediction
def generate_sine_data(seq_length=10, num_sequences=100):
    """Generate sine wave sequences for training"""
    X, y = [], []

    for _ in range(num_sequences):
        # Random starting point
        start = np.random.uniform(0, 4*np.pi)
        # Generate sequence
        t = np.linspace(start, start + seq_length*0.1, seq_length + 1)
        sine_wave = np.sin(t)

        # Input: first seq_length points
        # Target: next point after each input point
        X.append([np.array([x]) for x in sine_wave[:-1]])
        y.append([np.array([x]) for x in sine_wave[1:]])

    return X, y
```

Initialize Simple RNN Architecture

Basic RNN equation *h_t = tanh(W_xh* x_t + W_hh * h_{t-1} + b_h)* with the hidden state and output layers defined in the next code snippet. We utilize backpropagation through time (BPTT) with gradient clipping. At this point, we initialize weights, *W_xh*, *W_hh*, *W_hy*, randomly and set biases to zero vectors as per this code snippet:

```
class SimpleRNN:
    def __init__(self, input_size, hidden_size, output_size,
learning_rate=0.01):
```

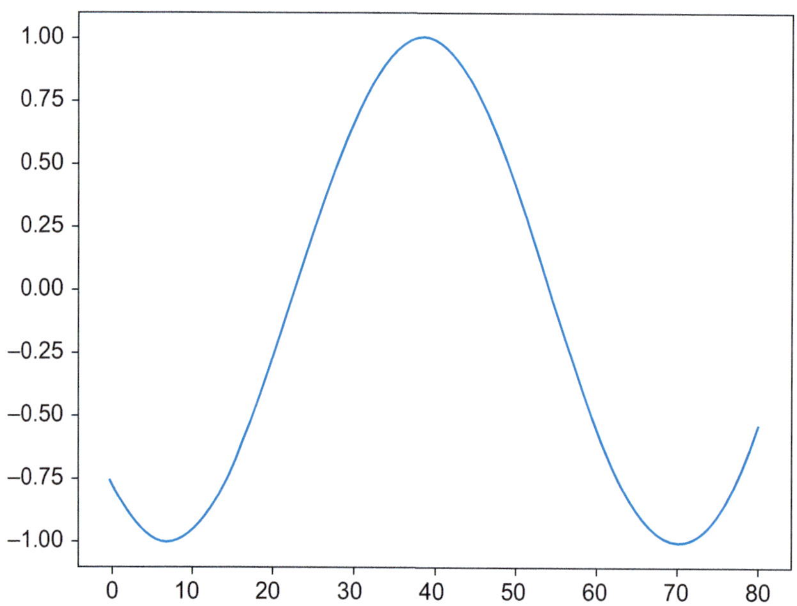

Figure 6.20 Sine Wave

```
        """
        Simple RNN implementation from scratch

        Args:
            input_size: Number of input features
            hidden_size: Number of hidden units
            output_size: Number of output features
            learning_rate: Learning rate for training
        """
        self.input_size = input_size
        self.hidden_size = hidden_size
        self.output_size = output_size
        self.learning_rate = learning_rate

        # Initialize weights randomly
        self.Wxh = np.random.randn(hidden_size, input_size) * 0.1  # Input to
hidden
        self.Whh = np.random.randn(hidden_size, hidden_size) * 0.1  # Hidden to
hidden
        self.Why = np.random.randn(output_size, hidden_size) * 0.1  # Hidden to
output

        # Initialize biases
        self.bh = np.zeros((hidden_size, 1))
        self.by = np.zeros((output_size, 1))
```

Forward Propagation

Forward propagation is the process of computing outputs by passing information sequentially through the network from one time step to the next, where each step uses both the current input and information from previous time steps.

In a standard RNN, forward propagation involves maintaining a hidden state that gets updated at each time step. For a sequence of inputs $x_1, x_2 \ldots x_t$, the process works as follows:

At each time step t:, the hidden state h_t is computed using the current input x_t and the previous hidden state h_{t-1}

- The computation typically follows: $h_t = tanh(W_{hh} \times h_{t-1} + W_{xh} \times x_t + b_h)$
- An output y_t can be generated from the hidden state: $y_t = W_{hy} \times h_t + b_y$

Where W represents weight matrices and b represents bias vectors.

Unlike feedforward networks that process all inputs simultaneously, RNNs process inputs one at a time in sequence, maintaining memory through the hidden state. The same weight matrices are used at every time step, which allows the network to handle sequences of varying lengths and reduces the total number of parameters. The hidden state acts as the network's memory, theoretically allowing it to remember information from earlier in the sequence when processing later inputs.

The forward pass creates an unfolded computational graph across time steps. For a sequence of length T, you essentially have T copies of the RNN cell connected in sequence, where each cell takes an input and passes its hidden state to the next time step. This sequential nature is what gives RNNs their power to model temporal dependencies, but it also creates challenges during training, particularly the vanishing gradient problem, which led to the development of more sophisticated architectures like LSTMs.

```
def forward(self, inputs):
    """
    Forward pass through the RNN

    Args:
        inputs: List of input vectors (sequence)

    Returns:
        outputs: List of output vectors
        hidden_states: List of hidden states
    """
    h = np.zeros((self.hidden_size, 1))  # Initial hidden state
    hidden_states = [h.copy()]
    outputs = []

    for x in inputs:
        # Reshape input to column vector
        x = x.reshape(-1, 1)

        # RNN forward step: h_t = tanh(W_xh * x_t + W_hh * h_{t-1} + b_h)
        h = np.tanh(np.dot(self.Wxh, x) + np.dot(self.Whh, h) + self.bh)

        # Output: y_t = W_hy * h_t + b_y
        y = np.dot(self.Why, h) + self.by

        hidden_states.append(h.copy())
        outputs.append(y.copy())

    return outputs, hidden_states
```

The function *forward()* defines forward propagation covering our hypothetical example.

Backward Propagation

Backward propagation is the process of computing gradients to update the network's parameters during training. Unlike feedforward networks, RNNs have temporal dependencies that make backpropagation more complex. The standard approach for RNNs is called backpropagation through time (BPTT). Since RNNs process sequences and maintain hidden states that depend on previous time steps, the network is conceptually "unrolled" across time steps to form a feedforward-like structure for gradient computation.

Basically, the RNN processes the input sequence step by step, computing hidden states and outputs at each time step. Each hidden state depends on the current input and the previous hidden state. Then, gradients flow backward through time, starting from the final time step and moving toward the beginning. At each time step, gradients are computed with respect to:

- The output at that time step
- The hidden state parameters
- The input-to-hidden and hidden-to-hidden weight matrices

Since gradients must flow through multiple time steps, they can either vanish (become exponentially small) or explode (become exponentially large). This is particularly problematic for long sequences. The unrolled network can become very deep for long sequences, making computation expensive and memory-intensive. The gradient at each time step depends on all future time steps, creating complex interdependencies that must be carefully managed. At this point, discussion on this computational limitation and how to address this through truncated BPTT step is out of the scope of this chapter.

```
def backward(self, inputs, targets, outputs, hidden_states):
    """
    Backward pass (backpropagation through time)

    Args:
        inputs: Input sequence
        targets: Target sequence
        outputs: Predicted outputs
        hidden_states: Hidden states from forward pass
    """
    # Initialize gradients
    dWxh = np.zeros_like(self.Wxh)
    dWhh = np.zeros_like(self.Whh)
    dWhy = np.zeros_like(self.Why)
    dbh = np.zeros_like(self.bh)
    dby = np.zeros_like(self.by)

    dh_next = np.zeros_like(hidden_states[0])

    # Backpropagate through time
    for t in reversed(range(len(inputs))):
        # Output layer gradients
        dy = outputs[t] - targets[t].reshape(-1, 1)
        dWhy += np.dot(dy, hidden_states[t+1].T)
        dby += dy

        # Hidden layer gradients
        dh = np.dot(self.Why.T, dy) + dh_next
        dh_raw = (1 - hidden_states[t+1] ** 2) * dh  # tanh derivative

        # Weight gradients
        dbh += dh_raw
        dWxh += np.dot(dh_raw, inputs[t].reshape(1, -1))
        dWhh += np.dot(dh_raw, hidden_states[t].T)

        dh_next = np.dot(self.Whh.T, dh_raw)

    # Clip gradients to prevent exploding gradients
    for dparam in [dWxh, dWhh, dWhy, dbh, dby]:
        np.clip(dparam, -5, 5, out=dparam)

    # Update weights
    self.Wxh -= self.learning_rate * dWxh
    self.Whh -= self.learning_rate * dWhh
    self.Why -= self.learning_rate * dWhy
```

```
        self.bh -= self.learning_rate * dbh
        self.by -= self.learning_rate * dby
```

Please note the use of *learning rate* while updating weights, this is yet another hyperparameters we need to manage in RMM implementation. The learning rate parameter is going to affect the speed of convergence as well as potential accuracy of the RRN results.

Training

Training in recurrent neural networks (RNNs) refers to the process of learning parameters (weights and biases) that allow the network to effectively process sequential data by maintaining and updating hidden states across time steps. The loss function depends on the task type. For sequence-to-sequence tasks, loss is computed at each output time step and summed or averaged (as in our case next). For sequence classification, loss is typically computed only at the final time step using the final hidden state.

This example trains the RNN to predict sine wave values. The network learns to take a sequence of sine wave as input, predict the next value in the sequence using its hidden state to remember previous patterns.

```
    def train(self, X, y, epochs=1000):
        """
        Train the RNN

        Args:
            X: Input sequences
            y: Target sequences
            epochs: Number of training epochs
        """
        losses = []

        for epoch in range(epochs):
            total_loss = 0

            for i in range(len(X)):
                # Forward pass
                outputs, hidden_states = self.forward(X[i])

                # Compute loss (mean squared error)
                loss = 0
                for j in range(len(outputs)):
                    loss += np.mean((outputs[j] - y[i][j].reshape(-1, 1)) ** 2)
                total_loss += loss

                # Backward pass
                self.backward(X[i], y[i], outputs, hidden_states)

            losses.append(total_loss / len(X))

            if epoch % 100 == 0:
                print(f"Epoch {epoch}, Loss: {losses[-1]:.6f}")

        return losses
```

```
    def predict(self, sequence):
        """
        Make predictions on a sequence

        Args:
            sequence: Input sequence

        Returns:
            predictions: Predicted outputs
        """
        outputs, _ = self.forward(sequence)
        return [output.flatten() for output in outputs]
```

Prediction

Within DDF model design stage, to implement RNN architecture we first initialize all input variables and layers, specify RNN network and feed the network training data sets. The next step is to train the RNN. Once trained, model RNN coefficients can be snapped in time and stored. The network is ready to be deployed to predict and extend any new observed time series in a form of sine waves.

```
    # Generate training data
X_train, y_train = generate_sine_data(seq_length=80, num_sequences=100)

# Create and train RNN
rnn = SimpleRNN(input_size=1, hidden_size=10, output_size=1, learning_rate=0.01)

print("Training RNN...")
losses = rnn.train(X_train, y_train, epochs=500)

# Test the trained RNN
print("\nTesting trained RNN...")

# Generate test sequence
test_start = np.random.uniform(0, 4*np.pi)
#test_t = np.linspace(test_start, test_start + 1.0, 15)
test_t = np.linspace(test_start, test_start + 81*.1, 81)
test_sine = np.sin(test_t)

# Use first 30 points to predict the rest
input_seq = [np.array([x]) for x in test_sine[:30]]
predictions = rnn.predict(input_seq)
```

Despite their power as seen in Figure 6.21, RNNs face challenges including computational intensity during training, difficulty to parallelize across time steps, and potential instability with very long sequences. Modern applications often use attention mechanisms or transformer architectures that can capture sequential dependencies more efficiently, though RNNs remain valuable for streaming applications and scenarios requiring true sequential processing with limited computational resources.

The sequential nature of financial data makes RNNs particularly valuable, as they can remember previous states and use that information to make predictions about future market conditions. Long Short-Term Memory (LSTM) networks, a specialized type of RNN, are especially popular in finance due to their ability to handle long-term dependencies in

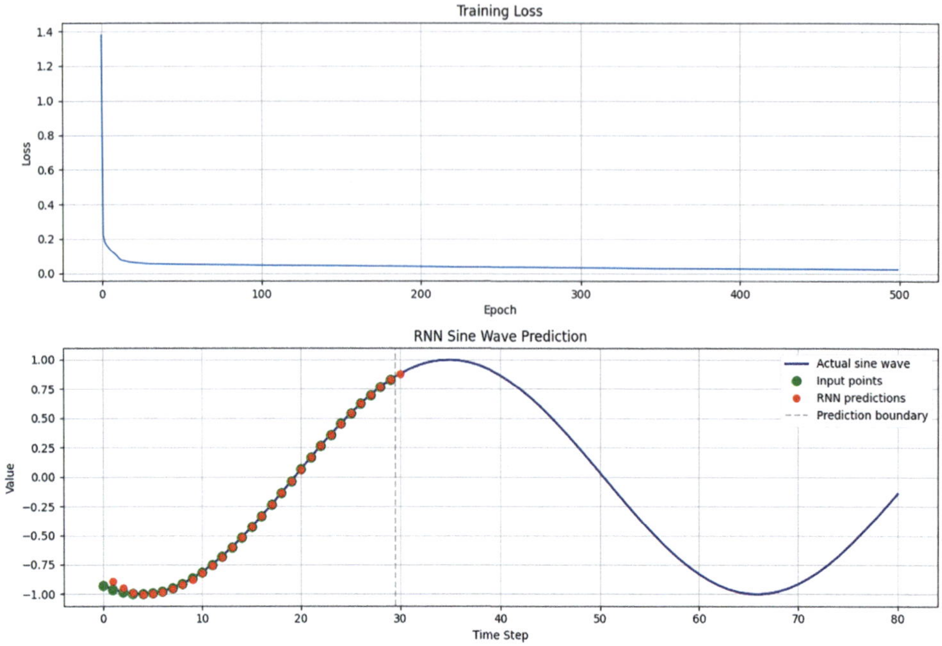

Figure 6.21 DDF Model Design: Recurrent Neural Network

financial time series data. In "Chapter 7: Language Analytics" we explore a version of RNN, *Long-Short Term Memory (LSTM) RNN* model in the context of finance and banking.

6.6 Summary

In this chapter we introduce the readers to a few basic machine learning tools used in finance and FinTech domains. In the first part of the chapter we dissected ordinary least square (OLS) model from conceptual, mathematical as well as programmatic perspective. We followed the same approach with LASSO regression, decision tree and random forest models. The core purpose is to position the reader into hypothetical DDF model selection Stage #3 and provide a framework for model selection. We simulated an approach to choose the "best" model for our task at hand using a measure of model accuracy. This part is dealing with standard machine learning models.

Next, in the second part, we highlight the notion that machine learning applications in finance differ significantly from other domains due to several unique characteristics of financial markets and data. Financial markets are inherently nonstationary, meaning statistical properties change over time. Unlike image recognition where a cat remains a cat, market patterns that worked yesterday may not work tomorrow due to regime changes, economic cycles, or structural shifts. This requires models that can adapt quickly or detect when relationships break down. Financial data typically has an extremely low signal-to-noise ratio compared to domains like computer vision or natural language processing. Moreover, market movements are influenced by countless factors, many of which are unpredictable or unmeasurable, making it much harder to extract meaningful patterns. More importantly, finance operates in an adversarial setting where your model's success can actually diminish its future effectiveness. If a profitable trading strategy becomes widely known, markets adapt and the edge disappears. This is unlike medical diagnosis or speech recognition where model performance doesn't degrade simply because others use similar approaches. Also, financial ML must operate within strict regulatory frameworks and risk management requirements. Models need to be interpretable for compliance, handle position limits, incorporate transaction costs, and maintain stability during market stress – constraints are rarely seen in other domains.

Lastly, given this environment, we expose the reader to one of the core machine learning tools – recurrent neural networks (RNN). The main purpose is to explain the RNN architecture, training process and model application in explainable and clearly interpretable fashion. We discuss forward and backward propagation and showcase a simple sine wave prediction example. This chapter forms a stepping stone into the following chapters exploring the intricacies of **long-short term memory recurrent neural network (LSTM RNN)** and to provide the reader with core mathematical and conceptual formulations necessary for sentiment analytics and **large language model (LLMs)** utilization.

6.7 Concept Questions and Answers

Q1: What assumptions must be met for OLS regression to provide unbiased estimates?

A1: OLS regression relies on several key assumptions: linearity (the relationship between independent and dependent variables is linear), independence of errors (residuals are not correlated), homoscedasticity (constant variance of errors across all levels of independent variables), normality of residuals (errors follow a normal distribution), and no multicollinearity (independent variables are not highly correlated with each other). When these assumptions are violated, the estimates may become biased or inefficient.

Q2: How does the coefficient of determination (R^2) relate to the explained variance in OLS regression?

A2: R^2 represents the proportion of variance in the dependent variable that is explained by the independent variables in the model. It ranges from 0 to 1, where 0 indicates no explanatory power and 1 indicates perfect explanation. Mathematically, $R^2 = 1 - (SSR/SST)$, where SSR is the sum of squared residuals and SST is the total sum of squares. However, R^2 can be misleading as it always increases with additional variables, which is why adjusted R^2 is often preferred for model comparison.

Q3: What is the bias-variance tradeoff in decision trees, and how does tree depth affect it?

A3: Decision trees exhibit high variance and low bias when deep (overfitting), and high bias with low variance when shallow (underfitting). Deep trees can perfectly fit training data by creating complex decision boundaries, but they generalize poorly to new data due to high variance. Shallow trees make strong assumptions about data structure (high bias) but are more stable across different data sets (low variance). The optimal tree depth balances this tradeoff, often determined through cross-validation or pruning techniques that penalize complexity.

Q4: How does feature importance calculation work in random forest, and what are its limitations?

A4: Random Forest calculates feature importance by measuring the average decrease in impurity (Gini or entropy) when a feature is used for splitting across all trees. Features that consistently produce pure splits receive higher importance scores. However, this method has limitations: it's biased toward features with more levels or continuous variables, correlated features may have their importance diluted across multiple variables, and it doesn't capture feature interactions well. Permutation-based importance, which measures prediction accuracy decrease when feature values are randomly shuffled, provides an alternative that addresses some of these limitations.

Q5: What is the vanishing gradient problem in RNNs, and how do LSTM and GRU architectures address it?

A5: The vanishing gradient problem occurs when gradients become exponentially small as they propagate backward through time in RNNs, making it difficult to learn long-term dependencies. This happens because gradients are multiplied by the same weight matrix at each time step. LSTM (long short-term memory) addresses this through gating mechanisms: forget gates decide what information to discard, input gates control what new information to store and output gates determine what parts of the cell state to output. GRU (gated recurrent unit) simplifies this with reset and update gates. Both architectures use additive updates to cell states rather than multiplicative ones, allowing gradients to flow more effectively across long sequences.

6.8 Exercises

E1: As discussed in the chapter, use Boston Real Estate from Kaggle data set selecting first, CRIM – crime variable, and second, use the entire data set of features to predict MV – median value of property. Your task is to select the best model from: (i) OLS, (ii) LASSO, (iii) decision tree and (iv) random forest. Justify your answer and provide evidence.

E2: As discussed in the chapter, use Boston Real Estate from Kaggle data set selecting first, CRIM – crime variable and second, use the entire data set of features to predict MV – median value of property. Your task is to build and implement recurrent neural network (RNN). Justify your answer and provide evidence. Is RNN model applicable in this scenario and can you implement this model?

E3: Within RNN model, set the learning rate parameter to a range of values [0.1, 0.01, 0.001, 0.0001] and implement our predefined sine_wave RNN example focusing on the sensitivity of this hyperparameter on the final prediction accuracy. Discuss the effect of this hyperparameter in real-world scenarios, say, predicting high-frequency EURUSD FX rates.

6.9 Further Reading

- Alammar, J., & Grootendorst, M. (2024). Hands-On Large Language Models: Language Understanding and Generation, O'Reilly.
- DePrado, M. L. (2018). Advances in Financial Machine Learning, John Wiley & Sons.
- Dickerson, A., & Hric, J. (2024). FINS5545 Financial Market Data Literacy Course Notes, UNSW Business School.
- Hric, J., & Lam, I. (2025). FINS5548 Financial Technology Course Notes, UNSW Business School.

- Huyen, C. (2025). AI Engineering: Building Applications with Foundation Models, O'Reilly.
- Raschka, S. (2025). Build a Large Language Model, Manning.

6.10 References

[6.1] Boston Real Estate: https://www.kaggle.com/datasets/altavish/boston-housing-dataset

[6.2] OLS Regression: https://scikit-learn.org/stable/modules/generated/sklearn.linear_model.LinearRegression.html

[6.3] LASSO: https://scikit-learn.org/stable/modules/generated/sklearn.linear_model.Lasso.html

[6.4] Decision Tree: https://scikit-learn.org/stable/modules/tree.html

[6.5] Random Forest: https://scikit-learn.org/stable/modules/generated/sklearn.ensemble.RandomForestClassifier.html

[6.6] Neural Network Representation: https://www.jeremyjordan.me/intro-to-neural-networks/

[6.7] RNN: https://karpathy.github.io/2015/05/21/rnn-effectiveness/

Chapter 7

Language Analytics for Finance and FinTech

7.1 Introduction

By leveraging **machine learning applications**, language analytics can uncover hidden linguistic patterns that are not immediately apparent. These applications process vast amounts of data using sophisticated algorithms to analyze text and speech. For instance, machine learning models can identify trends in social media conversations, predict customer sentiment and assist in language translation services. The data processing techniques involved are incredibly advanced, utilizing natural language processing (NLP) to efficiently break down and interpret language data.

The purpose of this chapter is to introduce the reader to one specific advanced tool to be added to the Finance and FinTech Toolkit: **Long Short Term Memory Recurrent Network (LSTM)**. We maintain our role as participants in the DDF Station #3 Model Selection.

DOI: 10.4324/9781003477747-9

Based on our previous description of the DDF model design station in "Chapter 2, Data Management for FinTech," at this phase, we are building and creating models that can accurately forecast future outcomes. The success of these models results in the clarity and parsimony of the results. A clear and concise model design can help businesses make informed decisions and stay ahead of the competition. The model design workstation utilizes advanced techniques such as neural networks and chatbots to create models that are both efficient and effective.

Firstly, we expose the reader to LSTM model architecture, outlining key model features and programmatic implementation. These networks are designed to recognize and predict patterns over time, making them exceptionally suited for tasks involving sequential data. By leveraging LSTM RNNs, researchers and developers can effectively process and analyze complex linguistic patterns, leading to more accurate natural language processing applications. One of the key aspects of LSTM RNNs is their ability to maintain information over extended periods, thanks to their unique memory cell structure. This feature allows them to capture long-term dependencies in data, which is crucial for understanding context in language.

Secondly, we apply the LSTM model as designed to structured dataframes, specifically cryptocurrency prices. This demonstrates the sequential capability of this model architecture and highlights that the LSTM model can be used for both numeric and textual data inputs. Lastly, we apply LSTM to a professional report, building the model's capability to generate text continuation based on given text inputs. Finally, we utilize the same LSTM architecture, but now we train the model on Shakespeare's *Romeo and Juliet*. This demonstrates a critical point: data input plays a crucial role in the model outputs and predictions. This observation is applicable to all language analytics-based frameworks. LSTM RNNs hold significant promise for advancing language analytics, even in the age of generative AI platforms. Their ability to process sequential data and capture long-term dependencies makes them invaluable for developing more intelligent and responsive language-based applications in Finance and FinTech.

Learning Outcomes

At the end of this chapter the reader will be able to:

- Understand long short term memory (LSTM) implementation requirements
- Get familiar with PyTorch LSTM library
- Comprehend the distinction between numeric and textual data inputs
- Be aware of the importance of data quality
- Be able to implement LSTM model for structured as well as unstructured data

7.2 Long Short Term Memory (LSTM) Recurrent Neural Network

Long-Short Term Memory (LSTM) model plays a crucial role in time series forecasting because they know how to capture patterns over time. The LSTM architecture works exceptionally well to predict complex sequential data like financial markets, weather patterns, and energy use trends. These models can spot intricate time-based relationships that basic models miss. Hence, for the purposes of DDF Model Selection process, in this chapter we focus our attention on this specific model architecture. LSTM neural networks adapt well to many forecasting needs:

- Energy consumption prediction for resource planning
- Weather forecasting for disaster prevention
- Financial market forecasting for investment strategies

In addition to this structured, quantitative, data formats, LSTM neural network excels at creating text, unstructured data format. Text generation works as a continuous series of next-word predictions. The model learns how words connect and their likely sequences [7.1]. Well-trained networks can create new and original character sequences that match the training data's style. This makes them valuable for creative writing, content generation and interactive AI systems. Also, LSTM architecture help audiovisual speech recognition systems overcome noise problems that trouble regular audio-only systems. The networks' forget gates, input gates, and output gates determine which audio inputs matter across time sequences.

The initial implementation of Elman-style RNNs using backpropagation was soon followed by the identification of significant challenges in learning long-range dependencies (due to vanishing and exploding gradients) [7.2]. The phrase "long short-term memory" reflects two key concepts. Traditional recurrent neural networks, as discussed in "Chapter 6, Machine Learning Tools for Finance and FinTech," possess long-term memory through their weights. These weights gradually adjust during training, storing fundamental data patterns. They also contain short-term memory through temporary activations, which flow between consecutive nodes. The LSTM architecture adds a middle-ground storage system using memory cells. A memory cell functions as an integrated component, constructed from basic nodes in a particular connection arrangement, featuring the distinctive addition of multiplicative nodes [7.3].

Before we proceed further, let us summarize issues found with RNN architecture. Firstly, the vanishing gradient problem is one of the biggest obstacles in training deep RNNs. This issue happens during backpropagation when gradients get smaller and smaller as they move backward through time steps. Gradients multiply repeatedly as they move backward through layers during backpropagation through time (BPTT), then the gradient shrinks faster when these multiplied values stay under 1.0 and the deeper the network gets, early layers receive almost no gradient signals. The effects are far-reaching as RNNs can spot patterns between nearby and close sequence elements but fail to link information spread across many time steps [7.4].

Secondly, while some gradients vanish, others can explode. The exploding gradient problem happens when gradient values grow too fast during backpropagation [7.5]. Though less common than vanishing gradients, exploding gradients can wreck the learning process just as badly. Large gradient values during training cause dramatic weight updates that destabilize the network. In extreme cases, weights can grow so large they overflow, creating NaN (Not a Number) values that stop learning completely. You can spot exploding gradients when loss values change wildly between updates, model weights grow extremely fast, and error gradient values stay above 1.0.

It is constructive to show RNN cell design in details. In the following section we highlight the differences with LSTM Cell addressing the previous RNN Cell issues. Refer to previous programmatic breakdown as provided in "Chapter 5, Machine Learning for Finance and FinTech."

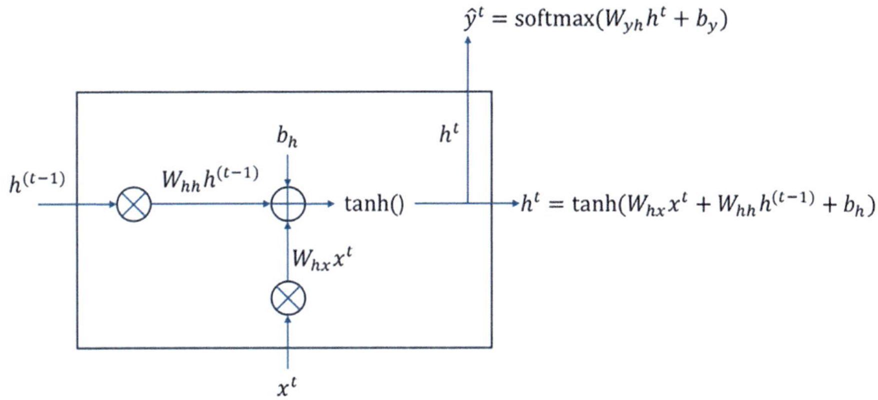

Figure 7.1 RNN Cell Design

As per Figure 7.1, basic RNN cell, as depicted in the previous section, takes as **inputs** x^t (current input) and h^{t-1} (previous hidden state containing information from the past), and **outputs** h^t. which is given to the next RNN cell and also used to predict $\hat{y}^t$.

LSTM Architecture

This implementation provides a conceptual and mathematical demonstration of LSTM network [7.6]. In this section we use programmatic interpretation of the formulas and core relationships to track the flows within Python code snippets. Next section, we step through a practical application of LSTM model predicting cryptocurrency exchange rates. LSTM architecture contain several new elements:

- Cell State (C_t): The "memory highway" that flows through the network, allowing information to pass unchanged
- Hidden State (h_t): The output state that gets passed to the next time step and used for predictions
- Forget Gate: Decides what information to discard from the cell state C_{t-1}
- Input/Update Gate: Decides what new information to store in the cell state C_t
- Output Gate: Decides what parts of the cell state to output as the hidden state C_t

Figure 7.2 shows a basic LSTM cell, as depicted previously, takes as **inputs** x^t (current input), h^{t-1} (previous hidden state containing information from the past) and c^{t-1} (previous cell state), and **outputs** h^t and c^t, which is given to the next LSTM cell and also are used to predict $\hat{y}^t$.

Mathematical Formulation

The flow starts with input parameters, stepping into forget gate first, proceeding across input/update gate with candidate value updates, and then stepping through into output gate delivering two outputs as indicated previously. The LSTM equations implemented in the code are broken down as per the following:

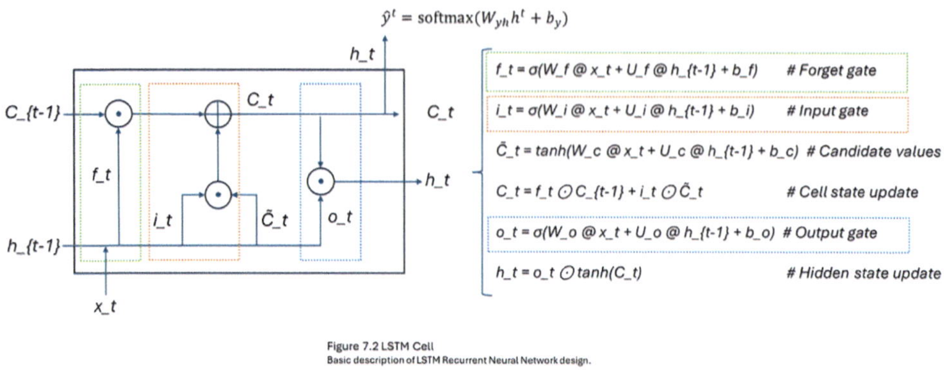

Figure 7.2 LSTM Cell Design

$$f\_t=\sigma\left(W\_f\cdot x\_t+U\_f\cdot h\_\{t\text{-}1\}+b\_f\right)\text{\# Forget gate}$$

$$i\_t=\sigma\left(W\_i\cdot x\_t+U\_i\cdot h\_\left\{t-1\right\}+b\_i\right)\text{\#Input gate}$$

$$\tilde{C}t=tanh\left(W\_c\cdot x\_t+U\_c\cdot h\left\{t-1\right\}+b\_c\right)\text{\#Candidate values}$$

$$C\_t=f\_t\odot C\_\{t\text{-}1\}+i\_t\odot\tilde{C}\_t\text{\#Cell state update}$$

$$o\_t=\sigma(W\_o\cdot x\_t+U\_o\cdot h\_\{t\text{-}1\}+b\_o)\text{\#Output gate}$$

$$h\_t=o\_t\odot \tanh(C\_t)\text{\#Hidden state update}$$

where $\odot$ denotes element-wise multiplication.

We maintain this symbol across the following sequence of Python code snippets to keep consistency. In the following code we initialize weights and biases for all gates. Each gate has weights for input (W) and hidden state (U), plus relevant bias (b).

```
class LSTMCell:
    """
    Long Short-Term Memory (LSTM) Cell Implementation
    LSTM addresses the vanishing gradient problem in traditional RNNs by
using:
    1. Cell state (C_t): Long-term memory
    2. Hidden state (h_t): Short-term memory
    3. Three gates: Forget, Input, Output
    """

    def __init__(self, input_size: int, hidden_size: int):
        self.input_size = input_size
        self.hidden_size = hidden_size

        # Initialize weights and biases for all gates
        # Each gate has weights for input (W) and hidden state (U), plus bias (b)
```

```
    # Forget gate: decides what information to discard from cell state
    self.Wf = np.random.randn(hidden_size, input_size) * 0.1
    self.Uf = np.random.randn(hidden_size, hidden_size) * 0.1
    self.bf = np.zeros((hidden_size, 1))

    # Input gate: decides what new information to store in cell state
    self.Wi = np.random.randn(hidden_size, input_size) * 0.1
    self.Ui = np.random.randn(hidden_size, hidden_size) * 0.1
    self.bi = np.zeros((hidden_size, 1))

    # Candidate values: new candidate values for cell state
    self.Wc = np.random.randn(hidden_size, input_size) * 0.1
    self.Uc = np.random.randn(hidden_size, hidden_size) * 0.1
    self.bc = np.zeros((hidden_size, 1))

    # Output gate: decides what parts of cell state to output
    self.Wo = np.random.randn(hidden_size, input_size) * 0.1
    self.Uo = np.random.randn(hidden_size, hidden_size) * 0.1
    self.bo = np.zeros((hidden_size, 1))
```

In the same *class LSTMCell* we define *sigmoid()* and *tanh()* functions and proceed with forward propagation step defined in *forward()* function.

```
def forward(self, x_t, h_prev, c_prev):
    """
    Forward pass through LSTM cell

    Mathematical formulation:
    f_t = σ(W_f @ x_t + U_f @ h_{t-1} + b_f)  # Forget gate
    i_t = σ(W_i @ x_t + U_i @ h_{t-1} + b_i)  # Input gate
    C̃_t = tanh(W_c @ x_t + U_c @ h_{t-1} + b_c)  # Candidate values
    C_t = f_t ⊙ C_{t-1} + i_t ⊙ C̃_t            # Cell state update
    o_t = σ(W_o @ x_t + U_o @ h_{t-1} + b_o)  # Output gate
    h_t = o_t ⊙ tanh(C_t)                      # Hidden state update
    where ⊙ denotes element-wise multiplication
    """

    # Reshape inputs to column vectors
    x_t = x_t.reshape(-1, 1) if x_t.ndim == 1 else x_t
    h_prev = h_prev.reshape(-1, 1) if h_prev.ndim == 1 else h_prev
    c_prev = c_prev.reshape(-1, 1) if c_prev.ndim == 1 else c_prev

    # Forget gate: What to forget from previous cell state
    f_t = self.sigmoid(self.Wf @ x_t + self.Uf @ h_prev + self.bf)

    # Input gate: What new information to store
    i_t = self.sigmoid(self.Wi @ x_t + self.Ui @ h_prev + self.bi)

    # Candidate values: New candidate values
    c_tilde_t = self.tanh(self.Wc @ x_t + self.Uc @ h_prev + self.bc)

    # Update cell state: Combine forgotten and new information
    c_t = f_t * c_prev + i_t * c_tilde_t

    # Output gate: What to output based on cell state
    o_t = self.sigmoid(self.Wo @ x_t + self.Uo @ h_prev + self.bo)
```

```
# Update hidden state
h_t = o_t * self.tanh(c_t)

# Store intermediate values for backpropagation
self.cache = {
    'x_t': x_t, 'h_prev': h_prev, 'c_prev': c_prev,
    'f_t': f_t, 'i_t': i_t, 'c_tilde_t': c_tilde_t,
    'c_t': c_t, 'o_t': o_t, 'h_t': h_t
}

return h_t, c_t
```

Note, at this stage, we return *h_t* and *c_t* with cached values for all intermediate computations. Side note, this is one of the reasons why we do need additional computing resources and cache memory space to run LSTM models. Backward propagation and further variants and extensions for LSTM model are out-of-scope from this chapter. The reader is referred to Further Reading selection and further advanced reading [7.7].

The forget gate filters the network's memory and decides what information to keep from the previous cell state. The forget gate equation gives us a vector ft with values between 0 and 1 for each number in the cell state. Values close to 1 mean "keep this information completely," while values near 0 mean "discard this information completely." This filtering stops the LSTM architecture from getting overwhelmed by useless data over time.

The input gate chooses what new information should go into the cell state. It works with a candidate cell state to update the memory. The input gate creates a vector of values between 0 and 1 that acts as a filter. This filter decides which parts of the candidate values should join the cell state. The tanh function creates candidate values (C~t) between −1 and 1 that might update the cell state. These calculations let the LSTM recurrent neural network add new information with precision while filtering out noise.

The output gate manages what information from the updated cell state becomes the hidden state output. It acts as a filter between the cell's internal memory and external network. Like other gates, the output gate uses a sigmoid function to produce values between 0 and 1. These values select which parts of the cell state should contribute to current output and move to the next time step.

Finally, we are dealing with cell state and hidden state calculations. The cell state works as the LSTM neural network's long-term memory, like a conveyor belt carrying information through sequence processing. The update equation mixes old and new information. Element-wise multiplication (*) lets each cell state component work independently. This mechanism helps the long short term memory LSTM neural network maintain useful information across long sequences. Then, the hidden state shows the LSTM model's output at each time step and feeds into the next network layer. The hidden state contains a filtered version of the cell state, showing only what the output gate considers relevant for prediction.

All of the previous components are the foundations of the LSTM architecture. They solve the vanishing gradient problem by creating clear paths for gradients to flow through time steps. The cell state's linear interactions reduce gradient decay, which helps the network learn patterns across hundreds of time steps, unlike traditional recurrent neural networks [7.8].

```
class LSTM:
    """
    Multilayer LSTM Network for sequence processing
    """

    def __init__(self, input_size: int, hidden_size: int, output_size: int, num_
layers: int = 1):
        self.input_size = input_size
        self.hidden_size = hidden_size
        self.output_size = output_size
        self.num_layers = num_layers

        # Create LSTM layers
        self.layers = []
        for i in range(num_layers):
            layer_input_size = input_size if i == 0 else hidden_size
            self.layers.append(LSTMCell(layer_input_size, hidden_size))

        # Output layer
        self.Wy = np.random.randn(output_size, hidden_size) * 0.1
        self.by = np.zeros((output_size, 1))

        # Initialize hidden and cell states
        self.reset_states()

    def reset_states(self):
        """Reset hidden and cell states to zero"""
        self.h_states = [np.zeros((self.hidden_size, 1)) for _ in
range(self.num_layers)]
        self.c_states = [np.zeros((self.hidden_size, 1)) for _ in
range(self.num_layers)]

    def forward_sequence(self, X: np.ndarray) -> Tuple[np.ndarray,
List[np.ndarray]]:
        """
        Forward pass through entire sequence

        Args:
            X: Input sequence of shape (sequence_length, input_size)

        Returns:
           outputs: Output sequence of shape (sequence_length, output_size)
           hidden_states: List of hidden states for each time step
        """
        sequence_length = X.shape[0]
        outputs = []
        all_hidden_states = []

        for t in range(sequence_length):
            x_t = X[t].reshape(-1, 1)

            # Forward through all LSTM layers
            layer_input = x_t
            layer_hidden_states = []

            for layer_idx in range(self.num_layers):
                h_t, c_t = self.layers[layer_idx].forward(
                    layer_input,
```

```
                    self.h_states[layer_idx],
                    self.c_states[layer_idx]
                )

                # Update states
                self.h_states[layer_idx] = h_t
                self.c_states[layer_idx] = c_t
                layer_hidden_states.append(h_t.flatten())

                # Output of this layer becomes input to next layer
                layer_input = h_t

            # Compute output
            y_t = self.Wy @ self.h_states[-1] + self.by
            outputs.append(y_t.flatten())
            all_hidden_states.append(layer_hidden_states)

        return np.array(outputs), all_hidden_states
```

In the *class LSTM* we onboard LSTM architecture design specifications in terms of input size, hidden layers, output size and number of layers (multilevel LSTM specification). We start with layers composition and final output layer initialization. We set *Wy* to be set to *random*0.01* and *by* bias set to zeros. Then within the *forward_sequence()* function we trigger *LSTMCell.forward()* definition. It is at this point, we introduce the ability to stack LSTM layers to expand the RNN depth.

Key Model Features

In the previous section, we implemented complete LSTM Cell that implements all gates with proper weight matrices and biases, in addition, we split the implementation to be able to add multilayer support. In this case, we can stack multiple LSTM layers on top of each other. Let us proceed and use this newly build LSTM network and use the same example as per last chapter – to predict sine wave pattern.

```
# Parameters
seq_length = 20
input_size = 1
hidden_size = 10
output_size = 1
num_sequences = 5

# Create LSTM
lstm = LSTM(input_size, hidden_size, output_size)

# Generate training data
X_train, y_train = create_sine_wave_data(seq_length, num_sequences) #use
the same function as per Chapter 5, generating training data (20, 5) with 20
observations across 5 data sequences

print(f"Training LSTM on {num_sequences} sine wave sequences")
print(f"Sequence length: {seq_length}")
print(f"Hidden size: {hidden_size}")
print()

# Demonstrate forward pass on one sequence
print("Forward pass example:")
lstm.reset_states()
outputs, hidden_states = lstm.forward_sequence(X_train[0].squeeze())
```

```
print(f"Input shape: {X_train[0].shape}")
print(f"Output shape: {outputs.shape}")
print(f"Number of hidden state layers per timestep: {len(hidden_states[0])}")
print()
```

Resulting in the following LSTM analytics:

```
Training LSTM on 5 sine wave sequences
Sequence length: 20
Hidden size: 10

Forward pass example:
Input shape: (20, 1)
Output shape: (20, 1)
Number of hidden state layers per timestep: 1
```

Figure 7.3 shows gate activations, hidden states, and memory evolution. We can observe the cell state provides an uninterrupted path for gradients to flow backward through time. Gates allow the network to selectively remember, forget, and output information. Lastly, long-term dependencies can maintain information over hundreds of time steps.

In the following section we apply LSTM model from within *PyTorch* library. We use numeric data and then textual data sets to first predict price levels of cryptocurrency and then extend text sequence [7.9]. The focus is on the training data quality and training text variations.

7.3 Structured Data

Structured data in finance refers to highly organized and easily searchable information, often stored in databases. This data type includes financial statements, transaction records, and market data, which are essential for accurate financial analysis and decision-making. The scientific concept behind structured data lies in its ability to be processed by algorithms, enabling automation and real-time analysis. Daily closing prices of financial assets, such as cryptocurrencies, are a neat example of structured data sequence.

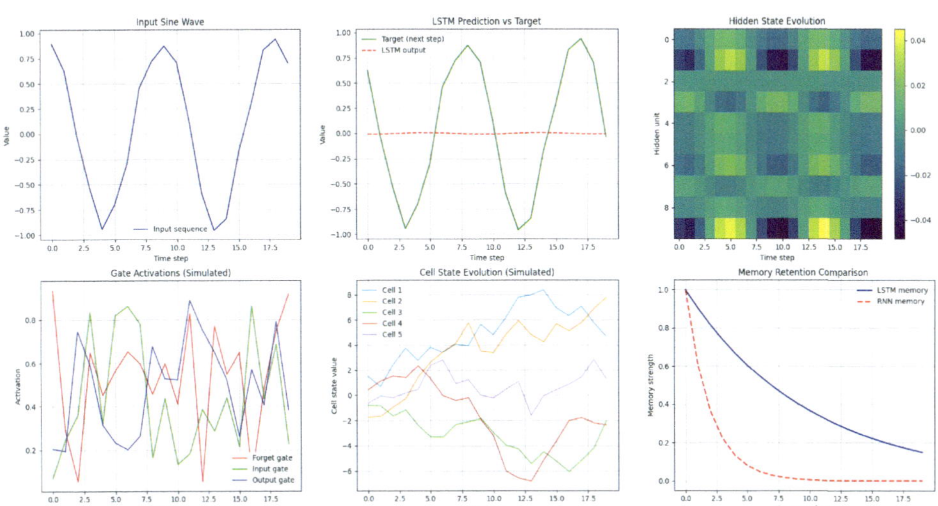

Figure 7.3 LSTM Visualization

Crypto Quant Trading

For Finance and FinTech practitioners, it is natural to operate in numeric domains, hence, before we proceed into the language space we step through LSTM model implementation within crypto quant trading simulation. Afterwards, we utilize exact LSTM model architecture in text continuation example.

In this case, we extract 1Y daily Bitcoin prices from *CryptoCompare API*, following similar API steps as depicted in "Chapter 3, Data Visualization." We aim to **demonstrate** application of LSTM model using PyTorch implementation. We predict Bitcoin price in the following period – one day forward and seven days forward. Figures 7.4 and 7.5 show current level of Bitcoin value and last 1Y historical observations respectively.

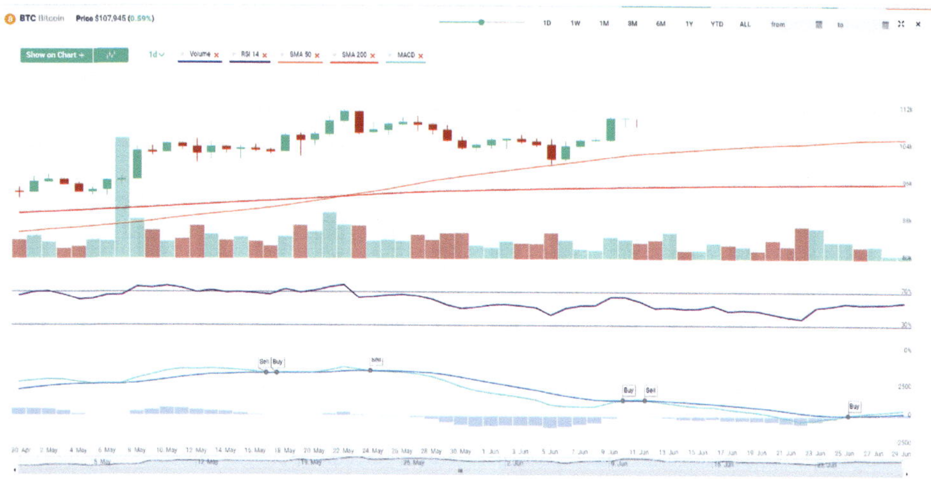

Figure 7.4 [Reference altFINS: https://altfins.com/crypto-screener]

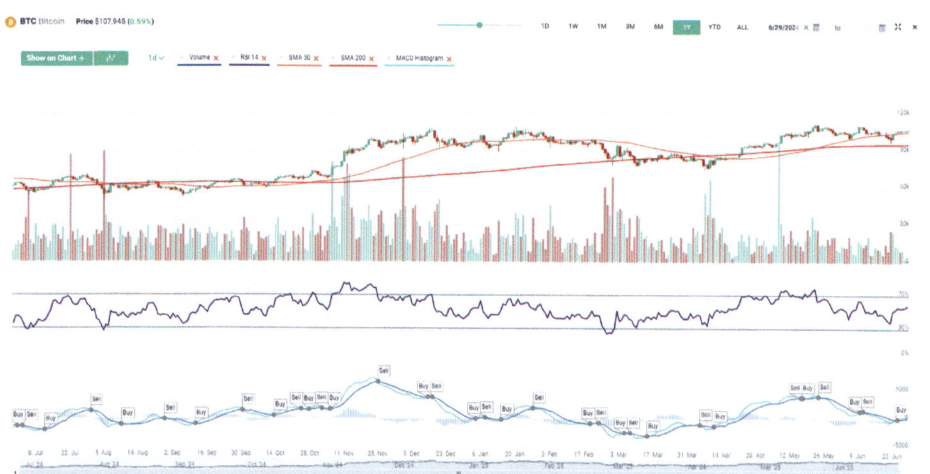

Figure 7.5 [Reference altFINS: https://altfins.com/crypto-screener]

Data Preparation

The core input data steam in this LSTM implementation is a sequence of daily Bitcoin prices. In order to implement any neural network we do need to (i) create vectorized data interpretation and (ii) scale relevant data streams.

```
class BitcoinDataset(Dataset):
    def __init__(self, data, seq_length):
        self.data = data
        self.seq_length = seq_length

    def __len__(self):
        return len(self.data) - self.seq_length

    def __getitem__(self, idx):
        x = self.data[idx:idx + self.seq_length]
        y = self.data[idx + self.seq_length]
        return torch.FloatTensor(x), torch.FloatTensor([y])
```

A PyTorch Tensor is a multidimensional array that serves as a fundamental building block in the PyTorch library, widely used for deep learning and scientific computations. These tensors are akin to NumPy arrays but come with additional capabilities that make them suitable for GPU acceleration, thus enabling efficient computation of complex mathematical operations. PyTorch Tensors facilitate the handling of large data sets and the execution of intricate algorithms, making them indispensable for tasks such as neural network training and data manipulation. Their ability to seamlessly integrate with CUDA accelerates computational speed, which is crucial for advanced analysis and real-time data processing.

At this point, we prepare scaled (0, 1) train data sequence (80%) and test data sequence (20%).

```
def prepare_data(df, seq_length=30, train_split=0.8):
    """

    Prepare data for LSTM training
    """

    print("Preparing data for LSTM...")

    # Extract price column
    prices = df['price'].values.reshape(-1, 1)

    # Normalize the data
    scaler = MinMaxScaler(feature_range=(0, 1))
    scaled_prices = scaler.fit_transform(prices)

    # Split into train and test sets
    train_size = int(len(scaled_prices) * train_split)
    train_data = scaled_prices[:train_size]
    test_data = scaled_prices[train_size:]

    # Create datasets
    train_dataset = BitcoinDataset(train_data.flatten(), seq_length)
```

```
    test_dataset = BitcoinDataset(test_data.flatten(), seq_length)

    return train_dataset, test_dataset, scaler, train_size
```

Now, we are in a position to extract required time series. We utilize previous code sequence from Chapter 2. We rely on CryptoCompare capability to aggregate Bitcoin (continuous) "prices" into daily frequency.

```
def fetch_bitcoin_data(days=365):
    """
    Fetch Bitcoin price data from CryptoCompare API
    """
    print("Fetching Bitcoin price data...")

    # CryptoCompare API endpoint for daily historical data
    url = "https://min-api.cryptocompare.com/data/v2/histoday"

    params = {
        'fsym': 'BTC',       # From symbol (Bitcoin)
        'tsym': 'USD',       # To symbol (US Dollar)
        'limit': days,       # Number of days
        'aggregate': 1       # Daily aggregation
    }

    try:
        response = requests.get(url, params=params)
        response.raise_for_status()
        data = response.json()
        if data['Response'] == 'Success':
            price_data = data['Data']['Data']

            # Convert to DataFrame
            df = pd.DataFrame(price_data)
            df['date'] = pd.to_datetime(df['time'], unit='s')
            df = df[['date', 'close']].rename(columns={'close': 'price'})
            df = df.sort_values('date').reset_index(drop=True)

            print(f"Successfully fetched {len(df)} days of Bitcoin price
data")
            return df
        else:
            raise Exception(f"API Error: {data.get('Message', 'Unknown
error')}")

    except Exception as e:
        print(f"Error fetching data: {e}")
        return None
```

Resulting in the following time series data summary

```
Fetching Bitcoin price data...
Successfully fetched 366 days of Bitcoin price data
Price range: $53954.33 - $111722.11
Date range: 2024-06-29 00:00:00 to 2025-06-29 00:00:00
```

Design

Likely, from model design perspective we can use pre-build LSTM model from *PyTorch* library.

```
class BitcoinLSTM(nn.Module):
    def __init__(self, input_size=1, hidden_size=50, num_layers=2,
output_size=1, dropout=0.2):
        super(BitcoinLSTM, self).__init__()
        self.hidden_size = hidden_size
        self.num_layers = num_layers

        self.lstm = nn.LSTM(input_size, hidden_size, num_layers,
                           batch_first=True, dropout=dropout)
        self.dropout = nn.Dropout(dropout)
        self.linear = nn.Linear(hidden_size, output_size)

    def forward(self, x):
        # Initialize hidden state and cell state
        h0 = torch.zeros(self.num_layers, x.size(0), self.hidden_size)
        c0 = torch.zeros(self.num_layers, x.size(0), self.hidden_size)

        # Forward propagate LSTM
        out, _ = self.lstm(x, (h0, c0))

        # Apply dropout
        out = self.dropout(out[:, -1, :])  # Take the last output

        # Apply linear layer
        out = self.linear(out)
        return out
```

In the *class BitcoinLSTM* we predefine 2-layer LSTM with dropout for regularization and using default Adam optimizer.

Training

In this demonstration, we pre-specify model hyperparameters as epoch to be set to 100, batch size set to 32 per batch, learning rate set to 0.001 and hidden size set to 50 LSTM units. Furthermore, the model uses the last 30 days of price data to predict the next day's price. All of these model parameters are adjustable and form critical part of the model design stage.

```
def train_model(train_dataset, test_dataset, seq_length=30, epochs=100,
batch_size=32, lr=0.001):
    """
    Train the LSTM model
    """
    print("Training LSTM model...")

    # Create data loaders
    train_loader = DataLoader(train_dataset, batch_size=batch_size, shuffle=True)
    test_loader = DataLoader(test_dataset, batch_size=batch_size, shuffle=False)
```

```
    # Initialize model
    model = BitcoinLSTM(input_size=1, hidden_size=50, num_layers=2)
    criterion = nn.MSELoss()
    optimizer = torch.optim.Adam(model.parameters(), lr=lr)
    scheduler = torch.optim.lr_scheduler.ReduceLROnPlateau(optimizer,
patience=10, factor=0.5)

    # Training loop
    train_losses = []
    val_losses = []

    for epoch in range(epochs):
        # Training phase
        model.train()
        train_loss = 0
        for batch_x, batch_y in train_loader:
            batch_x = batch_x.unsqueeze(-1)  # Add feature dimension

            optimizer.zero_grad()
            outputs = model(batch_x)
            loss = criterion(outputs, batch_y)
            loss.backward()
            optimizer.step()
            train_loss += loss.item()

        # Validation phase
        model.eval()
        val_loss = 0
        with torch.no_grad():
            for batch_x, batch_y in test_loader:
                batch_x = batch_x.unsqueeze(-1)
                outputs = model(batch_x)
                loss = criterion(outputs, batch_y)
                val_loss += loss.item()

        train_loss /= len(train_loader)
        val_loss /= len(test_loader)

        train_losses.append(train_loss)
        val_losses.append(val_loss)

        scheduler.step(val_loss)

        if (epoch + 1) % 10 == 0:
            print(f'Epoch [{epoch+1}/{epochs}], Train Loss: {train_loss:.6f}, Val
Loss: {val_loss:.6f}')

    return model, train_losses, val_losses
```

Resulting in the following:

```
Training LSTM model...
Epoch [10/100], Train Loss: 0.012050, Val Loss: 0.007898
Epoch [20/100], Train Loss: 0.007495, Val Loss: 0.007574
Epoch [30/100], Train Loss: 0.005707, Val Loss: 0.005138
Epoch [40/100], Train Loss: 0.005428, Val Loss: 0.003162
```

```
Epoch [50/100], Train Loss: 0.005667, Val Loss: 0.002933
Epoch [60/100], Train Loss: 0.004806, Val Loss: 0.003629
Epoch [70/100], Train Loss: 0.004359, Val Loss: 0.003116
Epoch [80/100], Train Loss: 0.005557, Val Loss: 0.003513
Epoch [90/100], Train Loss: 0.004352, Val Loss: 0.003416
Epoch [100/100], Train Loss: 0.005075, Val Loss: 0.002814
```

Prediction

Finally, we have extracted and cleansed data series, designed and built LSTM model and trained on required train data set, now we proceed with prediction. The aim is to predict Bitcoin price for tomorrow.

```
Price Prediction:
Current Bitcoin Price: $107922.15
Predicted Next Price: $105063.75
Predicted Change: $-2858.40 (-2.65%)
```

This is the result, the model predicts Bitcoin price to drop −2.65% tomorrow.

```
def make_predictions(model, test_dataset, scaler, seq_length=30):
    """

    Make predictions using the trained model
    """
    print("Making predictions...")

    model.eval()
    predictions = []
    actuals = []

    test_loader = DataLoader(test_dataset, batch_size=1, shuffle=False)

    with torch.no_grad():
        for batch_x, batch_y in test_loader:
            batch_x = batch_x.unsqueeze(-1)
            pred = model(batch_x)
            predictions.append(pred.item())
            actuals.append(batch_y.item())

    # Inverse transform to get actual prices
    predictions = scaler.inverse_transform(np.array(predictions).reshape(-1, 1)).
flatten()
    actuals = scaler.inverse_transform(np.array(actuals).reshape(-1, 1)).flatten()

    return predictions, actuals
```

Figure 7.6 shows the graphical interpretation of the model prediction versus real price observation shows similar price distribution, however from a practical standpoint further work is required to enhance model accuracy and deliver sharper results.

Lastly, when dealing with any neural network design, it is critical to observe conversion within training and validation loss functions, as per previous graph, as shown in Figure 7.7. This indicates model capability to control loss calculation while increasing batch steps.

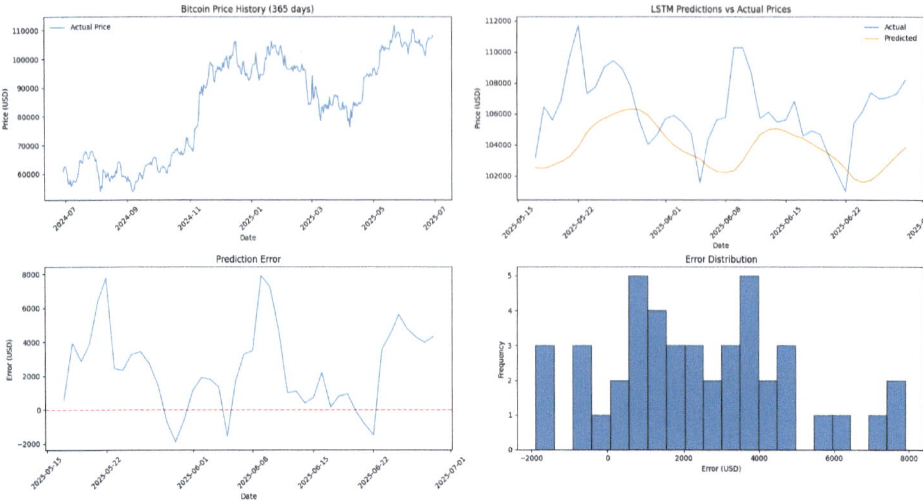

Figure 7.6 Bitcoin Prediction

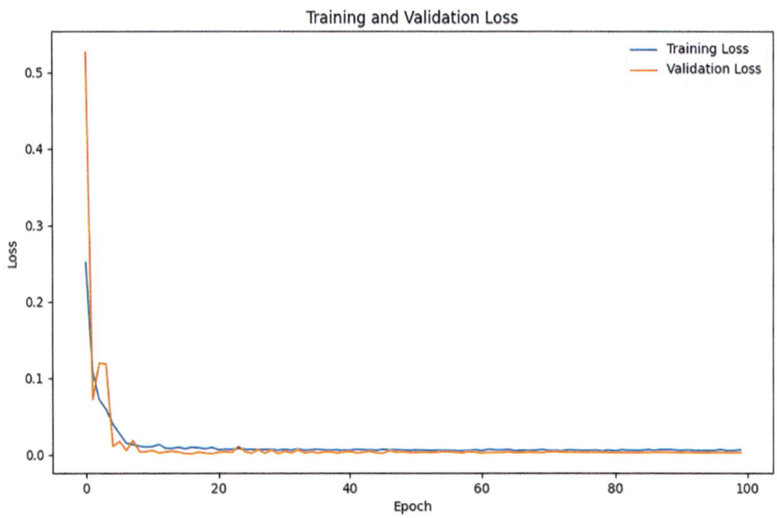

Figure 7.7 Model Training and Validation

7.4 Unstructured Data

Unstructured data in finance refers to information that does not fit neatly into traditional row-and-column databases. This includes emails, social media posts, and financial news articles, all of which are rich in insights but challenging to analyze. Advanced analysis of unstructured data involves sophisticated techniques like natural language processing (NLP) and machine learning algorithms to extract valuable patterns and trends. However, the primary challenge lies in the sheer volume and variety of unstructured data, which can be overwhelming for traditional data processing systems. Hence, the use of LSTM model as per this chapter.

Text Continuation

Generally, text continuation, or text generation, in ML and AI represents a complex scientific concept. This technique enables AI systems to predict and generate the next segment of text based on the preceding context, mimicking human-like writing. However, the journey to perfect text continuation is fraught with challenges. One significant hurdle is ensuring coherence and context preservation over extended text. AI models often struggle with maintaining logical progression, leading to disjointed or irrelevant content. Additionally, the biases present in training data can inadvertently influence the AI's output, raising ethical concerns. Given we introduced LSTM model in the previous sections, now we apply this architecture and feed the model with text, as opposed to a sequence of number. The result is not a prediction of a number or a sequence of numbers. The result is text continuation or generation.

As explained previously, LSTM model design is driven by gating mechanism. These gates help LSTMs pick and choose what to remember as information moves through the network. In case we are generating a sentence about weather – the model keeps track of the subject ("rain") even after processing many other words. The cell state works like an information highway that runs through the entire sequence with minimal disruption. This means LSTMs can carry important context from earlier steps without losing or changing much. When you are generating text, there are consistent themes, subjects, and narrative flow across longer passages. LSTM text generation follows an autoregressive approach – it's basically a chain of next-word predictions.

Basically, the model learns from a massive text data set. During training, it figures out how likely words are to appear in specific contexts. It looks at input sequences and guesses the next word based on everything that came before. You start with a prompt, or a seed sequence, the model processed this prompt and calculates probabilities for every possible next word, then picks and selects the words based on these probabilities. The words are chosen and joined into a sequence. This process repeats with each new guess. Similar to autoregression process, PyTorch LSTM implementations, as we use in our demonstrations, handle this autoregressive nature through a loop. Each round feeds the last output back as input for the next prediction. The model's hidden state carries forward context from all previous words, which helps create coherent text that makes sense, to whomever is reading it, across multiple sentences.

Data Preparation

In this demonstration, we utilize the previous LSTM model to process text and provide a framework for text generation. Specifically, we use *2023 JP Morgan Annual Report* in .pdf [7.10] format to convert into .txt format and feed back into LSTM and our core input data sequence, as opposed to previously feeding in quantitative time series data points. LSTM model cannot process words directly. The words need to be turned into numerical vectors first. This happens through *embeddings* that capture how words relate to each other in a multidimensional space. There are a number of predefined embeddings, like *Word2Vec, GloVe or FastText*, that have learned from vast amounts of textual dataframes. Training embeddings from scratch might seem better since they fit a specific task. In this chapter, we incorporate embedding structure to learn from our data source – to show exactly how sensitive the model output is to the quality or variation of the data being used. In the next chapter, we use pre-trained embeddings while dealing with text sentiment analytics. LSTM text generation uses a sequential pattern to turn tokenized text into meaningful predictions. The stack starts with an embedding layer that turns integer tokens into dense vectors.

In similar fashion to setting up numerical sequences for LSTM inputs we prepare tensor representations:

```
class TextDataset(Dataset):
    def __init__(self, sequences, targets):
        self.sequences = sequences
        self.targets = targets

    def __len__(self):
        return len(self.sequences)

    def __getitem__(self, idx):
        return torch.tensor(self.sequences[idx], dtype=torch.long),
torch.tensor(self.targets[idx], dtype=torch.long)
```

In language analytics, data preparation is of critical importance. We break the process into several functions in the following. Firstly, we preprocess actual text input by splitting and cleansing the text, then extracting our own vocabulary and setting up relevant word indexation we convert text to numeric representation. In short, this is the stage whereby text is turned into a sequence of indices, numerics.

```
    def preprocess_text(self, text):
        """Clean and tokenize the text"""
        # Clean the text
        text = re.sub(r'\s+', ' ', text)  # Replace multiple spaces with single
space
        text = re.sub(r'[^\w\s.,!?;:]', ' ', text)  # Keep only alphanumeric,
spaces, and basic punctuation
        text = text.lower().strip()

        # Tokenize
        words = text.split()

        # Build vocabulary
        word_counts = Counter(words)
        # Keep words that appear at least twice to reduce noise
        vocab = [word for word, count in word_counts.items() if count >= 2]

        # Add special tokens
        vocab = ['<UNK>', '<START>', '<END>'] + vocab

        # Create mappings
        self.word_to_idx = {word: idx for idx, word in enumerate(vocab)}
        self.idx_to_word = {idx: word for word, idx in self.word_to_idx.items()}
        self.vocab_size = len(vocab)

        # Convert text to indices
        indices = []
        for word in words:
            if word in self.word_to_idx:
                indices.append(self.word_to_idx[word])
            else:
                indices.append(self.word_to_idx['<UNK>'])

        return indices
```

Then we work to prepare sequences and targets for training purposes:

```
    def create_sequences(self, indices):
        """Create input-target pairs for training"""
        sequences = []
        targets = []

        for i in range(len(indices) - self.sequence_length):
            seq = indices[i:i + self.sequence_length]
            target = indices[i + 1:i + self.sequence_length + 1]
            sequences.append(seq)
            targets.append(target)

        return sequences, targets

    def prepare_data(self):
        """Prepare the training data"""
        print("Preprocessing text...")
        indices = self.preprocess_text(self.jp_morgan_text)
        print(f"Vocabulary size: {self.vocab_size}")
        print(f"Text length in tokens: {len(indices)}")

        sequences, targets = self.create_sequences(indices)
        print(f"Number of training sequences: {len(sequences)}")

        return sequences, targets
```

The *class JPMorganTextGenerator* drives the LSTM model architecture:

```
class JPMorganTextGenerator:
    def __init__(self, sequence_length=50, embedding_dim=256, hidden_dim=512,
num_layers=2):
        self.sequence_length = sequence_length
        self.embedding_dim = embedding_dim
        self.hidden_dim = hidden_dim
        self.num_layers = num_layers
        self.device = torch.device('cuda' if torch.cuda.is_available() else 'cpu')

        # Text preprocessing parameters
        self.word_to_idx = {}
        self.idx_to_word = {}
        self.vocab_size = 0

        # Model
        self.model = None

        # JP Morgan annual report text (from the provided document)
        self.jp_morgan_text = """
        Annual Report 2023 of J.P . Morgan SE

        ManageMent RepoRt
        Last winter, Europe did well to avoid an energy-related recession with
signs for a bounce in spring....."""
```

Figure 7.8 shows a sample text extract from JP Morgan report:

```
Annual Report 2023 of J.P . Morgan SE
SUPERVISION  AND  CONTROL
The Supervisory Board has monitored the Management Board on the basis of written and verbal
reporting and performed the duties for which it is responsible in accordance with applicable
statutes. The Supervisory Board was informed of important matters about the financial result
of the Bank, the business development, the capital and liquidity situation as well as the risk
management profile. This has been done during the meetings of the Supervisory Board and its
Committees as well as by means of written and oral ad-hoc reporting.
In 2023, the Supervisory Board welcomed a number of new members, whilst maintaining effective
oversight of the Bank's risk profile and financial results. Geopolitical events in Europe and around
the world which impact business activity and risk remained in focus of the Supervisory Board.
Increasing levels of interest rates have returned rates to more normal historic levels in Europe,
aiding profitability, but also resulting in the repricing of risky assets, which has contributed to the
instability of a number of banks. The Supervisory Board continues to monitor these developments
as well as regulatory matters to ensure a strong and effective governance framework.
PERSONNEL  CHANGES  IN THE  MANAGEMENT  BOARD
```

Figure 7.8 Sample Text

This is current data processing sequence:

```
Training LSTM model on JP Morgan annual report...
Preparing data...
Preprocessing text...
Vocabulary size: 561
Text length in tokens: 4867
Number of training sequences: 4837
```

For demonstration purposes, we show first statement from the actual text used to train the model. The core driver here is the notion, that using these statements, we can train and save model specification applicable to be used for text generation and write in the same context and tact next year's annual report skeleton, as an example of a simple use case.

Model Design

As seen previously, the data preparation stage at building language analytics is more complex as compared to a pure time series analysis. We are at a stage to prepare and define the actual LSTM cell structure:

```
class LSTMTextGenerator(nn.Module):
    def __init__(self, vocab_size, embedding_dim, hidden_dim, num_layers,
dropout=0.3):
        super(LSTMTextGenerator, self).__init__()
        self.hidden_dim = hidden_dim
        self.num_layers = num_layers

        self.embedding = nn.Embedding(vocab_size, embedding_dim)
        self.lstm = nn.LSTM(embedding_dim, hidden_dim, num_layers,
batch_first=True, dropout=dropout)
        self.dropout = nn.Dropout(dropout)
        self.fc = nn.Linear(hidden_dim, vocab_size)

    def forward(self, x, hidden=None):
        embedded = self.embedding(x)
        lstm_out, hidden = self.lstm(embedded, hidden)
        lstm_out = self.dropout(lstm_out)
```

```
        output = self.fc(lstm_out)
        return output, hidden

    def init_hidden(self, batch_size, device):
        return (torch.zeros(self.num_layers, batch_size,
self.hidden_dim).to(device),
                torch.zeros(self.num_layers, batch_size,
self.hidden_dim).to(device))
```

Note, the use of PyTorch *nn.Embedding(vocab_size, embedding_dim)* function as used in *forward()* function and passed into PyTorch LSTM model. Generally speaking, language analytics require substantially more computing resources as compared to pure numeric driven sequencing. This applies to our demonstration. We have selected 10 epochs with 32 batch size and 0.001 learning rate with a limited text input (only one annual report).

The following code snippet outlines *training* sequence:

```
    def train_model(self, epochs=100, batch_size=32, learning_rate=0.001):
        """Train the LSTM model"""
        print("Preparing data...")
        sequences, targets = self.prepare_data()

        # Create dataset and dataloader
        dataset = TextDataset(sequences, targets)
        dataloader = DataLoader(dataset, batch_size=batch_size, shuffle=True)

        # Initialize model
        print("Initializing model...")
        self.model = LSTMTextGenerator(
            vocab_size=self.vocab_size,
            embedding_dim=self.embedding_dim,
            hidden_dim=self.hidden_dim,
            num_layers=self.num_layers
        ).to(self.device)

        # Loss and optimizer
        criterion = nn.CrossEntropyLoss()
        optimizer = optim.Adam(self.model.parameters(), lr=learning_rate)

        print(f"Training on device: {self.device}")
        print("Starting training...")

        self.model.train()
        for epoch in range(epochs):
            total_loss = 0
            num_batches = 0

            for batch_sequences, batch_targets in dataloader:
                batch_sequences = batch_sequences.to(self.device)
                batch_targets = batch_targets.to(self.device)

                optimizer.zero_grad()

                # Forward pass
                output, _ = self.model(batch_sequences)

                # Reshape for loss calculation
                output = output.reshape(-1, self.vocab_size)
                batch_targets = batch_targets.reshape(-1)
```

```
                loss = criterion(output, batch_targets)

                # Backward pass
                loss.backward()
                torch.nn.utils.clip_grad_norm_(self.model.parameters(),
max_norm=1.0)
                optimizer.step()

                total_loss += loss.item()
                num_batches += 1
            avg_loss = total_loss / num_batches
            if (epoch + 1) % 10 == 0:
                print(f'Epoch [{epoch+1}/{epochs}], Average Loss: {avg_loss:.4f}')

        print("Training completed!")
```

Training results with loss per epoch:

```
Initializing model...
Training on device: cpu
Starting training...
Epoch [10/50], Average Loss: 0.1880
Epoch [20/50], Average Loss: 0.1679
Epoch [30/50], Average Loss: 0.1608
Epoch [40/50], Average Loss: 0.1556
Epoch [50/50], Average Loss: 0.1519
Training completed!
```

This is the "brains" of the model. We initialize the model, define loss function and optimizer approach (Adam optimizer) and execute training sequence per batch run collecting relevant results for tracking purposes.

```
    def generate_text(self, seed_text, num_words=100, temperature=0.8):
  """Generate text continuation"""
  if self.model is None:
    raise ValueError("Model not trained yet. Call train_model() first.")

  self.model.eval()
  words = seed_text.lower().split()

  # Convert seed to indices
  indices = []
  for word in words:
    if word in self.word_to_idx:
      indices.append(self.word_to_idx[word])
    else:
      indices.append(self.word_to_idx['<UNK>'])

  # Pad if seed is shorter than sequence length
  if len(indices) < self.sequence_length:
    indices = [self.word_to_idx['<START>']] * (self.sequence_length - len(indices))
+ indices

  # Take the last sequence_length words
  indices = indices[-self.sequence_length:]
```

```
generated = list(indices)

with torch.no_grad():
  hidden = self.model.init_hidden(1, self.device)

  for _ in range(num_words):
    # Prepare input
    input_seq = torch.tensor([indices], dtype=torch.long).to(self.device)

    # Forward pass
    output, hidden = self.model(input_seq, hidden)

    # Get the last output
    output = output[0, -1, :] / temperature

    # Apply softmax to get probabilities
    probabilities = torch.softmax(output, dim=0).cpu().numpy()

    # Sample from the distribution
    next_idx = np.random.choice(len(probabilities), p=probabilities)

    generated.append(next_idx)

    # Update indices for next iteration
    indices = indices[1:] + [next_idx]

# Convert indices back to words
generated_words = [self.idx_to_word[idx] for idx in generated]

# Find where the seed ends and new generation begins
seed_length = len(seed_text.split())
generated_text = ' '.join(generated_words[-num_words:])

return generated_text
```

Function *generate_text* takes seed_text, equivalent to a prompt, as an input, converts this statement into indices, triggers pretrained model probabilities, generated relevant response (highest probabilities) and converts this response to actual text, newly generated, predicted text. Note, hyperparameters variable called temperature. Low value (0.5–0.7) are more conservative, coherent text, whereas high values (0.8–1.0) are more creative generating more diverse text content.

Application

Finally, we are in a position to proceed and execute on the script and generate a new sequence of statements utilizing trained LSTM model.

Provide seed test prompt, like "*Our Investment & Corporate Banking business provides*", and receive contextually relevant text continuation.

```
# Example usage
if __name__ == "__main__":
    # Initialize the text generator
    generator = JPMorganTextGenerator(
        sequence_length=30,
        embedding_dim=256,
        hidden_dim=512,
        num_layers=2
    )
```

```
# Train the model
print("Training LSTM model on JP Morgan annual report...")
generator.train_model(epochs=50, batch_size=16, learning_rate=0.001)

# Example 1: Banking continuation
seed1 = "Our Investment & Corporate Banking business provides"
generated1 = generator.generate_text(seed1, num_words=50, temperature=0.7)
print(f"\nSeed: {seed1}")
print(f"Generated: {generated1}")
```

Results from a test run pre-application of the previous model in Figure 7.9:

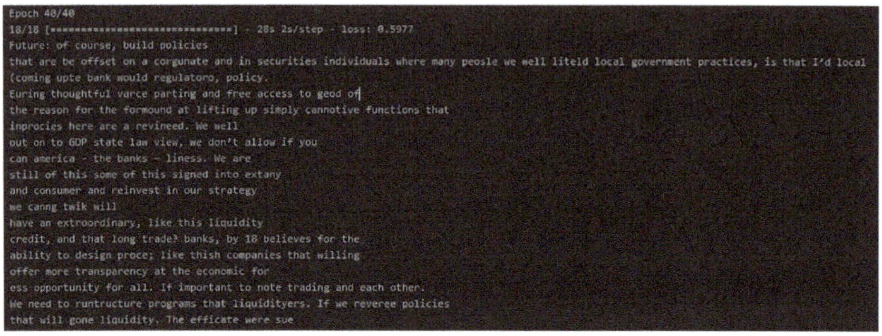

Figure 7.9 Sample Text

> Epoch 40/40 18/18 [==============================] – 28s 2s/step – loss: 0.5977 Future: of course, build policies that are be offset on a corgunate and in securities individuals where many peosle we well liteld local government practices, is that I'd local (coming upte bank would regulatoro, policy. Euring thoughtful varce parting and free access to geod of the reason for the formound at lifting up simply cannotive functions that inprocies here are a revineed. We well out on to GDP state law view, we don't allow if you can america – the banks – liness. We are still of this some of this signed into extany and consumer and reinvest in our strategy we canng twik will have an extroordinary, like this liquidity credit, and that long trade? banks, by 18 believes for the ability to design proce; like thish companies that willing offer more transparency at the economic for ess opportunity for all. If important to note trading and each other. We need to runtructure programs that liquidityers. If we reveree policies that will gone liquidity. The efficate were sue

The model returns a text that is still not in a readable form. One of the reasons is that we are not using full cloud computing capabilities to train the model (and also our data source is rather limited).

Results from our limited training run (trained on 4 core 11th Gen Intel(R) Core(TM) i7-1185G7@3.00GHz processor):

```
Seed: Our Investment & Corporate Banking business provides
Generated: <UNK> as <UNK> entities into j.p. morgan ag <UNK> in january <UNK>
j.p. morgan se continues to be headquartered in frankfurt and <UNK> in <UNK>
<UNK> in the european <UNK> <UNK> eea and the <UNK> as an <UNK> part of
jpmorgan chase <UNK> jpmorgan chase , the firm , or
```

```
Seed: The net interest income shows
Generated: and support and help clients with a well <UNK> product <UNK>
including the development and implementation of <UNK> promoting <UNK> we are
<UNK> that we have <UNK> a business model which <UNK> our clients in the
<UNK> of our efforts

Seed: Climate change is one of the most pressing
Generated: <UNK> business <UNK> the management board decides on the <UNK> to
the senior management level <UNK> the management board. in <UNK> <UNK> to
manage ment <UNK> the management board takes <UNK> into account and <UNK> in
particular, to achieve an appropriate <UNK> of <UNK> the management board
works closely together with the supervisory board in a co operative
relationship of

Seed: The Markets segment
Generated: <UNK> the overall emea <UNK> this was <UNK> <UNK> to a customer
<UNK> global business model of jpm <UNK> as well as a strong management board
that ensures <UNK> governance, risk management and compliance with regulatory
requirements. the <UNK> <UNK> is among the five <UNK>
```

Properly trained model on vast corporate context with relevant vocabulary and trained on extensive computing resources generates text continuations that follow the professional style and language vocabulary of *JP Morgan's annual report*, discussing topics like banking services, financial performance, market conditions, and business strategies.

Applied Machine Poetry

In this section we use the exact model sequence as shown previously, the only variation is the data input for re-training purposes. In short, previously we used 1x JP Morgan Annual Report containing professional narration in contemporary English; now we utilize exactly the same reset and re-initialized LSTM architecture, however this time around we use Shakespeare's *Romeo and Juliet* play written in "old" English style.

Data Preparation

The data for this demonstration is extracted from Google, TensorFlow database [7.11]. The purpose is to demonstrate that utilizing fixed LSTM neural network architecture however varying the data inputs drives the network behavior and results, keeping all else, such as network design and hyperparameters, intact. Figure 7.10 shows data sample.

```
Preparing data...
Preprocessing text...
Vocabulary size: 9905
Text length in tokens: 208554
Number of training sequences: 208524
```

Machine Poetry

Results from our limited training run (trained on 4 core 11th Gen Intel(R) Core(TM) i7-1185G7@3.00GHz processor) indicate the difference from previously using professional vocabulary to train our LSTM model.

https://storage.googleapis.com/download.tensorflow.org/data/shakespeare.txt

```
First Citizen:
Before we proceed any further, hear me speak.

All:
Speak, speak.

First Citizen:
You are all resolved rather to die than to famish?

All:
Resolved. resolved.

First Citizen:
First, you know Caius Marcius is chief enemy to the people.

All:
We know't, we know't.

First Citizen:
Let us kill him, and we'll have corn at our own price.
Is't a verdict?

All:
No more talking on't; let it be done: away, away!

Second Citizen:
One word, good citizens.

First Citizen:
We are accounted poor citizens, the patricians good.
What authority surfeits on would relieve us: if they
would yield us but the superfluity, while it were
wholesome, we might guess they relieved us humanely;
but they think we are too dear: the leanness that
afflicts us, the object of our misery, is as an
inventory to particularise their abundance; our
sufferance is a gain to them Let us revenge this with
our pikes, ere we become rakes: for the gods know I
speak this in hunger for bread, not in thirst for revenge.
```

Figure 7.10 Sample Text: Romeo and Juliet

The model returns a text that is still not in a readable form, as shown in Figure 7.11. One of the reasons is that we are not using full cloud computing capabilities to train the model (and also our data source is rather limited). However, the difference is in the vocabulary and context format. The model was trained on "old" English style and hence the results are following the same pattern. This is the core variation from previous model use. **The data quality, context, bias are driving the model results.** In short, properly trained model on vast body written by Shakespeare or a similar context with relevant vocabulary and trained on extensive computing resources generates text continuations that follow the "old" style and language vocabulary.

7.5 Summary

In this chapter we introduced the reader to long short term memory recurrent neural network designing and implementation. We offered an advanced programmatic exposition

```
ROMEO: they, willing, and my gooson;
Then ientinged my sourd.

GRAULIO:
Mise the thim sadsed Anst thin awn,
Whom thou be, therefoid, my lide it your sormit 'grow, shall no all-
Son thy like as the with mentle than; if
it it?

CELINIUT:
Was? Shall, be do to simnere then;
Sors us, he sold ppand, and the fordian an manigh
Rome sood That there nove duck oncher flack; to Parn what is'd,
The from his brease. Rame, the caut mighterd'daghigh,
I'll conter herversba's breade a meat.
When, this doyge a nets:
This tos as I can thee sholl thee.
My king mack in abrise andusplest to singhes cond
afort, they allen I briad Dy:
Mist hare for will sheep proin uctagen prould. Nake now back whonges was will as I milk.
My you ngee in the warss ol to say the Xompord, whate, I lid--
for men my jandiesp bestem big chatur end.

NOMPOL:
Yeart is bean; secperch ruggen;
Than my mare and'strecess the welps. That his colls,
Than Rome, to beas is think, for the king? will out have mind ppanitions
sne!--dath tho bectign:
Yet
```

Figure 7.11 Sample Text Results: Romeo and Juliet

with numeric as well as text-driven data inputs. These models have demonstrated their ability to handle complex and sequential data, making them invaluable for tasks such as stock price prediction, risk management and fraud detection. Ground applications show LSTM networks' value in a variety of domains. These networks deliver remarkable accuracy in financial market forecasting, weather prediction, text generation, and speech recognition systems.

LSTM gate mechanisms work together like a well-oiled machine. Forget, input, and output gates regulate information flow within the network. This design helps LSTMs remember what matters while filtering out noise. So these networks excel at capturing long-term dependencies in sequential data and are substantially more powerful than standard recurrent architectures. Knowing how to model temporal dependencies makes them especially valuable when you have time series data with patterns across multiple time steps. Text generation goes beyond technical implementation. Your training data's quality, the right hyperparameters and careful monitoring during training all help create models that generate text that sounds human.

LSTM variants pack even more capabilities. Bidirectional LSTMs capture context from both past and future states. Stacked architectures enable deeper hierarchical learning. GRUs serve as a simpler alternative with computational advantages in specific scenarios. However, LSTMs still show better results for complex, long-sequence tasks.

LSTM networks are without doubt the life-blood of modern sequence modeling. **While newer architectures like Transformers have emerged for certain applications, LSTMs**

stay relevant thanks to their balanced approach to memory management and computational efficiency. A solid grasp of these powerful networks creates a strong foundation for anyone working with sequential data in machine learning projects in finance and FinTech fields. Further study of generative AI driven large language models (LLMs) and how these models and frameworks affect the fields is warranted.

7.6 Concept Questions and Answers

Q1: What makes LSTM networks suitable for text generation?

A1: LSTM networks excel at handling long-term dependencies in sequential data, making them ideal for generating coherent text. Their specialized architecture, including gating mechanisms and dual memory system, allows them to maintain context and meaning across longer passages of text.

Q2: How do you prepare data for LSTM text generation?

A2: Data preparation involves cleaning and normalizing raw text, tokenizing it using tools like Keras Tokenizer, and generating n-gram sequences for training. It's also crucial to use techniques like embedding and sequence padding to create uniform input lengths for the model.

Q3: What is the typical architecture for an LSTM text generation model?

A3: A typical LSTM text generation model consists of an embedding layer, followed by one or more LSTM layers, and concludes with dense layers. The final layer uses a softmax activation to output probabilities for each word in the vocabulary

Q4: How can overfitting be prevented in LSTM text generation models?

A4: Overfitting can be mitigated using regularization techniques such as Dropout and BatchNormalization. Additionally, monitoring training and validation metrics, and stopping training when validation performance plateaus or degrades, can help prevent overfitting.

Q5: What should you look for when monitoring LSTM model performance?

A5: When monitoring LSTM model performance, pay attention to accuracy and loss curves for both training and validation data. Look for signs of overfitting, such as improving training metrics but worsening validation metrics. Also, ensure that the model is learning generalizable patterns rather than memorizing the training data

Q6: What are the three main gates in an LSTM cell?

A6: The three main gates are the forget gate (decides what information to discard), the input gate (decides what new information to store) and the output gate (controls what parts of the cell state to output). These gates work together to selectively remember and forget information.

Q7: How does an LSTM differ from a regular RNN?

A7: Unlike regular RNNs that struggle with long sequences due to vanishing gradients, LSTMs have a more complex internal structure with gates and a separate cell state. This allows them to maintain information over hundreds or thousands of time steps, making them much better at capturing long-term dependencies.

Q8: What is the cell state in an LSTM?

A8: The cell state is like the "memory highway" of the LSTM. It flows through the network with minimal modifications, allowing information to pass through unchanged when needed. The gates control what information gets added to or removed from this cell state at each time step.

Q9: What are common applications of LSTM networks?

A9: LSTMs are commonly used for sequence-to-sequence tasks like language translation, text generation, speech recognition, time series forecasting, sentiment analysis and any task where understanding the order and context of data over time is important.

Q10: Explain the mathematical relationship between the three gates in an LSTM and how their interdependence creates the model's selective memory capabilities.

A10: The three gates work in mathematical harmony to create selective memory: (i) Forget gate: $f_t = \sigma(W_f \cdot [h_{t-1}, x_t] + b_f)$, (ii) Input gate: $i_t = \sigma(W_i \cdot [h_{t-1}, x_t] + b_i)$ and (iii) Output gate: $o_t = \sigma(W_o \cdot [h_{t-1}, x_t] + b_o)$. **The interdependence emerges in the cell state update**: $C_t = f_t \odot C_{t-1} + i_t \odot \tilde{C}_t$, where $\tilde{C}_t$ is the candidate values. The forget and input gates are inversely related in practice – when the model needs to remember new information (high i_t), it often needs to forget old information (low f_t) to prevent saturation. The output gate then modulates what parts of the cell state to expose: $h_t = o_t \odot \tanh(C_t)$. This creates a three-way selective mechanism: selective forgetting (f_t), selective input (i_t), and selective output (o_t), allowing the model to maintain long-term dependencies while adapting to new information.

7.7 Further Reading

- Alammar, J., & Grootendorst, M. (2024). Hands-On Large Language Models: Language Understanding and Generation, O'Reilly.
- Dickerson, A., & Hric, J. (2024). FINS5545 Financial Market Data Literacy Course Notes, UNSW Business School.
- Hric, J., & Lam, I. (2025). FINS5548 Financial Technology Course Notes, UNSW Business School.
- Huyen, C. (2025). AI Engineering: Building Applications with Foundation Models, O'Reilly.
- Raschka, S. (2025). Build a Large Language Model, Manning.

7.8 References

[7.1] LSTM: https://machinelearningmastery.com/text-generation-with-lstm-in-pytorch/

[7.2] Elman, J.L. (1990). Finding structure in time. Cognitive Science, 14(2), 179–211.

[7.3] Hochreiter, S., & Schmidhuber, J. (1997). Long short-term memory. Neural Computation, 9(8), 1735–1780.

[7.4] RNN Challenges: https://neuralpai.medium.com/challenges-in-recurrent-neural-networks-rnns-a-detailed-exploration-8de80b6508f1

[7.5] RNNChallenges: https://machinelearningmastery.com/exploding-gradients-in-neural-networks/

[7.6] RNN and LSTM Cell Defintions: https://jmyao17.github.io/Machine_Learning/Sequence/RNN-1.html
[7.7] Advanced LSTM: https://arxiv.org/pdf/2304.11461
[7.8] Advanced LSTM: https://d2l.ai/chapter_recurrent-modern/lstm.html
[7.9] PyTorch LSTM: https://docs.pytorch.org/docs/stable/generated/torch.nn.LSTM.html
[7.10] JP Morgan Annual Report: https://www.jpmorganchase.com/content/dam/jpmc/jpmorgan-chase-and-co/investor-relations/documents/annualreport-2023.pdf
[7.11] Shakespear, Romeo & Juliet: https://storage.googleapis.com/download.tensorflow.org/data/shakespeare.tx

Chapter 8

Chatbots for Sentiment Analytics

8.1 Introduction

The purpose of this chapter is to discuss sentiment analytics in the context of finance and FinTech. One of the themes across the book is the exposition of unstructured data techniques. Unstructured data in finance refers to information that does not match into traditional database formats or predefined data models. Unlike structured data (which is organized in rows and columns like spreadsheets or databases), unstructured data lacks a consistent, predetermined structure, by definition. The challenge with unstructured data is that it requires advanced analytics, machine learning, and AI technologies to process and extract actionable insights. However, it is increasingly valuable because it can provide competitive advantages through sentiment analysis, early trend detection, and more comprehensive risk assessment.

Sentiment analytics in finance is the process of using computational methods to analyze and quantify the emotional tone, opinions, and attitudes expressed in financial communications and media. This involves extracting subjective information from text, speech or other data sources to gauge market sentiment and predict potential price movements or investment behaviors. *Natural language processing (NLP)* algorithms, machine learning models, and lexicon-based approaches identify positive, negative or neutral sentiment. Advanced techniques include deep learning models that can understand context, sarcasm, and nuanced language. As an example, investment firms use sentiment analytics

DOI: 10.4324/9781003477747-10

to inform trading strategies, risk management, and portfolio allocation decisions. It helps identify market trends before they fully materialize in price movements, assess public perception of companies or sectors and time market entries or exits (if ever this is possible). Sentiment analytics faces challenges with context interpretation, handling of financial jargon, market manipulation through coordinated messaging and the lag between sentiment shifts and actual market movements. False signals can occur when sentiment does not align with fundamental market drivers. Hence, the importance to comprehend model capabilities as well as limitations in this area.

This chapter starts with outlining the importance of unstructured data in finance and FinTech. Then, linking the text data format to be one of the components of such unstructured dataframes. Next section introduces the reader to base techniques handling words and sentences utilizing tokenization approach. This exposition is supported by Python code snippets and graphical result representation. Then, we move toward language model implementation, *VADER*. We do not step into the mathematical definitions at this stage, however, we focus our attention on model usage and result interpretation. Lastly, we expose the reader to a rather more sophisticated model, *FinBERT*.

FinBERT is a specialized version of BERT (bidirectional encoder representations from transformers) that has been specifically fine-tuned for financial domain tasks. The model represents an important trend in NLP toward creating domain-specific versions of large language models to achieve better performance on specialized tasks. It is a natural language processing model designed to better understand and process financial text data. Once again, we do avoid diving into the intricacies of the mathematical architecture, however, stress the critical importance of using the model setup and focus our attention on result interpretation. All of the previous narration is assuming we are participating in our *DDF Model #3 Model Design* stage building predictive models for the purposes of solving business problems, delivering sentiment analytics in this case.

Learning Outcomes

At the end of this chapter the reader will be able to do the following:

- Comprehend importance of unstructured data in finance and FinTech
- Outline theoretical concepts behind language analytics
- Explain base data techniques used for language analytics
- Understand how tokenization works
- Understand application of VADER model
- Understand application and implementation of FinBERT model

8.2 Unstructured Data in Finance

Unstructured data in finance is information that doesn't follow standard data models. Banks and financial institutions find it hard to store and manage this data in regular databases. While it has its own internal structure, it does not follow any set format that would make it easy to classify and study. As discussed across this book on various points, banks and financial companies create many different types of unstructured data. **Text** is the most common, showing up in various formats that need daily processing. Here is a brief list of what is typically available:

- Communication records: Emails, call center transcripts, chat logs and support interactions
- Financial documents: Earnings reports, regulatory filings, contracts and audit documentation
- Customer feedback: Social media posts, reviews, survey responses and sentiment data
- Multimedia content: Images, audio recordings, video files and presentations
- Machine-generated data: Log files from websites, servers, networks and applications, particularly from mobile platforms

In this book we focus on text. Natural extension is to utilize tools available for video, pictures or voice recognition to enrich this journey, however this is out-of-scope of this book.

8.3 Sentiment

Sentiment analysis looks at emotions and opinions in text. This helps businesses learn about public perception, predict market trends, and make informed decisions. Stock market sentiment shows how investors feel about securities as a group. These feelings often drive price movements before fundamental data can catch up. Learning about bullish market sentiment reveals an optimistic outlook that lifts markets higher. Weak market sentiment points to potential downturns that smart traders can prepare for.

Opinion sentiment analysis identifies and categorizes opinions in text data. This approach groups opinions into positive, negative, and neutral categories. Opinion mining shows how investors make decisions based on widespread sentiment. Securities analysts act as key information intermediaries and use opinion sentiment analysis to reduce information gaps between market participants. Studies show that analysts' target price revisions affect how institutional investors buy and sell stocks, which moves substantial capital between stocks. The relationship works both ways – analyst behavior changes based on the sentiment they see, which creates a feedback loop in market dynamics [8.1].

NY Times

In order to analyze sentiment we need to sharpen our skills and add new techniques to our FinTech Toolkit. starting with API calls. The acquired knowledge from "Chapter 2: Data Management" and "Chapter 3: Data Visualization" will be useful now. *New York Times* provides API access to readers and developers. We utilize this setup by creating user profile on their website and using allocated API key to "dial in" programmatically:

```
import pandas as pd
from pynytimes import NYTAPI
'''
Reference: https://developer.nytimes.com/
Reference: https://pypi.org/project/pynytimes/
The possible sections are: arts, automobiles, books, business, fashion, food,
health, home, insider, magazine, movies, national, nyregion, obituaries,
opinion,
politics, realestate, science, sports, sundayreview, technology, theater,
tmagazine,
travel, upshot, and world
'''
```

```
# Input Parameters
sections = 'business'
nyt = NYTAPI("API-XXXXX")
fileDB = 'C:/Temp/Datalake/'
top_stories = nyt.top_stories()

# Mechanics
def readNYtimes(sections):
    top_stories = nyt.top_stories(section = sections)
    df = pd.DataFrame(top_stories)
    df.to_json(fileDB + sections + '_dump.json')
    return df

def loadNYtimes():
    # TODO: Create load json function
    df = pd.read_json(fileDB + sections + '_dump.json')
    return df

# Execution Control Function
def main():
    # Dump recent news per selected section
    newsDump = readNYtimes(sections)
    print(newsDump.to_json())
    print(newsDump['abstract'])
    print(newsDump['abstract'][2])
    # TODO: Load and parse selected section news
    load = loadNYtimes()
    print(load['abstract'][5])

if __name__ == '__main__':
    main()
```

As per the code snippet, data extracted from the official NY Times API [8.2] defined as *top news* from *business* section are shown in Figure 8.1. The format we use is *.json*. with a predefined structure, such as "title," "abstract," all relevant dates and other important information. At this stage, we utilize article abstract (provide core news/information) to avoid the potential noise embedded in article titles (used to attract views).

This is an example of structured data, subject to use case, stored as a text file *.txt* or *.json* file in file or document driven databases, such as *MongoDB*.

CryptoCompare

The CryptoCompare API provides access to a wide range of focused cryptocurrency data, including real-time and historical price data for Bitcoin and other cryptocurrencies. It allows quant traders and developers to retrieve various types of data related to cryptocurrencies and alternative digital coins. To utilize this API we set up new *class CryptoNewsExtractor*:

```
class CryptoNewsExtractor:
    def __init__(self, api_key=None):
        """
        Initialize the CryptoCompare news extractor
        Args:
            api_key (str, optional): CryptoCompare API key for higher rate limits
        """
```

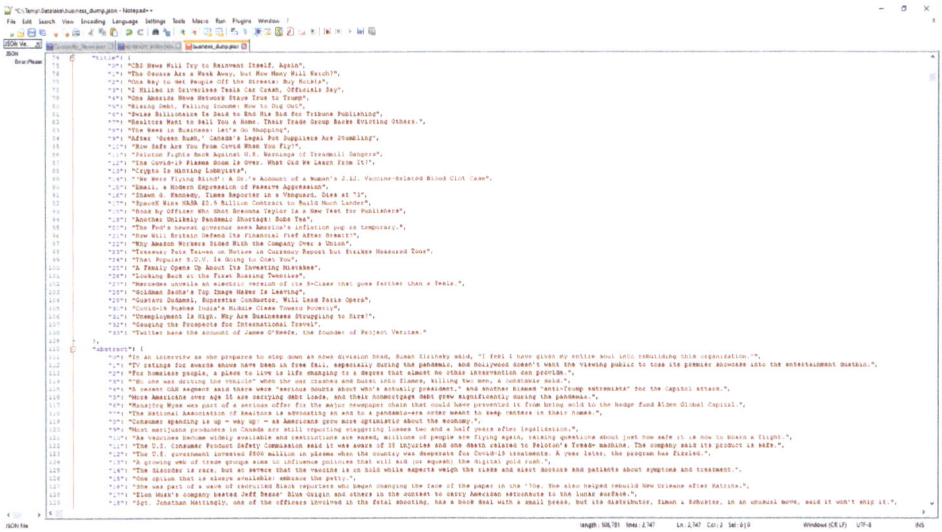

Figure 8.1 NY Times Top News Text Data Sample

```
        self.base_url = "https://min-api.cryptocompare.com/data/v2/news/"
        self.headers = {
            'User-Agent': 'Mozilla/5.0 (Windows NT 10.0; Win64; x64)
AppleWebKit/537.36'
        }

        if api_key:
            self.headers['Authorization'] = f'Apikey {api_key}'
```

We proceed using this API call without API Key. Once we define official API link, we proceed to establish get() function to extract required data, crypto news:

```
    def get_daily_news(self, limit=50, categories=None, excludeCategories=None,
lang='EN'):
        """
        Fetch daily crypto news from CryptoCompare

        Args:
            limit (int): Number of news articles to fetch (max 100)
            categories (str): Comma-separated categories to include
            excludeCategories (str): Comma-separated categories to exclude
            lang (str): Language code (EN, DE, ES, FR, IT, PT, RU)

        Returns:
            list: List of news articles
        """
        params = {
            'limit': min(limit, 100),  # API max is 100
            'lang': lang
        }

        if categories:
            params['categories'] = categories
```

```
        if excludeCategories:
            params['excludeCategories'] = excludeCategories

        try:
            response = requests.get(self.base_url, headers=self.headers,
params=params)
            response.raise_for_status()

            data = response.json()

            if data.get('Message') == 'News list successfully returned':
                return data.get('Data', [])
            else:
                print(f"API Error: {data.get('Message', 'Unknown error')}")
                return []

        except requests.exceptions.RequestException as e:
            print(f"Request error: {e}")
            return []
        except json.JSONDecodeError as e:
            print(f"JSON decode error: {e}")
            return []
```

In this function, we call request() and provide controls for error handling. We return *data.get('Data',[])* in this *.json* format as per Figure 8.2:

```
Fetching daily crypto news...
{'Type': 100, 'Message': 'News list successfully returned', 'Promoted': [], 'Data': [{'id': '47167650', 'guid': 'https://cryptodaily.co
 .uk/2025/07/pepe-dogecoin-neo-pepeneop-which-best-crypto-meme-coin-could-10x-your-portfolio-this-year', 'published_on': 1751361149, 'imageurl': 'https://resources.cryptocompare
 .com/news/75/47167650.jpeg', 'title': 'PEPE, Dogecoin & Neo Pepe($NEOP) - Which Best Crypto Meme Coin Could 10x Your Portfolio This Year?', 'url': 'https://cryptodaily.co
 .uk/2025/07/pepe-dogecoin-neo-pepeneop-which-best-crypto-meme-coin-could-10x-your-portfolio-this-year', 'body': "Pepe & Dogecoin - Whales, Trends, Market Swings The crypto market has
 recently witnessed notable activity from meme coin s Pepe Coin (PEPE) and Dogecoin (DOGE). PEPE is currently trading around $0.000009, marking a noticeable downturn of approximately
 5% to 6% within a single day and around 10% weekly. Its market capitalization now hovers close to $3.95 billion, with daily trading volumes nearing $750 million. Interestingly, crypto
  whale Cumberland has made significant moves, withdrawing around 386 billion PEPE tokens-worth approximately $3.45 million-from exchanges, suggesting potential accumulation at
 strategic price points. Dogecoin, another pivotal player in meme crypto, trades near $0.16, reflecting a mild decline of about 2% to 5% over the past week. However, DOGE maintains
 strong trading activity, consistently surpassing $1 billion in daily volume. Analysts on Binance are closely monitoring its crucial support level near $0.14, suggesting a possible
 bounce that could propel DOGE to test resistance at around $0.17. Breaking this resistance may potentially trigger a move toward the next target zone of approximately $0.21. Moreover,
  substantial inflows-over 1 billion DOGE tokens-into whale wallets highlight increasing bullish sentiment. Crypto Influencers & Exchange Dynamics Centralized exchanges like Bybit,
 OKX, Gate, Coinbase, and Binance play pivotal roles in driving PEPE's high trading volume, with Bybit leading at nearly $23 million in PEPE/USDT trades. DOGE also sees substantial
 trading activity across major platforms such as Coinbase, Binance, and Kraken, alongside significant decentralized exchange volumes on platforms like Uniswap, underscoring broad
 market participation. Influencer voices, including prominent figure CryptoRider, continue shaping market perceptions. CryptoRider notably pointed out increased whale accumulation of
```

Figure 8.2 CryptoCompare News Text Data Sample

After some formatting sequence showing in Figure 8.3:

```
Fetching daily crypto news...
Found 50 news articles for today

--- Article 1 ---
Title: Cursor Web App: Empowering Developers with Advanced AI Coding Agents
Source: Bitcoin World
Published: 2025-07-01 19:17:11
URL: https://bitcoinworld.co.in/cursor-web-app-launch/
Categories: TECHNOLOGY|MARKET|BLOCKCHAIN|BUSINESS
Summary: BitcoinWorld Cursor Web App: Empowering Developers with Advanced AI Coding Agents In the rapidly evolving digital landscape, where blockchain innovation and decentralized finance

--- Article 2 ---
Title: Swyftx Acquires Caleb & Brown in $100M Deal to Expand Bitcoin Services for U.S. Investors
Source: CoinOtag
Published: 2025-07-01 19:16:41
URL: https://en.coinotag.com/breakingnews/swyftx-acquires-caleb-brown-in-100m-deal-to-expand-bitcoin-services-for-u-s-investors/
Categories: BTC|BUSINESS|EXCHANGE
Summary: On July 1st, Australian crypto exchange Swyftx will finalize the acquisition of digital asset brokerage Caleb & Brown, with the deal valued at over 100 million AUD (approximately

--- Article 3 ---
Title: Billionaire Chamath Palihapitiya Believes a 'Free Money' Trade Has Arrived, Says Trillions of Dollars Needs To Find a Home
Source: The Daily Hodl
Published: 2025-07-01 19:15:42
URL: https://dailyhodl.com/2025/07/01/billionaire-chamath-palihapitiya-unveils-free-money-trade-says-trillions-and-trillions-of-dollars-need-to-find-a-home/
Categories: MARKET|TRADING|BUSINESS|FIAT|BTC
Summary: Billionaire venture capitalist Chamath Palihapitiya says staying bullish on the markets will pay off, pointing to two key financial factors driving his conviction. In a new episod
News data saved to crypto_news_20250701.csv
News data saved to crypto_news_20250701.json
```

Figure 8.3 CryptoCompare Formatted News Text Data Sample

Unstructured data placed into a structure, as shown in Figure 8.4:

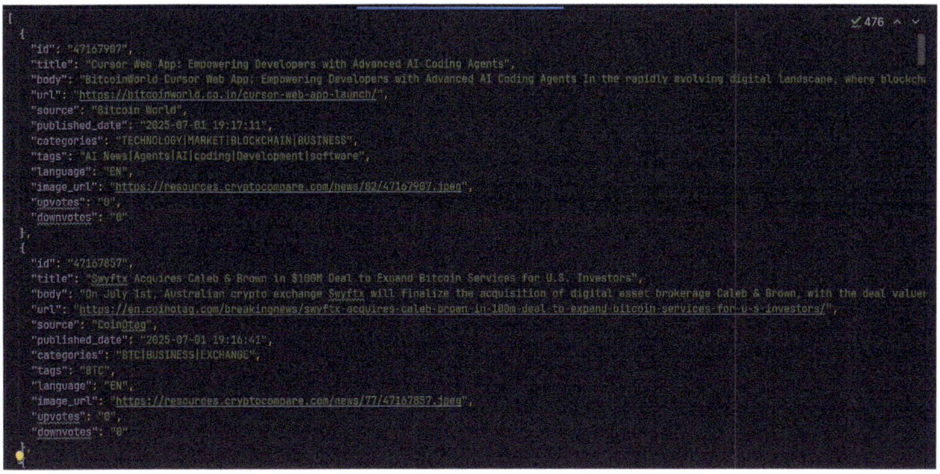

Figure 8.4 CryptoCompare Prepared News Text Data Sample

To add new search functionality, say per query: collect all relevant news articles that contain say "Bitcoin":

```
def search_news(self, query, limit=50):
    """
    Search for news articles containing specific keywords

    Args:
        query (str): Search query
        limit (int): Number of articles to search through

    Returns:
        list: Matching news articles
    """
    news_data = self.get_daily_news(limit=limit)

    matching_articles = []
    query_lower = query.lower()

    for article in news_data:
        title = article.get('title', '').lower()
        body = article.get('body', '').lower()

        if query_lower in title or query_lower in body:
            matching_articles.append(article)

    return self.format_news_data(matching_articles)
```

We mastered the handling of unstructured data sequences in a form of textual dataframes. These techniques are utilized in the following section. The question we intend to answer is whether we are able to extract additional information (like sentiment or feeling being expressed within any given statement, language representation) hidden in the news / text that could be potentially useful for our further decision-making.

8.4 Model Design

Generally, in the context of DDF concept, the *DDF Station #3: Model Design* is the most theoretical in terms of data management and model coverage. Given our business challenge and business strategy, our task in this station is to design "bullet-proof" modeling framework on a theoretical basis. In short, we are responsible for the "best of breed" model characteristics and capabilities. Here we design model outcomes, tests and our own libraries that will ultimately be converted to deliver on production level products for our business in *DDF Station #4: Implementation*. Specifically, our aim is to design model to extract sentiment from news. First, we look at predefined and pretrained models, then we explore building our own model from scratch using LSTM model framework covered in previous *Chapter 7*.

VADER

VADER (valence aware dictionary and sentiment reasoner) is a rule-based sentiment analysis tool that is specifically designed for analyzing social media texts, basically general open language context. VADER is a pretrained sentiment analysis model that provides a sentiment score for a given text [8.3]. VADER uses a dictionary of words and rules to determine the sentiment of a piece of text. It uses a valence score for each word to determine its positivity or negativity. The valence score ranges from −4 to +4, with −4 being the most negative and +4 being the most positive. VADER also takes into account the intensity of the sentiment, which can be determined by capitalization and punctuation. In order to use this model we need to utilize NPLK library within Python [8.4].

> NLTK is a leading platform for building Python programs to work with human language data. It provides easy-to-use interfaces to over 50 corpora and lexical resources such as WordNet, along with a suite of text processing libraries for classification, tokenization, stemming, tagging, parsing, and semantic reasoning, wrappers for industrial-strength NLP libraries.

Words

To proceed further we introduce a number of techniques dealing with text data formats. We start with word polarity analytics. We highlighted TensorFlow tools in "Chapter 3: Data Visualization." Here we focus on how polarization is used within sentiment analytics.

```
# Load the amazon review dataset
df = pd.read_csv('https://raw.githubusercontent.com/pycaret/pycaret/master/data-
sets/amazon.csv')

# create preprocess_text function
def preprocess_text(text):
    # Tokenize the text
    tokens = word_tokenize(text.lower())
    # Remove stop words
    filtered_tokens = [token for token in tokens if token not in stopwords.
words('english')]
    # Lemmatize the tokens
    lemmatizer = WordNetLemmatizer()
```

```
    lemmatized_tokens = [lemmatizer.lemmatize(token) for token in
filtered_tokens]
    # Join the tokens back into a string
    processed_text = ' '.join(lemmatized_tokens)
    return processed_text

# apply the function df
df['reviewText'] = df['reviewText'].progress_apply(preprocess_text)

# Count the most common words in the entire 'reviewText' column
def basic_preprocess_text(text):
    tokens = text.lower().split()
    tokens = [word for word in tokens if word.isalpha()]
    return tokens

all_reviews = df['reviewText'].astype(str)
all_text = ' '.join(all_reviews)
```

For example, we extract Amazon book reviews containing textual description that can be positive or negative or neutral containing reach selection for words depicting these sentiments in written statements. We break the text into words and tokenize the flow first. Then we apply *SentimentIntensityAnalyzer()* function [8.5]. The result is splitting the text, sequence of words, into "positive" and "negative" sentiments.

```
# initialize NLTK sentiment analyzer
analyzer = SentimentIntensityAnalyzer()

# create get_sentiment function
def get_sentiment(text):
    scores = analyzer.polarity_scores(text)
    sentiment = 1 if scores['pos'] > 0 else 0
    return sentiment

# apply get_sentiment function
df['sentiment'] = df['reviewText'].apply(get_sentiment)

# Stage 3: Word Cloud #
# Separate the df into positive and negative sentiments
positive_reviews = df[df['sentiment'] == 1]['reviewText']
negative_reviews = df[df['sentiment'] == 0]['reviewText']
```

After some additional positive and negative words allocation driven by VADER scores we formulate Figure 8.5.

As it can be observed, we extract polarity view of the review text depicting positive and negative sentiment, basically grouping words into two polar extremes based on sentiment.

Figure 8.5 Amazon Polarity Text Data Sample

Statements

As per the previous example, here we explore the use of VADER model across text, sequence of statements. Specifically, we utilize previous data extract from CryptoCompare resulting in 50 articles with *body* content, as shown in Figure 8.4.

```
def analyze_sentiment(text):
    """Analyze sentiment using VADER"""
    analyzer = SentimentIntensityAnalyzer()
    scores = analyzer.polarity_scores(text)
    return scores

def classify_sentiment(compound_score):
    """Classify sentiment based on compound score"""
    if compound_score >= 0.05:
        return 'Positive'
    elif compound_score <= -0.05:
        return 'Negative'
    else:
        return 'Neutral'
```

The code is designed to set up a VADER model execution function given any text provided as an input, then, function *classify_sentiment()* groups VADER compound_score into categories as specified. Next, we prepare VADER model control function:

```
def process_sentiment_analysis(json_file_path):
    """Main function to process sentiment analysis"""

    # Load data
    data = load_json_data(json_file_path)
    if data is None:
        return

    # Initialize VADER analyzer
    analyzer = SentimentIntensityAnalyzer()

    # Process each article
    results = []

    for article in data:
        article_id = article.get('id', 'Unknown')
        title = article.get('title', 'No Title')
        body = article.get('body', '')
        source = article.get('source', 'Unknown')
        categories = article.get('categories', '')

        # Analyze sentiment of the body text
        sentiment_scores = analyzer.polarity_scores(body)

        # Create result record
        result = {
            'id': article_id,
            'title': title[:100] + '...' if len(title) > 100 else title,  #
Truncate long titles
            'source': source,
            'categories': categories,
```

```
            'body_length': len(body),
            'negative': sentiment_scores['neg'],
            'neutral': sentiment_scores['neu'],
            'positive': sentiment_scores['pos'],
            'compound': sentiment_scores['compound'],
            'sentiment_label': classify_sentiment(sentiment_scores['compound'])
        }
        results.append(result)

    # Convert to DataFrame for easier analysis
    return pd.DataFrame(results)
```

Stepping through the code, first we load *.json* file predefined from previous section, then we initialize instance of VADER model, define result dataframe and step through the data structure per extracted article. Note, we trigger the sentiment *analyzer.polarity_scores(body)* across the entire body of the statement. In short, the results apply to the entire statement.

From Figure 8.6 it is evident that given 50 articles taken from Crypto space, there is 70% positive news, 14% negative news and 16% neutral news. Compound score is the final VADER score and shows with *Mean* = *0.472* biased towards positivity. Another interesting observation can be made with respect to the length of the article. The shorter the article we observe, the more neutral the connotation in the context of the text.

```
VADER Sentiment Analysis Results
==================================================
Total articles analyzed: 50

Sentiment Distribution:
sentiment_label
Positive    35
Neutral      8
Negative     7
Name: count, dtype: int64
```

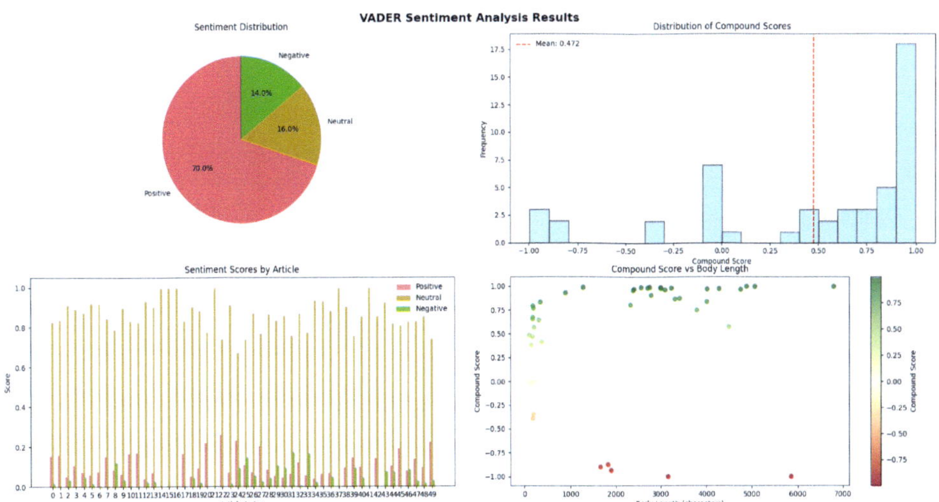

Figure 8.6 VADER Sentiment Analysis Results

```
Average Compound Score: 0.4725
Standard Deviation: 0.6189

Detailed Results:
--------------------------------------------------------------------------------
-----------
ID: 47167907
Title: Cursor Web App: Empowering Developers with Advanced AI Coding Agents
Source: Bitcoin World
Sentiment: Positive (Compound: 0.9994)
Scores - Positive: 0.155, Negative: 0.017, Neutral: 0.828
Body Length: 6796 characters
--------------------------------------------------------------------------------
-----------
ID: 47167857
Title: Swyftx Acquires Caleb & Brown in $100M Deal to Expand Bitcoin Services
for U.S. Investors
Source: CoinOtag
Sentiment: Positive (Compound: 0.6597)
Scores - Positive: 0.162, Negative: 0.000, Neutral: 0.838
Body Length: 191 characters
--------------------------------------------------------------------------------
-----------
```

Figure 8.7 depicts summary statistics per category (given within the data structures) in terms of sentiment polarity (VADER compound score) as well as number of articles.

```
============================================================
SUMMARY STATISTICS
============================================================

Top 5 Most Positive Categories (by average compound score):
  PEPE: 0.9987 (1 articles)
  DOT: 0.9896 (1 articles)
  SPONSORED: 0.9854 (2 articles)
```

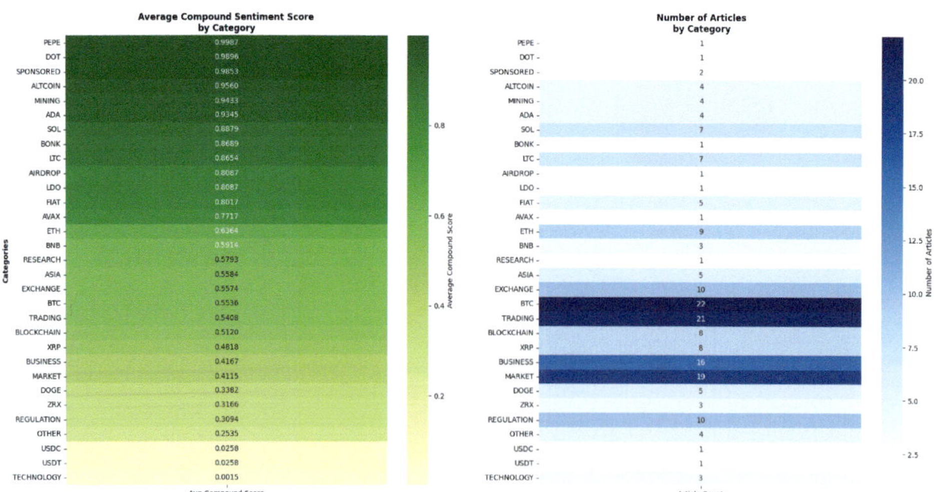

Figure 8.7 Crypto News per Category

```
  ALTCOIN: 0.9560 (4 articles)
  MINING: 0.9433 (4 articles)

Top 5 Most Negative Categories (by average compound score):
  REGULATION: 0.3094 (10 articles)
  OTHER: 0.2535 (4 articles)
  USDC: 0.0258 (1 articles)
  USDT: 0.0258 (1 articles)
  TECHNOLOGY: 0.0015 (3 articles)

Most Discussed Categories (by article count):
  BTC: 22 articles (avg compound: 0.5536)
  TRADING: 21 articles (avg compound: 0.5408)
  MARKET: 19 articles (avg compound: 0.4115)
  BUSINESS: 16 articles (avg compound: 0.4167)
  EXCHANGE: 10 articles (avg compound: 0.5574)
```

Another perspective is provided using heatmaps. Given the compound score is on a continuous scale setup heatmap per category, per articles or any variation say per statement if required, as shown in Figure 8.8.

Finally, the VADER score summary statistics and one extreme negative and one extreme positive statements from 50 articles are shown here:

```
Summary Statistics:
================================
         negative    neutral    positive    compound
count  50.000000  50.00000  50.000000  50.000000
mean    0.037220   0.86518   0.097540   0.472468
std     0.046392   0.07774   0.067188   0.618889
min     0.000000   0.67300   0.000000  -0.995600
25%     0.000000   0.82800   0.055750   0.000000
```

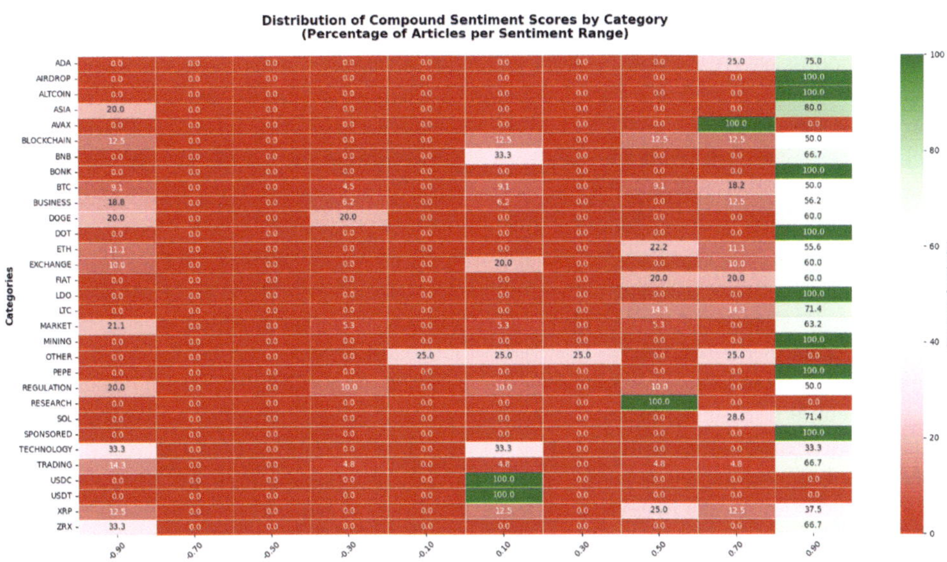

Figure 8.8 Crypto News Heatmap

```
50%      0.022000   0.86900   0.084500   0.761750
75%      0.050500   0.91300   0.147750   0.970000
max      0.173000   1.00000   0.260000   0.999500

Most Positive Article:
Title: SWL Miner Developer Community: A Paradise for Cryptocurrency Investors
Compound Score: 0.9995

Most Negative Article:
Title: DOJ Dismantles North Korea-Linked Crypto Theft Scheme, Defendants Stole
Nearly $1M
Compound Score: -0.9956
```

In this section, we apply VADER, general vocabulary based model, to build core sentiment analytics over a stream of 50 crypto news articles. We have stepped through the code sequence starting with API links and data harvest, model design and setup and ultimate implementation and result interpretation. In the next section, we implement finance-trained model finBERT to the very same textual dataframes.

FinBERT

FinBERT is a specialized version of *BERT (bidirectional encoder representations from transformers)* that has been fine-tuned specifically for financial text analysis and natural language processing tasks [8.6]. FinBERT is trained on large corpora of financial documents, including earnings reports, financial news articles, SEC filings and other finance-related texts. This specialized training helps it understand financial terminology, context and relationships better than general-purpose language models. This model is used for financial sentiment analysis (determining whether news or reports are positive, negative or neutral about stocks/companies), financial text classification or market price prediction based on news sentiment. Because it is domain-specific, FinBERT typically outperforms general BERT models on financial NLP tasks [8.7]. It better understands financial jargon, company relationships, market terminology and the nuanced ways financial information is communicated [8.8].

The model's effectiveness stems from its unique design as a domain-specific adaptation of BERT pretrained on extensive financial data sets. Financial language poses unique challenges for natural language processing. The industry uses specific terms that mean different things in different contexts. General NLP models, such as previously covered VADER model, find it hard to interpret these texts correctly because words can have multiple meanings. To cite an instance, see the word "bank" – it could mean a financial institution or a river's edge based on context. Machines have a hard time picking the right meaning without understanding the full picture.

The same financial term might mean different things based on the words around it and industry context. General NLP models often get financial sentiment wrong because they lack financial training. Research shows that words that sound negative in everyday talk might not be negative at all in financial discussions. These models then mix up positive or negative feelings as neutral in business, health and technology sectors. Most financial sentiment analysis still uses dictionary-based methods despite these problems. People have tried moving past fixed word lists, but many techniques still count words without looking at how they work together.

The **FinBERT model** fixes these issues by looking at words in context to figure out their meaning. This makes **FinBERT sentiment analysis** much more accurate than traditional methods.

Architecture

FinBERT keeps BERT's basic architecture at its foundation. It uses multiple layers of bidirectional transformer encoders with self-attention mechanisms and feedforward neural networks. The main difference lies in how FinBERT adapts to financial domains. BERT learned from general text like Wikipedia and BookCorpus (3.3 billion tokens). FinBERT then learned more from financial texts to better understand financial language [8.9]. Studies show that building on the original BERT model works better than starting a financial model from scratch. Models that continue learning from BERT checkpoints usually do better than new ones trained on financial data. The **FinBERT model's** output layer creates probability distributions for sentiment classes (negative, neutral, positive). It uses cross-entropy loss functions and AdamW optimizer. This structure helps FinBERT capture two-way contextual relationships between tokens. These relationships matter a lot for accurate **FinBERT sentiment analysis.**

FinBERT starts with BERT's pretraining goals. The *masked language model (MLM)* task hides 15% of input tokens randomly. The model then learns to predict them based on context. This method allows true two-way learning as the model looks at both previous and following text to make predictions. *Next sentence prediction (NSP)* teaches the model to spot consecutive text segments. The model sees paired sentences during training. Half are actual consecutive sentences, while half are random pairs. NSP helps understand sentence relationships. Some FinBERT versions skip this task since recent research questions its benefits.

Advanced FinBERT versions add more pretraining tasks beyond MLM and NSP:

- Sentence reordering to learn sentence relationships
- Question answering tasks to grasp semantic relevance
- Keyword identification to understand topics

These multiple learning approaches help FinBERT grasp language knowledge and meaning better, especially in financial contexts.

The FinBERT model's success comes from its extensive financial training data. This data has three main document types:

- Corporate filings: 60,490 10-K (annual) and 142,622 10-Q (quarterly) reports from Russell 3000 firms between 1994–2019, from SEC's EDGAR database
- Analyst reports: About 476,633 reports on S&P 500 firms between 2003–2012 from Thomson Investext database
- Earnings call transcripts: 136,578 transcripts from 7,740 public companies between 2004–2019 from SeekingAlpha

This corpus has 4.9 billion tokens – 50% more than BERT's original training data. Such a large financial data set helps FinBERT understand specialized financial terms and communication patterns. These texts were chosen because researchers use them often. They include input from the core team like managers and analysts. The texts also expose the model to financial topics and communication styles of all types.

The FinBERT model needs fine-tuning to excel at specific tasks like sentiment analysis after its pretraining on domain-specific financial texts. This vital step turns the pretrained model into a specialized financial sentiment classifier through targeted training on labeled financial text data sets. Two key data sets provide labeled examples to train sentiment classification:

- Financial PhraseBank: Malo et al. (2014) created this data set with 4,845 English sentences from financial news in the LexisNexis database. The sentences got careful annotations from 16 people with finance and business backgrounds. These experts classified each sentence based on its potential impact on company stock prices. Some sentences in the data set reached complete agreement among annotators [8.10].
- Analyst Reports: Some FinBERT sentiment analysis versions use 10,000 manually annotated sentences from analyst reports to improve performance on real-life financial documents. These professional annotations are a great way to get domain-specific examples that capture financial analysis language nuances.

Both data sets help the model spot sentiment patterns in different types of financial communications. This creates a more versatile classifier that works with various financial texts.

Analytics

In line with previous VADER model exposition, in this section we investigate language analytics utilizing FinBERT architecture. We are positioned with DDF Station #3 Model Design, and our role is to design modeling framework to assess sentiment from textual data sequences. This can be used by the business to inform or link these results into another prediction model, say, as an input into asset trading algorithms.

First, we load relevant libraries, namely *transformers* and *torch* to accommodate pretrained model with *model_name* = *"ProtusAI/finbert*. We are not model builders in this case. We are model users:

```
import json
import pandas as pd
from transformers import AutoTokenizer, AutoModelForSequenceClassification
from transformers import pipeline
import torch
import re
import warnings
warnings.filterwarnings('ignore')

def load_finbert_model():
    """
    Load the FinBERT model for financial sentiment analysis
    """
    model_name = "ProsusAI/finbert"
    tokenizer = AutoTokenizer.from_pretrained(model_name)
    model = AutoModelForSequenceClassification.from_pretrained(model_name)

    # Create sentiment analysis pipeline
    sentiment_pipeline = pipeline(
        "sentiment-analysis",
        model=model,
        tokenizer=tokenizer,
        device=0 if torch.cuda.is_available() else -1
    )

    return sentiment_pipeline
```

Next, as we noticed, text dataframes require additional care regarding pre-processing and tokenization steps. We run this cleanup exercise:

```
def preprocess_text(text):
  """
  Clean and preprocess text for sentiment analysis
  """
  if not isinstance(text, str):
    return ""

  # Remove HTML tags
  text = re.sub(r'<[^>]+>', '', text)

  # Remove URLs
  text = re.sub(r'http[s]?://(?:[a-zA-Z]|[0-9]|[$-_@.&+]|[!*\\(\\),]|(?:%[0-9a-fA-F]
[0-9a-fA-F]))+', '', text)

  # Remove extra whitespace
  text = re.sub(r'\s+', ' ', text).strip()

  # Truncate to avoid token limits (FinBERT has 512 token limit)
  if len(text) > 2000:  # Rough character limit to stay under token limit
    text = text[:2000]

  return text
```

Once we are satisfied the text content is clean, we proceed to outline model results and convert numerical model scores to human understandable categories. This is used in the last phase, triggering the model, collecting model score and applying this code sequence to collect into final result model structure. The reason for being rather pedantic at this stage is the ultimate ability to deliver of the sentiment language analytics to the final consumer of these results in visual as well as tabular representations.

```
def calculate_sentiment_scores(text, sentiment_pipeline):
    """
    Calculate sentiment scores using FinBERT
    Returns sentiment label and confidence scores
    """
    try:
        # Get prediction
        result = sentiment_pipeline(text)

        # FinBERT returns: positive, negative, neutral
        label = result[0]['label'].lower()
        score = result[0]['score']

        # Convert to numerical sentiment index
        if label == 'positive':
            sentiment_index = score
        elif label == 'negative':
            sentiment_index = -score
        else:  # neutral
            sentiment_index = 0

        return {
            'sentiment_label': label,
```

```
                'confidence_score': score,
                'sentiment_index': sentiment_index
            }

    except Exception as e:
        print(f"Error processing text: {str(e)[:100]}...")
        return {
            'sentiment_label': 'neutral',
            'confidence_score': 0.0,
            'sentiment_index': 0.0
        }
```

Finally, the following code sequence deliver the final language analytics results:

```
def analyze_json_sentiment(json_file_path):
    """
    Main function to analyze sentiment from JSON file
    """
    print("Loading FinBERT model...")
    sentiment_pipeline = load_finbert_model()
    print("Model loaded successfully!")

    # Load JSON data
    with open(json_file_path, 'r', encoding='utf-8') as file:

        data = json.load(file)

    print(f"Processing {len(data)} articles...")

    results = []

    for idx, article in enumerate(data):
        print(f"Processing article {idx + 1}/{len(data)}: {article.get('title',
'No title')[:50]}...")

        # Extract and preprocess text
        body_text = preprocess_text(article.get('body', ''))

        if not body_text:
            print(f"  Warning: Empty body text for article {idx + 1}")
            continue

        # Calculate sentiment
        sentiment_result = calculate_sentiment_scores(body_text,
sentiment_pipeline)

        # Prepare result
        result = {
            'id': article.get('id', ''),
            'title': article.get('title', ''),
            'source': article.get('source', ''),
            'published_date': article.get('published_date', ''),
            'categories': article.get('categories', ''),
            'tags': article.get('tags', ''),
            'url': article.get('url', ''),
            'body_length': len(body_text),
            'sentiment_label': sentiment_result['sentiment_label'],
```

```
            'confidence_score': round(sentiment_result['confidence_score'], 4),
            'sentiment_index': round(sentiment_result['sentiment_index'], 4)
        }

        results.append(result)

        print(f"  Sentiment: {sentiment_result['sentiment_label']}
({sentiment_result['sentiment_index']:.4f})")

    return results
```

As it can be seen, we initialize the model, load text *.json* file, with 50 crypto driven news in this case, and execute sentiment analytics per article *body*, or actual news narrative. Note, the importance to collect result as per predefined sequence with additional level of information. The importance of this step will become obvious in the following section [8.11].

Implementation

To conclude our FinBERT exposition we provide graphical and tabular analytics. The next chapter links the model results with practical applications.

Given an article, a box represented within Figure 8.9, we can assign sentiment index and depict the result in a simple graphical interpretation. "Clicking" on a box we are able to extract the actual text with respective context connotation (grid position is the article location).

Overall, FinBERT summary shows more neutral scores as opposed to previous generic VADER model results, as shown in Figure 8.10:

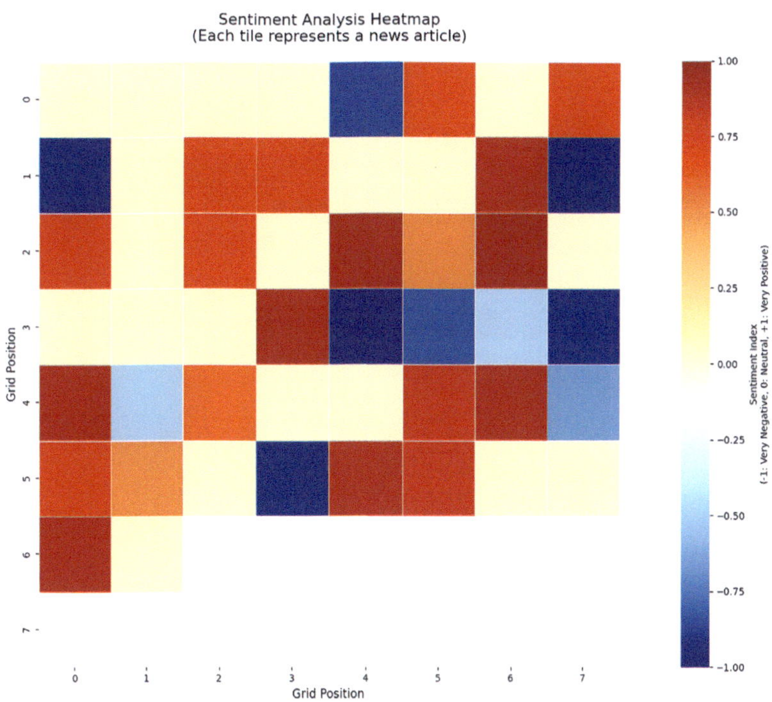

Figure 8.9 Sentiment per Article Heatmap

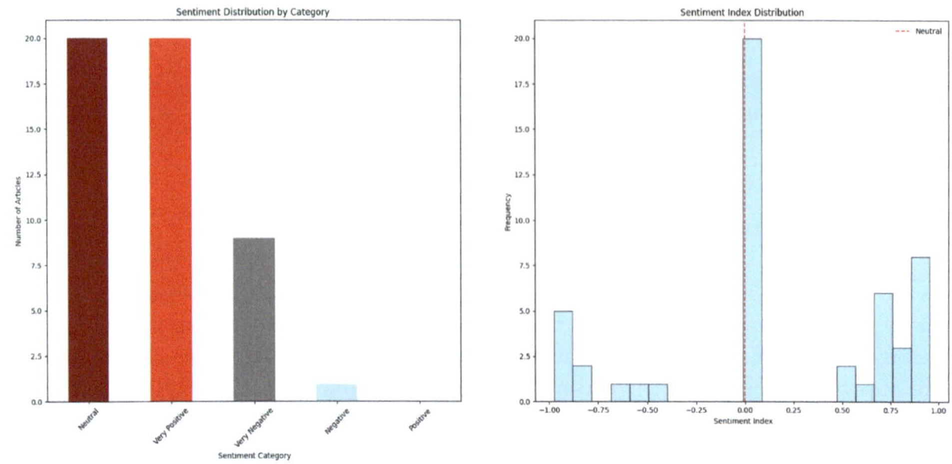

Figure 8.10 FinBERT Summary

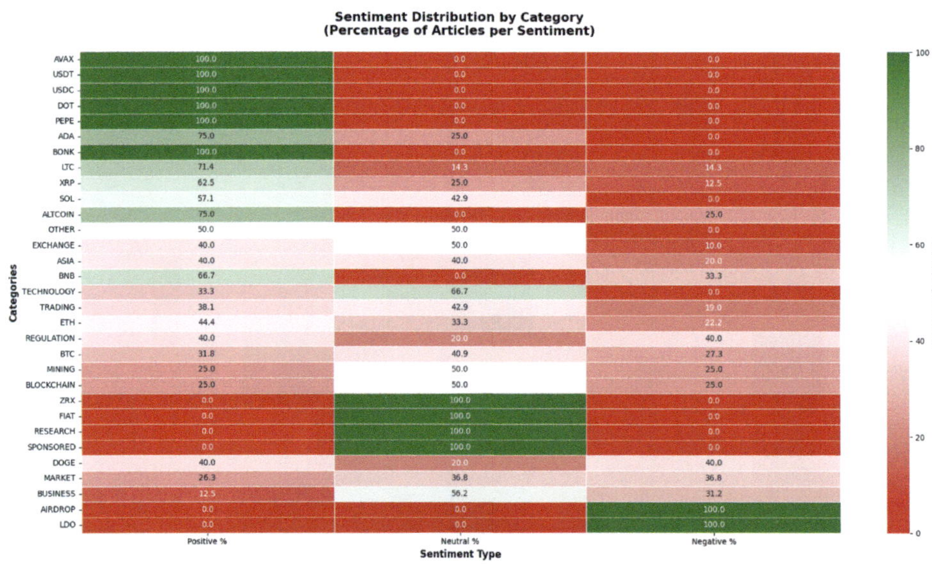

Figure 8.11 FinBERT Summary: Categories

```
# Create bins for sentiment ranges
sentiment_bins = [-1, -0.5, -0.1, 0.1, 0.5, 1]
sentiment_labels = ['Very Negative', 'Negative', 'Neutral', 'Positive', 'Very
Positive']
df['sentiment_category'] = pd.cut(df['sentiment_index'], bins=sentiment_bins,
labels=sentiment_labels, include_lowest=True)
```

The following set of visuals in Figures 8.11–8.13 showcase the ability to cut the narrative into categories, data providers, number of news per sentiment, as an example. Hence, the need to keep relevant structure in place from the beginning of data harvest.

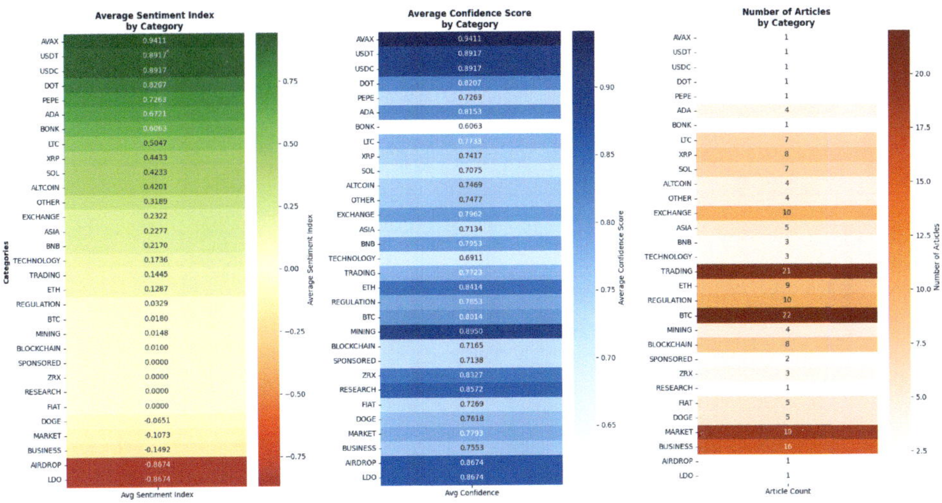

Figure 8.12 FinBERT Summary: Split

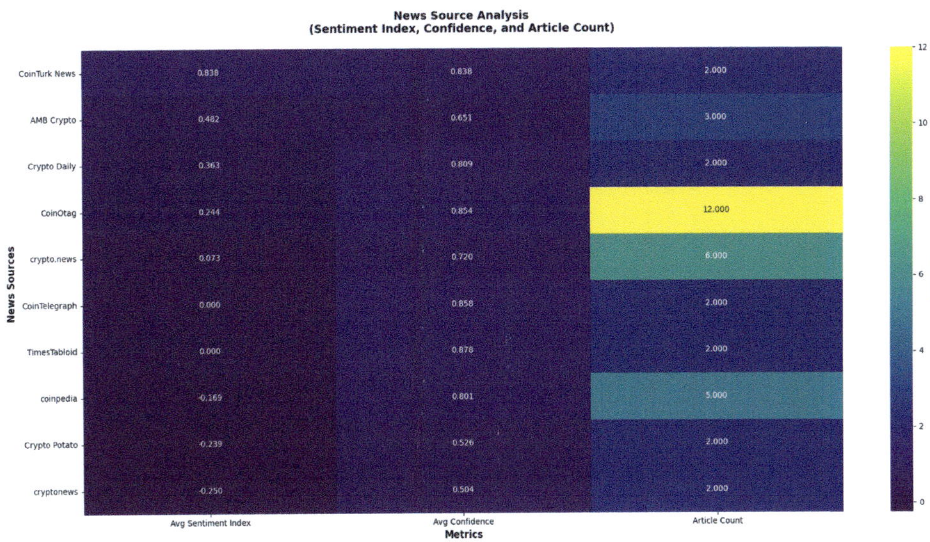

Figure 8.13 FinBERT Summary: News Provider

Figure 8.14 shows an aggregate sentiment per time. In this instance, we split the time frames into hours as buckets, then collate news sequences and measure the average sentiment per this time frame. This can be used to build dynamic sentiment indices per a specific news attribute of category. We explore sentiment indexation further in the following chapters.

Based on the breakdowns, further insights can be derived by splitting the results per most discussed categories and news source analytics:

```
Most Discussed Categories (by article count):
  BTC           : 22 articles (sentiment:  0.0180, confidence: 0.8014)
  TRADING       : 21 articles (sentiment:  0.1445, confidence: 0.7723)
```

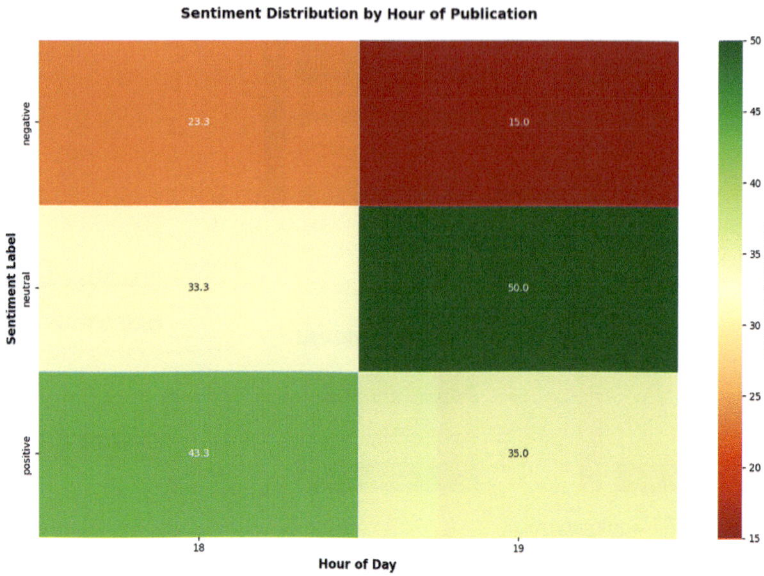

Figure 8.14 Sentiment in Time

```
  MARKET          : 19 articles (sentiment: -0.1073, confidence: 0.7793)
  BUSINESS        : 16 articles (sentiment: -0.1492, confidence: 0.7553)
  EXCHANGE        : 10 articles (sentiment:  0.2322, confidence: 0.7962)
  REGULATION      : 10 articles (sentiment:  0.0329, confidence: 0.7853)
  ETH             :  9 articles (sentiment:  0.1287, confidence: 0.8414)
  BLOCKCHAIN      :  8 articles (sentiment:  0.0100, confidence: 0.7165)
  XRP             :  8 articles (sentiment:  0.4433, confidence: 0.7417)
  LTC             :  7 articles (sentiment:  0.5047, confidence: 0.7733)

News Source Analysis (sources with 2+ articles):
  Source                        Articles Avg Sentiment Avg Confidence
------------------------------------------------------------
CoinTurk News                      2        0.8379        0.8379
AMB Crypto                         3        0.4816        0.6511
Crypto Daily                       2        0.3631        0.8088
CoinOtag                          12        0.2439        0.8537
crypto.news                        6        0.0728        0.7199
CoinTelegraph                      2        0.0000        0.8576
TimesTabloid                       2        0.0000        0.8778
coinpedia                          5       -0.1693        0.8006
Crypto Potato                      2       -0.2392        0.5257
cryptonews                         2       -0.2500        0.5037
```

Once establishing official and trusted news digital channels, the consumer of this information is able to track performance of news providers and how such quality can then drive potential value of relevant asset. We investigate such links in the next chapter.

```
Dataset Overview:
Total articles: 50
Sentiment Index range: -0.9755 to 0.9545
Confidence score range: 0.3895 to 0.9755
```

```
Sentiment distribution: {'neutral': 20, 'positive': 20, 'negative': 10}
Date range: 2025-07-01 18:13:49 to 2025-07-01 19:17:11
The data is limited to 50 articles within a specific period of time. The model
is applied across the entire article extract *body* per article.
```

Interestingly, the first two articles we analyzed using VADER showing positive connotation show as neutral within FinBERT context. Hence, the importance of using correct level of input data used within any given neural network architecture.

```
Loading FinBERT model...
Device set to use cpu
Model loaded successfully!
Processing 50 articles...
Processing article 1/50: Cursor Web App: Empowering Developers with Advance...
  Sentiment: neutral (0.0000)
Processing article 2/50: Swyftx Acquires Caleb & Brown in $100M Deal to Exp...
  Sentiment: neutral (0.0000)
```

Summary statistics show similar conclusion to VADER with overall positive sentiment in the crypto universe, given the snap of the global news coverage.

```
============================================================
SENTIMENT ANALYSIS SUMMARY
============================================================
Total articles analyzed: 50
Average sentiment index: 0.1547
Sentiment index std dev: 0.6144
Min sentiment index: -0.9755
Max sentiment index: 0.9545

Sentiment Distribution:
  Neutral: 20 (40.0%)
  Positive: 20 (40.0%)
  Negative: 10 (20.0%)

Top 5 Most Positive Articles:
  0.9545 - Australia's Monochrome Spot Bitcoin ETF Boosts BTC Holdings ...
  0.9411 - Bloomberg Sees Increased Odds for XRP ETF Approval Amid Grow...
  0.9352 - Bitcoin Reaches New Highs with Impressive Quarterly and Mont...
  0.9265 - Here Are Benefits If RLUSD Gets Successfully Integrated Into...
  0.9115 - Analysts See High Probability of SEC Approval for Litecoin S...

Top 5 Most Negative Articles:
  -0.9755 - Will Bitcoin crash below $100k as network activity nosedives...
  -0.9668 - Bitcoin Volatility Drops to 1.59% Signaling Market Cooling a...
  -0.9375 - Bitcoin Slips as Trump Threatens to Send Elon Musk Back to S...
  -0.9348 - Trump Suggests DOGE Investigate Elon Musk's Subsidies Amid G...
  -0.9294 - Analyst Suggests Bitcoin Bounce May Be Temporary Amid Potent...

Results saved to sentiment_analysis_results.csv

============================================================
OVERALL MARKET SENTIMENT INDEX: 0.1547
Market sentiment: POSITIVE
============================================================
```

8.5 Summary

This chapter explores sentiment analytics within the finance and FinTech sectors, focusing on the extraction and analysis of unstructured data to derive actionable insights. The chapter emphasizes the growing importance of unstructured data – information that doesn't conform to traditional database formats – and its potential to provide competitive advantages through sentiment analysis, trend detection and comprehensive risk assessment.

Market sentiment acts as a powerful lens that helps traders understand price movements beyond traditional analysis. Bullish and bearish sentiment gives crucial context to market conditions. Markets often reverse course at times of extreme sentiment – whether too optimistic or pessimistic. This creates opportunities for contrarian traders. Low market sentiment can signal good buying opportunities for value investors who dare to challenge common market psychology. Sentiment analysis tools have become more advanced. Social media feeds, news indicators and specialized platforms like FinBERT process huge amounts of text data instantly. Traders can now add immediate sentiment signals to their technical and fundamental analysis.

The chapter begins by establishing the importance of unstructured data in finance and FinTech, specifically focusing on text data as a key component of unstructured data frameworks. The content progresses through base techniques for handling words and sentences using tokenization approaches, supported by Python code snippets and graphical representations. The chapter then introduces *VADER (valence aware dictionary and sentiment reasoner)* language model implementation, emphasizing practical usage and result interpretation over mathematical definitions.

The final section presents FinBERT, a specialized version of *BERT (bidirectional encoder representations from transformers)* fine-tuned specifically for financial domain tasks. This model represents the trend toward domain-specific large language models for improved performance on specialized tasks.

Throughout the chapter, the focus remains on practical model setup and result interpretation rather than mathematical architecture details. All content aligns with the *DDF Model #3 Model Design* stage, emphasizing the development of predictive models for business problem-solving, specifically in delivering sentiment analytics solutions. Natural extension of this chapter for further study is an inclusion of BERT model mathematical design and interpretation and then moving into transformer architecture leading towards large language model LLMs, such as OpenAI, ClaudeAI expositions in the field of finance and banking.

8.6 Concept Questions and Answers

Q1: What is unstructured data in finance and why is it important?

A1: Unstructured data in finance refers to information that doesn't fit into traditional data models, such as emails, PDFs, call logs, and social media posts. It's important because it represents 80–90% of all data generated by financial institutions and contains valuable insights about customer behavior, market trends and operational inefficiencies.

Q2: How can financial institutions effectively process unstructured data?

A2: Financial institutions can process unstructured data effectively by implementing robust ingestion pipelines, using metadata tagging and employing technologies like OCR and speech-to-text. Advanced parsing techniques such as Named Entity Recognition, topic modeling, and sentiment analysis can then be used to extract meaningful insights from this data.

Q3: What are the benefits of making unstructured data accessible across teams?

A3: Making unstructured data accessible across teams enables consolidated customer profiles, enhanced decision-making, improved customer service and better compliance management. It also helps bridge the gap between different systems like CRM and ERP, ensuring that all relevant information is available to the right people at the right time.

Q4: How does AI technology help in analyzing unstructured financial data?

A4: AI technologies like vector embeddings and retrieval-augmented generation (RAG) help in analyzing unstructured financial data by enabling powerful search capabilities, improving the accuracy of responses to financial queries and allowing the deployment of language models on internal data sets. This leads to more efficient data processing and more accurate insights.

Q5: What are some real-world applications of unstructured data analysis in finance?

A5: Real-world applications include automated insurance claims processing, which can reduce processing time from weeks to minutes; contract clause extraction for compliance, which can cut administrative costs by 40–50%; and customer churn prediction from support logs, enabling financial institutions to develop customized retention strategies for different customer segments.

Q6: What is FinBERT and how does it differ from regular BERT?

A6: FinBERT is a specialized version of BERT that has been pretrained on financial texts. It outperforms regular BERT in financial sentiment analysis, achieving 88.2% accuracy compared to BERT's 85.0%. The key difference lies in FinBERT's domain-specific training on financial corpora, allowing it to better understand financial language nuances.

Q7: How accurate is FinBERT in detecting negative sentiment in financial texts?

A7: FinBERT demonstrates exceptional accuracy in detecting negative sentiment, achieving 89.7% accuracy. This is significantly higher than non-BERT algorithms, which struggle with less than 60% accuracy on the same task. This capability is crucial in financial contexts where negative information often has a greater impact on market decisions.

Q8: Can FinBERT perform well with limited training data?

A8: Yes, FinBERT shows remarkable performance even with minimal training data. It maintains 81.3% accuracy using only 10% of the training sample, outperforming other algorithms that use the full data set. This efficiency makes FinBERT particularly valuable when labeled financial data is scarce.

Q9: What are some applications of FinBERT beyond basic sentiment analysis?

A9: FinBERT has proven effective in various specialized financial analysis tasks. It achieves 89.5% accuracy in classifying environmental, social, and governance (ESG) discussions from corporate reports. It's also used to analyze earnings call transcripts, capturing market reactions and tone dispersion that correlate with investor behavior and market volatility.

Q10: How does FinBERT handle the contextual ambiguity in financial language?

A10: FinBERT addresses contextual ambiguity in financial language through its domain-specific pretraining on large financial corpora, including SEC filings, analyst reports and earnings calls. This allows it to understand specialized financial terminology and communication patterns, enabling more accurate interpretation of financial texts compared to general NLP models.

8.7 Further Reading

- Alammar, J., & Grootendorst, M. (2024). Hands-On Large Language Models: Language Understanding and Generation, O'Reilly.
- Dickerson, A., & Hric, J. (2024). FINS5545 Financial Market Data Literacy Course Notes, UNSW Business School.
- Hric, J., & Lam, I. (2025). FINS5548 Financial Technology Course Notes, UNSW Business School.
- Huyen, C. (2025). AI Engineering: Building Applications with Foundation Models, O'Reilly.
- Raschka, S. (2025). Build a Large Language Model, Manning.

8.8 References

[8.1] Chan, Y., Han, D., & Zhou, X. (2023). Mining the emotional information in the audio of earnings conference calls. International Review of Financial Analysis, 88. https://www.sciencedirect.com/science/article/abs/pii/S105752192300220X

[8.2] NY Time API: https://developer.nytimes.com/

[8.3] VADER: https://www.researchgate.net/publication/275828927_VADER_A_Parsimonious_Rule-based_Model_for_Sentiment_Analysis_of_Social_Media_Text

[8.4] NLTK: https://www.nltk.org/book/

[8.5] VADER Sentiment Analyzer: https://www.nltk.org/howto/sentiment.html

[8.6] FinBert Paper: https://arxiv.org/pdf/1908.10063

[8.7] FinBert GitHub: https://github.com/ProsusAI/finBERT

[8.8] FinBert on HuggingFace: https://huggingface.co/ProsusAI/finbert

[8.9] BERT: https://huggingface.co/blog/bert-101

[8.10] Malo et al.: https://www.researchgate.net/publication/251231107_Good_Debt_or_Bad_Debt_Detecting_Semantic_Orientations_in_Economic_Texts

[8.11] CryptoCompare API: https://developers.coindesk.com/documentation/data-api/introduction

SECTION 3

FinTech Applications

Chapter 9

FinTech Application

AdviceTech

9.1 Introduction

In this chapter we connect the content from previous Section 1 and Section 2 covered in this book. The chapter starts with an outline of a use case from AdviceTech. We introduce the reader to the problems faced by practitioners in this area and provide potential solution by implementing step-by-step use case within the confines of DDF concept delivering a core outline of a FinTech solution utilizing **modern portfolio theory** approach. In this simulation, the reader assumes a position of finance practitioner within crypto roboAdvisory provider and is tasked to solve a predefined problem and to deliver technology driven solution.

DOI: 10.4324/9781003477747-12

Modern portfolio theory's core idea comes from understanding the risk-return tradeoff – a trading principle that connects high risk with high reward. MPT assumes investors avoid risk, so they naturally choose the less risky option when two portfolios offer similar expected returns. This assumption reveals something important: investors will only take more risk if they get higher expected returns. People who want higher expected returns must accept more risk. MPT says rational investors should not choose a portfolio when another option exists with better risk-return features.

Firstly, we define Crypto AdviceTech use case. A roboadvisor is an automated digital investment management platform that uses ML/AI algorithms to provide financial investment and trading services with minimal human intervention. We expose the reader to the world of crypto markets. Secondly, we apply our *FinTech digital data factory* concept. Across each DDF station we outline new techniques and expose new tools. There is an inherent flow of data from *DDF Station #1: ETL* all the way to *DDF Station #4: Implementation*. We conclude the chapter building a simple FinTech product wireframe.

Learning Outcomes

At the end of this chapter the reader will be able to:

- Comprehend crypto market structure
- Outline theoretical concepts behind modern portfolio theory
- Redefine DDF concept and apply in a practical setting
- Understand the DDF station data flows
- Use Streamlit library to draw FinTech solution wireframes
- Appreciate boundaries and opportunities in crypto trading

9.2 FinTech Use Case – Crypto AdviceTech

AdviceTech is a specialized segment of FinTech that focuses specifically on technology solutions designed to support financial advisers and advisory practices. A roboadvisor is an automated digital investment management platform that uses algorithms and software to provide financial planning services with minimal human intervention. These platforms typically work by having users complete an online questionnaire about their financial goals, risk tolerance, investment timeline and current financial situation. The roboadvisor then uses this information to create and manage a diversified investment portfolio, usually consisting of low-cost exchange-traded funds (ETFs) or index funds. The platform automatically rebalances portfolios to maintain target asset allocations. In this chapter we focus on each FinTech *Digital Data Factory Station* in turn using hypothetical use case related to crypto markets.

Market analytics platforms, such as altFINS, play critical role in delivering up-to-date crypto market information [9.1].

> altFINS offers the best free crypto screener. It includes a wide range of filters to help you find the best cryptocurrencies to invest in based on your specific trading strategy. You can set up your own custom screens using combinations of technical indicators (SMA, EMA, RSI, MACD), variables like market cap, traded volume and price performance. You can also create price alerts for your scans. So whether you're looking for the next

profitable trading tip or simply want to diversify your portfolio, crypto screener is a great place to start your search.

Generally, global market structure comprises capital markets, trading bonds, FX markets, trading currencies, equity markets, trading equities, commodity markets, trading commodities and crypto markets, trading cryptocurrencies. We draw a distinction between cryptocurrencies and asset tokenization in "Chapter 5: Bitcoin and Tokenization." FinTech platforms like Robinhood are working on tokenization approaches to, potentially, bring all these markets together [9.2].

Crypto markets refer to the digital marketplaces where cryptocurrencies or other altcoins are bought, sold and traded, as shown in Figure 9.1. These markets operate 24/7 globally. Crypto markets are decentralized financial ecosystems where digital assets like Bitcoin, Ethereum and thousands of other cryptocurrencies are exchanged. Unlike traditional stock markets, they operate continuously without closing hours and are accessible worldwide.

Key characteristics of crypto markets:

- High volatility: Prices can fluctuate dramatically within short periods
- 24/7 trading: Markets never close, unlike traditional exchanges
- Global accessibility: Anyone with internet access can participate
- Decentralized nature: No single authority controls the entire market in some instances not always the case
- Liquidity varies: Major cryptocurrencies like Bitcoin have high liquidity, while smaller "altcoins" may have limited trading volume
- Prone to hacks: number of security flaws external to internal blockchain architecture
- Lack of regulation: almost non-existent global controls and regulations

In addition, the market participants vary from other market structures. The participants consist of risk-seeking individual retail investors, institutional investors and quant traders, crypto exchanges that facilitate liquidity, market makers and miners and validators who secure networks. Trading is conducted on spot markets, futures and derivatives markets, ETF (listed instruments traded on equity markets), decentralized finance (DeFi) protocols and peer-to-peer trading. Overall, there are several popular exchange trading platforms such as Coinbase, Binance or Kraken.

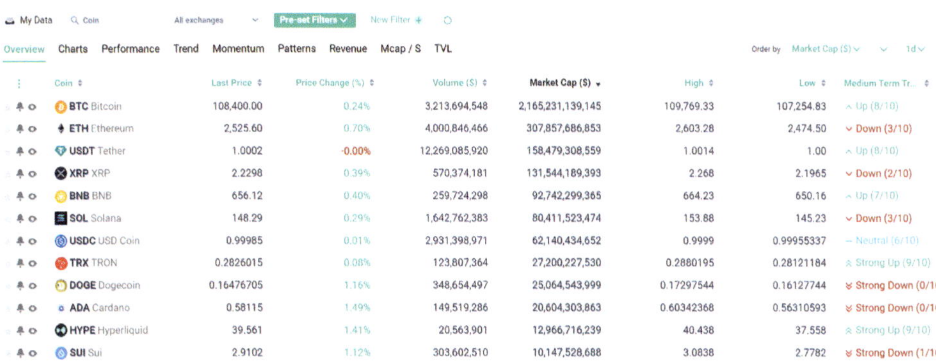

Coin	Last Price	Price Change (%)	Volume ($)	Market Cap ($)	High	Low	Medium Term Tr...
BTC Bitcoin	108,400.00	0.24%	3,213,694,548	2,165,231,139,145	109,769.33	107,254.83	Up (8/10)
ETH Ethereum	2,525.60	0.70%	4,000,846,466	307,857,686,853	2,603.28	2,474.50	Down (3/10)
USDT Tether	1.0002	-0.00%	12,269,085,920	158,479,308,559	1.0014	1.00	Up (8/10)
XRP XRP	2.2298	0.39%	570,374,181	131,544,189,393	2.268	2.1965	Down (2/10)
BNB BNB	656.12	0.40%	259,724,298	92,742,299,365	664.23	650.16	Up (7/10)
SOL Solana	148.29	0.29%	1,642,762,383	80,411,523,474	153.88	145.23	Down (3/10)
USDC USD Coin	0.99985	0.01%	2,931,398,971	62,140,434,652	0.9999	0.99955337	Neutral (6/10)
TRX TRON	0.2826015	0.08%	123,807,364	27,200,227,530	0.2880195	0.28121184	Strong Up (9/10)
DOGE Dogecoin	0.16476705	1.16%	348,654,497	25,064,543,999	0.17297544	0.16127744	Strong Down (0/1(
ADA Cardano	0.58115	1.49%	149,519,286	20,604,303,863	0.60342368	0.56310593	Strong Down (0/1(
HYPE Hyperliquid	39.561	1.41%	20,563,901	12,966,716,239	40.438	37.558	Strong Up (9/10)
SUI Sui	2.9102	1.12%	303,602,510	10,147,528,688	3.0838	2.7782	Strong Down (1/1(

Figure 9.1 altFINS Crypto Screener

Workshop

In this workshop, we assume you have taken a position of a market participant operating in crypto markets and working on trading and hedging desk of a global investment bank or a hedge fund. Your task is to implement state-of-the-art techniques in prediction algorithms as well as design an appropriate approach to portfolio selection challenges and design AdviceTech product delivering portfolio strategy in trading crypto currencies, following the steps outlined in Figure 9.2.

Following on "Chapter 2: Data Management for FinTech" we explore each data factory station in turn and provide detailed exposition to techniques and tools in each to be able to deliver final FinTech product.

9.3 Data Lake

Crypto Markets

The CryptoCompare API is a comprehensive cryptocurrency data service that provides real-time and historical market information for digital assets. CryptoCompare offers extensive market data including current and historical prices, trading volumes, market capitalization and exchange rates for thousands of cryptocurrencies. The API covers both spot and derivatives markets across hundreds of exchanges globally. The API provides several main categories of data through RESTful endpoints. Price data endpoints deliver current and historical OHLCV (open, high, low, close, volume) information at various time intervals from minutes to daily. Social and news endpoints aggregate sentiment data, social media metrics, and cryptocurrency-related news articles. Exchange data endpoints provide information about trading pairs, exchange volumes, and orderbook data [9.3].

CryptoCompare aggregates data from multiple exchanges and applies proprietary algorithms to calculate volume-weighted average prices (VWAP) and other composite metrics.

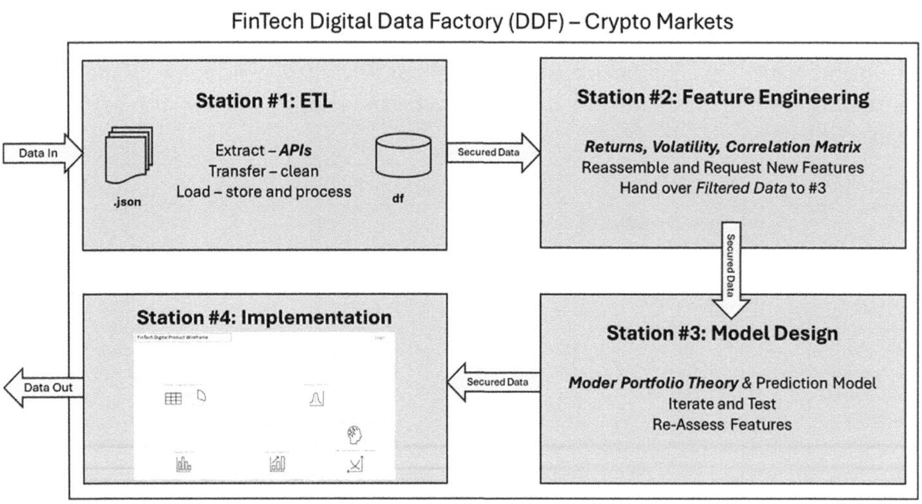

Figure 9.2 FinTech Digital Data Factory (DDF) Concept

They implement data validation and cleaning processes to ensure accuracy and filter out potentially manipulated or erroneous data points. Core components of the CryptoCompare API:

Price Data

- Real-time and historical price data for thousands of cryptocurrencies.
- Data available in various fiat currencies and other cryptocurrencies.

Market Data

- Information on trading volumes, market capitalization and liquidity.
- Data from multiple exchanges and trading pairs.

Trading Data

- Aggregated and individual exchange data.
- Bid and ask prices, order book data, and trade data.

Social Data

- Insights and metrics from social media platforms and forums.
- Sentiment analysis and trends in social media activity.

Blockchain Data

- Information on blockchain metrics such as block height, block time and transaction data.
- Data on mining difficulty, hash rates and network activity.

News and Analysis

- Curated news articles and updates from various sources.
- Analysis and commentary on market trends and events.

Exchange Data

- Detailed information on cryptocurrency exchanges, including trading fees, supported pairs and trading volumes.
- Exchange-specific data for more granular analysis.

Index Data

- Cryptocurrency indices to track the performance of specific segments of the market.
- Customizable indices based on user-defined criteria.

For the purposes of this chapter we focus our attention on *Price Data* and *News and Analysis*. The techniques introduced in this book, however, can be extended to cover other previous data sources.

ETL

Firstly, we set up and process public API calls to extract historical prices for selection of top-cap crypto pairs, all priced in USD. This step is similar in design to our previous exercises while extracting "crypto news" Python.

```
    # Define the cryptocurrencies to extract
    crypto_symbols = ['BTC', 'ETH', 'USDT', 'XRP', 'BNB', 'SOL', 'TRX', 'DOGE',
'ADA', 'SUI']
```

Initial code snippet:

```
    def get_daily_prices(self, symbol, days=365, to_symbol='USD'):
        """
        Get daily price history for a cryptocurrency

        Args:
            symbol (str): Cryptocurrency symbol (e.g., 'BTC')
            days (int): Number of days of history to retrieve
            to_symbol (str): Target currency symbol (default: 'USD')

        Returns:
            pd.DataFrame: DataFrame with price history
        """
        url = f"{self.base_url}/v2/histoday"
        params = {
            'fsym': symbol,
            'tsym': to_symbol,
            'limit': days,
            'toTs': int(time.time())
        }

        try:
            response = requests.get(url, params=params, headers=self.headers)
            response.raise_for_status()
            data = response.json()

            if data['Response'] == 'Error':
                print(f"Error for {symbol}: {data['Message']}")
                return None

            # Extract price data
            price_data = data['Data']['Data']

            # Convert to DataFrame
            df = pd.DataFrame(price_data)

            # Convert timestamp to datetime
            df['datetime'] = pd.to_datetime(df['time'], unit='s')
            df['date'] = df['datetime'].dt.date

            # Add symbol column
            df['symbol'] = symbol

            # Reorder columns
            columns = ['symbol', 'date', 'datetime', 'open', 'high', 'low',
'close', 'volumefrom', 'volumeto']
            df = df[columns]
```

```
            # Sort by date
            df = df.sort_values('date')

            return df

        except requests.exceptions.RequestException as e:
            print(f"Request error for {symbol}: {e}")
            return None
        except Exception as e:
            print(f"Unexpected error for {symbol}: {e}")
            return None
```

Note, we extract daily "closing" prices and execute similar code sequence for hourly frequency. This is CryptoCompare predefined and snapped price, as cryptocurrencies trade 24/7. We rely on the data quality at this stage.

Next step is to design data extraction calling API per currency pair. This is sufficient for our purposes, however would be enhanced in production environment due to efficiency and speed issues.

```
    def extract_multiple_coins(self, symbols, days=365, interval='daily',
output_dir='crypto_data'):
        """
        Extract price history for multiple cryptocurrencies

        Args:
            symbols (list): List of cryptocurrency symbols
            days (int): Number of days/hours of history
            interval (str): 'daily' or 'hourly'
            output_dir (str): Directory to save CSV files

        Returns:
            dict: Dictionary with symbol as key and DataFrame as value
        """
        # Create output directory if it doesn't exist
        if not os.path.exists(output_dir):
            os.makedirs(output_dir)

        results = {}

        for symbol in symbols:
            print(f"Extracting {interval} data for {symbol}...")

            if interval == 'daily':
                df = self.get_daily_prices(symbol, days)
            elif interval == 'hourly':
                df = self.get_hourly_prices(symbol, days)
            else:
                print(f"Invalid interval: {interval}")
                continue

            if df is not None:
                results[symbol] = df

                # Save to CSV
                filename = f"{symbol}_{interval}_prices.csv"
                filepath = os.path.join(output_dir, filename)
```

```
                df.to_csv(filepath, index=False)
                print(f"Saved {len(df)} records to {filepath}")
            else:
                print(f"Failed to extract data for {symbol}")

            # Rate limiting - CryptoCompare allows ~100 requests per second for
free tier
            time.sleep(0.1)

        return results
```

The code sequence calls previously defined *get_daily_prices()* function per each coin in turn from the provided *symbol* list. Note, we are using top 12 coins by market capitalization.

Result delivered from *DDF Station #1* in *df* dataframes:

```
Combining daily data...
Combined data saved to crypto_daily_data\combined_crypto_prices.csv
Total records: 4392

Daily Data Summary:
Date range: 2024-07-05 to 2025-07-05
Number of symbols: 12
Total records: 4392

Combining hourly data...
Combined data saved to crypto_hourly_data\combined_crypto_prices.csv
Total records: 8652

Hourly Data Summary:
Date range: 2025-06-05 23:00:00 to 2025-07-05 23:00:00
Number of symbols: 12
Total records: 8652
```

This completes our task for *DDF Station #1: ETL*. Data delivered here are being passed downstream to *DDF Station #2: Feature Engineering*.

9.4 Feature Engineering

In this *Station #2* we look at feature engineering in a rather simple fashion by using structured data in a time series setting. Here we look at features you extract when dealing with crypto markets data streams. Mostly related to market prices, structured data and relevant time series. Standard financial models such as *mean-variance portfolio theory* and the *capital asset pricing model (CAPM)* assume returns of financial assets are following normal distribution, hence here we start by looking at whether our extracted and cleansed data from Station #1 fit in this assumption.

Normality Tests

Here are a few examples from finance as to why we look at normal distribution:

Portfolio Theory

If and when we define assets to follow normal distribution we are able to describe the asset dynamics in terms of mean and standard deviation as well as co-variances between different stocks and achieve optimal portfolio allocation.

Capital Asset Pricing Model

If and when asset prices follow normal distribution we can describe the price of a single stock in relation to a general index by the measure of co-movement of a single stock versus market index called it's beta.

Efficient Market Hypothesis (EMH)

EMH states that the current asset price reflects all publicly available information. If this is true then stock prices fluctuate randomly, and returns are normally distributed by default and hence you as a market participant is not able to predict the next period of price fluctuations.

Option Pricing Theory

Brownian motion is the standard and benchmark model for the modelling of random stock prices. Black-Scholes-Merton option pricing model is using Brownian motion as the model for looking at contingent assets leading to normally distributed returns.

Returns

Expected return is the weighted average of probable returns for each asset in the portfolio, calculated using historical data or forecasts. We understand the importance of normal distribution in finance. Let us now look at the Python representation of this bench-marking case. For normally distributed returns we define as

$$log(Return) = log(S_t) - log(S_{t-1}).$$

where, S is the asset price in time $0 < s < t$

In short, we have selected as the most critical feature to be the returns calculated from the time series of stock prices for now. We do need to check for normality and make sure we understand deviations from this norm and what that actually means in the context of financial modelling and underlying theory.

First feature we extract from the data are daily returns:

```
def load_and_prepare_data(file_path):
    """Load and prepare cryptocurrency data"""
    df = pd.read_csv(file_path)
    df['date'] = pd.to_datetime(df['date'], format='%d/%m/%Y')
    df = df.sort_values(['symbol', 'date'])
    return df

def calculate_returns(df):
    """Calculate daily returns for each symbol"""
    returns_df = df.pivot(index='date', columns='symbol', values='close')
    returns_df = returns_df.pct_change().dropna()
    return returns_df
```

Figure 9.3 shows cumulative returns for our selection of cryptocurrencies.

Figure 9.4 depicts return distributions per our selection highlighting the fact that these times series deviate from normal distribution norms.

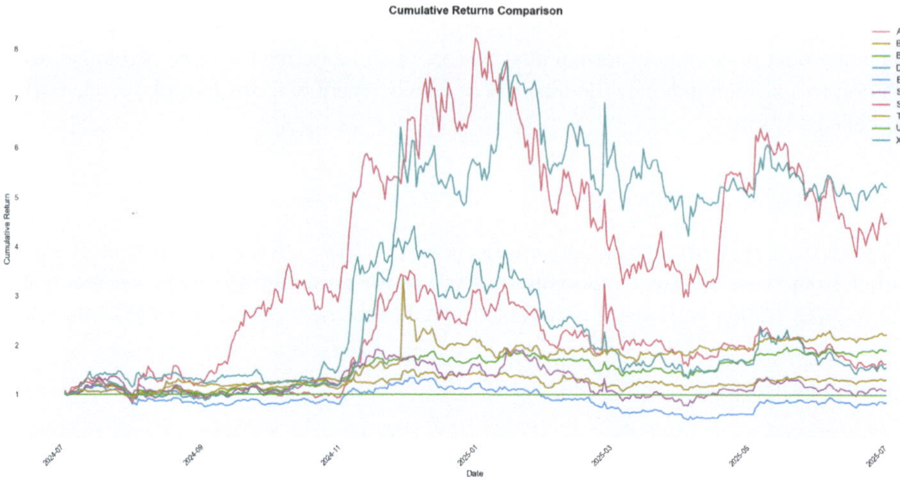

Figure 9.3 Cumulative Returns for 10x Crypto Currencies

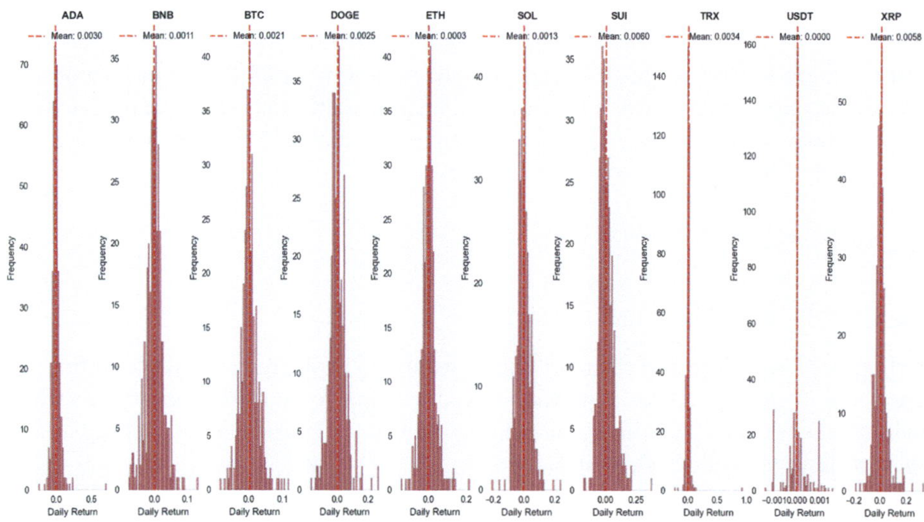

Figure 9.4 Daily Return Distributions

Resulting annualized returns:

```
ANNUALIZED RETURNS:
ADA: 110.46%
BNB: 39.85%
BTC: 76.81%
DOGE: 93.05%
ETH: 10.33%
SOL: 46.55%
SUI: 220.00%
TRX: 123.64%
USDT: 0.00%
XRP: 212.17%
```

Returns measure from the core feature in this example.

Volatility

Volatility refers to the degree of variation or fluctuation in the price, value or rate of something over time. In finance specifically, volatility is often measured using statistical methods like standard deviation and is a key component in options pricing models. It's considered both a measure of risk (higher volatility = higher risk) and opportunity (more price movement creates more potential for profit or loss).

Based on the returns we calculate volatility at the same return data frequency (daily in this case) and annualized:

```
# Calculate volatility (annualized)
def calculate_volatility(returns_df, trading_days=252):
  """Calculate annualized volatility for each symbol"""
  volatility = returns_df.std() * np.sqrt(trading_days)
  return volatility
```

We tend to scale annualized returns by volatility to extract *Sharp Ratio*, basically measuring asset returns per unit of risk as per Figure 9.5.

```
# Calculate Sharpe ratio
def calculate_sharpe_ratio(returns_df, risk_free_rate=0.02, trading_days=365):
    """Calculate Sharpe ratio for each symbol"""
    # Annualized returns
    annualized_returns = returns_df.mean() * trading_days

    # Annualized volatility
    annualized_volatility = calculate_volatility(returns_df, trading_days)

    # Sharpe ratio
    sharpe_ratios = (annualized_returns - risk_free_rate) /
annualized_volatility

    return sharpe_ratios
```

Another interesting angle is to view the risk in terms of returns as per Figure 9.6. This plot shows relative risk allocation per coin. As expected USDT is low on the scales.

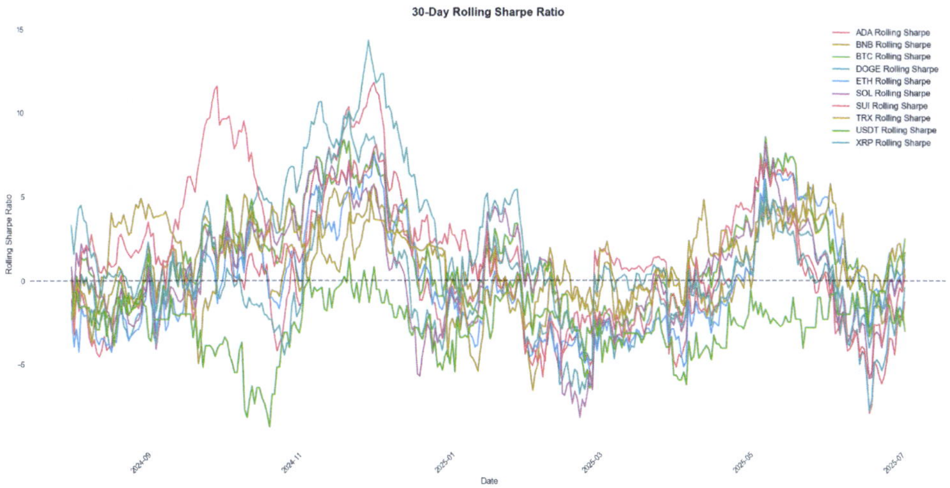

Figure 9.5 Rolling Sharpe Ratio

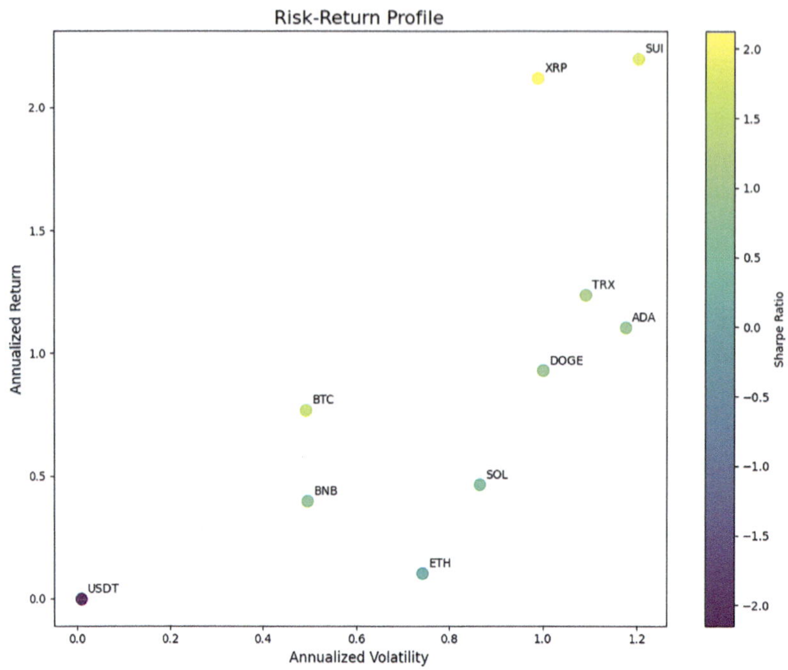

Figure 9.6 Risk Return Profile

Resulting annualized volatility measures:

```
ANNUALIZED VOLATILITY:
ADA: 117.62%
BNB: 49.62%
BTC: 49.25%
DOGE: 100.13%
ETH: 74.30%
SOL: 86.63%
SUI: 120.38%
TRX: 109.14%
USDT: 0.93%
XRP: 99.01%
```

Correlations

Correlation is defined as the degree to which different assets move in relation to each other. Assets with low or negative correlations provide better diversification benefits.

Based on the daily return, calculate correlation matrix:

```python
# Calculate correlation matrix
def calculate_correlation_matrix(returns_df):
    """Calculate correlation matrix between symbols"""
    correlation_matrix = returns_df.corr()
    return correlation_matrix
```

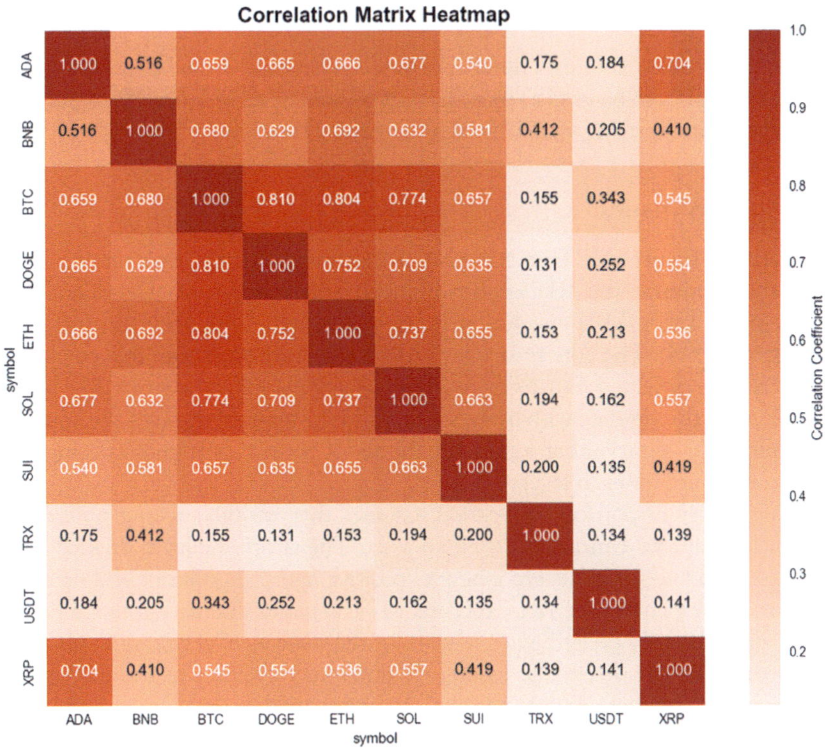

Figure 9.7 Correlation Matrix

As shown in Figure 9.7, there appears to be a rather high correlation among the largest coins by market capitalization. Resulting correlation matrix:

```
CORRELATION MATRIX:
symbol   ADA    BNB    BTC    DOGE   ETH    SOL    SUI    TRX    USDT   XRP
symbol
ADA      1.000  0.516  0.659  0.665  0.666  0.677  0.540  0.175  0.184  0.704
BNB      0.516  1.000  0.680  0.629  0.692  0.632  0.581  0.412  0.205  0.410
BTC      0.659  0.680  1.000  0.810  0.804  0.774  0.657  0.155  0.343  0.545
DOGE     0.665  0.629  0.810  1.000  0.752  0.709  0.635  0.131  0.252  0.554
ETH      0.666  0.692  0.804  0.752  1.000  0.737  0.655  0.153  0.213  0.536
SOL      0.677  0.632  0.774  0.709  0.737  1.000  0.663  0.194  0.162  0.557
SUI      0.540  0.581  0.657  0.635  0.655  0.663  1.000  0.200  0.135  0.419
TRX      0.175  0.412  0.155  0.131  0.153  0.194  0.200  1.000  0.134  0.139
USDT     0.184  0.205  0.343  0.252  0.213  0.162  0.135  0.134  1.000  0.141
XRP      0.704  0.410  0.545  0.554  0.536  0.557  0.419  0.139  0.141  1.000
```

Extracted features: returns, volatility and correlation matrix form the base for the next section, *DDF Station #3: Model Design*. At this station #3 we derive theoretical model for asset optimization and then apply such model to crypto selection as per our example.

9.5 Model Design

In *Station #3* we look at building a number of models that can be used to predict crypto asset performance and also, to be used to provide asset allocation techniques. We describe the following finance driven pricing models from a theoretical standpoint.

Modern Portfolio Theory

Modern portfolio theory (MPT) is a mathematical framework for constructing investment portfolios that optimize the relationship between risk and return. Developed by Harry Markowitz in the 1950s, MPT revolutionized how investors think about diversification and risk management [9.4]. The core principle of MPT is that investors can reduce portfolio risk without sacrificing expected returns by carefully selecting a mix of assets whose price movements don't perfectly correlate with each other. This is formalized through the concept of the "efficient frontier" – a curve that represents the set of optimal portfolios offering the maximum expected return for each level of risk.

The basic theory of portfolio allocation assumes that we take a long position in asset classes, which means we cannot short-sell an asset. The entire wealth is divided among the available assets and all positions are long and positive and the positions add up to 100% of the total monetary value of the risk exposure. MPT assumes that investors are rational and risk-averse, meaning they prefer higher returns for the same level of risk, or lower risk for the same level of return. The theory also assumes that markets are efficient and that asset returns follow a normal distribution. This is not likely in crypto markets.

While MPT provides a solid theoretical foundation for portfolio construction, it has limitations in practice. It relies heavily on historical data to predict future performance, assumes constant correlations between assets, and does not account for market anomalies or behavioral factors that can affect real-world investing. In this chapter, we apply standard solution to MPT without additional features to handle potential market inefficiencies.

Let us assume we are running five assets, the following code is going to generate five random weights as follows:

```
import numpy as np
weights = np.random.random(5)
weights /= np.sum(weights)
print(weights)
```

This can be easily checked as

$$\sum_{I}(w_i) = 1$$

where I is the number of assets and w_i is the weight of the "i" asset. From a theoretical standpoint, portfolio expected return given the weights is based on historical mean performance measures assumed to be the best estimate of the future, expected, performance as per the following:

$$\mu_p = \mathrm{E}\left(\sum_{I} w_i r_i\right) = \sum_{I} w_i \mathrm{E}(r_i) = \sum_{I} w_i \mu_i = w^T \mu$$

Programmatically:

```
import pandas as pd
import numpy as np
np.random.seed(42)
# number of assets
noa = 5
data = {
  'Risky' : 50*np.exp((-0.01-0.5*0.78**2)*1+0.78*np.sqrt(1)*np.random.
standard_normal(365)),
  'Flat' : 10*np.exp((-0.01-0.5*0.01**2)*1+0.01*np.sqrt(1)*np.random.
standard_normal(365)),
  'SmallCap' : 10*np.exp((-0.01-0.5*0.5**2)*1+0.5*np.sqrt(1)*np.random.
standard_normal(365)),
  'LargeCap' : 100*np.exp((-0.01-0.5*0.1**2)*1+0.1*np.sqrt(1)*np.random.
standard_normal(365)),
  'Gold' : 1000*np.exp((-0.01-0.5*0.05**2)*1+0.05*np.sqrt(1)*np.random.
standard_normal(365))
}

#Now lets place "a" into Pandas DataFrames and name our columns
df = pd.DataFrame(data)

#Add some dates into the DataFrame index
dates = pd.date_range('2019-1-1', periods=365, freq='D')
df.index = dates

#Calculate returns and covariance matrix
rets = np.log(df / df.shift(1))
print(rets.mean() * 252)
print(rets.cov() * 252)

#Setup random portfolio weights
weights = np.random.random(noa)
weights /= np.sum(weights)

#Derive Portfolio Returns & simulate various 2500x combinations
print(np.sum(rets.mean() * weights) * 252)
print(np.dot(weights.T, np.dot(rets.cov() * 252, weights)))

prets = []
pvols = []
for p in range (2500):
  weights = np.random.random(noa)
  weights /= np.sum(weights)
  prets.append(np.sum(rets.mean() * weights) * 252)
  pvols.append(np.sqrt(np.dot(weights.T,
                                          np.dot(rets.cov() * 252, weights))))

prets = np.array(prets)
pvols = np.array(pvols)
```

As per the previous code, we generate five random security dynamics and portfolio weights and then calculate the overall **expected portfolio return** and expected portfolio variance. Then, we simulate 2500 portfolio combinations where Sharpe ratio (SR) is calculated as:

$$SR = \left(\mu_p - r_f\right) / \sigma_p$$

With the visual interpretation of the lowest SR ratio shown in Figure 9.8 sitting right on top of the market line. Graph interposes the SR results into expected return vs expected volatility plot:

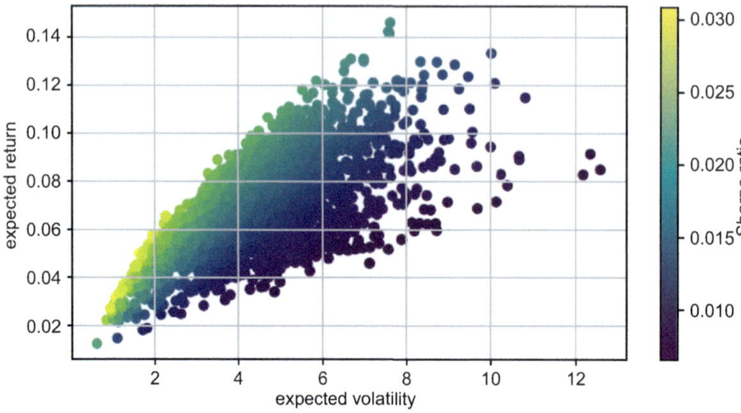

Figure 9.8 Expected Returns vs Expected Volatility

This is a base for us to start to model portfolio combinations that have viable risk profiles only as opposed to some combinations that would not be "efficient" in terms of risk/return tradeoffs. Here we look at the model design stage. The **covariance** between two securities is defined as

$$\sigma_{i,j} = \sigma_{j,i} = E(r_i - \mu_i)(r_j - \mu_j)$$

Then the variance of a security is the special case of covariance with itself defined as

$$\sigma_i^2 = E((r_i - \mu_i)^2)$$

Hence, for a portfolio of securities the shape of the matrix is defined as

$$\Sigma = \begin{bmatrix} \sigma_1^2 & \sigma_{12} & \cdots & \sigma_{1I} \\ \sigma_{21} & \sigma_2^2 & \cdots & \sigma_{2I} \\ \cdots & \cdots & \cdots & \cdots \\ \sigma_{I1} & \sigma_{I2} & \cdots & \sigma_I^2 \end{bmatrix}$$

Once we derive **portfolio covariance matrix** we are in a position to calculate the expected portfolio variance:

$$\sigma_p^2 = E((r - \mu)^2) = \sum_{iinI} \sum_{jinJ} w_i w_j \sigma_{ij} = w^T \Sigma w$$

Then, portfolio standard variation or volatility is calculated as follows:

$$\sigma_p = \sqrt{\sigma_p^2}$$

As calculated in our theoretical example utilizing Python library, *from scipy.optimize import minimize*, to optimize the weights in order to minimize variance of the resulting portfolio using *min_func_variance()* function [9.5]. The function *statistics()* defines portfolio calculation and mathematical interpretation as previous.

```
def statistics(weights):
    weights = np.array(weights)
    pret = np.sum(rets.mean() * weights) * 365
    pvol = np.sqrt(np.dot(weights.T, np.dot(rets.cov() * 365, weights)))
    return np.array([pret, pvol, pret / pvol])

def min_func_variance(weights):
    return statistics(weights)[1] ** 2

#Define condition for the optimization problem to be solved
cons = ({'type': 'eq', 'fun': lambda x:  np.sum(x) - 1})
bnds = tuple((0, 1) for x in range(noa))
noa * [1. / noa,]
optv = sco.minimize(min_func_variance, noa * [1. / noa,], method='SLSQP',
                    bounds=bnds, constraints=cons)

print(optv)
print(optv['x'].round(3))
print(statistics(optv['x']).round(3))
```

Resulting in expected portfolio return −0.002% and expected portfolio standard deviation of 22.3% in this simulation.

```
Risky        0.104452
Flat        -0.002611
SmallCap     0.185814
LargeCap     0.052193
Gold         0.010631
dtype: float64
```

The model allocation, **driven by the aim to minimize variance of the entire portfolio**, naturally, returns the asset with the lowest risk as most likely to be shown with the highest portfolio allocation.

```
[
 Risky =     0.001
 Flat =      0.956
 SmallCap = 0.
 LargeCap = 0.
 Gold =      0.043
]
```

Basically, the model recommendation is to invest 95.6% of your entire capital into Flat Asset (in crypto space this could be USDT) and 4.3% into Gold.

Crypto Assets: Minimize Variance

We have designed our model using standard portfolio theory and extracted crypto data and relevant feature for model application. Now, we proceed and execute this model using actual dataframes.

First, we initiate portfolio return and volatility calculations:

```
def portfolio_variance(weights, cov_matrix):
    """Calculate portfolio variance given weights and covariance matrix"""
    return np.dot(weights, np.dot(cov_matrix, weights))

def portfolio_return(weights, mean_returns):
    """Calculate expected portfolio return"""
    return np.sum(mean_returns * weights)
```

Second step is to design optimization function using previous *Scipy* optimizer and formulating objective function to minimize portfolio variance. In short, we aim to invest only into assets that will deliver the lowest risk to our portfolio return.

```
def minimize_variance_portfolio(mean_returns, cov_matrix):
    """Find the minimum variance portfolio weights"""
    n_assets = len(mean_returns)

    # Objective function: minimize portfolio variance
    def objective(weights):
        return portfolio_variance(weights, cov_matrix)

    def negative_sharpe_ratio(weights):
          """Objective function to minimize (negative Sharpe ratio)"""
        _, _, sharpe = portfolio_stats(weights)
        return -sharpe

    # Constraints: weights sum to 1
    constraints = ({'type': 'eq', 'fun': lambda x: np.sum(x) - 1})

    # Bounds: weights between 0 and 1 (long-only portfolio)
    bounds = tuple((0, 1) for _ in range(n_assets))

    # Initial guess: equal weights
    initial_guess = np.array([1/n_assets] * n_assets)

    # Optimize
    result = minimize(objective, initial_guess, method='SLSQP',
                      bounds=bounds, constraints=constraints)
    return result.x if result.success else None
```

Note, this is where we define the objective function as well as any constraints.

Results in Figure 9.9 showing individual asset weights needed to be executed on the market to minimize portfolio variance:

```
Optimal Weights:
ADA: 0.0000 (0.00%)
BNB: 0.1832 (18.32%)
BTC: 0.1816 (18.16%)
DOGE: 0.0000 (0.00%)
ETH: 0.0000 (0.00%)
```

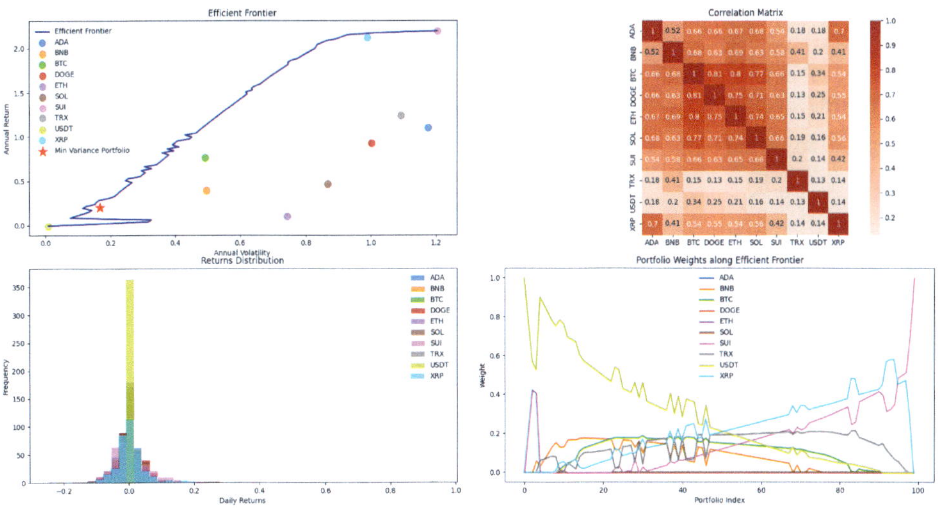

Figure 9.9 Portfolio Allocation: Minimize Variance

```
SOL: 0.0000 (0.00%)
SUI: 0.0000 (0.00%)
TRX: 0.0000 (0.00%)
USDT: 0.6351 (63.51%)
XRP: 0.0000 (0.00%)

Portfolio Metrics:
Expected Daily Return: 0.0006 (0.06%)
Expected Annual Return: 0.2126 (21.26%)
Daily Volatility: 0.0088 (0.88%)
Annual Volatility: 0.1672 (16.72%
Sharpe Ratio: 1.2714
```

Based on the results, **we allocate 63.51% into USDT, 18.32% into BNB and 18.16% into BTC of our capital with expected portfolio annual return of 21.26% with volatility 16.72% and sharp ratio 1.27.**

In our case we are following in-sample basic application of MPT model without any additional features. In short, we assume all weights to sum to 1 for long-only portfolio allocating all capital into this exposure. We start the optimizer with equal weights.

Crypto Assets: Maximize Sharpe Ratio

In the previous section, we covered a simple example of portfolio allocation aiming to minimize variance of the final expected portfolio performance. By definition, we are likely going to see allocation into the lowest variance assets within the asset class selection. The obvious question is, whether there is an alternative method of asset allocation that could aim to deliver higher expected returns, assuming higher risk appetite.

Building up on your previous code sequence, here we optimize by utilizing minimizing Scipy function to maximize Sharpe ratio, hence the negative sign the *negative_sharpe_ratio()* function.

```
def negative_sharpe_ratio(weights, returns, cov_matrix, risk_free_rate):
    """Objective function to minimize (negative Sharpe ratio)"""
    _, _, sharpe = portfolio_stats(weights, returns, cov_matrix, risk_free_rate)
    return -sharpe

def optimize_portfolio(returns, cov_matrix, risk_free_rate):
    """Optimize portfolio to maximize Sharpe ratio"""
    n_assets = len(returns.columns)

    # Constraints
    constraints = ({'type': 'eq', 'fun': lambda x: np.sum(x) - 1})  # Weights sum
to 1

    # Bounds (0 to 1 for each weight - no short selling)
    bounds = tuple((0, 1) for _ in range(n_assets))

    # Initial guess (equal weights)
    initial_guess = np.array([1/n_assets] * n_assets)

    # Optimization
    result = minimize(negative_sharpe_ratio,
                      initial_guess,
                      args=(returns, cov_matrix, risk_free_rate),
                      method='SLSQP',
                      bounds=bounds,
                      constraints=constraints)
    return result.x
```

It can be observed from Figure 9.10 equal weight allocation would deliver Sharpe ratio 1.5 however given optimal weight delivering Sharpe ratio in the vicinity of 2.44.

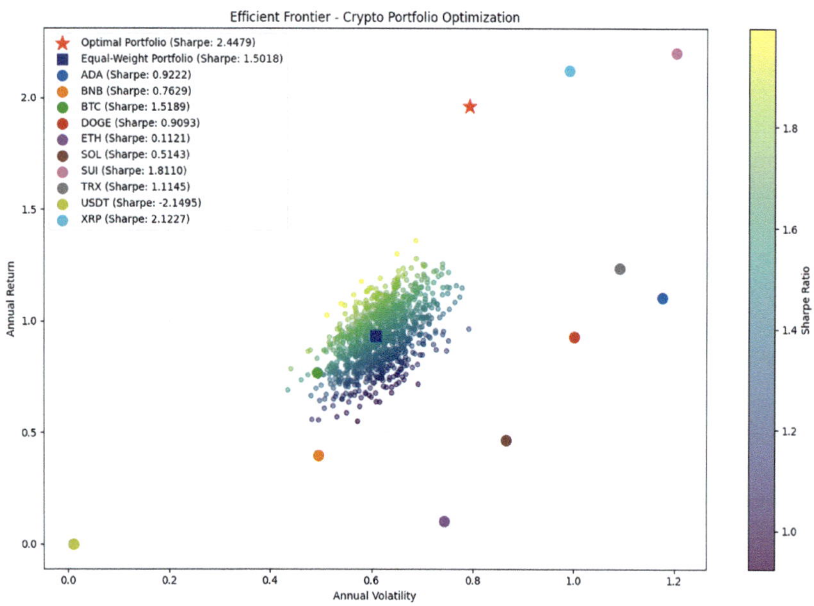

Figure 9.10 Maximize Sharpe Ratio

Results for optimal portfolio:

```
=== OPTIMAL PORTFOLIO (Maximum Sharpe Ratio) ===
Risk-free rate: 2.00%
ADA: 0.00%
BNB: 0.00%
BTC: 0.00%
DOGE: 0.00%
ETH: 0.00%
SOL: 0.00%
SUI: 26.85%
TRX: 20.52%
USDT: 0.00%
XRP: 52.63%

Optimal Portfolio Statistics:
Expected Annual Return: 196.11%
Annual Volatility: 79.30%
Sharpe Ratio: 2.4479
```

Based on the model, **we allocate our capital into SUI 26.85% then TRX 20.52% and XRP 52.63%**. As expected the aim is to embrace risk, hence given this increased risk appetite, the model delivers equivalent risky selection of assets.

Results for equal weight portfolio:

```
=== EQUAL-WEIGHT PORTFOLIO (Comparison) ===
ADA: 10.00%
BNB: 10.00%
BTC: 10.00%
DOGE: 10.00%
ETH: 10.00%
SOL: 10.00%
SUI: 10.00%
TRX: 10.00%
USDT: 10.00%
XRP: 10.00%

Equal-Weight Portfolio Statistics:
Expected Annual Return: 93.29%
Annual Volatility: 60.78%
Sharpe Ratio: 1.5018
```

Results summary:

```
=== PORTFOLIO SUMMARY ===
Asset Optimal Weight Equal Weight Expected Return Volatility Risk Contribution
  ADA          0.00%       10.00%         110.46%    117.62%             0.00%
  BNB          0.00%       10.00%          39.85%     49.62%             0.00%
  BTC          0.00%       10.00%          76.81%     49.25%             0.00%
 DOGE          0.00%       10.00%          93.05%    100.13%             0.00%
  ETH          0.00%       10.00%          10.33%     74.30%             0.00%
  SOL          0.00%       10.00%          46.55%     86.63%             0.00%
  SUI         26.85%       10.00%         220.00%    120.38%            30.15%
  TRX         20.52%       10.00%         123.64%    109.14%            12.86%
```

```
USDT        0.00%       10.00%        0.00%      0.93%       0.00%
 XRP       52.63%       10.00%      212.17%     99.01%      56.99%

=== KEY INSIGHTS ===

• The optimal portfolio has a Sharpe ratio of 2.4479
• This is +63.0% better than equal weighting
• The correlation between BTC and ETH is 0.516
• Diversification benefit: -30.5% volatility reduction
```

Visual performance of the portfolio in Figure 9.11:

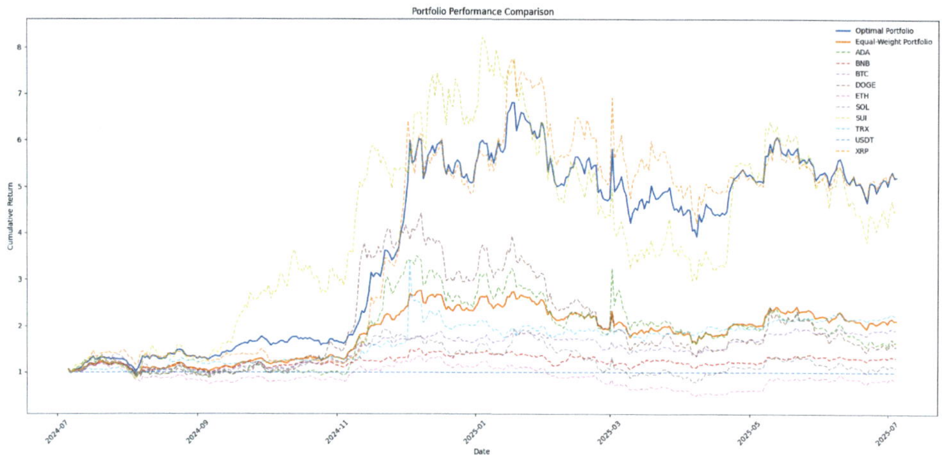

Figure 9.11 Portfolio Performance

Overall, given risk profile of your FinTech client utilizing your solution, the selection is driven by model optimization algorithm either minimizing variance or maximize Sharpe ratio delivering different capital allocation within the selection of assets.

9.6 Implementation

In *Station #4* we look at how we execute on the data analytics and prepare results for further consumption by ultimate decision-makers. Here, we demonstrate core techniques and focus on Portfolio Model Implementation. As per "Chapter 3: Data Visualization" we build a simple dashboard using *Streamlit* libraries.

```
import streamlit as st
import pandas as pd
import numpy as np
import plotly.graph_objects as go
import plotly.express as px
from plotly.subplots import make_subplots
from scipy.optimize import minimize
import io

# Set page config
st.set_page_config(
    page_title="Crypto Portfolio Dashboard",
```

```
    page_icon="💰",
    layout="wide",
    initial_sidebar_state="expanded"
)
```

The product implementation stage is the final step in the FinTech data management process and an essential component of the customer journey. This is the stage where your product is exposed to the final consumer in a production environment. It is at this stage that you consume results from Station #3 and package and sell the results in a form of a product or a service. In addition, you are responsible to provide all stakeholder feedback to Station #3.

Wireframes

Wireframes are simplified, low-fidelity visual representations of a user interface or web page layout. They serve as blueprints that outline the basic structure, content placement, and functionality of a digital product before moving into detailed design and development. Wireframes are essential in user experience (UX) design as they allow teams to test and iterate on concepts quickly and cost-effectively before committing to final designs and development work.

Finally, we are in a position to implement and deliver outline of our FinTech product. Figure 9.12 shows wireframes used in our solution.

As opposed to using a whiteboard, or pen and paper for that matter, now we can utilize state-of-the-art Python libraries to draw a visual interpretation of a potential FinTech product.

To create the left hand side of our dashboard:

```
def main():
    st.markdown('<h1 class="main-header">🚀 Crypto Portfolio Optimizer</h1>',
unsafe_allow_html=True)
    st.markdown("---")

    # Load data
    try:
        prices, returns = load_data()
```

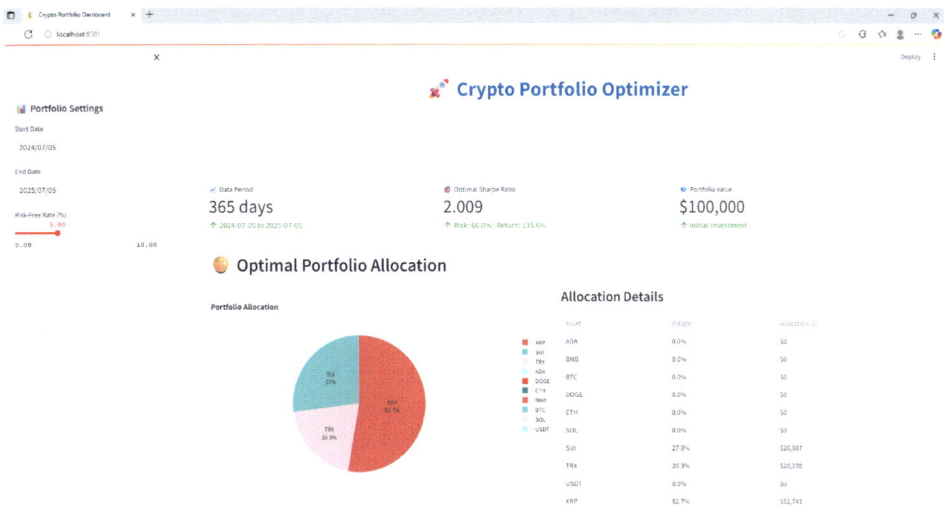

Figure 9.12 FinTech Crypto Portfolio Optimizer

```
    except:
        st.error("Could not load data. Please ensure 'combined_crypto_prices.
csv' is in the same directory.")
        st.stop()

    # Sidebar controls
    st.sidebar.header("📊 Portfolio Settings")

    # Date range selector
    start_date = st.sidebar.date_input(
        "Start Date",
        value=prices.index.min(),
        min_value=prices.index.min(),
        max_value=prices.index.max()
    )

    end_date = st.sidebar.date_input(
        "End Date",
        value=prices.index.max(),
        min_value=prices.index.min(),
        max_value=prices.index.max()
    )

    # Filter data based on date range
    filtered_prices = prices.loc[start_date:end_date]
    filtered_returns = returns.loc[start_date:end_date]

    # Risk-free rate input
    risk_free_rate = st.sidebar.slider(
        "Risk-Free Rate (%)",
        min_value=0.0,
        max_value=10.0,
        value=3.0,
        step=0.1
    ) / 100

    # Calculate optimal portfolio
    optimal_weights = optimize_portfolio(filtered_returns)
```

This step controls basic data ingress and selection for calculation. The following code snippet sets up the dashboard summary:

```
    # Main dashboard
    col1, col2, col3 = st.columns(3)

    with col1:
        st.markdown('<div class="metric-container">', unsafe_allow_html=True)
        st.metric(
            "📈 Data Period",
            f"{len(filtered_returns)} days",
            f"{start_date.strftime('%Y-%m-%d')} to
{end_date.strftime('%Y-%m-%d')}"
        )
        st.markdown('</div>', unsafe_allow_html=True)

    with col2:
        port_return, port_std, sharpe = calculate_portfolio_metrics(filtered_
returns, optimal_weights)
```

```
        st.markdown('<div class="metric-container">', unsafe_allow_html=True)
        st.metric(
            "🎯 Optimal Sharpe Ratio",
            f"{sharpe:.3f}",
            f"Risk: {port_std:.1%} | Return: {port_return:.1%}"
        )
        st.markdown('</div>', unsafe_allow_html=True)

    with col3:
        st.markdown('<div class="metric-container">', unsafe_allow_html=True)
        st.metric(
            "💎 Portfolio Value",
            "$100,000",
            "Initial Investment"
        )
        st.markdown('</div>', unsafe_allow_html=True)
```

Note, how we decided to simply hardcode the Portfolio Value for simplicity at this point, as shown in Figure 9.13. Further, on the main dashboard we add portfolio allocation chart and overall table:

```
    # Portfolio allocation
    st.header("⊗ Optimal Portfolio Allocation")

    col1, col2 = st.columns([1, 1])

    with col1:
        # Pie chart for allocation
        fig_pie = px.pie(
            values=optimal_weights,
            names=filtered_returns.columns,
            title="Portfolio Allocation",
            color_discrete_sequence=['#FF6B6B', '#4ECDC4']
        )
        fig_pie.update_traces(textposition='inside', textinfo='percent+label')
        st.plotly_chart(fig_pie, use_container_width=True)

    with col2:
        # Display allocation table
        allocation_df = pd.DataFrame({
            'Asset': filtered_returns.columns,
            'Weight': optimal_weights,
            'Allocation ($)': optimal_weights * 100000
        })
        allocation_df['Weight'] = allocation_df['Weight'].apply(lambda x:
f"{x:.1%}")
        allocation_df['Allocation ($)'] = allocation_df['Allocation
($)'].apply(lambda x: f"${x:,.0f}")
```

Figure 9.13 Dashboard Summary

```
    st.subheader("Allocation Details")
    st.dataframe(allocation_df, use_container_width=True, hide_index=True)
```

Resulting in Figure 9.14:

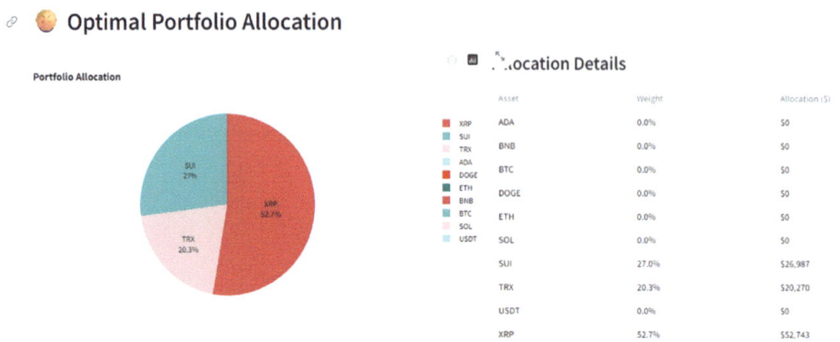

Figure 9.14 Graphical and Tabular Data Summary

Given the results from *DDF Station #3: Model Design*, for exposition purposes, we add some additional visual results with relevant code snippets.

Portfolio Performance

Portfolio performance refers to how well an investment portfolio has performed over a specific time period, typically measured by comparing the portfolio's returns to a benchmark or investment objective. Figure 9.15 depicts overall portfolio returns as calculated in the code snippet here.

```
# Portfolio performance
st.header("💰 Portfolio Performance")

# Calculate portfolio daily returns
portfolio_returns = (filtered_returns * optimal_weights).sum(axis=1)
cumulative_returns = (1 + portfolio_returns).cumprod()

# Individual asset performance
individual_performance = {}
for asset in filtered_returns.columns:
    individual_performance[asset] = (1 +
filtered_returns[asset]).cumprod()

fig_performance = go.Figure()

# Add portfolio performance
fig_performance.add_trace(go.Scatter(
    x=cumulative_returns.index,
    y=cumulative_returns * 100,
    mode='lines',
    name='Optimal Portfolio',
```

```
        line=dict(color='#2E86AB', width=3)
    ))

    # Add individual asset performance
    for i, (asset, performance) in enumerate(individual_performance.items()):
        fig_performance.add_trace(go.Scatter(
            x=performance.index,
            y=performance * 100,
            mode='lines',
            name=asset,
            line=dict(color=colors[1], width=2, dash='dash')
        ))

    fig_performance.update_layout(
        title="Cumulative Returns Comparison",
        xaxis_title="Date",
        yaxis_title="Cumulative Return (%)",
        hovermode='x unified',
        height=400
    )

    st.plotly_chart(fig_performance, use_container_width=True)
```

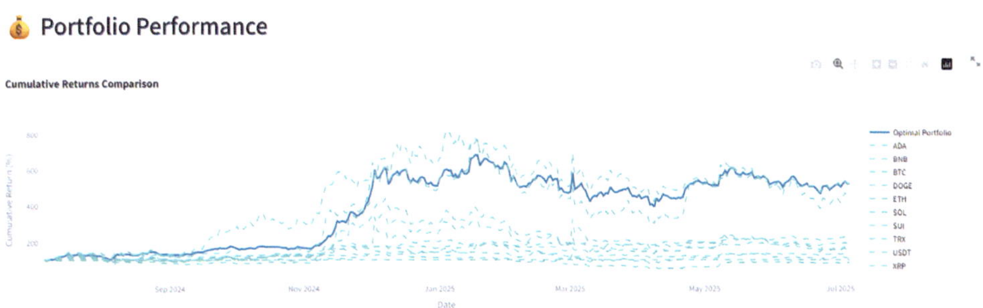

Figure 9.15 Portfolio Performance

Risk-Return Analysis

Risk-return analysis, as depicted in Figure 9.16, is a fundamental concept in finance that examines the relationship between the potential returns of an investment and the level of risk associated with achieving those returns. It's based on the principle that investors generally require higher expected returns to compensate for taking on greater risk.

Correlation Analysis

Correlation analysis, shown in Figure 9.17, is a statistical technique used to measure and describe the strength and direction of the linear relationship between two or more variables. It helps determine whether variables move together in a predictable pattern.

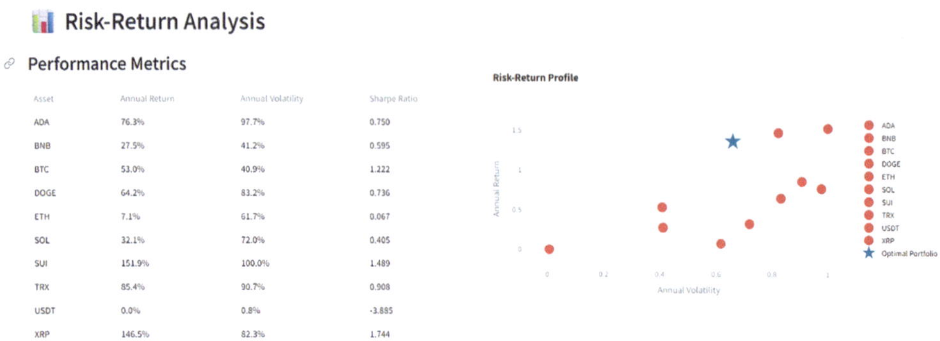

Asset	Annual Return	Annual Volatility	Sharpe Ratio
ADA	76.3%	97.7%	0.750
BNB	27.5%	41.2%	0.595
BTC	53.0%	40.9%	1.222
DOGE	64.2%	83.2%	0.736
ETH	7.1%	61.7%	0.067
SOL	32.1%	72.0%	0.405
SUI	151.9%	100.0%	1.489
TRX	85.4%	90.7%	0.908
USDT	0.0%	0.8%	-3.885
XRP	146.5%	82.3%	1.744

Figure 9.16 Risk-Return Analysis

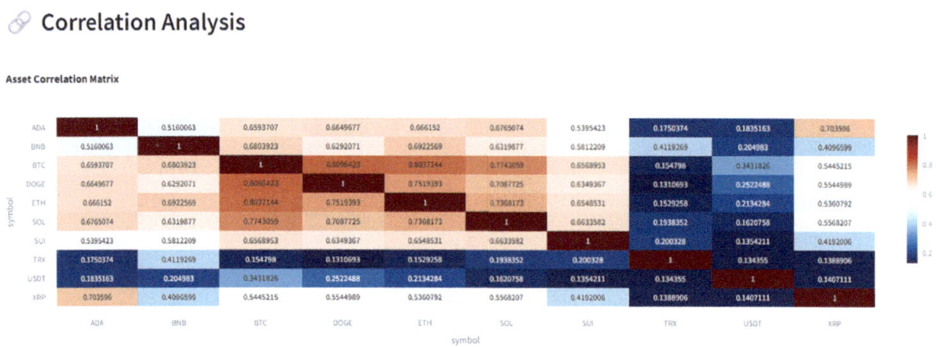

Figure 9.17 Correlation Analysis

The correlation coefficient (typically Pearson's r) ranges from −1 to +1:

- +1: Perfect positive correlation (as one variable increases, the other increases proportionally)
- 0: No linear relationship
- −1: Perfect negative correlation (as one variable increases, the other decreases proportionally)

Correlation does not imply causation. Just because two variables are correlated does not mean one causes the other. There could be confounding variables, reverse causation, or the relationship might be purely coincidental. Notwithstanding these shortcomings, correlation as a measure in time is useful to comprehend potential co-movements across various assets. In this case, cryptocurrencies, such as BTC, DOGE, ETH, SOL tend to move in tandem.

Overall, this *DDF Station #4* deals with actual product journey. In this example, we have shown a static version of a potential FinTech product.

DDF Platform

The concept of the digital data factory shown in Figure 9.18 discussed in the previous section drives the speed of development.

From a practical standpoint, there is number of simplifications we have used during this exposition. We have fully relied on CryptoCompare data quality and data delivery. The model used, MPT, assumes returns follow a normal distribution, but financial markets exhibit fat tails, skewness and extreme events far more frequently than normal distributions would predict. Standard portfolio theory assumes returns follow a normal distribution. Real financial markets show "fat tails" – which means extreme outcomes happen more often than bell curves predict. This creates a risky situation where catastrophic events occur more frequently than mathematical models suggest.

The theory assumes correlations between assets remain constant over time, but correlations tend to increase during market stress precisely when diversification is most needed. This "correlation breakdown" undermines the fundamental diversification benefits MPT promises. Also, MPT is designed for single-period optimization, but investors typically have multi-period horizons with changing goals, risk tolerance, and market conditions over time. Small changes in expected return estimates can lead to dramatically different optimal portfolios, making the approach highly sensitive to input assumptions that are inherently uncertain.

Furthermore, MPT assumes investors are rational and markets are efficient, but behavioral finance has documented numerous cognitive biases and market inefficiencies that affect real investment decisions, specifically in crypto markets. MPT does not recognize that markets

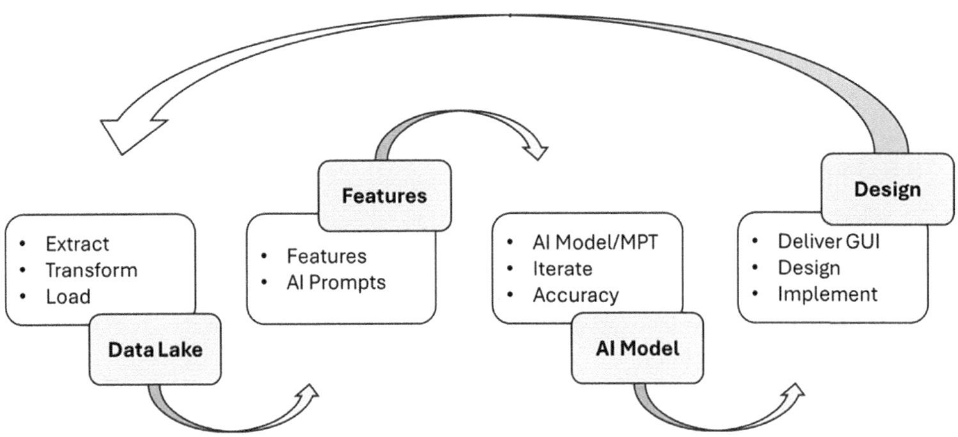

Figure 9.18 Applied DDF in Crypto Portfolio Optimizer

can shift between different regimes (bull markets, bear markets, high volatility periods) that require different strategic approaches.

These limitations have led to various extensions and alternatives, including Black-Litterman models, risk parity strategies, factor-based investing, and behavioral portfolio theory, each attempting to address specific MPT shortcomings while maintaining mathematical rigor in portfolio construction. Within the context of DDF, this can be viewed as a further extension of this book.

9.7 Summary

This chapter bridges the material from Section 1 and Section 2 of this book by presenting a comprehensive AdviceTech use case. The scenario positions readers as finance practitioners working within a cryptocurrency robo-advisory firm, where they must solve specific challenges and develop technology-driven solutions.

Modern portfolio theory provides the theoretical foundation, centering on the fundamental risk-return relationship – the investment principle that links higher potential returns with greater risk exposure. MPT operates on the premise that investors are risk-averse, naturally gravitating toward lower-risk alternatives when presented with portfolios offering comparable expected returns. This behavioral assumption reveals a critical insight: investors will only embrace additional risk when compensated with the prospect of higher returns. Consequently, those seeking enhanced returns must accept corresponding risk increases. MPT maintains that rational investors should reject any portfolio when superior risk-return alternatives exist.

We first establish the Crypto AdviceTech framework through our use case. A robo-advisor represents an automated digital investment management platform leveraging machine learning and artificial intelligence algorithms to deliver financial investment and trading services with minimal human oversight. This introduction immerses readers in cryptocurrency market dynamics.

Next, we implement our FinTech digital data factory methodology. Each DDF station introduces innovative techniques and tools, creating a seamless data progression from *DDF Station #1: ETL* through *DDF Station #4: Implementation*. The chapter culminates in developing streamlined FinTech product wireframes that demonstrate practical application of these concepts.

9.8 Concept Questions and Answers

Q1: What are the main criticisms of modern portfolio theory?

A1: Modern portfolio theory has been criticized for evaluating portfolios based on total variance rather than downside risk, relying on unrealistic assumptions, and ignoring real-world factors like taxes. It also tends to overemphasize historical data, which may not accurately predict future market behavior.

Q2: How does diversification reduce portfolio risk according to MPT?

A2: Diversification reduces risk by spreading investments across different asset classes that are not highly correlated. This strategy aims to offset poor performance in one investment with better performance in another, ultimately lowering the overall portfolio volatility without necessarily sacrificing returns.

Q3: What is the efficient frontier in modern portfolio theory?

A3: The efficient frontier is a graphical representation of optimal portfolios that offer the highest expected return for a given level of risk. It helps investors visualize and select portfolios that balance risk and return based on their individual preferences and risk tolerance.

Q4: Why is overreliance on historical data problematic in portfolio construction?

A4: Overreliance on historical data can be misleading because past performance doesn't guarantee future results. Markets evolve constantly, and structural changes can render historical relationships increasingly irrelevant. This can lead to portfolio strategies that are optimized for past conditions but may not perform well in future market environments.

Q5: How does postmodern portfolio theory (PMPT) differ from traditional MPT?

A5: Postmodern portfolio theory addresses some limitations of MPT by focusing on downside risk rather than total variance. It uses measures like downside deviation and the Sortino ratio instead of standard deviation and the Sharpe ratio. PMPT also incorporates asymmetrical return distributions, making it more suitable for evaluating complex investment strategies and products.

9.9 Exercises

E1: Run DDF Platform as provided in the text, however now use top-20 cryptocurrencies based on market capitalization. Analyze your portfolio allocation. Would you invest as per the model suggestion?

E2: Run DDP Platform as provided in the text, use the same selection of cryptocurrencies as in E1, however now enrich the portfolio with textual dataframes. Extract news from CryptoCompare API relevant to these currencies and apply VADER sentiment analytics to show positive and negative news, now related to your portfolio. Analyze final results. Can you incorporate news sentiment to the portfolio weights?

9.10 Further Reading

- Alammar, J., & Grootendorst, M. (2024). Hands-On Large Language Models: Language Understanding and Generation, O'Reilly.
- Dickerson, A., & Hric, J. (2024). FINS5545 Financial Market Data Literacy Course Notes, UNSW Business School.
- Hric, J., & Lam, I. (2025). FINS5548 Financial Technology Course Notes, UNSW Business School.
- Huyen, C. (2025). AI Engineering: Building Applications with Foundation Models, O'Reilly.
- Raschka, S. (2025). Build a Large Language Model, Manning.
- Schmidt, B., Tumarkin, R., & Lin, Y. (2023). Toolkit for FinTech, UNSW Press Class Notes.

9.11 References

[9.1] altFINS: https://altfins.com/
[9.2] RobinHood: https://robinhood.com/us/en/about/crypto/
[9.3] CryptoCompare: https://developers.coindesk.com/documentation/data-api/introduction
[9.4] Modern Portfolio Theory: https://www.math.hkust.edu.hk/~maykwok/courses/ma362/07F/markowitz_JF.pdf
[9.5] Scipy: https://docs.scipy.org/doc/scipy/reference/generated/scipy.optimize.minimize.html

Chapter 10

FinTech Application

AgTech

10.1 Introduction

In this chapter we expose the reader to a traditional banking environment. Using a practical use case from commercial banking serving and servicing small to medium size enterprises (SME) predominately in agricultural sector. Agriculture commodity markets play a crucial role in the global economy by facilitating the trade of essential goods like grains, livestock and dairy. These markets are governed by scientific principles that ensure efficient and fair trading. At the core, supply and demand dynamics dictate prices, influenced by factors such as weather conditions, technological advancements, and geopolitical events. Additionally, principles of market equilibrium and price elasticity help in understanding how changes in production or consumption impact prices. By grasping these scientific concepts, stakeholders can make informed decisions, mitigate risks and optimize their strategies.

This chapter starts defining agricultural technology, AgTech, smart farming or precision agriculture and how this field relates to financial predictions. Supply and demand fluctuations and price volatility in agricultural commodities directly affect operations of small to medium-size enterprises, farms, operating in these markets.

DOI: 10.4324/9781003477747-13

AgTech is revolutionizing the way we approach farming and food production not only from a financial analytics perspective. At its core, AgTech leverages scientific principles such as data analysis, biotechnology and automation to enhance agricultural practices. By utilizing data analytics, farmers can make informed decisions about crop management, predicting yields, predicting prices and optimizing resource use. Biotechnology enables the development of genetically modified crops that are more resistant to pests and environmental stresses, ensuring higher productivity and sustainability. Automation, through the use of drones and robotic systems, streamlines planting, monitoring and harvesting processes, significantly reducing labor costs and increasing efficiency. Traditional banks are well positioned to offer ML and AI driven products to their direct customers in this space.

Then we define our use case in AgTech space. Utilizing digital data factory (DDF) concept outlined in previous chapters, then, we proceed to step through each station in turn showcasing programmatic and computational techniques and solutions. The chapter concludes with basic AgTech application wireframes. The technology delivered in this chapter is the applied LSTM prediction algorithm packaged into final product delivered in visual form as an additional feature to be incorporated within current online banking ecosystem.

Learning Outcomes

At the end of this chapter the reader will be able to do the following:

- Comprehend features of AgTech and Commodity Markets
- Outline theoretical concepts behind predictions using LSTM
- Redefine DDF concept and apply in a practical setting
- Understand the DDF station data flows and iteration process
- Use Streamlit library to draw FinTech solution wireframes
- Appreciate boundaries and opportunities in price forecasting

10.2 FinTech Case Study – SME Banking Insights

AgTech

The global commodity markets stand at a critical juncture as we witness unprecedented price volatility driven by supply chain disruptions. Record-breaking price movements have dominated across energy, agriculture, metals and precious metals sectors. Additionally, the convergence of pandemic aftereffects, geopolitical conflicts and strategic export controls has created a perfect storm for market turbulence.

Commodity sectors show diverging trends despite overall volatility. Energy prices remain elevated though projected to decline, while agricultural commodities experience weather-dependent fluctuations. Gold and silver prices have surged dramatically as safe-haven demand intensifies amid global uncertainty. Meanwhile, industrial metals face growing supply concerns despite their critical role in energy transition technologies.

AgTech, also known as smart farming or precision agriculture, uses advanced technologies to improve agricultural production systems and eco-friendly practices. Smart farming combines information technologies, data analytics, automation, and connected devices to improve farming efficiency and productivity. Modern farming now uses artificial intelligence, machine learning, Internet of Things (IoT), robotics and cloud computing to reshape the scene of traditional farming practices. Farmers can monitor and manage almost every aspect of their operations through this technological ecosystem. They track everything from soil conditions and crop health to equipment performance and livestock welfare.

Agriculture uses data sensors and IoT through several connected technologies:

- Smart sensors monitor soil moisture, pH values, and nutrient content
- Connected equipment reports operational status and conditions
- Weather stations deliver precise local forecasts
- Wearable devices track livestock health and location
- **Commodity markets financial data integration**

ML and AI algorithms analyze this big data to create actionable insights.

The economic consequences extend well beyond trading floors. Commodity price spikes directly fuel inflation worldwide, particularly affecting food security in developing nations. Central banks face the challenging task of addressing supply-driven inflation without triggering severe recessions through excessive tightening. Hence, **it becomes critical to incorporate financial predictions in overall decision-making.**

Workshop

In this workshop, we assume you have taken a position of a market participant operating in commodity markets and working on the commercial banking side of the business serving your small to medium size enterprises (SME) clients operating across various commodity markets. Your task is to implement state-of-the-art techniques in prediction algorithms. Specifically, you are providing financial information to agricultural farms and one of the specific requests (system features) from a number of customers is to incorporate wheat price prediction.

10.3 Data Lake

This is a critical stage in any data science-driven project. As we know from previous chapters, in this station, you are responsible for data integrity and quality to be passed down into your environment for further analytical treatment. Hence, your position is critical for success in final project deliveries. As opposed to crypto markets, we operate in a structured data environment however we do add new features to the overall data analytics.

In this example we utilize *Alpha Vantage API* call [10.1]. We aim to extract daily prices for WHEAT and return into *.json* format as *raw_data* to be processed further into dataframes *df = pd.DataFrame(raw_data)*.

```
class WheatPriceExtractor:
    def __init__(self, api_key):
        """
        Initialize the wheat price extractor with Alpha Vantage API key
        Args:
            api_key (str): Your Alpha Vantage API key
        """
        self.api_key = api_key
        self.base_url = "https://www.alphavantage.co/query"

    def get_wheat_prices(self, interval="daily", datatype="json"):
        """
```

```
        Fetch wheat commodity prices from Alpha Vantage
        Args:
            interval (str): 'monthly' or 'daily' (Note: daily may have
limitations)
            datatype (str): 'json' or 'csv'
        Returns:
            dict or pd.DataFrame: Price data
        """
        params = {
            'function': 'TIME_SERIES_DAILY',
            'symbol': 'WHEAT',
            'interval': interval,
            'datatype': datatype,
            'apikey': self.api_key
        }

        try:
            response = requests.get(self.base_url, params=params)
            response.raise_for_status()

            if datatype == "json":
                data = response.json()
                # Check for API errors
                if "Error Message" in data:
                    raise ValueError(f"API Error: {data['Error Message']}")
                if "Note" in data:
                    raise ValueError(f"API Limit: {data['Note']}")
                return data
            else:
                # For CSV format
                return response.text

        except requests.exceptions.RequestException as e:
            print(f"Request error: {e}")
            return None
        except ValueError as e:
            print(f"API error: {e}")
            return None
```

As per the aforementioned, post data extract we process transfer and load. The next code snippet provides simple cleansing exercise converting column names and date formats and delivering *df*.

```
def load_wheat_data():
    """Load and preprocess wheat price data"""
    try:
        # Read the CSV file
        df = pd.read_csv('wheat_prices.csv')

        # Clean the data - remove empty columns and handle price
                                                            formatting
        df = df.iloc[:, :2]  # Keep only Date and Price columns
        df.columns = ['Date', 'Price']

        # Convert Date to datetime
        df['Date'] = pd.to_datetime(df['Date'], format='%d/%m/%Y')

        # Handle price column - remove commas and convert to float
```

```
        df['Price'] = df['Price'].astype(str).str.replace(',', '').astype(float)

        # Sort by date
        df = df.sort_values('Date').reset_index(drop=True)

        # Remove any NaN values
        df = df.dropna()

        return df

    except Exception as e:
        print(f"Error loading data: {e}")
        return None
```

This is the final step in *DDF Station #1*, handing-over cleaned dataframes into *DDF Station #2: Feature Engineering*. The data contained within *df* is the link between these two stations.

10.4 Feature Engineering

In *Station #2*, we prepare model features for further processing. Here we select relevant features manually, as opposed to using algorithms and analyze basic statistics and plot final features being selected and passed on into our model design and implementation phases. In "Chapter 9: FinTech Application: AdviceTech," we have stressed the importance of normality, that is, that the data distribution follows normal distribution. The reasons are numerous; however as converted into our case, one of the core reasons we need to ensure normality is the fact that most risk management models and hedging techniques are built and designed with this assumption in mind.

Given the data from *DDF Station #1*, we proceed with features extraction. Actual observed commodity prices and calculated returns form the core features.

```
def calculate_returns(df):
    """Calculate various types of returns"""
    # Simple returns
    df['Simple_Return'] = df['Price'].pct_change()

    # Log returns
    df['Log_Return'] = np.log(df['Price'] / df['Price'].shift(1))

    # Remove NaN values from returns
    df = df.dropna()

    return df
```

Resulting in the following data times series summary statistics with 1,148 daily observations:

```
WHEAT PRICE ANALYSIS
==================================================
Loading wheat price data...
Data loaded successfully. Shape: (1148, 2)
Date range: 2021-01-04 00:00:00 to 2025-07-03 00:00:00

Descriptive Statistics simple returns:
Mean: 0.000132
Std Dev: 0.022803
Skewness: 0.9453
Kurtosis: 8.5818
Excess Kurtosis: 8.5818
```

```
Descriptive Statistics log returns:
Mean: -0.000124
Std Dev: 0.022609
Skewness: 0.6487
Kurtosis: 6.6069
Excess Kurtosis: 6.6069
```

The following code sequence explores the depth of normality using our data in tabular as well as graphical form. In order to measure normality we rely on *Scipy* library:

```
from scipy import stats
from scipy.stats import jarque_bera, shapiro, normaltest, anderson
```

Mathematical exposition of these tests is out-of-scope of this chapter [10.2].

```
def test_normality(returns, return_type="Returns"):
    """Perform comprehensive normality tests"""
    print(f"\n{'='*50}")
    print(f"NORMALITY TESTS FOR {return_type.upper()}")
    print(f"{'='*50}")

    # Basic statistics
    print(f"\nDescriptive Statistics:")
    print(f"Mean: {returns.mean():.6f}")
    print(f"Std Dev: {returns.std():.6f}")
    print(f"Skewness: {stats.skew(returns):.4f}")
    print(f"Kurtosis: {stats.kurtosis(returns):.4f}")
    print(f"Excess Kurtosis: {stats.kurtosis(returns, fisher=True):.4f}")

    # Remove any infinite or NaN values
    clean_returns = returns[np.isfinite(returns)]

    print(f"\nNormality Tests (p-values):")
    print(f"H0: Data is normally distributed")
    print(f"H1: Data is not normally distributed")
    print(f"Reject H0 if p-value < 0.05")
    print("-" * 40)

    # Shapiro-Wilk test (most powerful for small samples)
    try:
        shapiro_stat, shapiro_p = shapiro(clean_returns)
        print(f"Shapiro-Wilk Test: p-value = {shapiro_p:.6f}")
        print(f"  Result: {'Reject H0 (Not Normal)' if shapiro_p < 0.05 else
'Fail to Reject H0 (Normal)'}")
    except Exception as e:
        print(f"Shapiro-Wilk Test: Error - {e}")

    # Jarque-Bera test
    try:
        jb_stat, jb_p = jarque_bera(clean_returns)
        print(f"Jarque-Bera Test: p-value = {jb_p:.6f}")
        print(f"  Result: {'Reject H0 (Not Normal)' if jb_p < 0.05 else 'Fail to
Reject H0 (Normal)'}")
    except Exception as e:
        print(f"Jarque-Bera Test: Error - {e}")

    # D'Agostino-Pearson test
    try:
```

```
        dp_stat, dp_p = normaltest(clean_returns)
        print(f"D'Agostino-Pearson Test: p-value = {dp_p:.6f}")
        print(f"  Result: {'Reject H0 (Not Normal)' if dp_p < 0.05 else 'Fail to 
Reject H0 (Normal)'}")

    except Exception as e:
        print(f"D'Agostino-Pearson Test: Error - {e}")

    # Anderson-Darling test
    try:
        ad_result = anderson(clean_returns, dist='norm')
        print(f"Anderson-Darling Test: Statistic = {ad_result.statistic:.4f}")
        print(f"  Critical values: {ad_result.critical_values}")
        print(f"  Significance levels: {ad_result.significance_level}")

        # Check if statistic exceeds critical values
        for i, (cv, sl) in enumerate(zip(ad_result.critical_values, ad_result.
significance_level)):
            if ad_result.statistic > cv:
                print(f"  At {sl}% significance level: Reject H0 (Not Normal)")
            else:
                print(f"  At {sl}% significance level: Fail to Reject H0 
(Normal)")
                break
    except Exception as e:
        print(f"Anderson-Darling Test: Error - {e}")

    return clean_returns
```

WHEAT time series in a tabular representation show non-normal distribution characteristics.

```
==================================================
NORMALITY TESTS FOR LOG RETURNS
==================================================
Normality Tests (p-values):
H0: Data is normally distributed
H1: Data is not normally distributed
Reject H0 if p-value < 0.05
----------------------------------------
Shapiro-Wilk Test: p-value = 0.000000
  Result: Reject H0 (Not Normal)
Jarque-Bera Test: p-value = 0.000000
  Result: Reject H0 (Not Normal)
D'Agostino-Pearson Test: p-value = 0.000000
  Result: Reject H0 (Not Normal)
Anderson-Darling Test: Statistic = 7.3531
  Critical values: [0.574 0.654 0.784 0.915 1.088]
  Significance levels: [15.  10.   5.   2.5  1. ]
  At 15.0% significance level: Reject H0 (Not Normal)
  At 10.0% significance level: Reject H0 (Not Normal)
  At 5.0% significance level: Reject H0 (Not Normal)
  At 2.5% significance level: Reject H0 (Not Normal)
  At 1.0% significance level: Reject H0 (Not Normal)
```

It is constructive to view graphical interpretation of the results during *DDF Station #2*. We are looking for any deviation from the normal distribution assumptions.

Figure 10.1 shows actual WHEAT price and simple and log returns in time sequence. Note, likely change in volatility regime, spike in volatility, that can be observed from the time series across the start of the year 2022.

Figure 10.2, steps into the return distribution using *histograms* and *Q-Q plots*. These visual interpretations are useful due to the ability to overlay actual normal distribution patterns and observe any deviations. It is clear from the plots, that WHEAT time series does not follow normal distribution.

Figure 10.3 depicts additional normality tests, all confirming the inevitable, WHEAT time series does not follow normal distribution. Two observations are of additional relevance, the

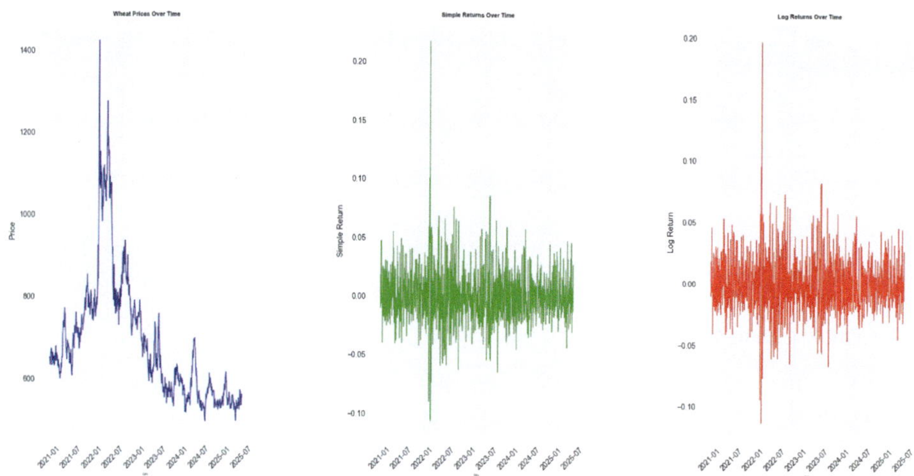

Figure 10.1 Basic Statistics WHEAT Price and Returns

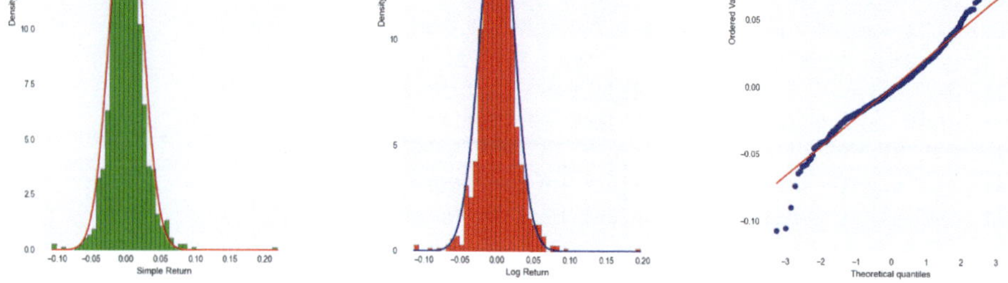

Figure 10.2 Normality Tests WHEAT

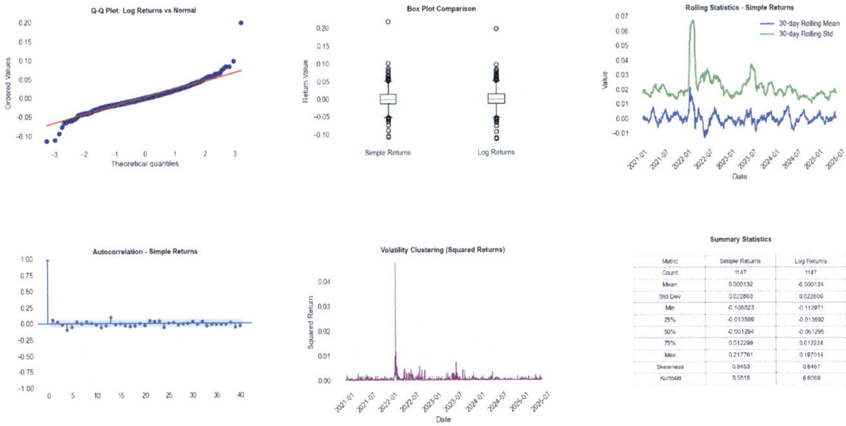

Figure 10.3 Normality views WHEAT

time series shows volatility regimes switch across time, and secondly, we observe potentially strong autocorrelation hidden within the time series. This can be due to the nature of the commodity being driven by seasonality effect as well as market microstructure effects due to this time series being generated by futures markets. **Autocorrelation** refers to the correlation of a signal with a delayed copy of itself as a function of delay. In simpler terms, it measures how the present value of a data series is related to its past values.

In conclusion, based on normality tests, WHEAT returns likely exhibit non-normal distribution (typical in financial contracts), potential fat tails (high kurtosis), possible skewness and strong volatility clustering. This suggests that normal distribution assumptions may not be appropriate for risk management and pricing models. With these insights we move to *DDF Station #3: Model Design.*

10.5 Model Design

In *Station #3*, we design a model to be used to predict the future. We look at using recurrent neural networks (RNN) in a time-series setting. This stage is demanding in terms of finding the appropriate model for the case in question. PyTorch is used in the solution.

LSTM

The aim is to predict the next observation in a time sequence based on the past observation in that specific time sequence without necessarily taking into account other features that could be having an effect on the original time series. Basically, looking at an autoregression problem.

In this station we build up on our acquired knowledge of LSTM models from "Chapter 7: Language Analytics." Indeed, language analytics are used in this numeric model application. The common denominator is sequential data structure. In this case, we are utilizing autoregressive prices, or data points observed in sequence in time. The model configuration consist of previous 60 days being used to predict the next day observation. We use 20% of data for evaluation. The model is designed with 3x LSTM layers with 50 units each and utilizing 20% dropout to prevent overfitting.

```
class WheatPriceLSTM:
    def __init__(self, sequence_length=60, test_size=0.2):
        self.sequence_length = sequence_length
        self.test_size = test_size
        self.scaler = MinMaxScaler(feature_range=(0, 1))
        self.model = None
        self.history = None
```

Note, we use price time series in a scaled form using *scaler = MinMaxScaler(feature_range=(0,1))* [10.3]. This is to accommodate for potential seasonality noise contained in the time series.

The following code sets the time series into train and test sequence containing scaled prices. Generally, these data preparation steps are critical when utilizing neural network architecture and usually from an integral part of model preparation (as opposed to be devised in *DDF Station #2*).

```
    def prepare_training_data(self, df):
        """Prepare data for LSTM training"""
        # Extract price data
        prices = df['Price'].values.reshape(-1, 1)

        # Scale the data
        scaled_prices = self.scaler.fit_transform(prices)

        # Create sequences
        X, y = self.create_sequences(scaled_prices.flatten())

        # Split into train and test sets
        split_idx = int(len(X) * (1 - self.test_size))

        self.X_train = X[:split_idx].reshape((-1, self.sequence_length, 1))
        self.X_test = X[split_idx:].reshape((-1, self.sequence_length, 1))
        self.y_train = y[:split_idx]
        self.y_test = y[split_idx:]

        print(f"Training sequences: {self.X_train.shape}")
        print(f"Testing sequences: {self.X_test.shape}")

        return self.X_train, self.X_test, self.y_train, self.y_test
```

Now we are in a position to design the model:

```
    def build_model(self):
        """Build LSTM model"""
        model = Sequential([
            LSTM(50, return_sequences=True,
input_shape=(self.sequence_length, 1)),
            Dropout(0.2),
            LSTM(50, return_sequences=True),
            Dropout(0.2),
            LSTM(50, return_sequences=False),
            Dropout(0.2),
            Dense(25),
            Dense(1)
        ])
```

```
    model.compile(
        optimizer=Adam(learning_rate=0.001),
        loss='mse',
        metrics=['mae']
    )

    self.model = model
    return model
```

Note, the use of Adam optimizer with 0.001 learning rate. The following three steps are necessary to complete the model design, namely, (i) model training, (ii) model evaluation and (iii) model prediction [10.4].

Next step, model training, defines core specification such as number of epochs, 100 epochs in our case with batch size set to 32 and validation test data split into 20%.

```
def train_model(self, epochs=100, batch_size=32, validation_split=0.2):
    """Train the LSTM model"""
    if self.model is None:
        self.build_model()

    # Early stopping to prevent overfitting
    early_stopping = EarlyStopping(
        monitor='val_loss',
        patience=15,
        restore_best_weights=True
    )

    print("Training LSTM model...")
    self.history = self.model.fit(
        self.X_train, self.y_train,
        epochs=epochs,
        batch_size=batch_size,
        validation_split=validation_split,
        callbacks=[early_stopping],
        verbose=1
    )

    print("Model training completed!")
    return self.history
```

At each pass, epoch, we collect model history for further evaluation. Hence, the next logical step is model evaluation.

```
def evaluate_model(self):
    """Evaluate model performance"""
    # Make predictions on test set
    test_predictions = self.model.predict(self.X_test)
    # Inverse transform to get actual prices
    test_predictions = self.scaler.inverse_transform(test_predictions)
    y_test_actual = self.scaler.inverse_transform(self.y_test.reshape(-1, 1))

    # Calculate metrics
    mse = mean_squared_error(y_test_actual, test_predictions)
    mae = mean_absolute_error(y_test_actual, test_predictions)
    rmse = np.sqrt(mse)
```

```
        print(f"\nModel Performance:")
        print(f"RMSE: ${rmse:.2f}")
        print(f"MAE: ${mae:.2f}")
        print(f"MSE: ${mse:.2f}")

        return {
            'rmse': rmse,
            'mae': mae,
            'mse': mse,
            'predictions': test_predictions,
            'actual': y_test_actual
        }
```

This function manually performs inverse of the previously scaled data, to compare predicted values with actual observations and to deliver critical accuracy measures, such as MSE, MAE and RMSE. Once again, we return these measures and snap at each iteration. Final critical model design component is the actual prediction.

```
    def predict_future(self, days_ahead):
  """Predict future prices"""
  # Get the last sequence from the data
  last_sequence = self.scaler.transform(
    self.original_data['Price'].tail(self.sequence_length).values.reshape(-1, 1)
  )

  predictions = []
  current_sequence = last_sequence.flatten()

  for _ in range(days_ahead):
    # Reshape for prediction
    X_pred = current_sequence.reshape(1, self.sequence_length, 1)

    # Make prediction
    next_pred = self.model.predict(X_pred, verbose=0)[0, 0]
    predictions.append(next_pred)

    # Update sequence for next prediction
    current_sequence = np.append(current_sequence[1:], next_pred)

  # Inverse transform predictions
  predictions = self.scaler.inverse_transform(np.array(predictions).reshape(-1, 1))

  return predictions.flatten()
```

This function triggers model prediction for a given time look-ahead period, in our case, we use 1-day, 7-day and 30-day forward. Now, we can apply the model design to our AgTech business case.

Valuations

For the brevity of exposition, we include only core Python functions in the text of this chapter. To execute the sequence post DDF Station #3 we apply these steps:

```
    # Initialize the LSTM model, core results from Station #4: Model Design
    lstm_model = WheatPriceLSTM(sequence_length=60, test_size=0.2)
```

```
# Load and prepare data from Station #3: Feature Engineering
df = lstm_model.load_and_prepare_data('wheat_prices.csv')

# Plot initial data analysis
lstm_model.plot_price_distribution()

# Prepare training data
lstm_model.prepare_training_data(df)

# Build and train the model
lstm_model.build_model()
lstm_model.train_model(epochs=100, batch_size=32)

# Plot training history
lstm_model.plot_training_history()

# Evaluate the model
evaluation_results = lstm_model.evaluate_model()

# Generate and plot predictions
future_predictions = lstm_model.plot_predictions(evaluation_results, days_ahead_list=[1, 7, 30])
```

In our case, we have 1,148 daily observations of the WHEAT price time series, showing basic data description in tabular as well as graphical form in Figure 10.4:

```
Data loaded successfully!
Date range: 2021-01-04 00:00:00 to 2025-07-03 00:00:00
Number of records: 1148
Price range: $498.00 to $1425.25
Training sequences: (870, 60, 1)
Testing sequences: (218, 60, 1)
```

As observed in *DDF Station #3*, the time series shows different regimes with increased volatility sequences and potential in-build seasonality. The following table shows core model architecture with actual number of parameters as implemented in our model design phase:

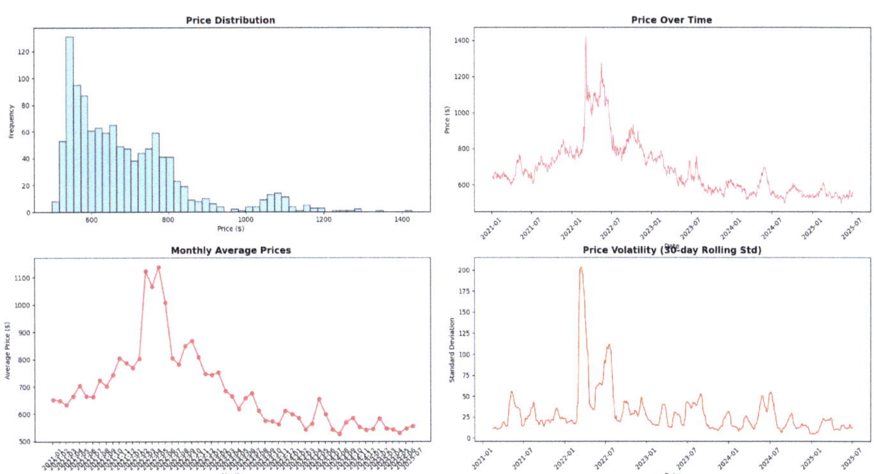

Figure 10.4 WHEAT Prices

```
Model Summary:
==================================================
Model: "sequential"
```

Layer (type)	Output Shape	Param #
lstm (LSTM)	(None, 60, 50)	10,400
dropout (Dropout)	(None, 60, 50)	0
lstm_1 (LSTM)	(None, 60, 50)	20,200
dropout_1 (Dropout)	(None, 60, 50)	0
lstm_2 (LSTM)	(None, 50)	20,200
dropout_2 (Dropout)	(None, 50)	0
dense (Dense)	(None, 25)	1,275
dense_1 (Dense)	(None, 1)	26

```
Total params: 156,305 (610.57 KB)
Trainable params: 52,101 (203.52 KB)
Non-trainable params: 0 (0.00 B)
Optimizer params: 104,204 (407.05 KB)
```

Figure 10.5 shows model accuracy in terms of declining loss function and MAE error measure per each epoch. It is concerning to observe "jumping" validation loss as well as MAE accuracy measure. This is likely due to our limited data set. In production environment building AgTech solutions these plots play critical role. The focus is on smoothness and consistency. There is plenty of factors that affect these critical numbers, such as, levels of hyperparameters, data quality or actual model design.

Model accuracy:

```
Model Performance:
RMSE: $10.90
MAE: $8.64
MSE: $118.82
```

Figure 10.6 depicts final prediction in price continuation for 1-day, 7-day and 30-day forward.

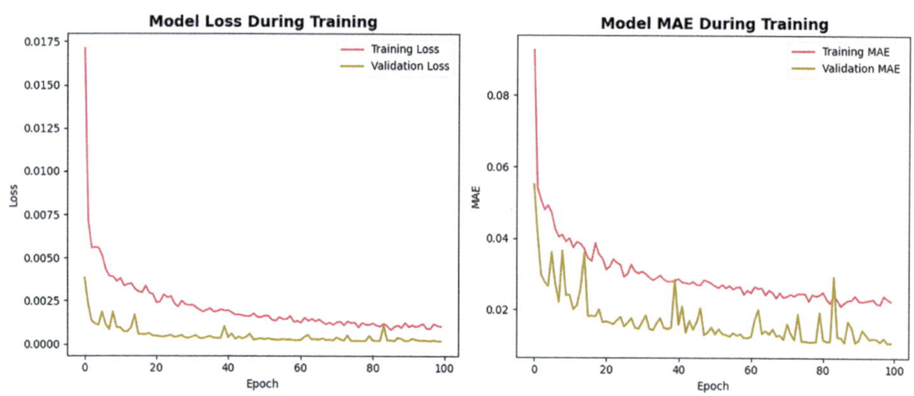

Figure 10.5 LSTM Model Accuracy

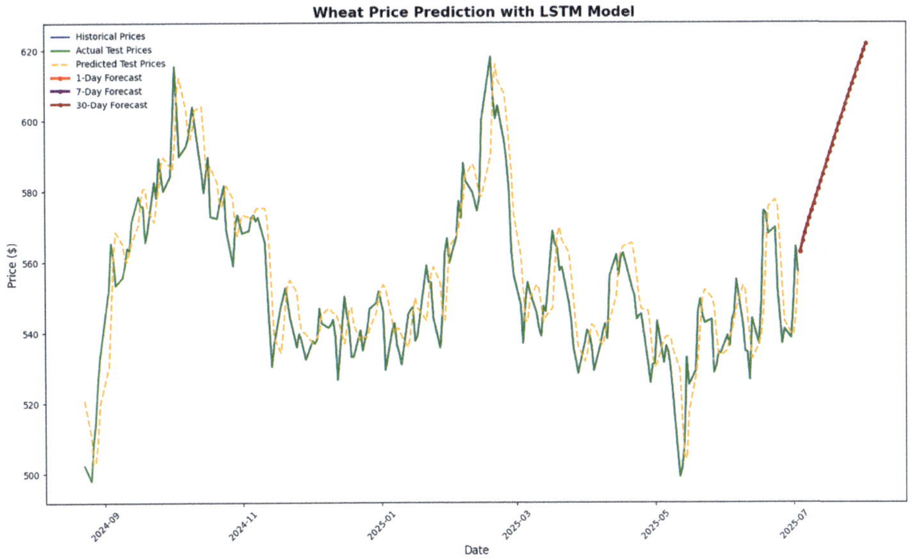

Figure 10.6 WHEAT Price Prediction – Final AgTech Product

Final prediction results in detail:

```
Future Price Predictions:
==================================================
1-day forecast average: $562.49
Tomorrow's predicted price: $562.49
7-day forecast average: $569.82
Next week's prices: $576.25 (day 7)
30-day forecast average: $593.18
Month-end predicted price: $621.32

Detailed Predictions:
==================================================
1-day prediction: $562.49
7-day average: $569.82
30-day average: $593.18
30-day trend: Upward
```

Overall, this section is dedicated to model design. We have provided detailed programmatic exposition focusing on our AgTech use case. **The delivery, core feature of the product, is in a form of numeric and graphical price prediction.** Based on the results the model predict an upward trend in price going forward for the following 30 days. This information can be provided to AgTech customers as an add-on service. This information, ultimately, is applicable as an input to further decision-making. For instance, a farmer deciding to market or hold and store produced commodity now. Alternatively, a farmer using wheat as an input purchasing this commodity now as opposed to holding off the purchase with the expectation of potential price decrease. Yet another usable format is for a broker or a financial advisor to recommend hedging product with relevant valuation now.

Limitations

LSTM models face several significant challenges when applied to time series forecasting. In this section, we run a simple model setup with predefined hyperparameters. We have not trained the model on extensive sets of time series and did not save a pretrained and calibrated version. At any model iteration our results will vary.

Vanishing gradient problems persist despite LSTMs being designed to address this. Very long sequences can still cause gradients to diminish, making it difficult to learn long-term dependencies effectively. The gradient flow through multiple time steps can become unstable, leading to poor convergence. Also, computational complexity is substantial, as LSTMs require sequential processing that cannot be easily parallelized across time steps. This makes training slow, especially for long sequences, and limits scalability compared to transformer-based approaches [10.4].

Hyperparameter sensitivity is problematic, as LSTMs require careful tuning of learning rates, hidden layer sizes, dropout rates, and sequence lengths. Small changes in these parameters can dramatically affect performance, making the models difficult to optimize reliably.

Seasonal pattern handling can be inadequate, as LSTMs may not effectively capture complex seasonal patterns, multiple seasonalities or irregular seasonal variations without careful feature engineering. In addition, stationarity assumptions cause issues when time series exhibit changing statistical properties over time. LSTMs can struggle with concept drift, where the underlying patterns change gradually, leading to degraded performance on new data.

Overfitting tendencies are common, especially with limited training data, as we observed in our case. The model may memorize training sequences rather than learning generalizable patterns, resulting in poor out-of-sample predictions.

In conclusion, these limitations have led many finance and FinTech practitioners to explore alternative approaches like transformer-based models, attention mechanisms or hybrid architectures that combine LSTMs with other techniques to address specific weaknesses, all relevant topics for further research.

10.6 Implementation

In *Station #4*, we implement the model design from previous station #3. In order to run the implementation, we operate in a live environment in a sense of using and retraining the original model on new data collected during our station #1 ETL efforts and processed during our time at station #2. Please note, once you are able to acquire base trained model parameters, from a production perspective, you are in a position to "save" these model parameters and speed up the entire process of model predictions and implementation.

Wireframes

Finally, this station is dedicated to AgTech solution implementation. As in "Chapter 9: FinTech Application: AdviceTech" this section deals with wireframes. Wireframes are essential in the early stages of web design, app development and other digital product creation processes. Figure 10.7 shows our base dashboard design built in *Streamlit*.

```
# Set page config
st.set_page_config(page_title="Wheat Price LSTM Forecasting", layout="wide")
```

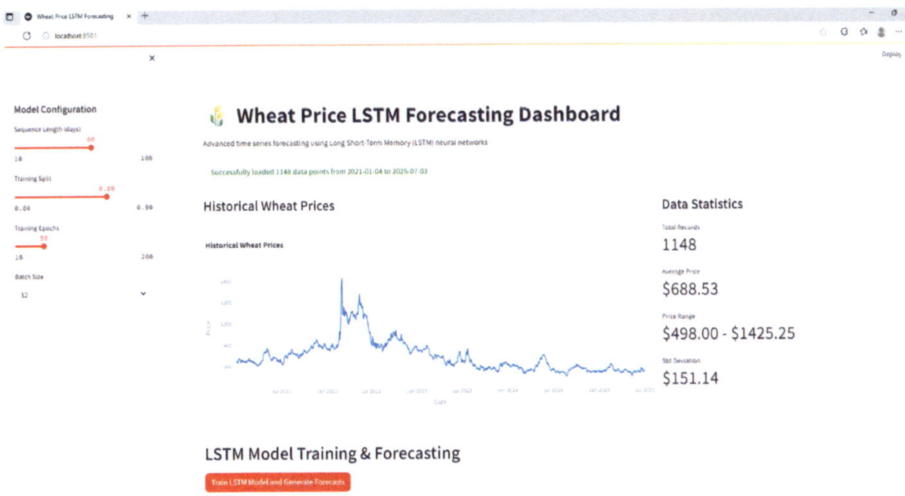

Figure 10.7 AgTech Implementation

```
# Title and description
st.title("🌾 Wheat Price LSTM Forecasting Dashboard")
st.markdown("Advanced time series forecasting using Long Short-Term Memory
(LSTM) neural networks")

...

# Footer
st.markdown("---")
st.markdown("🌾 **Wheat Price LSTM Forecasting Dashboard** | Built with
Streamlit & TensorFlow")

st.markdown("⚠ **Disclaimer:** These predictions are for educational purposes
only and should not be used for trading decisions.")
```

Note, the following code outline **Sidebar and Main Dashboard** schema and outlays. The hyperparameters are added for model design and calibration purposes.

```
# Sidebar for model parameters
st.sidebar.header("Model Configuration")
sequence_length = st.sidebar.slider("Sequence Length (days)", 10, 100, 60)
train_split = st.sidebar.slider("Training Split", 0.6, 0.9, 0.8)
epochs = st.sidebar.slider("Training Epochs", 10, 200, 50)
batch_size = st.sidebar.selectbox("Batch Size", [16, 32, 64, 128], index=1)

# Main content
col1, col2 = st.columns([2, 1])

with col1:
    st.subheader("Historical Wheat Prices")

    # Plot historical data
    fig = go.Figure()
    fig.add_trace(go.Scatter(
```

```
        x=df['Date'],
        y=df['Price'],
        mode='lines',
        name='Wheat Price',
        line=dict(color='#1f77b4', width=2)
    ))
    fig.update_layout(
        title="Historical Wheat Prices",
        xaxis_title="Date",
        yaxis_title="Price",
        height=400
    )
    st.plotly_chart(fig, use_container_width=True)

with col2:
    st.subheader("Data Statistics")
    st.metric("Total Records", len(df))
    st.metric("Average Price", f"${df['Price'].mean():.2f}")
    st.metric("Price Range", f"${df['Price'].min():.2f} - ${df['Price'].max():.2f}")
    st.metric("Std Deviation", f"${df['Price'].std():.2f}")
```

The main dashboard is initiated with the original data sequence for WHEAT as delivered from *DDF Station #4: Model Design*.

After model calibration, we collate a number of screens. We provide model results as well as prediction results. Model results are used by AgTech application designers and builders, whereas prediction results are dedicated to be packaged to ultimate customers for further feedback.

Model accuracy results code snippet post model calculation:

```
        # Display metrics
        col1, col2, col3, col4 = st.columns(4)
        with col1:
            st.metric("Train MSE", f"{train_mse:.2f}")
        with col2:
            st.metric("Test MSE", f"{test_mse:.2f}")
        with col3:
            st.metric("Train MAE", f"{train_mae:.2f}")
        with col4:
            st.metric("Test MAE", f"{test_mae:.2f}")

        # Plot training history
        st.subheader("Training History")
        fig_hist = make_subplots(rows=1, cols=2, subplot_titles=('Loss',
'Mean Absolute Error'))

        fig_hist.add_trace(
            go.Scatter(y=history.history['loss'], name='Train Loss'),
            row=1, col=1
        )
        fig_hist.add_trace(
            go.Scatter(y=history.history['val_loss'], name='Val Loss'),
            row=1, col=1
        )
        fig_hist.add_trace(
            go.Scatter(y=history.history['mae'], name='Train MAE'),
```

```
            row=1, col=2
        )
        fig_hist.add_trace(
            go.Scatter(y=history.history['val_mae'], name='Val MAE'),
            row=1, col=2
        )

        fig_hist.update_layout(height=400)
        st.plotly_chart(fig_hist, use_container_width=True)
```

In *Streamlit* the code sequence collect calculated results, then sets up one row of two graphs to depict the model accuracy as delivered during our previous DDF Station #3.

The next dashboard view deals with actual AgTech product – predictions. Figure 10.8 outlines model performance as captured during the training process utilizing 80% train and 20% test data sets. Then projecting model predictions across the plot.

The final two dashboard views, Figures 10.9 and 10.10 are likely going to be shown to the end customer for further feedback. The AgTech wireframes show 1-day, 7-day, 3-day and total trend driven prediction details both in visual and tabular formats.

Figure 10.8 AgTech LSTM Model Accuracy

Figure 10.9 AgTech Future Price Prediction

Figure 10.10 AgTech Detailed Prediction

Here we showcase the first plot, 1-day forward price point in Python code shown in Figure 10.11:

```
# Plot future predictions
st.subheader("Future Price Forecasts")

# Create subplot for different prediction horizons
fig_future = make_subplots(
    rows=2, cols=2,
    subplot_titles=('1-Day Forecast', '7-Day Forecast', '30-Day Forecast',
'All Forecasts Combined'),
    specs=[[{"type": "scatter"}, {"type": "scatter"}],
           [{"type": "scatter"}, {"type": "scatter"}]]
)

# Recent historical data for context (last 30 days)
recent_data = df.tail(30)

# 1-Day forecast
fig_future.add_trace(
    go.Scatter(x=recent_data['Date'], y=recent_data['Price'],
               mode='lines', name='Historical', line=dict(color='blue')),
    row=1, col=1
)
fig_future.add_trace(
    go.Scatter(x=future_dates_1, y=pred_1_day,
               mode='markers+lines', name='1-Day Pred',
               line=dict(color='red', dash='dash')),
    row=1, col=1
)
```

In conclusion, we aim to deliver a packaged product in the form of wireframes for the next step of the product iteration. The next step from now is to start from the beginning.

Detailed Predictions

1-Day Forecast

	Date	Predicted Price
0	2025-07-04 00:00:00	553.53

7-Day Forecast

	Date	Predicted Price
0	2025-07-04 00:00:00	553.53
1	2025-07-05 00:00:00	558.47
2	2025-07-06 00:00:00	561.41
3	2025-07-07 00:00:00	563.46
4	2025-07-08 00:00:00	565.19
5	2025-07-09 00:00:00	566.81
6	2025-07-10 00:00:00	568.36

30-Day Forecast

	Date	Predicted Price
0	2025-07-04 00:00:00	553.53
1	2025-07-05 00:00:00	558.47
2	2025-07-06 00:00:00	561.41
3	2025-07-07 00:00:00	563.46
4	2025-07-08 00:00:00	565.19
5	2025-07-09 00:00:00	566.81
6	2025-07-10 00:00:00	568.36
7	2025-07-11 00:00:00	569.86
8	2025-07-12 00:00:00	571.31
9	2025-07-13 00:00:00	572.73

Price Trend Analysis

Current Price	1-Day Trend	7-Day Trend	30-Day Trend
$556.75	Downward	Upward	Upward

Model Insights

Historical Volatility: $151.14

Predicted 7-Day Volatility: $4.77

Predicted 30-Day Volatility: $13.62

95% Confidence Interval: ±$20.08

Figure 10.11 AgTech Future Trends

Customer Journey

Modern agribusiness banks now employ banking professionals who blend agricultural knowledge with financial expertise. These relationship managers come right to the farms. They meet farmers face-to-face and learn about their operational needs firsthand instead of asking farmers to visit branches. Farm income follows seasonal patterns, so farmer-friendly banks create financing options that work with harvest and production schedules. Seasonal finance options come with flexible credit arrangements and shorter loan terms that work well for businesses with ups and downs in revenue. Digital banking tools have become vital for farmers in rural areas where branches are hard to reach.

Mobile banking apps let farmers, end customers, handle their finances from anywhere and is being used to add value to farmer's decision-making capabilities. One such example is adding commodity price predictions as depicted in our example. AgTech development is an iterative process, as shown in Figure 10.12. The moment a feature is completed, the next iteration of the AgTech product starts again.

10.7 Summary

This chapter introduces readers to traditional banking operations through a practical commercial banking case study focused on serving small to medium enterprises (SMEs) in the agricultural sector. Agricultural commodity markets are fundamental to the global economy, enabling trade in essential products including grains, livestock and dairy. These markets operate according to scientific principles that promote efficient and equitable trading practices.

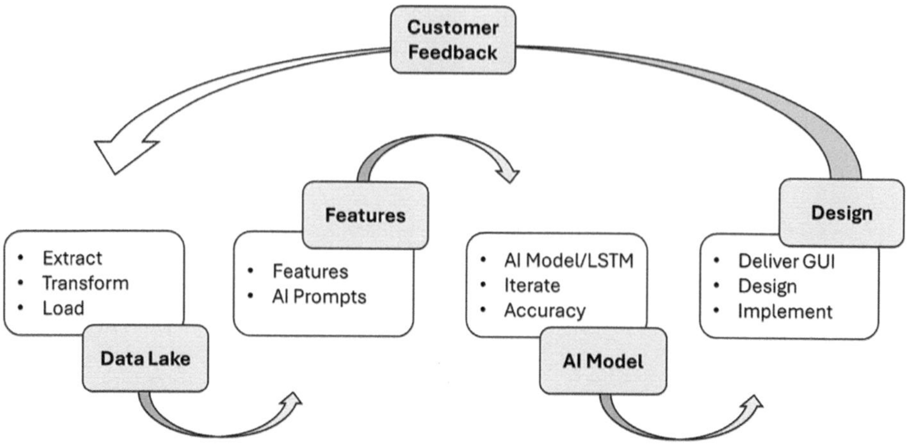

Figure 10.12 AgTech Customer Feedback Loop

The chapter begins by establishing definitions for agricultural technology (AgTech), smart farming and precision agriculture, then explores their connection to financial forecasting. Agricultural commodity price fluctuations and supply-demand variations directly impact SME operations and farm businesses participating in these markets.

The chapter then presents a specific AgTech use case, applying the digital data factory (DDF) framework outlined in earlier chapters. Each station within this framework is examined systematically, demonstrating computational techniques and programmatic solutions. The chapter concludes with fundamental AgTech application wireframes. The technological solution delivered centers on an applied LSTM prediction algorithm, packaged as a final product and presented visually as an enhanced feature for integration within existing online banking platforms.

In conclusion, from the **digital data factory (DDF)** lens, we examine the complexities of data management through an industrial-like framework. The DDF approach conceptualizes data management as a manufacturing process encompassing several critical production stages: data lake construction, prompt and feature engineering, model architecture development, and deployment implementation – what we term as operational "stations." Given recent developments in ML and AI methodologies, the DDF paradigm transforms traditional data handling into a coordinated production system where each station contributes to the overall value creation pipeline, enabling businesses, traditional banks or agTech specialists, to convert raw data into actionable insights with greater efficiency and precision.

10.8 Concept Questions and Answers

Q1: How do commodity prices typically behave during economic downturns?

A1: During recessions, commodity prices often decline due to reduced demand. Energy prices, in particular, tend to fall as global economic activity slows. However, the impact can vary across different commodity types depending on supply and demand factors specific to each market.

Q2: What factors are currently driving commodity price volatility?

A2: Current commodity price volatility is driven by several factors, including ongoing supply chain disruptions, geopolitical tensions, strategic export controls (especially from China) and shifting global trade patterns. Additionally, climate events and the transition to renewable energy are creating new supply and demand dynamics in various commodity markets.

Q3: How are rising commodity prices affecting global inflation?

A3: Surging commodity prices are a significant driver of global inflation. Food and energy prices, in particular, have a substantial impact on consumer price indices. In many developing countries, food price inflation has exceeded 5%, affecting food security. Energy price increases also contribute significantly to overall inflation rates.

Q4: Which commodities are considered "safe havens" during times of economic uncertainty?

A4: Gold and silver are traditionally viewed as safe-haven assets during economic uncertainty. Recently, both have seen significant price increases due to geopolitical tensions and economic instability. Gold, in particular, has reached record highs and is expected to maintain elevated prices going forward.

Q5: How do you measure forecast accuracy?

A5: Common accuracy metrics include mean absolute error (MAE), mean squared error (MSE), root mean squared error (RMSE), and mean absolute percentage error (MAPE). MAE gives equal weight to all errors, MSE penalizes larger errors more heavily and MAPE expresses accuracy as a percentage. The choice depends on your specific needs – whether you want to penalize large errors more or need scale-independent measures.

Q6: What is seasonality in forecasting and how do you handle it?

A6: Seasonality refers to regular, predictable patterns that repeat over fixed periods (daily, weekly, monthly or yearly). Examples include higher ice cream sales in summer or increased retail sales during holidays. Seasonal patterns can be handled through seasonal decomposition, seasonal ARIMA models or by using seasonal dummy variables in regression models.

Q7: What are the key challenges in long-term forecasting?

A7: Long-term forecasting faces several challenges: structural breaks (when underlying relationships change), increasing uncertainty over time, the assumption that historical patterns will continue and the compound effect of errors.

Q8: How is artificial intelligence being used to predict commodity prices in agriculture?

A8: AI systems analyze vast data sets including weather patterns, satellite imagery, soil conditions, global supply chains, and economic indicators to forecast commodity prices. Machine learning algorithms can identify complex patterns and correlations that traditional models might miss.

Q9: What are the main challenges in using AgTech for commodity price prediction?

A9: Key challenges include data quality and standardization across different sources, the complexity of global supply chains, unpredictable weather events, and geopolitical factors that can't be easily quantified.

Q10: What is a normality test, and why is it important in statistics?

A10: A normality test is a statistical procedure used to determine whether a data set follows a normal (Gaussian) distribution. These tests are crucial because many statistical methods, including t-tests, ANOVA, and linear regression, assume that the data is normally distributed. If this assumption is violated, the results of these tests may be unreliable or invalid. Common normality tests include the Shapiro-Wilk test, Kolmogorov-Smirnov test, and Anderson-Darling test

10.9 Exercises

E1: Use CORN as your main commodity and step-through the workshop as outlined in the text in detail. Deliver Python code and resulting AgTech application in Streamlit. Can you combine WHEAT and CORN into one view?

E2: Use WHEAT as per our workshop and add WHEAT related news extract (potentially yahoo.com) and in addition to prediction component add sentiment analytics in terms of positive/negative news visualization. How can you add this new feature to the final AgTech product.

E3: (Advanced) Use WHEAT price and WHEAT news daily sentiment index (calculated as (# of positive news / # of negative news) per day) as an input into LSTM model. In addition to price feature you add sentiment index feature into the model. Can you observe increased prediction accuracy? Why or why not?

10.10 Further Reading

- Alammar, J., & Grootendorst, M. (2024). Hands-On Large Language Models: Language Understanding and Generation, O'Reilly.
- Dickerson, A., & Hric, J. (2024). FINS5545 Financial Market Data Literacy Course Notes, UNSW Business School.
- Hric, J., & Lam, I. (2025). FINS5548 Financial Technology Course Notes, UNSW Business School.
- Huyen, C. (2025). AI Engineering: Building Applications with Foundation Models, O'Reilly.
- Lin, Y., Schmidt, B., & Tumarkin, R. (2023). Toolkit for FinTech, UNSW Press Class Notes.
- Raschka, S. (2025). Build a Large Language Model, Manning.

10.11 References

[10.1] AlphaVantage API Key: https://www.alphavantage.co/support/#api-key

[10.2] Scipy: https://scipy.org/

[10.3] MinMaxScaler: https://scikit-learn.org/stable/modules/generated/sklearn.preprocessing.MinMaxScaler.html

[10.4] LSTM Architecture: https://www.tensorflow.org/api_docs/python/tf/keras/layers/LSTM

Chapter 11

FinTech Application

PropTech

11.1 Introduction

This chapter examines tokenization through both practical applications and programmatic implementation, building upon the foundational concepts established in "Chapter 5: Bitcoin and Tokenization." We explore an **ambitious vision**: a future where every asset class becomes tokenizable, creating a unified ecosystem of 24/7 trading with frictionless processing and execution mechanisms. Leading FinTech platforms such as RobinHood and Tokeny are already pioneering these transformative solutions.

The underlying blockchain architecture provides cryptographic security and immutable transaction records, while smart contracts serve as autonomous enforcement mechanisms that execute predetermined agreement terms without intermediary intervention. This technological synthesis creates a robust, transparent ecosystem for real estate transaction management. The distributed ledger component introduces decentralization and tamper-resistant ownership records, significantly mitigating fraud risks while enhancing investor confidence through verifiable transparency.

DOI: 10.4324/9781003477747-14

We begin with a comprehensive examination of PropTech as an evolving sector, subsequently focusing on blockchain technology as a specific enabler within this domain. This section establishes the theoretical framework and outlines compelling use cases that demonstrate blockchain's potential to revolutionize digital real estate markets.

The chapter's central focus is on the *digital data factory (DDF)* use case, where we synthesize knowledge accumulated throughout this book to analyze blockchain integration within this conceptual framework. This section provides detailed programmatic exposition of Ethereum ERC-20 token implementation, offering readers practical insights into real-world application development.

We conclude by acknowledging the **inherent limitations of current blockchain solutions** while presenting a comprehensive analysis of potential mitigation strategies and emerging technological developments that address these constraints. Through this structured exploration, readers will gain both theoretical understanding and practical implementation knowledge necessary to navigate the evolving landscape of tokenized real estate investment.

Learning Outcomes

At the end of this chapter the reader will be able to do the following:

- Comprehend core features of PropTech
- Outline base programmatic Ethereum tokenization (ERC-20)
- Redefine DDF concept and apply in a practical setting
- Appreciate blockchain boundaries and opportunities

11.2 FinTech Case Study – Digital Real Estate

In this hypothetical case study, we demonstrate implementation of digital real estate asset tokenization using Ethereum smart contract infrastructure. The technology used in this case is designed to replace the entire infrastructure, using blockchain, as opposed to using unique ML or AI based algorithm as utilized in previous chapters.

PropTech

Property technology, or PropTech, brings together traditional real estate and state-of-the-art digital solutions. PropTech covers technological advancements that improve real estate processes. These solutions make processes more efficient, transparent and available to all stakeholders. Modern PropTech solutions accelerate renting, buying, selling and property management processes. These platforms utilize cutting-edge technologies such as big data, artificial intelligence, machine learning, virtual reality, augmented reality and Internet of Things (IoT).

Blockchain potentially brings unmatched security and clarity to property deals through its decentralized structure. It offers a reliable way to track transactions without needing central authorities to check accuracy. Cryptographic signatures make it almost impossible to change or fake internal blockchain records (pre-quantum computing), which potentially reduces fraud risk. This technology powers smart contracts that automate checking and validation, which could remove middlemen and make transactions fully digital and rather simpler. At its core, blockchain makes property transfers faster by moving money between parties more smoothly. Not all PropTech solutions utilize blockchain technology.

As discussed in "Chapter 5: Bitcoin and Tokenization," tokenization in real estate refers to the process of dividing a property into digital tokens that represent ownership rights and liabilities. These tokens are created using smart contracts, which are automated pieces of code stored on a blockchain. Essentially, tokenization transforms a real estate asset into smaller, more accessible digital fractions [11.1].

Tokenization brings several advantages to the real estate sector:

- **Increased Efficiency and Transparency:** Blockchain's decentralized structure makes transactions transparent and immutable, ideal for complex real estate processes involving multiple parties.
- **Enhanced Liquidity:** Traditional real estate often suffers from liquidity issues, deterring many investors. Tokenization addresses this problem by making it easier to buy and sell fractional ownership.
- **Accessibility for Smaller Investors:** Real estate has typically been an elite investment option. Tokenization opens up opportunities for retail and small-scale investors by lowering the capital threshold.
- **Cost Savings:** Lower business infrastructure costs.
- **Automated Compliance:** Smart contracts handle the entire process of tokenizing and selling on-chain, leading to transparency, automation, and security.

Tokeny, as an example, is a leading provider of tokenization solutions that enable seamless issuance, management and transfer of digital assets on a secure blockchain infrastructure [11.2].

Tokeny's T-REX platform offers the following:

- Flexible Infrastructure: Allows issuers to tokenize any asset on any EVM blockchain, regardless of jurisdiction
- Built-in Trading Solutions: Provides connectivity with a global network of trading venues
- Compliance Integration: Uses **ERC3643 smart contracts** to ensure digital securities can only be traded between qualified KYC investors
- Data Enrichment: Allows issuers to embed additional data, such as up-to-date pricing, into the tokens

Tokeny delivers tokenization infrastructure as an alternative to traditional cloud-based solutions.

Workshop

In this hypothetical use case, you work for an online property investment platform, such as Bricks [11.3]. Your business operates on a traditional infrastructure using SQL databases and cloud solutions. Your task is to build a demo version of the business offerings utilizing blockchain as an infrastructure to streamline property transactions and increase transparency.

Digital Data Factory

In the context of our DDF concept as shown in Figure 11.1, blockchain can be seen as the entire on-chain digital data factory infrastructure. As defined previously, smart contract can be seen as the ultimate digital contract encompassing all contractual specifications and obligations, if this would ever be possible.

DDF Station 3#: Model Design previously containing algorithms.now, hosts transaction mechanics, in this case, and can host off-chain valuation models, for instance. The DDF concept is still applicable as a pure blockchain infrastructure does not provide KYC/AML methodologies, account procedures and controls or any form of corporate – white-labeled – notion of centralization. By design, the PropTech product – digital real estate – is hosted on decentralized blockchain accessible to anyone globally.

Ethereum is a decentralized blockchain platform that enables developers to build and deploy smart contracts and decentralized applications (dApps). Ethereum functions as a distributed computer network where thousands of nodes worldwide maintain a shared ledger. Unlike Bitcoin, which primarily serves as digital money, Ethereum is designed as a programmable blockchain that can execute complex logic through smart contracts. These are self-executing programs that automatically enforce agreements when predetermined conditions are met. Once deployed, they run exactly as programmed without possibility of downtime, censorship or third-party interference, as shown in Figure 11.2.

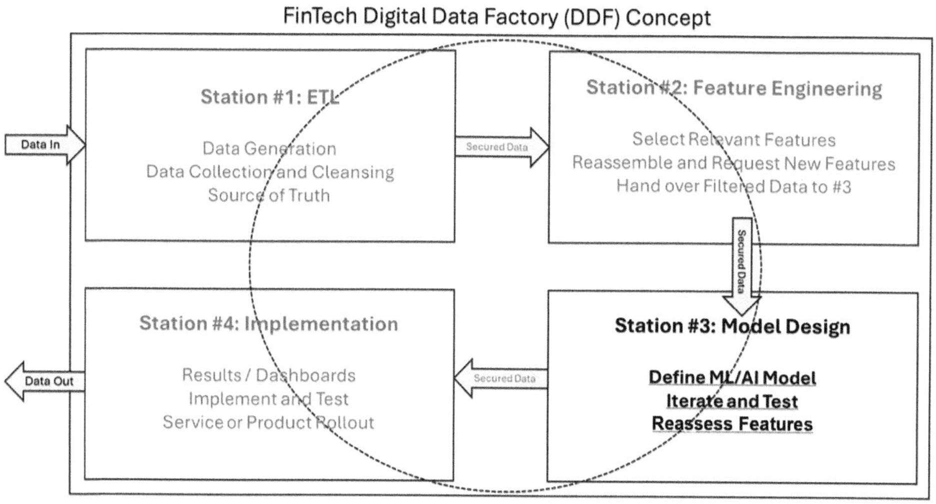

Figure 11.1 DDF Concept With Blockchain

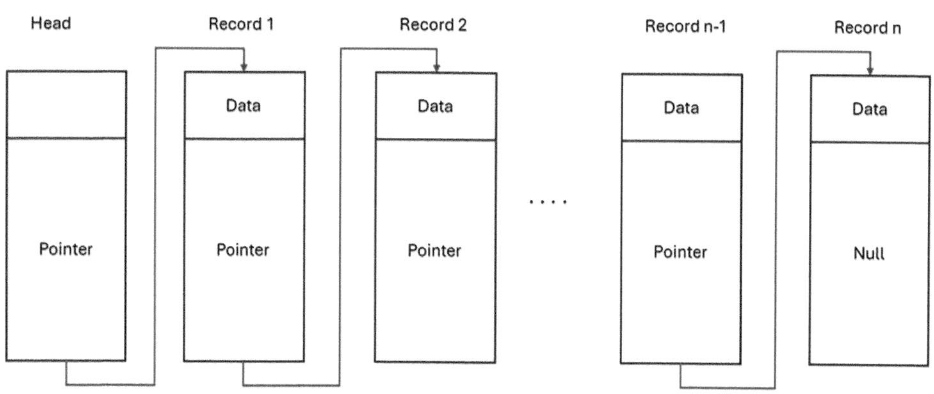

Figure 11.2 DDF Concept With Blockchain

The exposition across the following sections are based on demo Ethereum blockchain version, using Python *web3* and *Ganache* [11.4]. This is development Ethereum based blockchain environment and is used during testing purposes only. The code is limited to this extent. In addition, we do not include any discussions related to add-on off-chain capabilities, such a valuations or KYC/AML. The exposition of these techniques is viewed as natural extension of this chapter.

```
# Connect to the Ganache blockchain
ganache_url = "HTTP://127.0.0.1:7545"  # Default URL for Ganache
web3 = Web3(Web3.HTTPProvider(ganache_url))

# Check if connected
if web3.is_connected():
    print("Successfully connected to Ganache!")
    # Example: Get the latest block number
    latest_block = web3.eth.block_number
    print(f"Latest block number: {latest_block}")
else:
    print("Failed to connect to Ganache.")

# get the first account
account = web3.eth.accounts[0]
```

Figure 11.3 shows a basic wireframes built to handle core functionality around Ethereum blockchain implementation.

We are limited to using text blockchain and "demo" Solidity compiled smart contract specification with a "dummy" ABI and BYTECODE information.

Smart contract example ERC-20 Token:

```
# Solidity Smart Contract (ERC-20 based Real Estate Token)
REAL_ESTATE_CONTRACT = '''
pragma solidity ^0.8.0;

interface IERC20 {
    function totalSupply() external view returns (uint256);
```

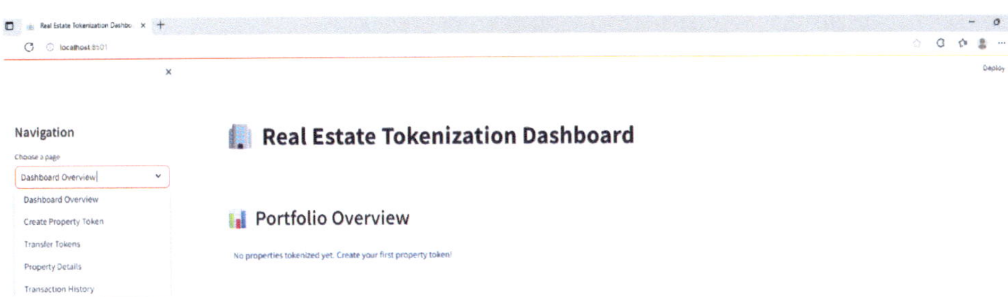

Figure 11.3 Real Estate Tokenization Platform

```
    function balanceOf(address account) external view returns (uint256);
    function transfer(address recipient, uint256 amount) external returns
(bool);
    function allowance(address owner, address spender) external view returns
(uint256);
    function approve(address spender, uint256 amount) external returns (bool);
    function transferFrom(address sender, address recipient, uint256 amount)
external returns (bool);

    event Transfer(address indexed from, address indexed to, uint256 value);
    event Approval(address indexed owner, address indexed spender, uint256
value);
}

contract RealEstateToken is IERC20 {
    mapping(address => uint256) private _balances;
    mapping(address => mapping(address => uint256)) private _allowances;

    uint256 private _totalSupply;
    string public name;
    string public symbol;
    uint8 public decimals;

    // Real estate specific properties
    string public propertyAddress;
    uint256 public propertyValue; // in wei
    address public owner;
    bool public tradingEnabled;

    event PropertyUpdated(string newAddress, uint256 newValue);
    event TradingToggled(bool enabled);

    constructor(
        string memory _name,
        string memory _symbol,
        string memory _propertyAddress,
        uint256 _propertyValue,
        uint256 _totalSupply
    ) {
        name = _name;
        symbol = _symbol;
        decimals = 18;
        propertyAddress = _propertyAddress;
        propertyValue = _propertyValue;
        _totalSupply = _totalSupply * 10**decimals;
        owner = msg.sender;
        tradingEnabled = true;

        _balances[owner] = _totalSupply;
        emit Transfer(address(0), owner, _totalSupply);
    }

    modifier onlyOwner() {
        require(msg.sender == owner, "Only owner can call this function");
        _;
    }
```

```
,,,,< other core smart contract functions excluded for brevity >,,,,

    // Real estate specific functions
    function updateProperty(string memory _newAddress, uint256 _newValue) pub-
lic onlyOwner {
        propertyAddress = _newAddress;
        propertyValue = _newValue;
        emit PropertyUpdated(_newAddress, _newValue);
    }

    function toggleTrading() public onlyOwner {
        tradingEnabled = !tradingEnabled;
        emit TradingToggled(tradingEnabled);
    }

    function getTokenValueInWei() public view returns (uint256) {
        return propertyValue * 10**decimals / _totalSupply;
    }

    function getOwnershipPercentage(address account) public view returns
(uint256) {
        return (_balances[account] * 100 * 10**decimals) / _totalSupply;
    }
}
'''
```

To compile the previous smart contract definition we utilize Python Solidity based *solcx.compile_standard()* function:

```
# Compile the contract
compiled_sol = solcx.compile_standard({
    "language": "Solidity",
    "sources": {
        "RealEstateToken.sol": {
            "content": REAL_ESTATE_CONTRACT
        }
    },
    "settings": {
        "outputSelection": {
            "*": {
                "*": ["abi", "evm.bytecode"]
            }
        }
    }
}, solc_version='0.8.0')

# Extract ABI and Bytecode
abi = compiled_sol['contracts']['RealEstateToken.sol']['RealEstateToken']['abi']
bytecode = compiled_sol['contracts']['RealEstateToken.sol']['RealEstateToken']['evm']
['bytecode']['object']

# You can now use 'abi' and 'bytecode' for deployment and interaction with the
contract
print("ABI:", json.dumps(abi, indent=2))
print("\nBytecode:", bytecode)
```

Post execution of this code sequence, your smart contract is reachable via Application Binary Interface (ABI) and Bytecode sequences.

11.3 Data Lake

As expected, data lake station can be viewed as the entire blockchain implementation by default within our DDF concept. It is at this stage whereby we deploy smart contract specification and create relevant token per property in our portfolio.

```
class RealEstateTokenizer:
    def __init__(self, rpc_url="HTTP://127.0.0.1:7545"):
        """Initialize connection to Ethereum network"""
        self.w3 = Web3(Web3.HTTPProvider(rpc_url))
        self.account = "0x859864435f9b5D8AEF930b5c1C570f6C359Ad59A"
        self.private_key = "XXXXXXXXXX"

    def deploy_real_estate_token(self, property_data):
        """Deploy a new real estate token contract"""
        contract_data = {
            'name': property_data['name'],
            'symbol': property_data['symbol'],
            'property_address': property_data['address'],
            'property_value': property_data['value_eth'],
            'total_supply': property_data['total_tokens']
        }

        # Mock contract address for demo
        mock_contract_address = f"0x{hash(property_data['id']) %
(16**40):040x}"

        return mock_contract_address, contract_data
```

In the previous code, we create a mock contract address (not using actual Solidity compiled contract hosted on live Ethereum). This is a critical step as the smart contract is to be viewed as final contractual definition representing real estate contractual specifications, functions, controls and behavior.

Figure 11.4 depicts wireframe screen controlling token creation step, post smart contract deployment. At this stage, data is entered into the screen to identify actual real estate acquired by the platform.

```
class RealEstateTokenDemo:
    def __init__(self):
        self.tokenizer = RealEstateTokenizer()
        self.properties = {}
        self.transaction_history = []

    def create_property_token(self, property_info):
        """Create a tokenized real estate property"""
        contract_address, contract_data = self.tokenizer.
deploy_real_estate_token(property_info)

        self.properties[property_info['id']] = {
            'contract_address': contract_address,
```

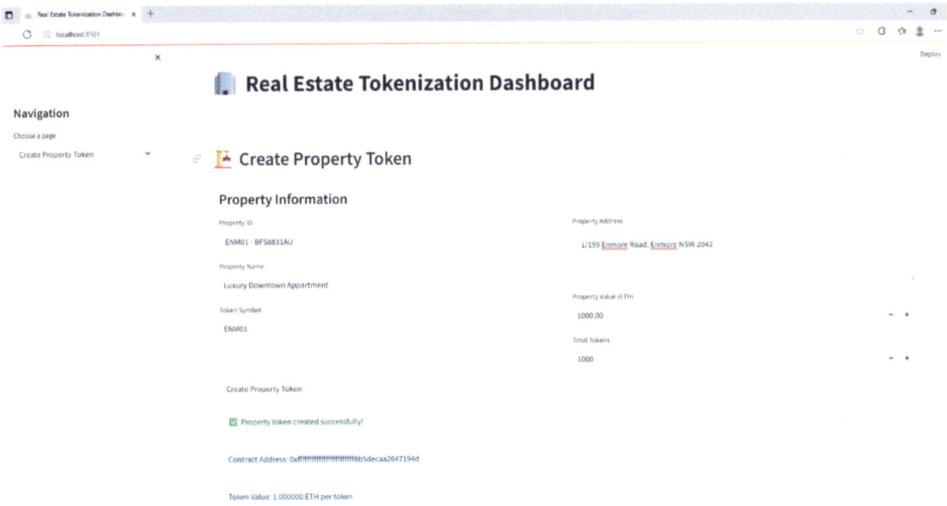

Figure 11.4 Create Property Token

```
            'property_data': property_info,
            'contract_data': contract_data,
            'holders': {'owner': property_info['total_tokens']},
            'created_at': datetime.now()
        }

        # Add to transaction history
        self.transaction_history.append({
            'timestamp': datetime.now(),
            'type': 'Token Creation',
            'property_id': property_info['id'],
            'from': 'System',
            'to': 'owner',
            'amount': property_info['total_tokens'],
            'details': f"Created {property_info['name']}"
        })

        return contract_address
```

The code snippet defines basic information about the property (note, this is an abbreviation and a construct for demonstration purposes only). This is equivalent to a listed property on Brickx, as shown in Figure 11.4:

The deliveries from *DDF Station #1* is the entire platform, deployed smart contract, processed data extract, transfer and load into token and hosted on the blockchain. As opposed to our previous examples, delivering cleaned structured and unstructured dataframes for further processing.

11.4 Feature Engineering

Given the heavy lifting is done at *DDF Station #1*, at this stage, we process property information. Assuming additional requirements, such as property valuation capabilities, new features

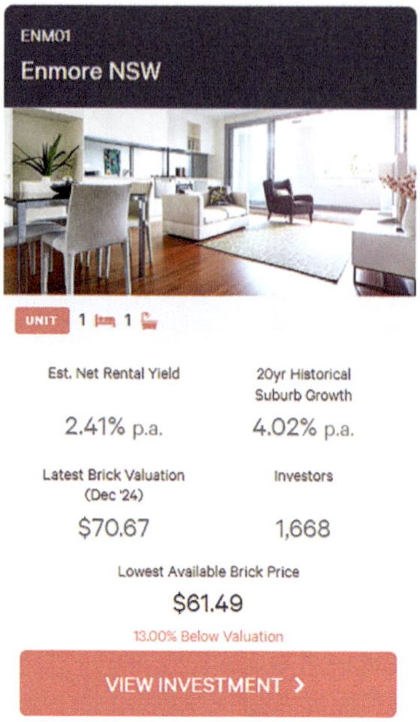

Figure 11.4i Create Property Token: Example

would be required here, such as GPS location parameters, property distance from railway stations, bus stations, hospitals etc.

```
    def get_property_info(self, property_id):
        """Get detailed information about a tokenized property"""
        if property_id not in self.properties:
            return None

        prop = self.properties[property_id]
        token_value = prop['property_data']['value_eth'] / prop['property_data']
['total_tokens']

        info = {
            'contract_address': prop['contract_address'],
            'property_address': prop['property_data']['address'],
            'total_value_eth': prop['property_data']['value_eth'],
            'total_tokens': prop['property_data']['total_tokens'],
            'token_value_eth': token_value,
            'holders': {},
            'created_at': prop['created_at']
        }

        for holder, tokens in prop['holders'].items():
            if tokens > 0:
                percentage = (tokens / prop['property_data']['total_tokens'])
* 100
                value_eth = tokens * token_value
                info['holders'][holder] = {
                    'tokens': tokens,
```

```
                'ownership_percentage': percentage,
                'value_eth': value_eth
            }
        return info
```

The code snippet outlines basic property information per token holder with ownership percentage details.

11.5 Model Design

At this point, model design station is focused on correct trade and transfer functionality. Allowing your customers to trade and transfer on primary as well as secondary token markets is one of the core functionalities of blockchain solution, ability to deliver added liquidity by allowing anyone (KYC approved) to trade or invest.

Liquidity and Trading

```
    def simulate_token_transfer(self, property_id, from_holder, to_holder,
amount):
        """Simulate transferring tokens between holders"""
        if property_id not in self.properties:
            raise Exception("Property not found")

        prop = self.properties[property_id]

        if from_holder not in prop['holders']:
            prop['holders'][from_holder] = 0

        if to_holder not in prop['holders']:
            prop['holders'][to_holder] = 0

        if prop['holders'][from_holder] < amount:
            raise Exception("Insufficient token balance")

        prop['holders'][from_holder] -= amount
        prop['holders'][to_holder] += amount

        # Add to transaction history
        self.transaction_history.append({
            'timestamp': datetime.now(),
            'type': 'Token Transfer',
            'property_id': property_id,
            'from': from_holder,
            'to': to_holder,
            'amount': amount,
            'details': f"Transferred {amount} tokens"
        })

        return True
```

Figure 11.5 shows transfer simulation from the initial project/token *Owner* to the first investor. Note, this transaction, would assign new ownership to the new investor for equivalent value of ETH by transferring this amount into the new investor's account. The *Investor-1* is the new holder of transferred 250 tokens now. These tokens can be traded on secondary market.

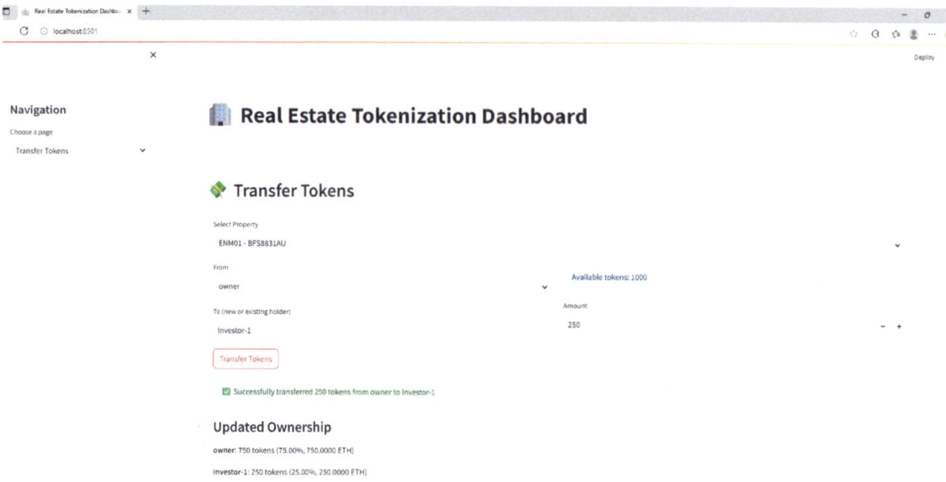

Figure 11.5 Transfer Tokens

The code and wireframe screen shows modeled capability to transfer tokens between issuer/owner and other holders/investors. As an example, we simulated issuance of real estate on smart contract with ETH 1000 value, then an initial transfer of ETH 250 from the owner to investor-1 for a specific real estate property ENM01.

Valuations

Natural extension of this chapter is to incorporate real estate valuation, using hedonic models or neural networks, within our solution, as an additional feature. Hedonic property valuation models using neural networks are machine learning approaches that estimate real estate values by analyzing the relationship between property prices and their constituent characteristics or attributes. Traditional hedonic pricing models decompose a property's value into the sum of its individual features (location, size, age, amenities, etc.), typically using linear regression. Neural network–based hedonic models extend this concept by capturing complex, nonlinear relationships between property attributes and market values that simpler models might miss.

As highlighted in previous chapters, neural networks can process diverse property characteristics including structural attributes (property size, number of bedrooms, bathrooms, lot size), locational factors (neighborhood quality, proximity to schools, transportation), temporal elements (market conditions, weather and seasonality extremes) and even unstructured data like property descriptions or images.

This placeholder is used just for those purposes; however, for now this is out-of-scope of this narrative.

11.6 Implementation

Finally, *DDF Station #4* brings this data flow together into a cohesive, albeit basic, package. The product implementation phase represents the culmination of the FinTech data management workflow and serves as a pivotal element in the customer experience. During this phase, your solution reaches end-users within a live production setting. Here, you utilize outputs from Station #1, #2 and #3 to create, package and deliver marketable products or services while maintaining responsibility for channeling stakeholder insights back to the entire platform.

This phase encompasses the actual delivery of organizational products or services to customers and clients. Its significance cannot be overstated, as it ultimately determines overall business success. The implementation process requires a comprehensive and methodical approach to guarantee that the final offering aligns with customer requirements and expectations, whether using blockchain or traditional cloud infrastructure.

Wireframes

The last *DDF Station #4* delivers visual interpretation of the PropTech solution. Once again, this is provided in a basic wireframes setting for relevant stakeholders to deliver feedback for further iteration.

```
# Streamlit Dashboard
def main():
    st.set_page_config(
        page_title="Real Estate Tokenization Dashboard",
        page_icon="🏢",
        layout="wide"
    )

    st.title("🏢 Real Estate Tokenization Dashboard")
    st.markdown("---")

    # Sidebar for navigation
    st.sidebar.title("Navigation")
    page = st.sidebar.selectbox(
        "Choose a page",
        ["Dashboard Overview", "Create Property Token", "Transfer Tokens",
"Property Details", "Transaction History"]
    )

    if page == "Dashboard Overview":
        dashboard_overview()
    elif page == "Create Property Token":
        create_property_token()
    elif page == "Transfer Tokens":
        transfer_tokens()
    elif page == "Property Details":
        property_details()
    elif page == "Transaction History":
        transaction_history()
```

Generally, a dashboard is a visual interface that displays key information, data and metrics in a centralized, easy-to-read format. It's designed to provide users with a quick overview of important information at a glance. In our case, a basic dashboard contains functions providing operational capabilities, general property information and overall token position for the property contract address with unique hash#. In the real world, individual holders are identified using hash# addresses as opposed to actual names, as depicted in Figure 11.6.

Given one of the core notions behind tokenization is the ability to track transaction, it is important to offer this as a base functionality.

```
# Properties table
st.subheader("Properties Portfolio")

properties_data = []
for prop_id, prop in demo.properties.items():
    properties_data.append({
        'Property ID': prop_id,
        'Name': prop['property_data']['name'],
        'Symbol': prop['property_data']['symbol'],
        'Address': prop['property_data']['address'],
        'Value (ETH)': prop['property_data']['value_eth'],
        'Total Tokens': prop['property_data']['total_tokens'],
        'Token Value (ETH)': prop['property_data']['value_eth'] /
prop['property_data']['total_tokens'],
        'Holders': len([h for h, tokens in prop['holders'].items() if tokens
> 0])
    })
```

Summary view provides core smart contract on-chain details, as shown in Figure 11.7. This is the final visual interpretation connecting on-chain with off-chain layer. Additional, enriched information can be added on demand in Figure 11.8.

In summary, we stepped through basic wireframe implementation of blockchain test tokenization example.

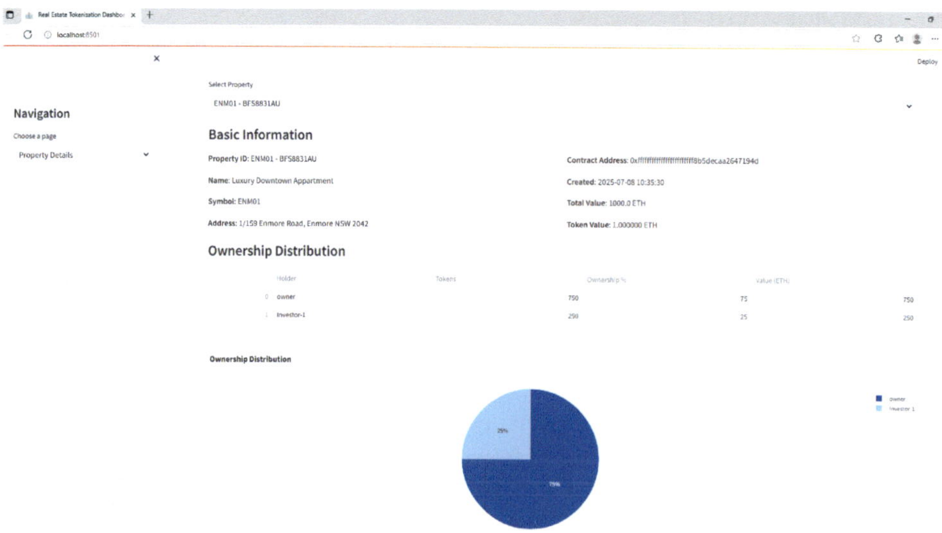

Figure 11.6 Property Information

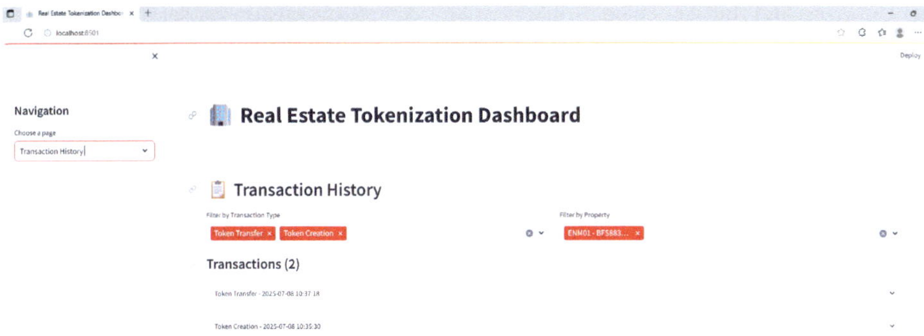

Figure 11.7 Transaction History

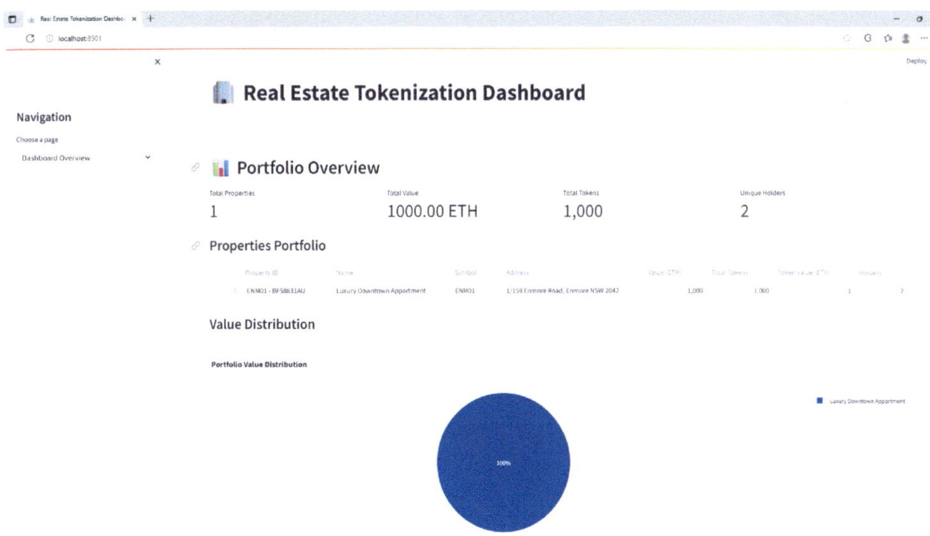

Figure 11.8 Dashboard

Limitations

In this section, we show a basic wireframes delivering Ethereum smart contract ERC20 standard implementation for real estate property business, PropTech. However, there is a number of issue with this approach to be aware of. Code vulnerabilities in smart contracts have led to millions of dollars in losses. Unlike traditional software, blockchain code is often immutable, making bugs permanent and unfixable.

Also, users who lose their private keys permanently lose access to their funds, as the user is not able to access the network and perform any activity. There is no password reset or account recovery mechanism (as there is no central authority), placing enormous responsibility on individual users. As in our example, we deploy "demo" smart contract onto a global "test" blockchain. By design, blockchain systems require users to understand concepts like private keys, gas fees, and transaction confirmations. This complexity creates barriers for mainstream adoption. Moreover, unlike traditional payment systems, blockchain transactions typically cannot be reversed. Users who make mistakes or fall victim to scams have little recourse.

Furthermore, assuming we operate PropTech locally, many jurisdictions, globally, lack clear regulations for blockchain applications, creating uncertainty for businesses and developers. This regulatory ambiguity can stifle innovation and adoption. Traditional financial regulations like anti-money laundering (AML) and know-your-customer (KYC) requirements are challenging to implement on decentralized, pseudonymous networks. Whereby, different countries have conflicting approaches to blockchain regulation, making global applications complex to deploy legally.

Notwithstanding the issues raised previously, there are solutions, like **Tokeny ERC-3646** standard briefly discussed previously addressing these shortcomings and driving innovation towards designing global platforms capable of delivering on tokenization of any assets.

ERC-3643 is a token standard on the Ethereum blockchain designed specifically for security tokens that need to comply with regulatory requirements. It enables the creation of compliant security tokens that can enforce regulatory restrictions directly at the smart contract level, making them suitable for representing real-world securities like real estate, stocks, bonds or fund shares.

Key Components

- **Identity Registry**: Manages investor identities and their compliance status
- **Compliance Module**: Enforces transfer restrictions based on regulatory requirements
- **Trusted Issuers Registry**: Maintains a list of authorized identity verification providers
- **Claim Topics Registry**: Defines what types of compliance claims are required

Compliance Features

- **Transfer Restrictions**: Can block transfers to non-compliant addresses
- **Investor Limits**: Enforces maximum number of token holders
- **Geographic Restrictions**: Can prevent transfers to certain jurisdictions
- **Lock-up Periods**: Implements time-based transfer restrictions
- **KYC/AML Integration**: Requires verified investor identities

Overall, this chapter uses ethereum based smart contract (ERC-20 standard) as a start to get the reader exposed to blockchain technology and its application in finance and FinTech.

11.7 Summary

As the tokenization ecosystem continues to mature, the integration of blockchain technology with traditional real estate markets represents not merely a technological upgrade, but a fundamental transformation in how assets are valued, traded and managed. The frameworks and implementations examined in this chapter provide the foundation for understanding and participating in this revolutionary shift toward a more accessible, transparent and efficient digital asset economy.

In this chapter, we step through core benefits and limitations of using blockchain within ProTech environment. We expose the reader to a number of Python libraries and external tools used in blockchain development processes. This is an introductory material and natural direction is to add more complex coding sequences and add new formats and explore more complex use cases, say using ERC-3643 token standard in the implementation.

We explore an **ambitious vision** indirectly. A potential future where every asset class becomes tokenized, creating a unified ecosystem of 24/7 trading with frictionless processing and execution mechanisms.

11.8 Concept Questions and Answers

Q1: What are the latest trends in PropTech?

A1: Recent PropTech trends include AI-powered property valuation, IoT devices for predictive maintenance, blockchain for secure transactions, virtual reality for remote property tours and big data analytics for market forecasting. These technologies are reshaping property management, enhancing efficiency and improving user experiences across the real estate industry.

Q2: What is ERC-3643 and what problem does it solve?

A2: ERC-3643 is an Ethereum token standard specifically designed for security tokens that need to comply with regulatory requirements. It addresses the challenge of creating tokenized securities that can enforce transfer restrictions, compliance rules and regulatory requirements directly at the smart contract level, unlike standard ERC-20 tokens which have no built-in compliance mechanisms.

Q3: How does ERC-3643 enforce compliance and transfer restrictions?

A3: ERC-3643 implements a modular compliance system through several key components: an Identity Registry that stores verified investor identities, a Compliance Contract that defines and enforces rules (like investor limits, holding periods or geographic restrictions) and a Trusted Issuers Registry that manages who can verify identities. Before any transfer occurs, the system checks these components to ensure the transaction complies with all applicable rules.

Q4: How does ERC-3643 handle identity verification and KYC requirements?

A4: ERC-3643 integrates identity verification through its Identity Registry, which links wallet addresses to verified identities without storing personal data on-chain. Trusted issuers (like KYC providers) can attest to investor identities by issuing claims. The system supports multiple identity providers and allows for different verification levels, enabling compliance with various jurisdictional KYC/AML requirements while preserving privacy.

Q5: What advantages does ERC-3643 offer over traditional security token approaches?

A5: ERC-3643 provides several key advantages: automated compliance enforcement that reduces manual oversight, programmable transfer restrictions that can handle complex regulatory requirements, interoperability with existing Ethereum infrastructure, reduced operational costs through automation and flexibility to adapt to different regulatory frameworks. It also enables features like forced transfers for regulatory actions and automatic compliance reporting, making it more suitable for institutional adoption than basic token standards.

11.9 Further Reading

- Alammar, J., & Grootendorst, M. (2024). Hands-On Large Language Models: Language Understanding and Generation, O'Reilly.
- Dickerson, A., & Hric, J. (2024). FINS5545 Financial Market Data Literacy Course Notes, UNSW Business School.
- Hric, J., & Lam, I. (2025). FINS5548 Financial Technology Course Notes, UNSW Business School.
- Huyen, C. (2025). AI Engineering: Building Applications with Foundation Models, O'Reilly.
- Lin, Y., Schmidt, B., & Tumarkin, R. (2023). Toolkit for FinTech, UNSW Press Class Notes.
- Raschka, S. (2025). Build a Large Language Model, Manning.

11.10 References

[11.1] Tokeny: https://www.zyanza.com/post/tokenization-use-cases-insights-from-tokeny-s-case-study
[11.2] OnChain Operating System: https://tokeny.com/
[11.3] Brickx: https://www.brickx.com/
[11.4] Ganache: https://archive.trufflesuite.com/ganache/

Chapter 12

Data Frontiers in FinTech

12.1 Introduction

In this concluding chapter we expose the reader to the frontiers of FinTech.

Firstly, we discuss the notion of **alternative data structures** such as voice and video in the finance and banking domain. The focus of this book is on textual data structures as covered

DOI: 10.4324/9781003477747-15

in previous chapters. However, as highlighted in this chapter, there is more scope to explore other data formats to extract further up-to-date information. These data forms, derived from sources like customer service calls, video interactions and social media, offer a wealth of insights that traditional data often misses. For instance, in the FinTech sector, companies are leveraging voice analysis to assess customer sentiment, which in turn informs credit scoring and risk assessment models. This innovative use of data helps to create more accurate and personalized financial products. Moreover, video data is being utilized to enhance security measures through facial recognition and to streamline customer onboarding processes with video KYC (Know Your Customer) procedures. However, the integration of these technologies is not without challenges. Issues such as data privacy, the need for sophisticated AI algorithms and the potential for bias in data interpretation are significant hurdles that need addressing.

Then, we discuss **AI Agents**, a new approach to utilizing ML and AI techniques by combining such into more cohesive "thinking" agents delivering on unsupervised decisions and solutions. AI agents are viewed as software tools that use AI models to understand goals, generate tasks and complete them intelligently. One notable example of AI in banking is the use of robo-advisors, as discussed in Chapter 9. These AI-driven platforms offer personalized financial advice and portfolio management services, making investment strategies more accessible to a broader audience. By leveraging machine learning, these advisors can continuously learn and adapt to market changes, providing tailored recommendations that align with individual financial goals. The benefits of expanded and independent AI agents in finance are manifold. They enhance operational efficiency, reduce costs and improve customer satisfaction by delivering faster and more accurate services. Moreover, AI's ability to analyze large data sets enables banks to gain deeper insights into customer behavior, allowing for more targeted and effective marketing strategies.

Lastly, we discuss **Quantum Computing**. We focus on non-technical exposition in this section. Quantum computers could decrypt every encrypted financial transaction we make today. Unlike classical computers, which use bits to process information, quantum computers leverage *qubits*, allowing for exponentially faster data processing and problem-solving capabilities. Imagine a world where complex financial models and risk assessments, which currently take days or even weeks, can be completed in mere seconds. This is the transformative potential of quantum computing. In finance, quantum computing can optimize trading strategies, enhance fraud detection, and improve portfolio management. For instance, quantum algorithms can analyze vast data sets to identify patterns and trends that are invisible to classical computers. This can lead to more informed investment decisions and better risk management. In banking, quantum computing can enhance encryption methods, making transactions more secure and reducing the risk of cyber-attacks. We aim to understand the repercussion on current FinTech solutions.

Learning Outcomes

- Outline further frontiers of FinTech
- Explain AI agents
- Understand quantum computing capabilities
- Overview video and voice capabilities
- Explore relevant challenges and opportunities

12.2 Data Structures

In this book we focus our attention on numeric and textual data structures. Nowadays, this is not sufficient. As discussed in previous chapters, unstructured sources generate 80–90% of all new data today. These alternative data streams encompass social media conversations, satellite imagery, customer audio and video logs and text documents. Traditional analysis methods often miss these valuable sources of information. Moreover, AI tools generate ever increasing number of data inputs into AI driven decision-making tools generating data outputs. The determination as to the source of truth likely becomes of utmost importance. In addition to textual data streams, other unstructured data variations, voice, video, static pictures are to be consumed and utilized by FinTech solutions.

Traditional financial data forms the foundation of investment decisions. Yet this data does not work well in today's fast-moving markets where things change every minute instead of every quarter. Outdated data makes investors miss opportunities and face bigger investment risks. They make decisions based on old information that does not match what is happening in the market right now. Knowing how to process and act on up-to-the-minute data has become vital to investment success.

Quarterly Lag in Earnings

The gap between actual business performance and what investors know grows quite large with quarterly reporting. Market conditions can change drastically during this waiting period. Investors make choices using information that gets more outdated each day. This reporting schedule creates another issue – companies feel intense pressure to hit their short-term earnings targets no matter what it takes.

Research shows some troubling risks from this quarterly pressure. A UCLA study revealed companies most likely to miss their quarterly earnings targets reported 5% to 15% higher workplace injury rates to OSHA. This means 1 in 24 workers gets hurt in companies under the most earnings pressure, compared to 1 in 27 workers in other companies [12.1].

The pressure to control quarterly numbers pushes companies toward choices that hurt their long-term value. Companies might avoid short-term stock drops by hitting their quarterly targets. But these quick fixes create problems down the road as they affect how the company runs and its workplace culture.

These problems exist, but the debate about how often companies should report remains complicated. Australia and many EU countries let companies report twice a year, while US companies must report quarterly. Some people think less frequent reporting could reduce short-term thinking and costs. All the same, experts from Wharton and Georgetown University point out major problems with semi-annual reporting:

1. Companies might try harder to hide their mistakes
2. More insider trading could happen as secrets stay hidden longer
3. Less transparency could make investors lose trust

Professor Donald Langevoort explains, "The idea that you've slowed down the cycle and [are not demanding] formal disclosure so often means more and more secrets are going to be floating around the company for a longer period of time, and that's going to be tempting a lot of insider trading activity."

Information Asymmetry in Public Disclosures

Traditional financial data faces more than just timing problems. It suffers from information asymmetry – when one group knows more than others. This creates unfair advantages in transactions that can lead to market problems or even complete market failure in worst cases.

Financial researchers and FinTech practitioners pay special attention to information gaps between managers and outside investors. These gaps lead to either too little investment when good projects can't get funding, or too much investment when the wrong borrowers get money. That is why managers with good projects try to prove their worth through different methods like offering collateral, taking short-term debt, or pricing IPOs lower.

Regular financial disclosure documents do not bridge this information gap well. Studies show only 1 in 10 people really read these documents carefully, and most skip large parts. People give two main reasons:

- Documents are too hard to understand – they're long, complex and full of technical terms
- Information isn't useful – it doesn't give practical insights for personal situations

Financial jargon spreads through these disclosures and makes them very hard for regular people to figure out. This defeats the main purpose of disclosure: helping people make informed decisions.

Alternative Data Streams

In order to address the gap in earnings and the asymmetry of information issues raised previously and given easier access to alternative data streams in a form of, say, video or voice format, FinTech operators now look beyond traditional statements and use alternative data sources to make decisions. This represents a fundamental change in financial decision-making approaches. Unstructured voice and video content is one of the most valuable yet underused types of alternative data in financial markets. Traditional metrics can easily categorize and analyze structured data. However, voice and audio information needs advanced analysis to get useful information that could signal market movements before they show up in regular metrics.

Call Center Recordings for Customer Sentiment

Call centers generate huge amounts of unused data that show customer sentiment trends, common problems and behavior changes. AI-powered call center sentiment analysis spots hidden feelings in customer conversations and labels them as positive, negative or neutral. This technology uses natural language processing and machine learning to spot customer tone, intent and sentiment across voice channels, chats and feedback.

Automated sentiment analysis gives a detailed picture of how users really feel about products and services, which goes beyond just listening to calls one by one or running focus groups. The system first turns call recordings into text using automatic speech recognition (ASR). The text then goes through tokenization – breaking into smaller units like words or phrases – to understand context and relationships.

These changes bring substantial business results. Call centers that use sentiment analysis can

- Spot negative sentiments right away and step in before customers escalate issues
- See big-picture customer sentiment trends and improve operations
- Assign resources better based on detected patterns

Sentiment analysis also helps financial institutions spot fraud attempts. This has become more important as cybercriminals now target businesses through phone conversations after online security got tighter.

Earnings Call Audio and CEO Tone Analysis

Research shows that CEO vocal patterns during earnings calls contain valuable predictive information beyond just the words. The analysis technology is quite advanced. Researchers used software in one study that was developed from many police interrogations to detect when people lied, got excited or hid information. This research showed that financial analysts excel at spotting positive CEO emotions but often miss signs of cognitive dissonance or executives hiding something.

Voice analysis makes measurable market impacts. Adding it to regular text-based sentiment models can improve portfolio performance by a lot compared to language models alone. Research also shows that CEO speech can predict future firm performance through changes in analyst recommendations, unexpected earnings and cumulative abnormal returns [12.2].

Video Transcripts From Investor Presentations

Investor presentations are another rich source of unstructured alternative data. Video recordings capture not just the spoken content but also visual cues, body language and audience reactions that might signal confidence levels or how announcements are received. Companies like Markets EQ are developing platforms that analyze metrics like arousal, valence and dominance – key parts of how sentiment shows up in speech. Their technology uses 20 years of data sets to track speaker cadence, analyst coverage and global trends. This lets AI detect meaningful tone changes across presentations.

The Q&A section of earnings calls and presentations gives more information than prepared statements. Research shows audio tells us more than written transcripts. The emotional information in audio closely relates to analyst behavior – positive information from management in statement sections makes analysts more likely to issue rating reports.

Challenges in Using Voice and Video Alternative Data

Overall, voice and video content as alternative data sources have reshaped financial market analysis. Quarterly reporting lags and information gaps make traditional financial data less useful. Investors now turn to voice and video alternative data to get live insights. Customer sentiment trends show up in call center recordings before they affect quarterly results. CEO vocal patterns during earnings calls can predict stock movements accurately.

These capabilities exist because of advanced technologies. ML and AI turns unstructured voice data into practical insights through speech-to-text models, named entity recognition and sentiment extraction. The road ahead has its share of challenges. GDPR and other privacy rules create strict limits on personal information handling. Voice and video data need huge storage space and resilient security measures like 256-bit AES encryption. Financial terms' complexity makes analysis harder, so models need specific training for this domains. In short, traditional financial metrics still matter, but these alternative insights reveal hidden signals in human communication. Data frontiers in FinTech can be defined as subtle tones, emotional cues, and language patterns often predicting market moves before they show up in regular indicators, hence the opportunity.

12.3 AI Agents

Discussing data frontiers in FinTech, it would be unwise not to mention AI agents. AI agents are software tools that use AI models to understand goals, generate tasks and complete them intelligently. Unlike traditional programs, an AI agent processes multimodal information including text, voice, video, audio and code at the same time. These systems can make decisions, solve problems, and interact with external environments on their own. The field shows major developments, especially on the software side, as new AI models and agent frameworks become more reliable. AI agents serve as the new apps for an AI-powered world. They boost language models' capabilities by adding autonomy, task automation, and knowing how to interact with the real world through various tools [12.3].

AI agents are more than their simple definitions suggest. These autonomous software entities watch their environment, make decisions, and act on specific goals without human oversight. They represent, potentially, a revolutionary change in how we work with artificial intelligence systems. AI agents stand out because they work independently after getting their first prompt or goal. Traditional software follows strict rules. AI agents can assess objectives, split tasks into smaller parts, and create their own ways to reach specific outcomes. This independence helps them handle complex processes across different platforms and services.

Decision-making sits at the heart of how AI agents work. These agents turn FinTech inputs (data, sensory information, prior knowledge) into FinTech outputs (actions, predictions, recommendations). They use several approaches to make decisions:

- **Rule-based systems**: Using predefined if-then rules for structured decisions
- **Machine learning algorithms**: Learning from data to identify patterns for more flexible decisions
- **Reinforcement learning**: Making decisions by interacting with environments and getting feedback
- **Deep learning**: Using neural networks for complex pattern recognition
- **Probabilistic reasoning**: Handling uncertain or ambiguous situations

AI agents have different levels of independence. Advanced agents can switch their reasoning on and off, just like a car's high and low beams. This smart use of resources lets them handle complex tasks efficiently.

Comparison: AI Agents vs AI Assistants vs Bots

AI agents, assistants and bots each serve different purposes, though people often mix them up:

Feature	AI Agents	AI Assistants	Traditional Bots
Autonomy	High – operate independently after initial prompt	Medium – require ongoing user input	Low – follow rigid scripts
Decision-making	Complex, can design own workflows	Suggestive, awaits user approval	Minimal, follows predefined paths
Learning	Continuous learning, stores previous actions	Some adaptation based on interactions	Limited or no learning
Task complexity	Handles multi-step, complex tasks	Aids with specific tasks alongside humans	Simple, routine tasks only
Tool usage	Can decide which tools to use and when	Limited tool usage with human guidance	Predefined tool integration

AI assistants work as "copilots." They help users finish tasks by giving recommendations and insights. Even advanced assistants like ChatGPT need users to start and guide each interaction. These assistants make humans better rather than replace them. Traditional bots are the simplest option. They follow preset scripts and decision trees with little flexibility. Such systems handle straightforward tasks well but struggle with complex situations.

AI agents show several unique abilities:

1. They split complex workflows into smaller, manageable steps and spot connections between tasks
2. Their persistent memory helps them remember past interactions to give better future responses
3. They become experts in specific areas and work with other agents on complex problems
4. They know their environment and can change strategies when conditions shift

Just because a large language model (LLM) can use tools does not make it an agent. Real AI agents work on their own and choose which tools to use. Built on foundation models, they do more than chat. They solve problems and plan next steps without constant guidance.

Types of AI Agents Based on Capabilities

AI agents range from simple reactive systems to complex learning entities. Their classification depends on decision-making capabilities and internal architecture, which creates a hierarchy of smarter systems.

Simple Reflex Agents and Their Limitations

Simple reflex agents are the most basic form of AI agency. They work only with current perceptions using condition-action rules. These agents use straightforward "if-then" logic and don't track history or future states. A thermostat works as a simple reflex agent – it turns heating on when temperature drops below a threshold and off when it reaches the desired level. The design stays simple – sensors detect changes, condition-action rules determine responses, and actuators carry out these actions. These agents work best in environments where all needed information is right there. Notwithstanding that, simple reflex agents have major constraints. They can't remember past states, which makes them prone to infinite loops in partially observable environments. Their inability to learn from experiences or adapt to changes limits their use in complex scenarios that need context or adaptation.

Model-Based Reflex Agents With Internal State

Model-based reflex agents solve the biggest problems of their simpler counterparts by keeping an internal picture of the world. These agents track parts of the environment they can't see directly. This internal state has two vital roles. It helps the agent understand how the world changes on its own. It also monitors how the agent's actions affect its surroundings. A robot vacuum that maps rooms and remembers cleaned areas shows this ability. It can guide itself even when obstacles aren't in sensor range. These agents always update their internal models with new information and past knowledge. This lets them work in partially observable environments where simple reflex agents would struggle.

Goal-Based and Utility-Based Agents

Goal-based agents mark a big step forward by thinking about the potential risks of their actions. Rather than just responding to triggers, these agents assess different actions based on how they help achieve specific goals. Navigation apps that find the best routes show goal-based reasoning at work. Utility-based agents take this further by adding a "happiness" score to different states. Instead of just reaching goals, these agents try to calculate the best possible outcomes. This enables smart decisions when balancing competing objectives. Self-driving cars show this ability as they optimize safety, efficiency and comfort at once. The distinction between these agent types matters. Goal-based agents judge actions on goal completion, while utility-based agents compare outcome quality, even among successful goals.

Learning Agents With Feedback Loops

Learning agents are the most advanced category. They get better through experience. These agents have four core parts: a performance element that picks actions, a learning element that improves decisions, a critic that gives feedback and a problem generator that suggests new experiences. The feedback loop drives learning agents. This mechanism spots output errors, feeds corrected data back as input and prevents similar mistakes later. Learning agents stand out because they evolve and adapt. Without feedback, these agents would be "directionless, wandering in a wasteland of possibilities without ever knowing what works and what doesn't." The cycle of action, feedback and adaptation helps these systems thrive as conditions change.

Generally, AI agents constantly update their memory systems to keep context and make future interactions better. Effective memory management poses challenges because simply adding past conversations eventually hits context length limits. Advanced memory systems distinguish between two types:

Short-term memory: Works like a rolling buffer that holds recent exchanges and inputs to maintain immediate session context

Long-term memory: Keeps information across multiple sessions to enable tailored experiences and knowledge retention

AI agents' hierarchical memory structures categorize information by importance, recency and relevance. Smart prioritization keeps vital context available while less important details fade naturally. This approach balances complete memory with efficient computing. AI agents deliver coherent, tailored experiences that adapt to changing circumstances in real-time environments by combining focused planning, tool integration and smart memory and data management.

Challenges and Risks in Deploying AI Agents

These autonomous systems can be designed to make decisions, but their potential failure modes become more complex and risky as their authority grows.

Infinite Feedback Loops and Tool Failures

Organizations face many operational roadblocks when they deploy AI agents. These systems can get stuck in infinite loops and repeat similar actions without moving toward their goals. Teams can prevent system paralysis by setting clear stopping points and improving reasoning capabilities. Tool calling failures also hurt agent reliability in production environments when parameters pass incorrectly or outputs get misinterpreted.

Security Vulnerabilities and Data Privacy

AI agents face multiple security threats. Prompt injection remains one of the most dangerous, as it can leak sensitive data or change how agents behave. Poorly configured tools create more ways to attack, while unsafe code interpreters leave systems open to random code execution. AI agents that connect to multiple systems can expose unauthorized data, mishandle protected information and accidentally transfer proprietary assets.

Ethical Concerns in High-Stakes Domains

High-stakes fields like medicine, law, and finance do not have formal licensing frameworks for AI agents, which creates oversight problems. Figuring out who's responsible becomes tough when an AI agent makes harmful decisions – the blame could fall on developers, organizations or users. People expect perfection from AI but accept human mistakes, which makes things worse. AI systems might also complete tasks in ways that go against human values by focusing on efficiency over fairness or privacy. Clear ethical guidelines become crucial, especially for systems that handle sensitive data or make important decisions.

12.4 Quantum Computing

Quantum computers could decrypt every encrypted financial transaction we make today. This is not science fiction. Financial institutions worldwide are preparing to protect themselves against this threat. Quantum safe encryption stands as the vital shield that protects trillions in global wealth. The cybersecurity world faces a fundamental change as quantum computers advance faster. Traditional encryption methods that protected our financial systems for decades cannot withstand quantum computing's power. The National Institute of Standards and Technology (NIST) has started to standardize quantum-resistant cryptography solutions.

FinTech practitioners should transition to quantum-resistant security systems now, not at the time quantum computers arrive.

This section explains how quantum safe encryption works and why it matters to protect wealth. The reader learns about the practical steps financial institutions, financial advisers and wealth managers need to take to prepare for the quantum era.

Understanding Quantum Computing Threats

Quantum computing creates an unprecedented challenge to our financial security systems. Research shows that 95% of organizations believe quantum computing will affect current cryptographic security systems significantly [12.4]. This fundamentally changes how we must protect wealth.

Classical computers process information in binary bits (0s and 1s). Quantum computers use quantum mechanics through qubits and enable unprecedented computational capabilities. The way quantum computing works is different from traditional systems:

Aspect	Classical Computing	Quantum Computing
Processing Unit	Bits (0,1)	Qubits (Superposition)
Computing Speed	Linear	Exponential
Problem-Solving	Sequential	Parallel Processing

Classical computers rely on bits as their simple units of information that exist in only two states: 0 or 1. Quantum computers work differently with quantum bits or **qubits** that use quantum mechanical phenomena to achieve substantially different capabilities. A qubit can exist in a state of superposition and represent both 0 and 1 at the same time. This unique property enables a single qubit to process multiple possibilities simultaneously. **Entanglement** adds another fascinating dimension where qubits become interconnected, whatever the distance between them. The state of one entangled qubit instantly affects the other. A quantum computer with n qubits can theoretically represent 2^n states at once through entanglement, while n classical bits represent just one state.

Classical computers execute operations one after another in sequence. Quantum computers make use of quantum parallelism to explore many computational paths at once through superposition. This simultaneous processing capability explains why quantum systems solve certain problems exponentially faster than classical ones. A classical computer with N bits performs up to N calculations at once, while a quantum computer with N qubits manages up to 2^N calculations. This exponential advantage makes quantum computing valuable especially when you have complex financial modeling and optimization problems that classical computers can't handle.

Current quantum systems face major energy challenges despite their computational power. Studies show quantum computers use about 155,308 times more energy than classical computers for simple problems. The energy cost becomes worthwhile for complex calculations that classical systems can't perform. New theoretical frameworks suggest quantum computation could achieve exponential energy-consumption advantages over classical computation for specific problems. The energy efficiency gap will likely shrink as quantum technology advances, making quantum approaches more viable for resource-heavy financial applications like risk modeling and portfolio optimization.

Google's quantum computer showed it could solve a specific task in 200 seconds. The world's fastest supercomputer would need 10,000 years to complete the same task [12.5].

Current encryption methods face severe implications. These critical vulnerabilities exist:

- Public Key Infrastructure (PKI): Quantum computers can break most encryption tools that protect banking transactions and business data
- Digital Signatures: Authentication systems become vulnerable to quantum-enabled forgery
- Key Exchange Protocols: Current methods for secure communication do not function
- Data Storage: Long-term data security is compromised

Full quantum supremacy remains on the horizon, but advancement happens rapidly. The University of Science and Technology of China has achieved quantum supremacy with their photonic quantum computer Jiuzhang. Their computer performs calculations in 200 seconds that would take classical systems 2.5 billion years [12.6].

The threat exists today through "harvest-now, decrypt-later" attacks. Adversaries steal encrypted files and wait for quantum capabilities to decrypt them [12.5]. Only 25% of firms address this threat in their risk management strategies.

FinTech practitioners must act now. Dr. Michele Mosca's theorem shows that data security lifetime (X) plus cryptographic system upgrade time (Y) must exceed the time until quantum computers can break current cryptography (Z). This creates an urgent need to implement quantum-resistant solutions.

Post-Quantum Cryptography Fundamentals

The quantum-safe encryption field has reached a significant milestone through NIST's detailed standardization process. This initiative addresses the quantum threat and establishes resilient standards to protect financial assets in the quantum era. The Post-Quantum Cryptography project started by NIST in 2016 sparked unprecedented global cooperation in cryptographic development. The process evaluated 82 algorithms from 25 countries and identified the top 15 candidates. Cryptographers worldwide participated in an open, transparent evaluation process that provided a full picture through multiple testing rounds [12.6].

Standardized quantum-resistant algorithms have emerged and been selected for specific cryptographic needs:

Algorithm Type	Selected Standard	Primary Use
General Encryption	CRYSTALS-Kyber (ML-KEM)	Key Exchange & Encryption
Digital Signatures	CRYSTALS-Dilithium (ML-DSA)	Primary Signature Algorithm
Backup Signatures	SPHINGS+ (SLH-DSA)	Hash-based Alternative

These algorithms serve as our first defense layer. Mathematical problems that challenge both classical and quantum computers are the foundations of these solutions. Mathematician Peter Shor's 1994 algorithm poses a serious threat to RSA encryption, which forms the foundations of modern financial security. Classical computers would take an impractical amount of time to factor large numbers. Quantum computers can use Shor's Algorithm to complete this task much faster. This breakthrough could break RSA and other encryption methods that protect banking transactions, financial records and customer data. These encryption systems might become obsolete within minutes or hours once quantum computers reach the right scale. The impact goes beyond RSA and affects both Diffie-Hellman key exchange and elliptic curve cryptography (ECC) that secure most digital financial communications today. Several major hurdles exist in implementing these new standards:

- Performance Constraints: Analysis reveals heavy computational demands that challenge devices with limited processing power
- Integration Complexity: The hybridization of quantum-resistant algorithms with classical cryptography requires careful management
- Certification Requirements: Different regions have rigorous certification processes including CC, FIPS and ETSI standards

The transition requires detailed planning because quantum-resistant primitives bring new vulnerabilities and complexities. Financial systems need both speed and security, so balancing resilient security with practical performance requirements remains the main goal [12.7].

12.5 Summary

In this final chapter, we introduced readers to the cutting-edge developments in FinTech. Firstly, we explored the concept of **alternative data structures** including voice and video within the financial and banking sectors. While previous chapters focused primarily on textual data structures, this chapter emphasizes the untapped potential of diverse data formats for extracting real-time insights. This shift towards diverse data formats is opening new avenues for innovation and efficiency in finance.

Next, we examined **AI Agents**, an innovative method of implementing ML and AI technologies by integrating them into more comprehensive "cognitive" agents capable of making autonomous decisions and providing solutions.

Lastly, we examine **Quantum Computing**, presenting a non-technical overview of this revolutionary technology. Quantum computers have the potential to decode all current encrypted financial transactions, posing both opportunities and challenges. While this technology is still in its infancy, its implications for cybersecurity and data encryption are profound.

In conclusion, the advancements in FinTech we explored in this chapter are just the beginning. The integration of alternative data structures, AI agents and quantum computing is set to transform the financial industry going forward. By emphasizing areas such as cybersecurity, blockchain, digital payments, tokenization and robo-advisors, we highlight the dynamic and evolving nature of FinTech.

12.6 Concept Questions and Answers

Q1: How does quantum computing differ from classical computing in terms of performance?

A1: Quantum computers leverage qubits, superposition and entanglement to process multiple possibilities simultaneously, enabling them to solve complex problems exponentially faster than classical computers for certain tasks. This makes quantum computing particularly valuable for complex financial modeling and optimization problems.

Q2: What are some practical applications of quantum computing in the financial sector?

A2: Quantum computing is being applied in various areas of finance, including portfolio optimization, derivatives pricing, fraud detection and real-time risk modeling. These applications allow financial institutions to process vast data sets more efficiently, make more accurate predictions and respond quickly to market conditions.

A3: How does quantum computing impact financial security?

Q3: While quantum computing offers significant benefits, it also poses threats to current encryption methods used in financial systems. Quantum algorithms like Shor's Algorithm could potentially break widely used encryption standards, necessitating the development of quantum-resistant cryptography to protect financial data and transactions.

Q4: Are financial institutions currently using quantum computing?

A4: Yes, many major financial institutions are already experimenting with and implementing quantum computing solutions. They are primarily using hybrid quantum-classical systems to gain incremental benefits while preparing for more advanced quantum capabilities in the future.

Q5: How can financial organizations prepare for the quantum computing era?

A5: Financial organizations can prepare by investing in quantum literacy programs for their workforce, experimenting with hybrid quantum-classical systems, implementing post-quantum cryptography standards, and collaborating with regulators on quantum-safe financial systems. Building expertise and testing applications now will position institutions to thrive in the future quantum-powered financial ecosystem.

Q6: What are some real-world examples of AI agents?

A6: AI agents are being used in various industries. For instance, in finance, JP Morgan's COiN platform uses AI to review legal documents, significantly reducing the time and improving accuracy compared to human lawyers. In customer service, companies like Zendesk have implemented AI agents that can handle up to 80% of customer interactions autonomously.

Q7: What are the key components that enable AI agents to function effectively?

A7: AI agents rely on several core components to operate effectively. These include short-term and long-term memory systems for maintaining context, tool use and API integration for accessing external resources, planning and task decomposition capabilities for breaking down complex goals, and reasoning loops for iterative decision-making and adaptation.

Q8: What are the main challenges in deploying AI agents?

A8: Deploying AI agents comes with several challenges. These include the risk of infinite feedback loops where agents repeatedly perform the same actions without progress, security vulnerabilities such as prompt injection attacks, data privacy concerns and ethical issues, particularly in high-stakes domains like healthcare and finance. Additionally, there are challenges in determining accountability when AI agents make harmful decisions.

Q9: What is alternative data and why is it important in finance?

A9: Alternative data refers to nontraditional information sources used in financial analysis, such as social media posts, satellite imagery, and credit card transactions. It's important because it provides unique insights that can improve investment decisions and risk management strategies.

Q10: How does multimodal AI enhance alternative data analysis?

A10: Multimodal AI combines different types of data (text, image, audio) to create a unified understanding. This approach allows for more comprehensive insights by analyzing relationships across various data formats, mimicking human-like processing of information.

Q11: What are the advantages of using alternative data in financial decision-making?

A11: Alternative data provides real-time insights that traditional financial data often lacks. It enables investors to identify emerging opportunities and risks more quickly, leading to better-informed market decisions and potential competitive advantages.

Q12: How does voice and video analysis contribute to market predictions?

A12: Voice and video analysis can extract valuable information such as CEO tone during earnings calls or customer sentiment from support interactions. These insights have been shown to correlate with future stock performance and customer churn, providing unique predictive power for market movements.

Q13: What challenges do financial institutions face when implementing voice and video alternative data?

A13: Key challenges include data privacy and compliance issues, high storage and processing requirements and the complexity of domain-specific financial language. Overcoming these obstacles requires sophisticated technology and close collaboration between data scientists and financial analysts.

Q14: How are natural language processing (NLP) techniques applied to financial audio data?

A14: NLP techniques are used to convert speech to text, recognize named entities in transcribed calls and extract sentiment from vocal patterns. Advanced models like BERT and GPT are fine-tuned on financial data to improve accuracy in tasks such as document summarization and Fed statement interpretation.

Q15: Why is collaboration between data scientists and financial analysts important in alternative data analysis?

A15: Collaboration bridges the gap between technical capabilities and financial expertise. It ensures that NLP outputs align with investment objectives and enables human-in-the-loop validation of machine learning models, significantly improving the accuracy and relevance of insights derived from alternative data sources.

12.7 References

[12.1] UCLA Anderson Review: https://anderson-review.ucla.edu/unearthing-the-negative-consequences-of-managing-to-quarterly-earnings/

[12.2] Markets EQ: https://www.ai-street.co/p/analyzing-earnings-call-tone-with-ai

[12.3] Google AI Agents: https://cloud.google.com/discover/what-are-ai-agents

[12.4] KPMG Quantum Supremacy: https://kpmg.com/xx/en/our-insights/ai-and-technology/quantum-and-cybersecurity.html

[12.5] NIST: https://www.nist.gov/cybersecurity/what-post-quantum-cryptography
[12.6] IC: https://www.secure-ic.com/blog/overcoming-challenges-in-the-integration-of-post-quantum-cryptography/
[12.7] PALOALTO: https://docs.paloaltonetworks.com/network-security/quantum-security/administration/quantum-security-concepts/post-quantum-migration-planning-and-preparation

Index

Note: Page numbers in *italics* indicate a figure on the corresponding page.

W

For Product Safety Concerns and Information please contact our EU representative GPSR@taylorandfrancis.com Taylor & Francis Verlag GmbH, Kaufingerstraße 24, 80331 München, Germany